The Insider's Guide To Buying *Home Furnishings*

BY KIMBERLY CAUSEY

HOME DECOR PRESS

Published by: Home Decor Press
P. O. Box 1514
Roswell, GA 30077

To order single copies of this book, or any other books published by Home Decor Press, call (800) 829-1203 or use the order form given in the back of this book. Credit cards are accepted.

Quantity discounts are available -- please call the publisher at (770) 643-0254 for a discount schedule.

If you have any questions or comments regarding this book, please write to the author at the above address.

Publisher's Cataloging-in-Publication Data

Causey, Kimberly, 1968-
The Insider's Guide To Buying Home Furnishings

Includes index.
1. Interior decoration--United States 2. Consumer education--United States 3. Shopping--United States

ISBN 1-888229-21-7 LC 95-081080

The author and publisher have made every reasonable effort to ensure the accuracy and completeness of the information contained in this book. However, we assume no responsibility for any errors, inaccuracies, or omissions herein. Also, we are not responsible for any changes in the information given in this book that may occur after the book has been printed. We shall have no responsibility or liability to any person or entity with respect to any loss or damage caused, or alleged to have been caused, directly or indirectly, by the information and advice contained in this book.

This book is designed to provide information about the home furnishings industry based upon the personal experience of the author. The information and recommendations given in this book strictly reflect only the author's opinions and personal knowledge of the products, services, people, companies, and all other topics discussed herein.

The author's sole purpose in writing this book is to present information and consumer advice that may benefit readers. The author and publisher do not intend to provide legal, accounting, or medical advice. If expert assistance is required, please consult a qualified professional.

M. L. McCamey 1/97

Overview

Part I teaches you how to get the best bargains on high-quality home furnishings: furniture, fabrics, wallpaper, carpeting, soft window treatments, bed treatments, lighting, and decorative accessories. You'll learn how to find the best bargains and how to make sure that the furnishings you buy are high-quality. You'll also learn how to spot shoddy merchandise and scams.

Part II tells you all about the middlemen: interior designers, interior decorators, and retail stores. You'll learn about less expensive (or free) alternatives to their services. You'll also learn about many middleman scams.

Part III tells you all about telephone ordering services, antique malls, and flea markets. These sources often have great deals, even though they are technically middlemen. However, you do need to know exactly what to look for.

Part IV is the heart of this book -- how to shop the way interior decorators shop when they are decorating their own homes. You'll learn all about being your own decorator and buying from wholesale sources.

Part V teaches you some insider techniques I have learned over the years for dealing with businesses that don't treat their customers properly.

Table of Contents

Introduction

Part I: Getting the Goods -- How To Get the Best Quality At the Best Price

Part III: Somewhere In-Between, With Great Prices!

Part IV: The Inside Scoop – How To Buy Home Furnishings At Wholesale Prices

Part V: What To Do When Things Go Wrong

Chapter 1

Introduction

How You Can Save 50% To 80% Off Retail When You Buy Home Furnishings

Have you ever wished that you knew someone in the design trade?

Have you ever wanted a shopping companion who could point out the best bargains and steer you away from merchandise and services that won't give you good value for your money?

Have you ever wished that you had a consumer expert on your side who could alert you to scams and rip-offs in the home furnishings industry?

Have you ever wanted to know exactly where all of the best sources for home furnishings are located -- factory outlets, deep discounters, and more?

Have you ever wanted to shop at a wholesale interior design center without having to pay an interior designer to accompany you while you browse?

Have you ever wanted to attend any of the hundreds of wholesale trade shows that feature all of the newest styles in furniture, fabrics, wallcoverings, lighting, decorative accessories, and other home furnishings -- such as the World of Window Coverings show and the Home Furnishings Markets at High Point, Dallas, Atlanta, and San Francisco?

You know -- the shows that are supposedly closed to consumers. Many consumers have been getting in anyway, and have bought quite a lot of wholesale merchandise at my family's wholesale trade center showrooms over the years.

Have you ever wanted a person who has years of factory and workroom experience to evaluate your custom furnishings so that you can be sure that they are well made and will look their best for many years to come?

Have you ever wondered how professional interior decorators shop when they are decorating their *own* homes? They certainly don't pay retail when they are spending their *own* money.

Is it possible for you to get the very same insider bargains and trade discounts that professional interior decorators have access to?

Yes.

That is the purpose of this book -- to help you apply insider knowledge of the home furnishings industry to all of your shopping and decorating decisions.

This book will take you inside the home furnishings industry and explain how the business of interior decorating works behind the scenes. You can draw on over twenty years of manufacturing experience to show you how to spot high-quality goods and services without having to hire (and pay) an interior designer.

By using your knowledge of the industry to eliminate unnecessary expenses (such as middleman commissions and markups), you can save 50% to 80% off retail when you decorate your home -- just like industry insiders do. This book will teach you to shop the way interior decorators shop when they are decorating their own homes. They certainly don't pay retail prices when they are shopping for themselves -- and neither should you!

You will even learn how you can buy home furnishings from wholesale design center showrooms, local wholesale workrooms, and manufacturers. You can be your own interior decorator and buy your home furnishings from wholesale sources at big trade discounts -- just like professional interior decorators do! It's easy!

This book not only shows you *how* to get the best deals on all types of home furnishings -- it shows you *where* to get them. This book discusses many different sources of home furnishings and shows you how to get the best deals at each one. You will learn how to get the best deals at wholesale sources, factory outlets, and deep discount stores, but you will also learn how to get the best possible deals from retail stores and interior designers. Then, you will receive a simple step-by-step-plan that will help you locate the lowest-priced sources for the particular types of home furnishings you wish to purchase.

Plus, names and addresses are listed for over one thousand factory outlets and deep discount sources for all types of home furnishings all over the U. S.

You'll also learn about the rip-offs and scams that exist in the home furnishings industry. As in all other industries, there are some businesses in the home furnishings industry that take advantage of their customers. I'll explain the little schemes that some home furnishings businesses use to cheat their customers -- so you won't be next.

I was born and raised in the home furnishings industry. My parents owned a top manufacturing company for over twenty years. I worked in our wholesale trade center showrooms at the Dallas Market Center, the Atlanta Market Center, and the High Point International Home Furnishings Market. I managed our wholesale custom window treatment and accessory workroom and factory outlet store, where I worked with interior designers and interior decorators on a daily basis. I also supervised our own staff of interior designers. I have seen all facets of the home furnishings industry from every possible angle. I know exactly where ALL of the savings opportunities are.

Read on, and use the buying strategies described in this book to save 50% to 80% off retail when you decorate your home.

The Three Laws of Smart Decorating

If I were to condense the advice in this book down to three simple laws, they would be these:

FIRST LAW

Never pay middleman markups and commissions when you can shop directly at the source.

SECOND LAW

Never pay for skills, materials, or advice that you don't need.

THIRD LAW

Never pay for advice you can get free.

It's that simple, and this advice has nothing to do with lowering your expectations or settling for less than the best. It has everything to do with preventing waste -- wasted time, wasted materials, and *wasted money.*

You can decorate your home beautifully without breaking the bank. You just have to know where all the possible pitfalls and potential savings are.

How Is This Possible?

How is it possible to save so much money without settling for inferior merchandise or scaling back your design ideas?

You might think that you would have to sew your own draperies, install your own wallpaper, or refinish your own furniture to save so much money. Not so. While doing your own custom work is certainly a good way to save money, this is not a "do-it-yourself" book.

This book will show you how to save at least 50% off retail on all types of home furnishings without sewing a single stitch or scraping off one smidgen of paint. On some types of furnishings, you can save as much as 80% off retail! This book is for people who want to hire professional seamstresses, upholsterers, wallpaper installers, and other craftspeople to do their custom work.

The advice in this book also has nothing to do with settling for lower-quality goods or off-brands. You will learn how to buy the very same new high-quality fabrics, wallpapers, furniture, lighting, carpeting, accessories, and other home furnishings that top interior designers sell.

You can buy the vast majority of the very same brands from the very same manufacturers. You just won't be paying top designer prices for them.

How To Use This Book

Part I -- Getting the Goods -- How To Get the Best Quality At the Best Price

This section is divided into chapters concerning each major category of home furnishings: furniture, fabrics, wallpaper, carpeting, window treatments, bed treatments, lighting, and decorative accessories.

Each chapter begins with a crash course on each type of home furnishing. You'll learn how to choose the right furnishings for your home and how to spot quality products when you see them. You will learn how to avoid sloppy workmanship and substandard materials. All of the practical information you need to know about home furnishings is in these chapters.

Then, each chapter discusses various sources from which these furnishings can be purchased: which sources have great deals, exactly how to get those great deals, how to get the best quality and service, and which sources you should avoid. Many wonderful discount sources are right under your nose, but, since they have small advertising budgets, you are probably unaware of many of them.

Interior designers know all about these discount sources, however. Ironically, many interior designers shop at these sources, which are also available to the general public, and then get away with charging a hefty added commission because their clients don't know that these discounters exist.

Each chapter in this section ends with a step-by-step plan you can use to track down the very best bargains for each type of furnishing.

Part II -- The Middlemen -- The Highest Prices and the Least Value

You will learn all about the middlemen -- retail stores, interior designers, and interior decorators. You'll learn why you don't need to pay them a hefty commission to buy the vast majority of furnishings that are advertised as being available only "to-the-trade". You shouldn't waste money on middleman markups when you can easily buy the very same furnishings directly from the source.

You will also learn about scams that a small percentage of these businesses use to rip off thousands of consumers every year. Most are avoidable, if you know what to look out for.

We will also discuss times when it may be appropriate for you to work through a middleman. It's fine to pay a middleman markup when you are receiving good value for your money. Some consumers really should hire professional help -- primarily those who have elaborate homes, plan to purchase antiques, or are decorating a historic home in period style.

These consumers receive necessary and valuable guidance in return for the money they pay to middlemen -- unlike most other consumers, who pay big middleman markups just to have their orders passed along to the manufacturers that actually make their furnishings. Don't waste your money on what really amounts to an overpriced messenger service.

Chapter 14 will teach you when it's a good idea to hire an interior designer -- and how to get every penny's worth out of the designer you hire.

Part III -- Somewhere In-Between, With Great Prices!

You will learn about telephone ordering services. Yes, technically these are middlemen, but their markups are very low -- far less than interior designers charge to process your order -- and they are the only way for consumers to obtain some brands of home furnishings without paying high middleman markups. Unless they become their own decorators and shop wholesale, that is.

You will also learn about antique malls and flea markets. Many small manufacturers and craftspeople who cannot afford to open a full-fledged factory outlet sell their irregulars and closeouts here. You can get some great deals on first-quality new merchandise, if you know what to look for.

Part IV -- The Inside Scoop -- How To Buy Home Furnishings At Wholesale Prices

This is the best part of the book -- how to be your own decorator and shop wholesale.

You *can* be your own decorator. It's just like being your own building contractor when you arrange to have your own home built. You get a city license and resale number, and then you can buy your furnishings directly from manufacturers and make your own direct arrangements with custom laborers, such as custom window treatment workrooms and upholsterers. You do need to know the basics about quality home furnishings (which are all explained in Part I) and how to work directly with wholesale home furnishings manufacturers, workrooms, and other wholesale sources.

Being your own decorator is slightly more work than just hiring a middleman to choose your furnishings and process your purchases for you, but it pays big dividends. The standard procedure in the trade is for the interior designer or decorator to keep one dollar for every dollar that actually goes to pay manufacturers and workrooms for your furnishings.

In most cases, half of the money you pay to an interior designer or decorator goes right in her pocket as a commission. Sometimes, they can keep more than half of your money for themselves, especially when they can get special discounts from wholesale suppliers (which are usually not

No Advertising?

None. No company or person has paid the author or publisher any money to be mentioned in this book. The publisher, Home Decor Press, derives its sole income from the sale of this and other books.

Companies identified in this book are listed at the sole discretion of the author and publisher, and no advertising fees are solicited or accepted. We believe that this policy is necessary to ensure objectivity in all of our books on consumer topics.

We welcome notices of new discount sources, for any type of product, that our readers may benefit from knowing about.

All sources must be verified before being considered for inclusion in future editions of this book or any of our other consumer-oriented books.

All opinions expressed in this book are solely those of the author.

passed along to the designer's client). Even building contractors usually don't make such high commissions.

I'll show you how to keep that big designer commission in your own pocket, plus I'll even show you how to get those extra discounts from wholesale suppliers on some types of furnishings. You can keep those for yourself, too.

I'll teach you how to get in wholesale trade shows (such as High Point and the World of Window Coverings Show), wholesale design centers, and wholesale manufacturer's showrooms. You probably thought you'd never be able to set foot in these "to-the-trade-only" places, but you can. I'll teach you the industry customs, price codes, and "designer lingo" so that you will know all of the right things to say and do.

Part V -- What To Do When Things Go Wrong

I'll teach you steps you can take to help protect yourself from being ripped off by any type of business, and possibly get your money back if your custom order isn't delivered correctly -- or isn't delivered at all!

Unfortunately, business arrangements do occasionally go wrong. Customer deposits are mishandled. Custom furnishings aren't made correctly. Businesses close without delivering merchandise. No matter how many precautions you take, you might still have a problem. What then?

This book wouldn't be complete without showing you how you can clear up many of these problems. I'll show you some insider strategies I have learned over the years that you can use to go after businesses that refuse to either fill your order correctly or refund your money.

How To Be Your Own Licensed Interior Decorator...

...And Receive All Of the Wholesale Buying Privileges and Discounts Available To Any Interior Decorator

In Chapter 19, I will even tell you how you can be your own interior decorator, with all of the big trade discounts and exclusive wholesale buying privileges available to any interior decorator.

All you need is a city license, a resale number, and business cards. In most cities, these cost about $110.00 (or less) combined. Think of it as a $110.00 backstage pass.

Of course, you also have to know how to properly shop wholesale in order to be able to use this buying advantage. This book will teach you how to conduct business with wholesale design center showrooms and manufacturers just like professional interior decorators do. I'll teach you all the designer lingo, price codes, and industry customs so that you will know exactly what to say and do.

Other decorating books have mentioned that consumers can buy home furnishings wholesale if they purchase a license and resale permit. However, this book tells you exactly how to obtain these business credentials. I haven't made any assumptions about what you do or don't know about business matters. Everything you need to know is explained in detail, step by step. Even if you have no prior knowledge of how small businesses are run, you will still be able to use this buying advantage.

About the Author

I have had an insider's view of the home furnishings industry throughout most of my life. My parents started their own manufacturing company when I was very young. It quickly grew into one of the finest high-end home furnishings factories in the United States.

For over twenty years, my parents designed and manufactured decorative pillows and chair cushions for the most exclusive interior designers and furniture stores in the U. S. and Canada. Their designs were carried in hundreds of the finest high-end furniture stores in the country, featuring many of the highest-quality furniture brands -- such as Drexel-Heritage, Baker, Henredon, Pennsylvania House, Thomasville, and Century.

For nearly a decade, they designed and manufactured decorative pillows and chair cushions carried in Ethan Allen stores all over the world. They designed and manufactured decorative pillows and chair cushions carried in Haverty's, Rhodes, and Castro Convertibles stores all over the U. S.

They have also designed and manufactured decorative pillows and chair cushions for many large wicker and rattan importers, such as St. John Imports, Rattan Arts, and Typhoon International. Their designs have also been featured in many mail order catalogs, such as Charles Keath.

Later, we also began making custom window treatments, bed treatments, upholstery, and other custom furnishings, for interior designers and interior decorators. Our custom workroom did hundreds of jobs every year for designers and decorators -- who turned around and charged their clients twice as much (sometimes even more!) as we charged to do the actual work, simply because they wrote up the work order and passed it along to us. For many years, I have watched designers and decorators collect 100% (or higher) commissions simply to function as order-taking middlemen.

I was allowed to participate in the business from an early age. I worked in our wholesale trade center showrooms at the World Trade Center in Dallas, the Atlanta Market Center, and the High Point International Home Furnishings Market.

I have traveled all over the country on business trips with my family. I especially enjoyed the fabric buying trips to New York City. I have spent many hours browsing through the to-the-trade-only fabric showrooms on Fifth Avenue. I managed our factory outlet store, and supervised our staff of interior designers.

I was even encouraged to try my hand at designing original pillows. Several of my designs were carried by Ethan Allen stores all over the world and featured in their catalog.

For over ten years, I have worked with interior designers, interior decorators, furniture stores, and home furnishings manufacturers. I was in constant contact with the interior designers and interior decorators who hired our workroom to manufacture custom home furnishings. I have spent many years listening to them talk about their clients.

I have seen sides of the interior design business that interior designers and interior decorators would never dare show the public. It has been quite an education.

How Recent Changes In the Industry Can Help You Save Money

This is a time of great upheaval in the home furnishings industry. Competition from foreign manufacturers has greatly increased since the late 1980's, due to expensive government mandates for U. S. manufacturers and eased trade sanctions on foreign manufacturers. NAFTA and GATT will probably encourage even more importing of home furnishings products.

On top of all of that, home furnishings purchases in the U. S. are down due to the general belt-tightening most families have been doing over the last several years. Domestic manufacturers are hurting for business. Many businesses are desperate to make up lost income and are going to great lengths to sell their products anywhere they can.

The home furnishings industry is rapidly becoming a free-for-all. Old customs between manufacturers and interior designers and furniture stores are no longer being observed. Designer fabrics that were once available only to interior designers and interior decorators can now be purchased by the general public in discount fabric warehouses. Furniture and accessories that were once only available in high-end furniture stores can now be ordered over the phone at deep discounts.

The home furnishings industry used to have a very strict set of unwritten rules designed to protect, and profit, the various levels of middlemen between the manufacturer and the retail customer. Back in the early and mid 1980's, when sales were high, manufacturers could afford to pick and choose their customers. Not anymore.

Now, many manufacturers have broken all of the old rules, selling directly to any wholesale customer who will buy. As a result, many of the old layers of middlemen are disappearing. The interior designer's and furniture store's loss can be your gain. There has never been a better time to be a home furnishings customer.

Never Pay Retail!

The 90's have been called the "never pay retail" decade. Nowhere is this more true than in the home furnishings business.

Manufacturers, furniture stores, and interior designers are all clamoring for your purchasing dollars and will make every effort to win your business.

It is up to you, however, to ask. You never get what you don't ask for. You have to know where the weaknesses are in the industry to get the best deals.

The insider tips given in this book will help you decorate your home beautifully without wasting a cent on waste, fraud, or middlemen.

PART I

GETTING THE GOODS:

HOW TO GET
THE BEST QUALITY AT
THE BEST PRICE

Chapter 2

Furniture

Most of your decorating budget will probably be spent on furniture, so bargain shopping is especially important here. Fortunately, there are a wide variety of discount sources. You don't ever have to pay retail for furniture.

In fact, you can usually save at least 50% off retail on new furniture in a wide variety of high-quality designer styles and brands -- just like professional interior decorators and designers do when they decorate their own homes. Most furniture brands that are carried in high-end furniture stores and featured in top interior design magazines can be ordered over the phone at huge discounts. You can also save up to 80% off irregulars, discontinued styles, and seconds.

If you decide to be your own decorator and shop wholesale, you can save at least 40% to 50% off retail on new furniture, plus you will be able to select from a much wider variety of brands and styles. Instead of only selecting from brands and styles carried by discounters and factory outlets, you can browse through all of the wholesale showrooms that are open to interior decorators.

I'll teach you all of the insider shopping strategies. I've been listening to designers and decorators brag for years about the great deals they found, and often resold to their clients at huge markups. You don't need to hire a designer to have access to the best furniture at the best prices.

How To Make Sure You Are Buying Quality Furniture

The main thing you want to look for when you are judging the quality of furniture is the type of wood used. We will discuss the various types of wood, along with the pros and cons of each specific type, in greater depth in the following section.

You will also want to examine the construction of the furniture, which we will discuss later in the chapter. I'll give you a list of specific quality checks that you can use to make sure that your furniture is solidly built.

Types Of Wood

Before you can know the true value of the furniture you are buying, you must understand the proper value of the base materials. If you are being asked to pay top dollar for a piece of furniture, you should make sure that the wood it is made from will last and remain attractive for the longest possible time.

Generally, you should choose wood that is strong, hard (which makes it resistant to damage such as dents and scrapes), doesn't swell or shrink due to humidity changes, doesn't warp, and stains evenly. Solid wood is best.

The best furniture uses the few types of wood that are very durable, easy to work with, and stain evenly -- cherry, mahogany, oak, teak, and walnut. Those five woods "have it all" and should be your preferred choices whenever possible.

The next best choices after that are maple and birch. These are very durable woods that stain evenly and will look good for many years. Their main flaw is that they are relatively difficult to work with. This means that they cannot be easily shaped into graceful curved lines or carved embellishments. However, if you want simple furniture with straight lines and no intricate carvings anyway, maple and birch are excellent choices that can save you money.

After that comes veneered furniture: furniture with a strong wood used in the frame and a beautiful, easily workable wood that stains evenly used for the visible decorative portions. Veneered furniture that has been well constructed is fine. In fact, there are some shapes, sizes, and types of furniture that cannot be made from solid wood. However, there are some poorly made veneers out there, so you must be careful. Later in the chapter, we will thoroughly discuss veneers.

Don't settle for furniture that is made from weak softwoods, such as fir or poplar. This is not a good way to cut costs. High-quality furniture can last a lifetime and is well worth the higher price. There are many other ways you can cut decorating costs without sacrificing quality.

Some of the woods listed below are normally used only for the exposed parts of furniture -- table tops, table legs, carved chair arms and legs, surfaces of dressers and cabinets, etc. -- because they stain evenly and are easy to work with but are not the most durable. Other woods are normally used only for the interior framework of furniture because they are very durable but difficult to stain or work with.

Alder Hardwood that stains evenly and has good resistance to shrinking, scrapes, and dents, but is not as strong as many other hardwoods. It is usually used in medium-priced furniture.

Ash Strong hardwood with good resistance to warping, scrapes, and dents. It is very durable but difficult to work with. It is usually used in furniture frames.

Beech Strong hardwood with poor resistance to warping, shrinking, swelling, and dry rot. It is usually used in medium-quality furniture, particularly curved parts.

Birch Strong hardwood that stains evenly and has good resistance to shrinking, swelling, and warping. It is usually used in furniture frames and some Scandinavian style furniture.

Birch is a cut below cherry, walnut, oak, mahogany, and teak because it cannot be worked with as easily. If you want delicate curved lines and carvings on your furniture, you will want to pay more for a better wood. However, if you want simple furniture with straight lines and no intricate carvings anyway, birch is a fine choice and can save you some money.

Sometimes, birch is stained and sold as ‘‘imitation mahogany’’, ‘‘imitation cherry’’, or ‘‘imitation walnut’’. It is a decent substitute for mahogany or walnut in some simple styles of furniture, although it will not look quite as nice or last as long.

Cedar Weak softwood. It is most often used for closet linings, decorative paneling, trellises, garden cedar chips, and shingles. Please note that only red cedar repels moths -- other types of cedar do not.

Cherry Strong hardwood that is easy to work with, wears well, stains evenly, and has good resistance to shrinking, swelling, and warping. It carves well, which makes it very well suited to furniture styles that have carved embellishments or curved lines. This is a very high-quality wood. It is also relatively expensive, but it is an excellent investment.

If you want very high-quality elegant furniture, but don't want to go to the extra expense of purchasing mahogany, teak, or English walnut, cherry is a very good choice. It is available in a wide variety of furniture styles.

If you love the look of cherry furniture, but you can't afford it, imitation cherry that is made of stained birch is a good substitute. It's only major drawback is that it is more difficult to work with and cannot be shaped or carved as well as cherry.

Ebony Strong hardwood that wears well and is easy to work with. It is extremely expensive due to its relative scarcity and the fact that it must be imported from a few tropical areas in Asia and Africa. It is normally used in decorative furniture inlays and small carved decorative accessories.

English walnut See "***Walnut-English***"

Fir Weak softwood with poor resistance to swelling and wear. It is difficult to work with and is usually used only in cheap furniture.

Gum Strong hardwood that is easy to work but has poor resistance to shrinking, swelling, warping, and dry rot. It is usually used in furniture frames.

Sometimes, gum is stained and sold as ‘‘imitation mahogany’’, ‘‘imitation cherry’’, or ‘‘imitation walnut’’. Gum is inferior to real mahogany, cherry, and walnut in durability. If you want to save money by purchasing imitation walnut, cherry, or mahogany -- buy the kind that is made from birch. It is a better investment.

Mahogany Strong hardwood that is easy to work with, stains evenly, wears well, looks gorgeous, and is basically perfect. It's also basically

Scam Alert!

Look out for so-called "Philippine mahogany". Sometimes, furniture salespeople try to pass this off as the real thing. This is NOT a variety of real mahogany -- it's from a completely different botanical family.

Real mahogany comes from trees of various species within the botanical family *Meliaceae*. Common names of the different varieties of real mahogany include: American mahogany, Cuban mahogany, sapele mahogany, New World mahogany, African mahogany, African scented mahogany, Honduran mahogany, cedar mahogany, and West Indian mahogany. All of these names refer to the real thing and are fine for you to buy.

Philippine mahogany comes from trees of a number of species within the botanical family *Dipterocarpaceae*. The various species within this family go by a variety of common names: Bagtikan, Philippine cedar, Lumbayao, Red Lauan, Tanguile, Almon, and Narra. This is a totally different, and inferior, type of tree.

Philippine "mahogany" is not as durable as real mahogany and it has problems with shrinking, swelling, and warping.

Philippine mahogany is a passable substitute for real mahogany if you can buy it at a lower price, but you certainly wouldn't want to get stuck with it when you are paying top dollar for what you believe is real mahogany.

If you want mahogany but you can't afford it, buy the kind of imitation mahogany that is made from birch. It is a better investment, and usually a better bargain.

expensive, but it's worth every penny.

The main reason why mahogany is so much more expensive than cherry, oak, and walnut is that it must be imported from Central America, South America, or Africa. American mahogany is marginally higher-quality than African mahogany.

Mahogany does have its own unique beauty, but it really does not wear any better than cherry, oak, and American walnut (which are grown in North America). So, if you want high-quality gorgeous furniture that will last a lifetime -- cherry, oak, and American walnut are fine. The only reason to pay a higher price for mahogany is for its unique look.

You might also consider purchasing imitation mahogany that has been made from birch, if you can't afford the real thing. Birch is a high-quality wood that will wear well for many years. It won't be quite as gorgeous or long-lasting as the real thing, but it makes a good substitute. Avoid imitation mahogany that has been made from lower-quality woods, such as gum or so-called "Philippine mahogany" (described in the box at left).

Maple Strong hardwood that is hard to work with but stains evenly and has good resistance to wear, shrinking, and swelling. You may have heard it called "hard rock maple", "sugar maple", or "black maple" -- these names all refer to the same type of wood. "Bird's eye maple" refers to maple with a particular naturally occurring decorative pattern in the wood grain.

Maple is usually used in medium to high-quality furniture that has simple straight lines and no curved portions or decorative carvings. If you are looking for simple furniture styles anyway, maple is a good choice that will wear well, look good, and save you some money.

Cherry, oak, walnut, mahogany, and teak are all a cut above maple because they carve well and can be worked into gently curving shapes. If you don't want curved lines and carved embellishments on your furniture anyway, why pay extra for wood that has that capability?

Oak Strong hardwood that is easy to work with, wears well, stains evenly, and has good resistance to swelling, shrinking, and warping. It carves well, which makes it very well suited to furniture styles that used carved embellishments or curved lines. This is a very high-quality wood. It is also a bit expensive, but it's well worth the money.

If you want very high-quality furniture, but don't want to go to the extra expense of purchasing mahogany, teak, or English walnut, oak is a very good choice. It is available in all types and styles of furniture.

Particle board This isn't technically a wood, but it is the main component of most cheap furniture. Particle board is actually pressure-treated, glued-together, sawdust.

Particle board furniture is a poor investment. It isn't very durable. It soaks up water (from the air) like a sponge and will eventually separate from the pretty veneers that often cover it.

Don't worry about properly identifying particle board -- you'll know it when you see it. It looks just like what it is -- sawdust. It is sometimes referred to as "wood product".

Pine Weak softwood that is easy to work with but has poor resistance to swelling, shrinking, and warping. It's normally used in medium-priced furniture.

Poplar Weak softwood that is easy to work with and stains evenly but has poor resistance to swelling, shrinking, and warping. It's normally used in relatively cheap furniture.

Rattan The lower, thick, segmented portion of the stem of the rattan palm. It is relatively cheap, although it is also quite durable and attractive. You can get some great deals on rattan furniture.

Rosewood Strong hardwood that is easy to work with, stains evenly, and has good resistance to wear. Rosewood is durable and beautiful, but it's also expensive because it must be imported from India or Brazil.

Satinwood Strong hardwood that has a high luster and is easy to work with. It is very expensive and is normally used only in fine cabinetry and furniture inlays.

Teak Strong hardwood that is easy to work with, stains evenly, and has good resistance to wear, swelling, warping, and shrinking. It carves well, which makes it very well suited to furniture styles that used carved embellishments or curved lines. This is a very high-quality wood, available in all types and styles of furniture.

Teak is quite expensive because it must be imported from Asia. Like mahogany and English walnut, the only reason to buy it is because it has a unique and beautiful look. Cherry, American walnut, and oak are just as durable and attractive and are less expensive because they are grown domestically.

Walnut-American Strong hardwood that is easy to work with, wears well, stains evenly, and has good resistance to shrinking, swelling, and warping. It carves well, which makes it very well suited to furniture styles that used carved embellishments or curved lines. This is a very high-quality wood. It is also relatively expensive, but it is well worth the price. It is also known as ''black walnut''.

If you want very high-quality elegant furniture, but don't want to go to the extra expense of purchasing mahogany, teak, or English walnut, American walnut is a good choice. It is available in all types and styles of furniture.

Walnut-English Strong hardwood that is easy to work with, wears well, stains evenly, and has good resistance to shrinking, swelling, and warping. It carves well, which makes it very well suited to furniture styles that used carved embellishments or curved lines. This is a very high-quality wood. It is also relatively expensive, partly because it must be imported from Europe, Asia Minor, or Asia, but it is worth every penny.

English walnut is a different, but very closely related, species of walnut than American walnut. Its other common names include: European walnut, Russian walnut, Persian walnut, Circassian walnut, etc. -- depending upon

Make Sure You Know What You're Buying

A few furniture manufacturers and salespeople will misrepresent veneered particle board furniture. For instance, I recently saw some teak-veneered particle board furniture being sold as ''teak furniture'' in a local retail store. Be careful. Check furniture over yourself to make sure that it isn't really particle board in disguise.

Usually, there will be places on the furniture where the manufacturer never expected you to look and the particle board has not been covered by a veneer:

1 Pull out an adjustable shelf from an armoire, entertainment center, or bookshelf -- there should be exposed wood (or particle board) on the short ends.

2 Pull out a drawer from a desk or cabinet -- there should be exposed wood on the back of the drawer.

3 Look underneath tables -- you can sometimes see exposed wood on the underside of the tabletop.

where the trees are harvested. All of these names refer to the same type of tree.

English walnut is marginally higher-quality than American walnut. It is even easier to carve, and, therefore, it can have more intricately carved embellishments. It also looks slightly different in color and grain than American walnut.

The only real reason to spend the extra money for imported English walnut is if you prefer the unique look of it. Otherwise, American walnut looks very similar, is essentially the same wood, and is less expensive.

Wicker The upper, thin, unsegmented portion of the stem of the rattan palm. Wicker furniture that is tightly woven looks great, will wear well with moderate care, and can last a lifetime.

There is, of course, an abundance of very cheap shoddy wicker out there, too, so you must look everything over carefully before you buy. The durability and attractiveness of wicker furniture depends largely on the intricacy and skill of the weaving.

Look for wicker that is tightly woven and has an inner frame of wood or metal to provide extra support.

Wood product See ''***Particle board***''.

Veneers

Unfortunately, veneers have gotten an undeserved bad reputation in some circles. Some people incorrectly believe that a veneer is a sure sign of cheap furniture. Not at all. There is cheap veneered furniture and there is quality veneered furniture, but you must know how to tell the difference.

Make sure that the veneer has been applied to a good-quality base wood. Birch, maple, gum, and ash are all good choices. Fir, poplar, and particle board are commonly used, but inferior, base woods. Avoid them.

Occasionally, veneers will be attached to their own base woods. Many manufacturers produce solid cherry furniture that is actually made of a cherry base and a cherry veneer. This allows large pieces of cherry furniture to be built, as described later in this section.

Choose a quality manufacturer. All of the major manufacturers listed on page 29 are very reputable and produce quality furniture. You should not experience any problems with veneered furniture from these companies. Veneered furniture from any design center, trade center, or independent wholesale showroom should also be fine.

Other than that, there's not much else you can do to check the quality of the veneer yourself. There is a certain amount of faith involved. However, if you stick with quality woods and quality manufacturers, you are unlikely to have any problems.

Veneers are not always used as a cost-cutting measure, although this is a primary reason for their use. Veneering does allow manufacturers to make the maximum use of a small amount of very expensive decorative wood. However, veneers are also used to create attractive patterns with wood grains.

There is also a special type of veneer called a ''rotary-cut veneer''. This type of veneer is made by slicing wood very thinly starting at the outside edge of the tree trunk and spiraling inward to the center. A thin sheet of veneer is peeled from the trunk, sort of like fabric being unrolled. This allows large sheets of veneer to be made for large pieces of furniture, such as a dining table top, from very small trees.

Cherry trees, for example, are fairly small trees. Rotary-cut veneers allow large pieces of cherry furniture to be made. How else could you have large pieces of furniture made from such a tiny tree?

So, don't be afraid of veneers. They are a perfectly acceptable cost-cutting measure, as long as you are dealing with quality woods and quality manufacturers, and they make many types of beautiful furniture available that would otherwise be impossible to build.

Upholstery Details

There are some additional considerations you should be aware of when you are shopping for upholstered furniture:

Fabric Consider the manufacturer's fabric choices carefully. Do you like the weight of the fabric? Is it appropriate for your family? You wouldn't want to choose a relatively delicate lightweight fabric for your family couch if you have young children who will subject the sofa to heavy wear, for instance.

You don't have to limit yourself only to the fabrics chosen by the manufacturer. You can often substitute your own fabrics on a C.O.M. basis, as discussed on page 22, but you should still stay close to the weights and types of fabrics used by the manufacturer. Fabric types and their durability are discussed in depth on pages 55-63.

Leather Leather is more expensive than many fabrics, but it is more durable than even the heaviest upholstery fabric. You should look for full grain or top grain leather -- these are most attractive and durable types of leather.

Durability Sit down. Then, get up again and look behind you. Can you still see where you were sitting? A quality sofa or chair should spring right back to its original shape. Cheap furniture often doesn't.

Cushions If the furniture has any removable seat cushions, find out what kind of stuffing has been used in them. The very highest-quality seat cushions are made with an inner core of springs inside a plain fabric cover, wrapped in a layer of polyester batting, all wrapped in a layer of polyurethane foam, enclosed in another plain fabric cover, and zipped into a decorative seat cushion cover. Whew! Naturally, all of this work is expensive -- but well worth it. The cushions will probably outlive you.

Next best are seat cushions are made with a solid piece of polyurethane foam wrapped in a layer of polyester batting, sewn inside a plain fabric covering, and then zipped into the decorative seat cushion cover. This is a very common way of making seat cushions, and furniture made this way is usually very durable. The cushions should last for many years.

Manufacturers of lesser-quality seat cushions usually use only the solid piece of foam and omit the zipper. Avoid purchasing furniture with seat cushions that have been made this way. Without polyester batting and a fabric cover, the inner foam core of the cushion will tend to shift around inside the decorative fabric cover -- with very unattractive results. Without a zipper, you can't remove the stuffing to have the cushion dry-cleaned.

The very lowest-quality seat cushions are filled with shredded polyurethane foam and have no zippers. Avoid buying furniture that has this type of cushion. It is a poor investment.

Any removable cushions that are designed to support your back are likely to be made with shredded polyurethane foam and button-tufted. This is fine. Back cushions don't shift and mat down nearly as badly as seat cushions.

Avoid buying furniture that has down-filled seat or back cushions. It does feel very rich and very plush (it ought to for what it costs), but the cushions aren't as durable as those that use synthetic stuffing materials. Those wonderful fluffy down cushions will start to flatten and mat down before you know it. Unless you don't mind fluffing the cushions every time you stand up, don't buy down.

Frame Make sure the frame is built from a strong hardwood such as birch, ash, gum, or maple. Avoid weak woods such as poplar, fir, and especially particle board.

Springs Eight-way hand-tied springs are best. Lesser-quality furniture may have springs that are only tied four ways.

Continuity Look at the pattern of the fabric. High-quality upholstered furniture should have all fabric patterns lined up nicely, like an expensive plaid shirt or suit.

If the fabric pattern looks as though it was applied haphazardly with no thought as to how the finished piece would look, find a different manufacturer. This is a sure sign of sloppy workmanship.

Other Quality Checks

There are a few other quality checks you should look out for on all types of furniture:

Sturdiness Gently lean against the side of a sofa or the footboard of a poster bed. Gently shake a chair or table. Did it move? Even worse -- did you hear it move? Does it feel like it isn't held together very well, or does it feel solid and sturdy?

All hardware should be firmly attached. Knobs, drawer pulls, and handles should be attached by a screw from the inside of the door or drawer front, instead of just being nailed or glued on.

Gently tap decorative panels, made from glass or other materials, inset in cupboard doors. They should not jiggle or shift in any way. They should feel snug.

Look underneath tabletops, chair seats, and sofa frames. You should see a small wooden brace in each corner, forming a triangle with the corner. This adds strength and stability to the furniture.

Finish Does the finish feel smooth, or does it feel rough, gritty, or bumpy?

Is the color attractive and even over the entire piece? Quality furniture should have a very smooth, evenly colored finish.

Smooth function Do drawers open and close smoothly and easily, or do they squeak and resist moving? Large drawers that may be heavy when they are filled should be mounted on metal tracks that have rollers to move the drawer back and forth.

Do doors open and close smoothly, or do they seem to be scraping against the frame? You shouldn't have to use any force to open or close the doors.

Joints Check the drawers. They should have dove-tailed joints at all four corners. If they are just nailed together, eventually they will pull apart.

Look at where table and chair legs are attached. Make sure that there isn't any excess glue dripping out and that there are no gaps in the joints.

Extras Chests of drawers should have a panel between each drawer to catch dust. You don't want dust to rain down on the contents of lower drawers each time you open or close drawers above them.

Entertainment centers and furniture designed to hold computer equipment should have small holes drilled in the back to allow power cords to pass through.

Drawers should have stops to prevent them from being accidentally pulled out of the frame.

Look at the bottom of any large piece of furniture, such as an entertainment center or armoire. Quality furniture will have small concealed casters to help you move the furniture around.

Finish

You will sometimes be given a choice of finishes on the furniture you are buying. In addition to protecting the wood, finishes usually determine the color of the finished furniture.

Unfortunately, most furniture manufacturers use a confusing system to label these finish choices. Finish choices are normally referred to by wood names "cherry finish", "oak finish", "walnut finish", etc.

The name of the finish has absolutely nothing to do with the type of wood that has been used. "Walnut finish" does not necessarily mean walnut furniture. Make sure you understand clearly what type of wood has been used. These finish names can create confusion.

Consider Updating the Furniture You Already Have

Chances are, unless you are just starting out in your first home, you are replacing existing furniture because it has either gone out of style or you are just tired of it, not because it is worn out or unusable. Most furniture is very durable, and it usually lasts far longer than the fashions it was made to coordinate with.

Finding ways to update your existing furniture, instead of attempting to sell it and buy new furniture, can save a lot of money when you are redecorating. Most of the various methods of updating furniture used by

Decorative Hardware Sources

Antique Hardware Store
9730 Easton Rd.
Kintnersville, PA 18930
(800) 422-9982

Ball & Ball
(Send $7.00 for catalog)
463 W. Lincoln Hwy
Exton, PA 19341
(800) 257-3711

Crown City
(Send $25.00 for catalog)
1047 N. Allen Ave.
Pasadena, CA 91104
(800) 950-1047

Horton Brasses
(Send $4.00 for catalog)
P. O. Box 120
Cromwell, CT 06416
(203) 635-4400

Jamestown Distributors
28 Narragansett Ave.
Jamestown, RI 02835
(800) 423-0030

Paxton Hardware
(Send $4.00 for catalog)
P. O. Box 256
Upper Falls, MD 21156
(410) 592-8505

The Renovator's Supply
Renovator's Old Mill
Millers Falls, MA 01349
(800) 659-2211

Van Dyke's
(Send $1.00 for catalog)
P. O. Box 278
Woonsocket, SD 57385

Wayne's Woods
(Send $2.00 for catalog)
39 N. Plains Industrial Rd.
Wallingford, CT 06492
(800) 793-6208

professional interior designers are not difficult for the average consumer to use. Much can be done to easily and inexpensively update the look of your current furniture:

Paint it A wide variety of painted finishes can radically change the look of your furniture. Marbling, sponge painting, stenciling, trompe l'oeil effects, and a wide variety of other painted finishes can have a dramatic effect. This is a great way to give your furniture a rich, expensive look at very little cost.

Many books on decorative painting techniques should be available at your local library and bookstore. Jocasta Innes has written several excellent books on the subject. Study them to decide what effects you may wish to attempt by yourself.

Some effects are very easy for anyone to do, but others, such as trompe l'oeil, require more skill. If you want help with your painting, contact a local art school. Many student painters will give you a very good price, and most do fine work. Often, someone in the financial aid office will be able to put you in touch with students who want to earn some extra money.

Embellish it Decorative hardware can transform a plain piece of furniture into something that looks like a treasured antique. There are a wide variety of sources for all types of decorative, restored antique, and antique-looking reproduction hardware, such as drawer pulls, handles, hinges, locks, etc.

Some of the major sources of decorative furniture hardware to interior designers are listed at left. All of these sources also sell to the public. If there is no specific charge noted for a catalog, then you may order one free by calling the 800-number provided.

Refinish it Advice and instruction on refinishing is very easy to come by. Some home centers and local colleges even offer free or very inexpensive classes on refinishing. There are many books available at your library on the subject. _The Furniture Doctor_ by George Grotz is an excellent source of information on repairing and refinishing furniture.

There is also a very informative television show completely devoted to ''rescuing'' old or used furniture. It is called "Furniture On the Mend", and it airs six days a week on the Learning Channel. Check your local TV schedule for show times.

Refinishing supplies are usually very inexpensive and can be found at most hardware stores and home centers. There are also a couple of catalogs, listed below, that carry refinishing supplies. These sources often have supplies used to create unusual effects that may be difficult for you to find locally.

Liberon
(Call for free catalog)
P. O. Box 86
Mendocino, CA 95460
(800) 245-5611

Wayne's Woods
(Send $2.00 for catalog)
39 N. Plains Industrial Rd.
Wallingford, CT 06492
(800) 793-6208

If you don't want to do your own refinishing, you can find a service to do it for you in the Yellow Pages under *Furniture -- Repairing and Refinishing*.

Rearrange it There are design services in some cities that do nothing but rearrange their customers' existing furniture -- for about $200.00 PER ROOM. A good example is the "Use-What-You-Have" interior design service in New York City, described on page 273.

You can do the same thing. Check out some design books at your local library and have a go at it yourself before you resort to paying an interior designer to do this for you.

It really can make a major difference in the look of your home. If you are considering redecorating because you are bored with your current surroundings, consider rearranging what you already have before you invest money in new furnishings.

Slipcover it Slipcovers can hide a multitude of decorating sins, without emptying your bank account. You can have your slipcovers professionally made by a local seamstress or workroom (read Chapter 18), buy them ready-made in a very limited variety of fabrics, or do-it-yourself. Professionally-made slipcovers will look far better than the free-form tuck-in kind you can buy ready-made or make yourself.

Having slipcovers made is usually much cheaper than reupholstering your furniture. However, custom-made slipcovers are still fairly expensive, so do be sure to buy a durable long-lasting fabric.

There is no simple way to estimate the yardage necessary to make your slipcovers. Every piece of furniture is different. If you hire a professional to make your slipcovers, you should arrange to have the seamstress or workroom to measure your furniture and estimate the necessary yardage.

A limited variety of inexpensive ready-made slipcovers are now available in linens stores. This is a new type of product, so you will want to browse through linens stores in your area to see the latest colors and designs available.

Some interior design books and magazines give basic instructions for making a loose, free-form slipcover that is tucked in around your furniture rather than being sewn. This is not a long-lasting solution and will have to be tucked in again fairly often, but if you are low on money and are looking for a short-term fix-up for your furniture, this might work for you.

If you are going to just tuck in a temporary slipcover around your furniture, it is fine to use sheets if you wish. Many magazine articles and television shows have suggested this. However, if you plan to pay a seamstress to sew them for you, don't use sheets. They aren't durable enough.

If you have your slipcovers custom-made, make sure you use a durable medium-weight decorative fabric -- preferably a sailcloth, medium-weight sateen, or medium-weight chintz. Don't use a heavy-weight fabric, such as a heavy upholstery boucle', because it will probably be too difficult for the seamstress to sew. Medium-weight fabrics are discussed in depth on pages 60-62.

Don't skimp on the quality of the fabric you choose for your custom-made slipcovers. You don't want to spend several hundred dollars to have slipcovers made, only to have them full of worn spots long before their useful life should be over.

Cover it, period If you have a really ugly table, a beautiful tablecloth can work wonders. No one is ever going to look underneath.

Accent it Often, your furniture really isn't the problem. Unless you have ornate or stylized furniture, you can often give your home a fresh look by changing the small accessories instead of buying all new furniture. If you want a more traditional look, for instance, try buying some pretty decorator pillows or pictures instead of changing your sofa.

Most of the design books and magazines available at your local library and bookstore will have plenty of ideas on how you can put together a wide variety of looks strictly by changing your accessories.

Before you go shopping, give some thought to sprucing up the furniture you already have. Furniture is usually the most expensive category of furnishings in any home. Making alterations to the furniture you already have and investing your money in smaller items, such as pictures or pillows, can greatly reduce your total decorating bill.

Custom Upholstered Furniture

You don't always have to limit your choices to the few fabrics that a particular furniture manufacturer might choose to make its upholstered furniture up in. Many major furniture manufacturers and furniture dealers offer a "C.O.M." option on some furniture styles. "C.O.M." means "customer's own material". Rarely, you might see a "C.O.F." notation which means "customer's own fabric". This is the same thing as C.O.M.

When you order upholstered furniture C.O.M., this means that you go out and buy your own fabric and ship it to the manufacturer to have your upholstered furniture made up in it. You can choose any appropriate fabric from any source to have your furniture upholstered.

C.O.M. is generally more expensive than choosing one of the furniture manufacturer's selected fabrics because manufacturers buy fabrics in bulk and, therefore, get a much better price. However, this method will allow you to order exactly what you want, without hiring an interior designer.

You can sometimes turn C.O.M. into a savings strategy if having your furniture custom upholstered allows you to buy your fabric in larger quantity directly from the fabric manufacturer as described on pages 79-82. If you are having several items made up in the same fabric, such as a sofa and several matching window treatments, you may wish to go this route. After you find out how much total fabric you need to order for your furniture and other furnishings, you can weigh your options and determine if becoming your own decorator and buying your fabric in bulk is the least expensive way to go in your particular situation. Chapter 19 explains in depth how to become your own decorator.

The furniture dealer (usually a telephone furniture ordering service or a wholesale design center showroom) will tell you how much fabric to order. Make sure that you find out how many fabric repeats are necessary in addition to the base yardage amount. Also, ask if there are any fabric patterns that don't work well on the particular piece of furniture you have in mind, such as plaids or stripes. When you place a C.O.M. order, you are solely responsible for choosing an appropriate and durable fabric. Use the guidelines on pages 55-62 to select fabrics that will wear well. Fabric repeats are discussed on page 66.

Make note of the fabrics that the manufacturer does offer. You should only be purchasing your own fabric to obtain a certain color or decorative pattern that the manufacturer does not offer. Stay close to the types and weights of fabrics that the manufacturer has chosen. If you want to provide your own fabric because you think that the manufacturer's fabric choices are too lightweight or too heavyweight, bear in mind that the manufacturer chose that fabric weight for a good reason. You might be on the verge of making an expensive mistake.

If a manufacturer only offers a certain sofa in black or white heavy boucle', buying a red heavy boucle' and having the sofa made up in it is fine. Buying a vastly different type or weight of fabric, such as a mediumweight chintz, and having the sofa made up in it is a big waste of money. You will almost certainly be unhappy with the looks and durability of the resulting furniture. Be your own decorator, by all means, but don't try to reinvent the wheel.

You are also responsible for shipping your fabric to the manufacturer. Normally, you will want to send it via a common package carrier, such as UPS. UPS has an information line that will help you arrange shipment: (800) 742-5877. They can pick the fabric up right from your home. Make sure that the fabric is well wrapped.

Ask the furniture dealer for its in-house procedures for processing your C.O.M. order. Procedures will vary from company to company. Waiting times to receive your furniture will vary from about two months to about six months, depending on the particular furniture manufacturer involved.

The furniture dealer will tell you what information to write down and send with your fabric. Normally, you will give your name, your address, your daytime phone number, the style name or number of the piece of furniture you are ordering, and usually some type of order identification number that the furniture dealer or manufacturer will assign to your order.

A good way to avoid mix-ups with C.O.M. orders is to staple your written order to the fabric itself. Make sure you staple the order to the selvage, not to the decorative portion of the fabric. If you just write your identifying information on the outside of the package or pack it inside without attaching it to the fabric, it may get lost.

Unfinished Furniture

In most areas, you will be able to find several local shops which carry unfinished furniture. This is just the plain furniture without any finish, paint, or decorative hardware. You can usually save at least 25% off of the cost of comparable finished furniture if you buy it in its unfinished state and do the finishing work yourself.

Unfinished furniture is often not the very highest-quality furniture available, although it is usually well made. Usually, this type of furniture works best in kitchens, family rooms, and children's rooms. You are unlikely to find unfinished furniture that would be formal enough to use in your living room or dining room.

Finishing, or refinishing, furniture is usually not difficult. The time and effort involved will vary according to the particular finish or effect you want to achieve. Find out exactly what will be involved before you buy the furniture. Many books and even television shows are devoted to this topic. If you have some free time and you want to save a lot of money, this is an alternative you should consider.

Any of the ideas given earlier in the chapter for revitalizing your current furniture with paint, new finishes, new hardware, or other embellishments can also be applied to unfinished furniture.

Antiques

Antique stores and auctions are very interesting places. After all, you aren't just buying furniture, you're making a good investment. And aren't you smart to invest your money in a unique treasure that will probably increase in value instead of just throwing it away on plain old furniture. So what if it costs more than you had planned to spend. You can resell it for twice as much as you paid for it in a few years. And, of course, such an obviously sophisticated person as yourself will have no problem picking out the real winners. After all, you have excellent taste.

If you have ever been to an antique store or auction, this might sound very familiar to you. Unscrupulous antique dealers have been taking advantage of naive customers (and making millions in the process) with this sort of ridiculous flattery for centuries. This may very well be the world's oldest scam.

Real expertise in judging the value of antiques takes years of study and experience to acquire. Unless you are truly an expert, put the idea of investing in antiques for profit out of your mind. Some antique dealers are sharks, and you don't want to swim with them unless you're a shark, too. Way too many guppies go home every day with $500.00 hat racks and $1000.00 coffee tables that they didn't even want and have no hope of ever increasing a nickel in value.

Besides, if a true gem really were lurking around somewhere, such as an original Hepplewhite chair, don't you think that the antique experts who purchased it, dusted it off, put a price tag on it, and put it out on display, might have noticed at some point that they had a genuine find? After all, that is what they have been trained and educated to do.

Phenomenal bargains and overlooked treasures are incredibly rare. You might as well invest your money in lottery tickets.

Many of us just love the *look* of antique furniture and other furnishings. They give an elegant, warm, and very stylish atmosphere to a home. Fortunately, reasonably priced reproductions of many antique furniture styles are widely available from factory outlets, wholesale showrooms, and telephone ordering services.

Many interior designers will tell you that reproductions are *tres gauche* and that you deserve "the real thing", but bear in mind that these people are usually being paid a straight percentage commission on whatever they can convince you to purchase. Of course they want you to buy the genuine $20,000.00 antique instead of a $500.00 copy, and the reason why doesn't have anything to do with the style police.

I have known a lot of interior designers over the years, and I can assure you that when they are decorating their own homes, at their own expense, they don't hesitate to grab a great reproduction when they see one.

If you love the look of antique furniture, but you can't afford it or don't feel qualified to properly judge its value, there are many good alternatives. You can shop for interesting older furniture that may not qualify as antique but is still perfectly attractive and well-made at charity thrift shops, estate sales, antique malls (the name is very misleading -- antique malls rarely sell true antiques), and flea markets.

Look for furniture that has possibilities. New hardware and finishes can make most used furniture look 100% better. New reproduction furniture is widely available through factory outlets, wholesale showrooms, and telephone ordering services. You might also consider buying new unfinished furniture and then adding antique or reproduction hardware and applying a finish with a nice, warm tone. These options are usually a lot cheaper than buying true antiques, or what you believe are true antiques, and will make your home look just as nice.

Whatever you do, don't let anyone talk you into buying something that you hadn't planned to buy and costs more than you had planned to spend because you think (or someone whispered in your ear) that it will increase in value. Buy only pieces that you think are attractive and reasonably priced. Don't try to speculate on their future value. If you must gamble, buy a $1.00 lottery ticket, not a $1000.00 credenza.

Special Safety Considerations For Children

There are some special safety concerns to consider when you are buying furniture for babies' and children's rooms. Some adult furniture, such as rockers and dressers, can also be used in a child's room, but you have to be more careful about what you buy.

Many of the discount sources, outlets, manufacturers, and other sources listed in this chapter sell cribs and other childrens' furniture in addition to their adult product lines. Some of the advice given in this chapter for getting great deals on adult furniture does not necessarily apply to buying furniture for your child.

Never buy a used, sample, discontinued, or second-quality crib. Always buy a new crib and make sure that it is a very recent model, not something that was manufactured five or ten years ago and then discontinued. Used or sample cribs may have been abused or damaged.

A discontinued crib might have been discontinued because it did not meet updated safety standards. Safety standards for cribs have been greatly improved in recent years, but that won't help you if the crib you purchase was manufactured before the most recent government safety standards went into effect.

Cribs and other types of furniture that have been declared unsafe aren't supposed to be sold, but there will always be some retailers and distributors that will sell off their existing stock anyway instead of taking a loss on it. Don't depend wholly on the government to protect you from unsafe products. There are hundreds of thousands of furniture distributors and retailers in the U. S. -- the government can't possibly inspect them all. Find out what the current safety standards are, as explained below, and check everything yourself.

Also, make sure that the crib was manufactured in the U. S. -- not overseas. Overseas companies are often not subject to the same regulations

Free Safety Brochure

You can also receive a free safety brochure by sending a self-addressed stamped envelope to the Juvenile Products Manufacturers Association at the following address:

JPMA Safety Brochure
236 Route 38 W., Suite 100
Moorestown, NJ 08057

You may also phone them at (609) 231-8500 if you have any concerns that are not addressed in the brochure.

The JPMA is a private association of juvenile products manufacturers that certifies all types of juvenile products, such as cribs and bedding, for safety.

and inspections as domestic companies. It is also very difficult for an average consumer to sue an overseas company for injuries caused by sloppy manufacturing. One positive aspect of the litigation frenzy in the U. S. is that it does tend to keep domestic manufacturers on their toes. Fear of being sued is a great motivation to test products thoroughly to make sure that they are safe.

Make sure that the mattress that comes with your child's crib is very firm. Soft mattresses, or any other soft surface, can cause a baby to smother. Also, check the slats underneath the mattress to make sure that they are firmly attached to the crib frame.

Make sure that any furniture used in a child's room is free of lead paint. That antique rocker you found at the local flea market might look wonderful in your baby's room, but you need to make absolutely sure that there is no lead in the paint. Not very long ago, lead paint was the standard for many types of furniture. If you have any doubt, strip the furniture and repaint or refinish it.

Make sure that all joints and slats are secure. Your child's fingers could get badly pinched if the legs or slats are wobbly. Check the width of any decorative cut-outs or spaces between slats, such as you might find on the back of a rocking chair. Make sure that there are no spaces wide enough for your child to put her head through.

Look for loose nails or splinters on an old piece of furniture. Explore every inch, just like a baby does, to make sure that there are no sharp points or edges. Don't forget to look underneath -- some companies put inspection stickers or law labels there. Look for any stickers, labels, loose nails, decorative tacks, or loose pieces of veneer, that a baby could pull off and put in his mouth.

Make sure that drawer and cabinet knobs and handles are tightly attached and cannot be easily unscrewed. While the knob or handle itself might be too large to pose a choking hazard, most of these types of knobs and handles have small screws in the reverse side that a child could easily choke on.

Check dresser drawers to make sure that they cannot be pulled completely out. Some dressers have stoppers that prevent the drawer from being accidentally removed from the frame. Otherwise, when you child starts pulling up on things, he might pull the drawers out on top of him. The same applies to removable bookshelves.

Be very careful about railings on bunk beds. The safety standards for bunk beds were recently revised due to the reported strangulation deaths of several children who became stuck between the railing and the bed frame. New federal safety guidelines state require that the space between the railing and bed frame is small enough not to allow this to happen. The updated safety standards are so new that you must be especially careful about this one when you are shopping. Unsafe bunk beds will probably remain on the market for some time.

This is by no means a complete list of safety concerns. These are only some concerns I have been made aware of over the years as I have spoken with parents about their decorating jobs. I am not an expert on child safety. I just felt that I should pass along the various concerns that I am aware of. You should not rely on this information alone as a means of keeping your child safe.

For further information on safety standards for childrens' furniture and other juvenile products and notices of product recalls, contact the U. S. Consumer Products Safety Commission at (800) 638-2772. This is an automated hotline, so you will not be able to speak to anyone personally, but it is incredibly detailed and comprehensive. Every parent should make a habit of calling this number for an update on unsafe products.

Your pediatrician or family doctor may also have more information about safety concerns when you are buying furniture for your child's room.

Retail Stores

Avoid buying furniture here unless you can find a good deal on seconds, floor samples, and returned merchandise. These can be great bargains. The best times to find floor samples on sale are January through early March and July through early September. Seconds and returned merchandise are available year-round at many stores.

Always ask. Many retail stores, especially the upscale ones, do not display marked-down merchandise because they do not wish to create an impression that they sell anything less than the best. If they were to put a table with a little scratch on it out in the middle of the showroom, their customers might think that everything else had some kind of damage, too.

So, they hide anything that looks less than perfect. As you can imagine, this makes their advertising options rather limited for imperfect furniture. Sometimes these bargains are just waiting in the back room for someone like you to speak up. You can get some great bargains, usually at least 50% to 80% off retail.

As noted in the box at right, be careful when you buy imperfect furniture. Sometimes, it doesn't conform to standard sizes. This can be a big problem, especially with beds. Imperfect furniture is normally not returnable, so be sure to check the size before you buy.

Retail stores are discussed thoroughly in Chapter 15.

Interior Designers and Interior Decorators

Avoid buying furniture here unless you can arrange to purchase something that another customer has failed to pay for. Most designers and decorators get stuck with something at some point.

Occasionally, the customer refuses to pay because the furnishings are second-quality or damaged in some way. More often, the designer or decorator ordered the wrong size or color and couldn't return it to the manufacturer. Usually the furnishings are fine, and might be just what you were looking for. If so, you can usually negotiate a big discount, at least 50% off retail and sometimes as much as 80% off retail.

There are enough of these "designer bloopers" out there to support a thriving industry of consignment stores that buy these furnishings from designers and decorators and then resell them to consumers. Cut out the middleman. These consignment stores aren't doing anything you can't do for yourself. Call around to designers and decorators in your area and see if they have anything you can use.

Don't Rely On "Standard" Sizes

Seconds and irregulars are often designated as such because they are not standard size. Also, the standard sizes of furniture have changed over the years. You must be careful when purchasing used, second-quality, or irregular furniture.

In general, the standard sizes have increased over the years as the average person's height has increased. This makes some older furniture too small. Some older bed frames are too short to accommodate a new mattress, for instance.

Don't assume anything. Always carry a small steel tape measure with you when you shop. These are very inexpensive and are available in any discount store. Don't use cloth or plastic tape measures because they sometimes stretch and give wrong measurements.

Modern mattress sizes are listed below. Try out all other types of furniture (desks, chairs, etc.) to be sure that they are comfortable for you before you buy.

Standard Mattresses

Twin: 39" X 75"
Extra-long twin: 39" X 80"
Full: 54" X 75"
Queen: 60" X 80"
Standard King: 78" X 80"

Waterbed mattresses

Single: 48" X 84"
Queen: 60" X 84"
King: 72" X 84"

Telephone Furniture Ordering Services

Telephone ordering services are one of the best sources for new furniture. Savings run up to 50% off retail. Unless you live near a factory outlet, or decide to become your own licensed decorator and buy your furniture wholesale, you will usually find the best bargains on new furniture from these services.

You can order furniture from almost any major manufacturer through the services listed in this section. Most of these services carry a wide variety of styles, unless there is a notation following the service name that indicates that it only carries one narrow category of furniture. Many carry hundreds of different brands. Call several services to compare prices and get the best deal on the particular brand and style of furniture you wish to order.

If the particular piece of furniture you want isn't available through any of the services, it is probably an exclusive product from an ultra-high priced designer. Exclusive products are discussed on page 286. If the snob-appeal of this exclusive furniture -- read "furniture with prices that have been vastly overinflated due to the elimination of open competition by monopolistic merchandising practices" -- is important enough to you to justify paying two prices (at least), you will have no choice but to buy it through an interior designer, and pay a hefty commission on top of the inflated price, of course.

However, if you are trying to keep costs down, look around carefully. No matter what furniture style or period you are interested in, you should be able to find high-quality furniture that looks very similar to the exclusive furniture and is available through a telephone ordering service at a far better price.

Many telephone ordering services can also order mattresses from major manufacturers. You may wish to compare their prices to those available in your city.

There are a few disadvantages to buying furniture over the phone. Waiting times are horrendous -- two months at the absolute least and sometimes as much as six months. Also, you are dealing with large amounts of money, out-of-state businesses, and an industry that has been infiltrated by a few con-artists. The savings can be wonderful, but there are risks. Many customers lose money every year to crooked telephone ordering services.

This doesn't mean that you shouldn't enjoy the savings that are available, just that you should be very careful. Virtually all of the risks are avoidable. Please read Chapter 16 (Telephone Ordering Services) and Chapter 20 ("Troubleshooting") carefully before ordering furniture over the phone.

Also, be sure to read the section later in the chapter on factory outlets. Many of these businesses also accept phone orders and allow customers to pay by credit card.

Ordering As with any telephone ordering service, you should have as much product information as possible at the ready when you call. Although some services publish catalogs, it is generally not necessary to refer to the catalog when you place your order. If you already have the product information discussed on the next page, most services will be able to process your order right away, assuming that they carry the particular brand you have in mind.

When you are shopping at local design centers and retail stores and looking through design magazines, you should record the following information (where applicable):

Manufacturer name	
Item number	
Type of wood	
Type of finish	Cherry, oak, walnut, etc. Don't forget that the finish refers to the color only, not to the type of wood used.
Color	
Upholstery details	You should note what specific touches you want, such as a skirt on sofas and chairs. You should also specify the name or number of the fabric you want.
Finished size	Specify the length, width, height, and depth of the furniture, where applicable.
Description	Give a general description of the furniture -- ''Queen Anne chair'', ''contemporary pillow-back sofa'', etc.

If you are in doubt as to whether a detail is important -- write it down!

Much of this information is usually recorded on a label underneath table tops, bed frames, and chair seats and on the backs of sofas, bookcases, dressers, entertainment centers, and mirrors. Always look carefully for this original label from the manufacturer. By law, it should not have been removed or altered -- although some businesses do this anyway.

Making sure you have the correct product information Some retail stores -- but not magazines and wholesale design center showrooms -- will alter or hide item numbers and manufacturer information to hinder competition from telephone ordering services. If the alterations are obvious (crossed out information, little stickers covering up the original manufacturer's product information, etc.), shop somewhere else.

If you suspect that the item numbers have been altered on a furniture sample, you can often call the manufacturer's home office to receive a brochure with pictures and information about its products -- including all of the correct item numbers. Some firms charge a nominal fee for their catalogs, but many will reimburse this fee upon making a furniture purchase.

If you do not wish to pay the catalog fee, or if a catalog is not available, the home office should be able to direct you to a number of retail stores in your area that carry the manufacturer's furniture free of charge. Chances are, at least one will not have altered the product information on its samples.

The home office phone numbers of some of the most prominent furniture manufacturers in the U. S. are listed in the box at right.

Major Furniture Mfrs

Baker	(800) 592-2537
Bassett	(703) 629-6000
Bernhardt	(800) 345-9875
Bieleck Bros.	(212) 753-2355
Broyhill	(800) 327-6944
Brueton	(800) 221-6783
Century	(800) 852-5552
Classic Rattan	(606) 885-3384
Cochrane	(704) 732-1151
Crawford	(716) 661-9100
Customcraft	(800) 624-6792
D. & F. Wicker	(201) 927-8530
Dinaire	(716) 894-1201
Donghia	(800) 366-4442
Drexel Heritage	(800) 916-1986
E. J. Victor	(704) 437-1991
Edward Ferrell	(910) 841-3028
Ethan Allen	(800) 228-9229
Grange	(800) 472-6431
Habersham Plantation	(800) 241-0716
Harden	(315) 245-1000
Hekman	(800) 253-5345
Henredon	(800) 444-3682
Hickory Chair	(800) 349-4579
Highland House	(704) 323-8600
Hooker	(704) 632-2133
Kittinger	(716) 876-1000
Kreiss	(800) 573-4771
La Barge	(800) 253-3870
La-Z-Boy	(313) 242-1444
Lane	(804) 369-5641
Levenger	(800) 544-0880
Lexington	(800) 544-4694
Ligne-Roset	(800) 297-6738
Lloyd-Flanders	(906) 863-4491
McGuire	(415) 626-1414
Modulus	(800) 486-2580
Pennsylvania House	(800) 782-9663
Roche-Bobois	(800) 972-8375
Sherrill	(704) 322-2640
Stickley	(315) 682-5500
Techline	(800) 356-8400
Tell City Chair	(812) 547-3491
Thomasville	(800) 225-0265
William Alan	(910) 885-6095
Woodhenge	(800) 225-3772

Payment The standard procedure with many of these services is to require a portion of the order to be paid at the time the order is placed, typically 20% to 50%, with the balance due at the time the order is ready to be shipped. Always make all payments with a credit card. Normally, the deposit will be charged to your credit card immediately, and the balance will be charged when the merchandise is actually shipped. If you don't live in the state where the service is located, you will normally not be charged sales tax.

A few services insist that customers pay the entire balance up front if they are using a credit card. Avoid these companies if you can -- there are some companies that do allow you to pay the balance with your credit card only when the furniture is actually shipped. Read pages 344-346 carefully before placing your order -- it explains credit card policies and potential problems that you want to make sure you avoid.

Reconfirm the payment policies of any service you contact before placing an order, as they can change from time to time, and ALWAYS use your credit card.

Most of the companies listed below and on the next page carry a wide assortment of traditional and contemporary furniture brands and styles. A few of these companies carry only one narrow category of furniture. Where applicable, the specific type of furniture carried by the company has been noted under the company name.

Telephone Ordering Services

Barnes & Barnes Fine Furniture
(Call for free brochure)
190 Commerce Ave.
Southern Pines, NC 28387
(800) 334-8174

Blackwelder's
Route 18, Box 8
Statesville, NC 28677
(800) 438-0201

Boyles Distinctive Furniture
Hickory Furniture Mart
Hickory, NC 28602
(704) 326-1740

Brass Bed Shoppe
Brass and iron beds only
12421 Cedar Rd.
Cleveland Heights, OH 44106
(216) 371-0400

Charles P. Rogers
Brass and iron beds only
899 First Ave.
New York, NY 10022
(800) 272-7726

Colfax Furniture Store
South Holden Rd.
Greensboro, NC 27407
(910) 855-0498

Corner Hutch Furniture
Highway 21 North
Statesville, NC 28677
(704) 873-1773

The Decorator's Edge
509 Randolph St.
Thomasville, NC 27360
(800) 289-5589

Telephone Ordering Services (cont.)

Designer Secrets
P. O. Box 529
Fremont, NE 68025
(800) 955-2559

Don Lamor
Hickory Furniture Mart
Hickory, NC 28602
(704) 324-1776

Edgar B.
(Call for free catalog)
P. O. Box 849
Clemmons, NC 27012
(800) 255-6589

Ellenburg's Furniture
I-40 and Stamey Farm Rd.
Statesville, NC 28677
(704) 873-2900

European Furniture Importers
(Send $3.00 for catalog)
2145 W. Grand Ave.
Chicago, IL 60612
(800) 283-1955

Furniture Barn of Forest City
Hwy. 74 Bypass
Spindale, NC 28160
(704) 287-7106

Furniture Choices
2501 Peters Creek Parkway
Greensboro, NC 27107
(910) 720-9700

Genada Imports
Scandinavian and Danish furniture only
(Send $1.00 for catalog)
P. O. Box 204
Teaneck, NJ 07666
(201) 790-7522

Harvest House Furniture
Highway 109 S.
Denton, NC 27239
(704) 869-5181

Hunt Galleries
(Send $8.00 for catalog)
2920 Hwy. 127 N
Hickory, NC 28601
(800) 248-3876

Loftin-Black Furniture
111 Sedgehill Dr.
Thomasville, NC 27360
(800) 334-7398

Mallory's Fine Furniture
2153 Le Jeune Blvd.
Jacksonville, NC 28546
(910) 353-1828

Mecklenburg Furniture
7203 Statesville Rd.
Charlotte, NC 28213
(800) 541-9877

Midamerica Furniture
100 E. Lincoln St.
Hamburg, AR 71646
(800) 259-7897

National Furniture Distributors
Hickory Furniture Mart
Hickory, NC 28602
(704) 322-1115

Plaza Furniture
P. O. Box 1150
North Myrtle Beach, SC 29598
(800) 262-9898

Plexi-Craft Quality Products
Acrylic furniture only
(Send $2.00 for catalog)
514 W. 24th St.
New York, NY 10011
(212) 924-3244

Quality Furniture Market
2034 Hickory Blvd. SE
Lenoir, NC 28645
(704) 728-2946

Reflections Contemporary Furniture
Hickory Furniture Mart
Hickory, NC 28602
(704) 327-8485

Sutton-Councill Furniture
421 S. College Rd.
Wilmington, NC 28403
(910) 799-9000

Triad Furniture Discounters
9770 North Kings Hwy.
Magnolia Plaza
Myrtle Beach, SC 29577
(800) 323-8469

Turner Tolson Furniture
U. S. Hwy. 17 S
New Bern, NC 28562
(919) 638-2121

Tyson Furniture
109 Broadway St.
Black Mountain, NC 28711
(704) 669-5000

Wicker Warehouse
(Send $5.00 for catalog)
195 S. River St.
Hackensack, NJ 07601
(800) 274-8620

Factory Outlets

Factory outlets definitely bear investigating. Prices are normally at least 50% off retail on new first-quality furniture, and are sometimes as low as 75% to 80% off retail on irregulars, seconds, floor samples, and discontinued items.

Many manufacturers do not operate their own outlets, as this is an expensive undertaking and is often not cost-effective for a small manufacturer to do alone. Many liquidate their seconds, irregulars, showroom samples, and discontinued styles through a consolidated outlet store that carries merchandise from many different manufacturers or through a deep discount store (usually the stores in North Carolina). You will find a number of consolidated outlets listed in this section and many deep discount stores listed in the next section.

A few manufacturers, typically the very small and very high-brow ones, do not liquidate any imperfect merchandise to the public at all. They price their seconds, returns, and samples low enough to sell all of it to their own employees or to well connected people in the industry. They don't want their brand names to be associated with discount stores or outlets in any way. Even so, you can still occasionally purchase floor samples or returns from these brands through local wholesale showrooms and retail stores.

If you cannot locate furniture from a specific manufacturer through an outlet or discount store, you may wish to call wholesale showrooms in your local area, if there are any. Keep in mind that some of these high-brow manufacturers won't sell to the public at all, even samples and seconds.

You could switch to a different manufacturer, instead. Most of the very finest major furniture manufacturers do liquidate imperfect merchandise to the public through outlets and discount stores -- Henredon, Century, Baker, Thomasville, Drexel-Heritage, Bernhardt, and many more. You should have no difficulty finding beautiful furniture that suits your tastes perfectly at bargain prices. You don't have to pay retail in order to have the finest quality furniture.

If you place a phone order with an outlet that is not in the state where you live, you will usually not be charged sales tax. However, if you make your purchase in person at any outlet, you will be charged that state's sales tax.

Virtually all furniture factory outlets are in North Carolina, which makes traveling to them too inconvenient and expensive for many of you. Fortunately, some of them accept phone orders and allow payment by credit card.

Some outlets accept phone orders -- some don't. Some accept credit cards -- some require payment by check. Policies change from time to time, so it's best to call and find out what the current policies are when you are ready to place your order with the outlet. Outlets are listed on pages 33 and 34.

These outlets are typically real no-frills operations. Of course, the prices are much lower partly due to the relative lack of service and sales help. This is all part of buying at deep discounts.

Consolidated outlets are marked with a ***(C)*** after the outlet name. These outlets carry merchandise from many different manufacturers. All of the other outlets only carry furniture from one particular manufacturer.

If a consolidated outlet specializes in certain types of furniture, this will be noted in italics below the outlet name. All of the other consolidated outlets carry a wide variety of furniture types and styles.

Factory Outlets

California

Brass Beds Direct ***(C)***
Brass beds only
3410 Harcourt Ave.
Los Angeles, CA 90016
(800) 727-6865

Delaware

Wicker Outlet ***(C)***
Wicker and rattan only
Ocean Outlets Factory
Outlet Center
Route 1
Rehoboth Beach, DE 19971
(302) 226-9223

Missouri

Vermillion
Factory Merchants
Hwy. 76 and U. S. Hwy. 65
Branson, MO 65616
(417) 335-6686

North Carolina

Brass and Iron Beds/
Furniture & Accessories Outlet ***(C)***
Brass and iron beds only
711 E. Harden St.
Graham, NC 27253
(910) 228-6903

Classic Leather Factory Outlet
Ramada Rd.
Burlington, NC 27216
(910) 570-0444

Hickory White Factory Outlet
Ramada Rd.
Burlington, NC 27216
(910) 229-0831

North Carolina (cont.)

Pennsylvania House Factory Outlet
Ramada Rd.
Burlington, NC 27216
(910) 226-8466

Rattan and Wicker Factory Outlet ***(C)***
Rattan and wicker only
200 E. Seneca Rd.
Greensboro, NC 27406
(910) 273-1683

Beacon Hill Factory Outlet
Hickory Furniture Mart
Hickory, NC 28602
(704) 324-2220

Century Factory Outlet
Hickory Furniture Mart
Hickory, NC 28602
(704) 326-1740

Drexel-Heritage Factory Outlet
Hickory Furniture Mart
Hickory, NC 28602
(704) 324-2220

Henredon Factory Outlet
Hickory Furniture Mart
Hickory, NC 28602
(704) 322-7111

Hickorycraft Factory Outlet
Hickory Furniture Mart
Hickory, NC 28602
(704) 324-2220

Home Outfitters ***(C)***
Hickory Furniture Mart
Hickory, NC 28602
(704) 324-2220

Hunt Galleries
2920 Hwy. 127 N
Hickory, NC 28601
(800) 248-3876

North Carolina (cont.)

La Barge Factory Outlet
Hickory Furniture Mart
Hickory, NC 28602
(704) 324-2220

Maitland-Smith Factory Outlet
Hickory Furniture Mart
Hickory, NC 28602
(704) 324-2220

Marge Carson Factory Outlet
Hickory Furniture Mart
Hickory, NC 28602
(704) 324-2220

The Baker Factory Store
Cannon Village
146 West Ave.
Kannapolis, NC 28081
(704) 938-9191

Carolina Interiors ***(C)***
Cannon Village
200 West Ave.
Kannapolis, NC 28081
(704) 933-1888

Century Furniture Clearance
Center
Cannon Village
200 West Ave.
Kannapolis, NC 28081
(704) 938-9191

Thomasville Furniture Factory Store
401 E. Main St.
Thomasville, NC 27360
(910) 476-2211

Factory Outlets (cont.)

Ohio

Aurora Furniture & Interiors ***(C)***
Aurora Farms Factory Outlets
Exit 13 off Ohio Turnpike
Aurora, OH 44202
(216) 562-9400

Forty Winks Beds & Bedding ***(C)***
Beds and mattresses only
Aurora Farms Factory Outlets
Exit 13 off Ohio Turnpike
Aurora, OH 44202
(216) 562-2350

Wayside Workshop ***(C)***
Reproduction and unfinished only
Aurora Farms Factory Outlets
Exit 13 off Ohio Turnpike
Aurora, OH 44202
(216) 562-4800

Tennessee

Furniture Factory Outlet ***(C)***
Belz Factory Outlet Mall
3536 Canada Rd.
Lakeland, TN 38002
(901) 386-3180

Virginia

Lane Furniture Factory Outlet
Williamsburg Outlet Mall
Exit 234 off I-64
Lightfoot, VA 23090
(804) 565-0241

Rowe Showplace Gallery
Potomac Mills Outlet Center
Exit 156 off I-95
Prince William, VA 22192
(800) VA-MILLS

Deep Discount Stores

By "deep discount store", I'm not talking about the stores in your area that sell cheap, particle-board furniture. I am talking about enormous warehouses filled with high-quality designer brands -- Henry Link, Baker, Henredon, Thomasville, Drexel-Heritage, Century, Bernhardt, and literally hundreds of other top-quality furniture lines -- at unbelievable discounts. These are the very same lines that interior designers and interior decorators make a killing on every day by charging huge mark-ups to consumers who probably have no idea that they can shop direct for much less.

Most of the deep discount furniture stores are located in North Carolina. Over 60% of the furniture produced in the entire United States is made here, and outlet stores and discount stores are on virtually every street corner. If you are planning to purchase a significant amount of furniture and you are within a reasonable distance, you may wish to travel to North Carolina to choose your furniture right at the source. This is the mother lode. There are some discounters in other cities throughout the United States, as well.

Be sure to check out the Hickory Furniture Mart, described at right. It has about 60 deep discount stores and factory outlets all under one roof (13 acres of furniture on display!) that carry an amazing variety of top-quality furniture and other home furnishings. There are also some true factory outlets in the Mart that carry seconds, samples, discontinued styles, and irregulars from a variety of manufacturers. These are listed on page 33.

Many catalogs, such as Bloomingdale's and Spiegel, and department stores, such as Macy's and Haverty's, have outlet centers all across the country that stock furniture and other types of home furnishings. Normally, these are customer returns, floor samples, and canceled special orders. The furniture is usually of medium to high quality and well worth checking out. These stores are included in the list of discount stores, as well.

You will often have to pay by cash or check -- although some stores do accept credit cards. Most of the furniture will be sold on an "as-is" basis, meaning that it cannot be returned and any defects are your responsibility. This is fine as long as you carefully inspect all furniture personally before you buy.

Typical discounts at these stores are up to 50% on new furniture. Seconds, irregulars, floor samples, customer returns, and discontinued styles can run up to 80% off retail.

One extra advantage to buying furniture at these sources, in addition to the added savings, is that you don't have to wait for months to get your furniture home. It's all there. Right now. Just pick out what you want and load it up.

You should be well-prepared in advance of your trip, as the best stores will often be some distance from where you live. Make sure you have researched the basic styles and finishes you want. Measure spaces in your home for sofas, bookcases, entertainment centers, dressers, and other large items. Don't forget to measure the height of your ceiling -- this is important for some wall units.

Measure door dimensions, too. You don't want to get your unreturnable purchases home just to find that they won't fit where you want to use them, or can't be brought into the room at all. Bring along any necessary fabric or carpet swatches to match upholstered furniture.

The Hickory Furniture Mart

This is discount central. The most prestigious furniture manufacturers in the industry -- Bernhardt, Century, Henredon, and Drexel-Heritage, among many others -- have factory outlet stores here. Most of the stores and outlets accept credit cards and telephone orders. In addition to the furniture lines listed here, there are also many outlets and discounters for other types of furnishings, which are listed in the appropriate chapters later in this book.

Some of the manufacturers that only have discount showrooms at the Mart also operate true factory outlets at other locations, listed on pages 33-34.

The only furniture factory outlets at the Mart are Drexel-Heritage, La Barge, Henredon, Century, Beacon Hill, Frederick Edward, Hickorycraft, Maitland-Smith, Marge Carson, and Home Outfitters. Home Outfitters sells seconds, irregulars, discontinued styles, and floor samples from many different manufacturers. The rest of the showrooms are discount stores.

Some of the showrooms also accept phone orders. Please call each showroom directly at the phone number listed next to the brand name to find out if that particular manufacturer is currently accepting phone orders.

There is a general number that can give you directions to the Mart and help arrange shipping -- (800) 462-MART. It is often possible to combine orders from several separate showrooms and have them packed and shipped together, which can save you a substantial amount on your freight bill. They can also mail you a free buyer's guide that will be very helpful in planning your trip.

The Mart is located at 2220 Highway 70 SE in Hickory, NC. The Mart is open Monday through Friday from 9 to 6 and Saturday from 9 to 5.

Furniture

Bassett	(704) 322-6602
Beacon Hill	(704) 324-2220
Beka Cast	(704) 345-0882
Benchcraft	(704) 345-0882
Benicia Daybeds	(704) 328-8855
Berkline	(704) 322-4440
Bernhardt	(704) 322-1740
Boyles	(704) 326-1740
Bradington Young	(704) 328-5257
Brown Jordan	(704) 345-0882
Broyhill	(704) 324-9767
Century	(704) 326-1740
Classic Leather	(704) 324-1776
Clayton Marcus	(704) 328-8688
Cochrane	(704) 322-6602
Comfort Zone	(704) 322-4440
Conover Chair	(704) 328-8855
Councill Craftsmen	(704) 326-1740
D & F Wicker	(704) 345-0882
Designer Creations	(704) 327-9933
Distinction Leather	(704) 328-8855
Don Lamor	(704) 324-1776
Drexel-Heritage	(704) 324-2220
Dura Wicker	(704) 345-0882
Ekornes	(704) 327-8485
Emerson Leather	(704) 327-8485
Executive Leather	(704) 322-6602
Franklin Place	(704) 322-5539
Frederick Edward	(704) 324-2220
Generations Youth	(704) 322-7275
Glencraft	(704) 327-8485
Habersham Plantation	(704) 328-8855
Halcyon	(704) 345-0882
Hammary	(704) 322-4440
Hancock and Moore	(704) 326-1740
Hekman	(704) 322-4440
Henkel-Harris	(704) 326-1740
Henredon	(704) 322-7111
Hickory Chair	(704) 326-1740
Hickory Home	(704) 323-8893
Hickory Park	(704) 322-4440
Hickory White	(704) 322-6602
Hickorycraft	(704) 324-2220
Hitchcock Chair	(704) 328-8855
Holiday Patio Shoppe	(704) 345-0882
Home Outfitters	(704) 324-2220
Homecrest	(704) 345-0882
J. Royale	(704) 322-6602
Kincaid	(704) 322-4440
Lane	(704) 326-1740
Lane Action	(704) 322-4440
La Barge	(704) 324-2220
LeatherMark	(800) 345-1599
Lexington	(704) 322-6602
Lloyd-Flanders	(704) 345-0882
Lyon Shaw	(704) 345-0882
Maitland-Smith	(704) 324-2220
Marge Carson	(704) 324-2220
Meadowcraft	(704) 345-0882
Molla	(704) 345-0882
Nat'l Furniture Dist.	(704) 322-1115
National Mt. Airy	(704) 324-1776
Natuzzi	(704) 327-8485
Old Hickory Tannery	(704) 327-8485
Pacific Rattan	(704) 345-0882
Palliser	(704) 324-7742
Park Place	(704) 327-9933
Pennsylvania Classics	(704) 324-1776
Pennsylvania House	(704) 324-1776
Precedent	(704) 326-1735
Polywood	(704) 345-0882
Reflections	(704) 327-8485
Rex Oak Dining Rms	(704) 328-8855
Rhoney Furniture Hse	(704) 328-8688
Rowe	(704) 327-9933
Samsonite	(704) 345-0882
Sherrill	(704) 326-1740
Skillcraft Glider Rockers	(704) 328-8855
Southern Designs	(704) 328-8855
Southern Furniture Reproductions	(704) 328-8855
Southwood	(704) 326-1740
Statesville Chair	(704) 324-1776
Statton	(704) 326-1740
Stratford	(704) 326-9224
Stratolounger	(704) 322-4440
Summer Classics	(704) 345-0882
Telescope	(704) 345-0882
Thomasville	(704) 326-1740
Tricomfort	(704) 345-0882
Tropitone	(704) 345-0882
Universal	(704) 322-6602
Vanguard	(704) 324-1776
Vargas	(704) 327-9933
Virginia House	(704) 328-8855
Weathercraft	(704) 345-0882
Weiman	(704) 324-1776
Wildermere	(704) 322-6602
Windsor Design	(704) 345-0882
Winner's Only	(704) 327-9933
Winston	(704) 345-0882
Wisconsin Furniture	(704) 328-8855
Woodard	(704) 345-0882
Zagaroli Classics	(800) 887-2424

Mattresses

Serta	(704) 322-6602

How Do You Get That Great Bargain Home?

If you shop at a discount store or factory outlet in person, you may have to make your own arrangements to get your furniture home.

Some outlets and discount stores can help you arrange delivery of your furniture, others don't establish any system to help you get your furniture home. If you are shopping at a real absolutely-no-frills operation, you will probably have to borrow or rent a truck and transport the furniture home yourself.

Depending upon the brand and quantity of furniture you plan to buy, you may find that it would be more cost-effective to pay slightly more for your furniture by ordering it over the phone from an outlet or service that accepts credit cards and having them arrange shipment.

It won't do you any good to save an extra $50.00 on a discontinued dining room table if you have to spend $200.00 to get it home. Of course, if you are buying furniture for every room in your house and you can save several thousand dollars by buying seconds and floor samples in person at the outlet or discount store, it would probably be cost-effective to rent a truck. You must consider your own particular situation and decide.

Deep discount stores such as these do have very good prices, but they don't match the factory outlets listed in the previous section. Factory outlets tend to have slightly lower prices and offer seconds, irregulars, floor samples, and discontinued furniture in addition to new merchandise. Discount stores typically only offer new merchandise from those manufacturers that have their own outlet stores.

However, some furniture manufacturers (especially the smaller ones) do not operate their own outlets and liquidate their new and imperfect merchandise through these discount stores instead. If you are interested in a particular brand of furniture, see if a true factory outlet is available first. That will usually be your best option.

If no factory outlet is available, or if the outlet won't take credit cards, a discount store or telephone ordering service can be a good alternative.

Discount stores normally carry furniture from a wide variety of manufacturers. Many also carry other home furnishings such as fabrics, artwork, mirrors, etc. Call each store directly to find out if they currently carry a specific manufacturer's products.

Shopping at these stores is very much like shopping at a factory outlet -- no frills whatsoever. Merchandise is generally sold "as-is". Returns are virtually never allowed. You will often have to load up your own purchases, so bring help if you need it. You may also need to borrow or rent a truck, as discussed at left. You will be charged sales tax.

Bring your magnifying glass. Check everything very carefully. Some of the products you will see are irregulars, seconds, and (in the case of catalog and department store liquidators) customer returns. Make sure that you know about any problems with the furniture and that you can either fix them or live with them because, no matter how bad the problems are, you can't return the furniture.

Discount stores are listed beginning at right, organized by state and city. Most stores are open 9-5 Monday through Saturday. Please call the store directly for current store hours, payment policies, and specific directions within the city.

"Do Y'all Validate?"

A new trend among outlets and discount stores in North Carolina is to reimburse you for all or part of your lodging bill if you purchase a certain minimum amount of furniture during your stay.

This perk is only available from a smattering of stores at this writing, but the intense competition in the furniture industry will certainly make many more stores follow along very soon. You should ask about lodging reimbursements when you contact an outlet or store in order to get the most up-to-date information.

Ask about any other new perks that might be available. As soon as this gimmick becomes routine, the stores are bound to come up with a new one.

Deep Discount Stores

Arkansas

Midamerica Furniture
100 E. Lincoln
Hamburg, AR 71646
(800) 259-7897

California

Sears Catalog Clearance Center
14500 E. Hatch Rd.
Modesto, CA 95351
(209) 538-0579

Sears Catalog Clearance Center
3450 College Ave.
San Diego, CA 92115
(619) 583-9802

Sears Catalog Clearance Center
2750 E. Main St.
Ventura, CA 93003
(805) 643-8661

Colorado

Spiegel Catalog Clearance Center
Rocky Mountain Factory Stores
I-25 and U. S. Hwy. 34
Loveland, CO 80538
(970) 663-1717

Delaware

Wicker Outlet
Ocean Outlets
Route 1
Rehoboth Beach, DE 19971
(302) 226-9223

Florida

Haverty's Direct Clearance Center
7720 Phillips Hwy.
Jacksonville, FL 32216
(904) 731-9160

Florida (cont.)

Spiegel Catalog Clearance Center
8427 Cooper Creek Blvd.
University Park, FL 34201
(813) 359-0519

Georgia

Ballard's Backroom
Catalog Clearance Center
1670 De Foor Ave.
Atlanta, GA 30318
(404) 352-2776

Rich's Furniture Clearance Center
2841 Greenbriar Parkway
Atlanta, GA 30331
(404) 346-2790

Rich's Furniture Clearance Center
2731 Candler Rd.
Decatur, GA 30034
(404) 243-2650

Haverty's Direct Clearance Outlet
5600 Buford Hwy.
Doraville, GA 30340
(404) 458-6700

Rhodes Furniture Clearance Center
4363 NE Expressway Access Rd.
Doraville, GA 30341
(404) 934-9350

J. C. Penney Catalog Outlet
5500 S. Expressway
Forest Park, GA 30050
(404) 363-3855

Bombay Company Clearance Center
4101 Roswell Rd., Suite 401
Marietta, GA 30062
(770) 509-7008

Georgia (cont.)

Charles Keath Clearance Center
1265 Oakbrook Dr.
Norcross, GA 30093
(800) 241-1122

Design Center Outlet
6315 Spalding Dr.
Norcross, GA 30092
(770) 825-0020

Roberds Clearance Center
I-85 and Jimmy Carter Blvd.
Norcross, GA 30093
(770) 449-4214

J. C. Penney Catalog Outlet
2434 Atlanta Rd.
Smyrna, GA 30080
(770) 432-5231

Rich's Furniture Clearance Center
2144 South Cobb Dr.
Smyrna, GA 30080
(770) 433-4790

Illinois

European Furniture Importers
2145 W. Grand Ave.
Chicago, IL 60612
(800) 283-1955

Spiegel Clearance Center
9950 Joliet Rd.
Countryside, IL 60513
(312) 357-3370

Bombay Company Clearance Center
1734 Sherman Ave.
Evanston, IL 60201
(708) 328-6171

J. C. Penney Clearance Center
I-94 and Route 132
Gurnee, IL 60031
(800) YES-SHOP

Deep Discount Stores (cont.)

Illinois (cont.)

Spiegel Clearance Center
Gurnee Mills
I-94 and Route 132
Gurnee, IL 60031
(800) YES-SHOP

Indiana

Kittle's Outlet
7150 E. Washington
Indianapolis, IN 46219
(317) 356-5400

Kentucky

Spiegel Clearance Center
1108 Fashion Ridge Rd.
Dry Ridge, KY 41035
(606) 824-9224

Maryland

Wicker Outlet
Chesapeake Village Outlet
Center
441 Chesapeake Village Rd.
Queenstown, MD 21658
(410) 827-8699

Massachusetts

Bombay Company Clearance
Center
9 Pleasant Valley St.
Methuen, MA 01844
(508) 685-2660

Michigan

Spiegel Clearance Center
12330 James St. and
U. S. Highway 31
Suite H-20
Holland, MI 49424
(616) 396-4446

Michigan (cont.)

Spiegel Clearance Center
14500 La Plaisance Rd.
Suite D-10
Monroe, MI 48161
(313) 457-2530

Minnesota

Dayton Hudson Distribution Center
701 Industrial Blvd.
Minneapolis, MN 55413
(612) 623-7111

New Jersey

Macy's Furniture Clearance Center
Route 4
Paramus, NJ 07652
(201) 487-1917

Macy's Furniture Clearance Center
Route 22 West
Springfield, NJ 07081
(201) 376-8699

Macy's Furniture Clearance Center
Route 46
Wayne, NJ 07470
(201) 785-0407

New York

Bloomingdale's Clearance Center
155 Glen Cove Rd.
Carle Place, NY 11514
(516) 248-1400

Macy's Furniture Clearance Center
174 Glen Cove Rd.
Carle Place, NY 11514
(516) 746-1490

New York (cont.)

Bombay Company Clearance
Center
439 Central Ave.
Cedarhurst, NY 11516
(516) 374-5020

Macy's Furniture Clearance
Center
1640 Broad Hollow Rd.
Farmingdale, NY 11735
(516) 293-7260

Charles P. Rogers
Brass and iron beds only
899 First Ave.
New York, NY 10022
(800) 272-7726

Major Furniture Showroom
16 W. 19th St.
New York, NY 10011
(212) 691-9885

Plexi-Craft Quality Products
Acrylic furniture only
514 W. 24th St.
New York, NY 10011
(212) 924-3244

North Carolina

Sobol House of Furnishings
141 Richardson Blvd.
Black Mountain, NC 28711
(704) 669-8031

Tyson Furniture
109 Broadway St.
Black Mountain, NC 28711
(704) 669-5000

Deep Discount Stores (cont.)

North Carolina (cont.)

Wellington's Fine Leather Furniture
Hwy. 321 Bypass
Blowing Rock, NC 28605
(800) 262-1049

The Furniture Patch
10283 Beach Dr. SW
Calabash, NC 28467
(910) 579-2001

Boyle's Furniture
7607 Nations Ford Rd.
Charlotte, NC 28217
(704) 522-8081

E. L. Mincey Furniture
600 W. Sugar Creek Rd.
Charlotte, NC 28213
(704) 596-2341

Haverty's Direct Clearance Center
3900 E. Independence Blvd.
Building B
Charlotte, NC 28205
(704) 536-5570

Mecklenburg Furniture
7203 Statesville Rd.
Charlotte, NC 28213
(800) 541-9877

Harvest House Furniture
Highway 109 S.
Denton, NC 27239
(704) 869-5181

Blowing Rock Furniture Co.
Highway 321 N.
Granite Falls, NC 28630
(704) 396-5356

North Carolina (cont.)

Center Court Furniture Mall
76 Wood Lane St.
Granite Falls, NC 28630
(704) 396-4803

Coffey Discount Furniture and Auction
Highway 321
Granite Falls, NC 28630
(704) 396-2900

Lake Hickory Furniture
405 Hwy. 321 S
Granite Falls, NC 28630
(704) 396-2194

Mackie Furniture
N. Main St.
Granite Falls, NC 28630
(704) 396-3313

Oak City
Hwy. 321 S.
Granite Falls, NC 28630
(704) 396-8320

Plaza Furniture Gallery
241 Timber Brook Lane
Granite Falls, NC 28630
(704) 396-8150

Sofa World
2171 Highway 70 SE
Granite Falls, NC 28630
(704) 496-1010

Thomas Home Furnishings
401 Hwy. 321 S.
Granite Falls, NC 28630
(704) 396-2147

A Classic Design
1703 Madison Ave.
Greensboro, NC 27403
(910) 274-2922

North Carolina (cont.)

Colfax Furniture Store
South Holden Rd.
Greensboro, NC 27407
(910) 855-0498

Fields Furniture Co.
2700 Randelman Rd.
Greensboro, NC 27406
(910) 273-7629

Furniture Choices
2501 Peters Creek Parkway
Greensboro, NC 27107
(910) 720-9700

House Dressing International Furniture
3608 W. Wendover
Greensboro, NC 27407
(800) 322-5850

L. F. Shaw Furniture
3208 Summit Ave.
Greensboro, NC 27405
(910) 621-3675

Priba Furniture Sales
5-A Wendy Ct.
Greensboro, NC 27409
(910) 855-9034

Spring Valley Discount Furniture
429 W. Meadowview Rd.
Greensboro, NC 27406
(910) 272-9655

Bonita Furniture Galleries
210 13th St. SW
Hickory, NC 28602
(704) 324-1992

Farm House Furnishings
1432 First Ave. SW
Hickory, NC 28602
(704) 324-4595

Deep Discount Stores (cont.)

North Carolina (cont.)

Hunt Galleries
2920 Hwy. 127 N
Hickory, NC 28601
(800) 248-3876

Interior Furnishings Ltd.
1308 Hwy. 64
Hickory, NC 28602
(704) 328-5683

Rhoney Furniture House
2401 Highway 70 SW
Hickory, NC 28602
(704) 328-2034

A. Windsor Furniture Galleries
607 Idol St.
High Point, NC 27262
(910) 883-9000

Alan Ferguson Associates
422 S. Main St.
High Point, NC 27260
(910) 889-3866

Arts By Alexander
701 Greensboro Rd.
High Point, NC 27260
(910) 884-8062

Bennington Furniture Galleries
1300 S. Main St.
High Point, NC 27260
(910) 884-1894

Black's Furniture
2800 Westchester St.
High Point, NC 27262
(910) 886-5011

Boyles Furniture Co.
727 N. Main St.
High Point, NC 27262
(910) 889-4147

North Carolina (cont.)

Dallas Furniture Store
215 N. Centennial St.
High Point, NC 27260
(910) 882-2654

Furniture Clearance Center
1107 Tate St.
High Point, NC 27260
(910) 882-1688

Gibson Interiors
417 S. Wrenn St.
High Point, NC 27260
(910) 883-4444

High Point Furniture Sales
2000 Baker Rd.
High Point, NC 27260
(800) 334-1875

Main St. Galleries
430 S. Main St.
High Point, NC 27260
(910) 883-2611

Paynes Furniture
2904 N. Main St.
High Point, NC 27265
(910) 887-4444

Rose Furniture
916 Finch Ave.
High Point, NC 27263
(910) 886-6050

Rose Furniture Clearance Center
1813 S. Main St.
High Point, NC 27260
(910) 886-8525

Utility Craft Inc.
2630 Eastchester Dr.
High Point, NC 27265
(910) 454-6153

North Carolina (cont.)

Wood Armfield Furniture
460 S. Main St.
High Point, NC 27260
(910) 889-6522

Young's Furniture and Rug Co.
1706 N. Main St.
High Point, NC 27262
(910) 883-4111

Cedar Rock Home Furnishings
Highway 321 S
Hudson, NC 28638
(704) 396-2361

Furniture Dealers Clearance Center
Route 3
Hudson, NC 28638
(704) 396-1648

Holiday Patio Showcase
Patio, wicker, and rattan only
Highway 321
Hudson, NC 28638
(704) 728-2664

The Leather Shop
Hickory St.
Hudson, NC 28638
(704) 396-6294

Smoky Mountain Furniture Outlet
Highway 321
Hudson, NC 28638
(704) 726-1434

Mallory's Fine Furniture
2153 Le Jeune Blvd.
Jacksonville, NC 28546
(910) 353-1828

Deep Discount Stores (cont.)

North Carolina (cont.)

Furnitureland South
5635 Riverdale Rd.
Jamestown, NC 27282
(910) 841-4328

Carolina Interiors
200 West Ave.
Kannapolis, NC 28081
(704) 938-3200

Village Furniture House
146 West Ave.
Kannapolis, NC 28081
(704) 938-9171

Quality Furniture Market
2034 Hickory Blvd. SE
Lenoir, NC 28645
(704) 728-2946

Triplett's Furniture Fashions
2084 Hickory Blvd. SE
Lenoir, NC 28645
(704) 728-8211

Nite Furniture
611 S. Green St.
Morganton, NC 28655
(704) 437-1491

Spiegel Clearance Center
1001 Airport Blvd.
Suite 280-285
Morrisville, NC 27560
(scheduled to open fall 1995)

Homeway Furniture
121 West Lebanon St.
Mount Airy, NC 27030
(800) 334-9094

Turner Tolson Furniture
U. S. Hwy. 17 S
New Bern, NC 28562
(919) 638-2121

North Carolina (cont.)

A. & H. Wayside Furniture
1086 Freeway Dr.
Reidsville, NC 27320
(910) 342-0717

Trott Furniture
Hwy. 258
Richlands, NC 28574
(910) 324-4660

Barcalounger Gallery/
Interior Images
1010 Winstead Ave.
Rocky Mount, NC 27804
(919) 937-2067

Bulluck Furniture Co.
124 S. Church St.
Rocky Mount, NC 27804
(919) 446-1138

Hardee's Furniture Warehouse
Highway 301 S
Sharpsburg, NC 27878
(919) 291-3105

Barnes and Barnes Furniture
190 Commerce Ave.
Southern Pines, NC 28387
(800) 334-8174

Furniture Barn of Forest City
Hwy. 74 Bypass
Spindale, NC 28160
(704) 287-7106

Corner Hutch Furniture
Highway 21 North
Statesville, NC 28677
(704) 873-1773

Ellenburg's Furniture
I-40 and Stamey Farm Rd.
Statesville, NC 28677
(704) 873-2900

North Carolina (cont.)

The Decorator's Edge
509 Randolph St.
Thomasville, NC 27360
(800) 289-5589

Holton Furniture
805 Randolph St.
Thomasville, NC 27361
(800) 334-3183

Loftin-Black Furniture
111 Sedgehill Dr.
Thomasville, NC 27360
(800) 334-7398

Murrow Furniture
3514 S. College Rd.
Wilmington, NC 28412
(910) 799-4010

Sutton-Councill Furniture
421 S. College Rd.
Wilmington, NC 28403
(910) 799-9000

Ohio

Aurora Furniture and Interiors
Aurora Farms Outlet Center
Hwy. 43
Aurora, OH 44202
(216) 562-2000

Brass Bed Shoppe
12421 Cedar Rd.
Cleveland Heights, OH 44106
(216) 371-0400

Oklahoma

Sears Catalog Clearance Center
5644 W. Skelly Dr.
Tulsa, OK 74107
(918) 446-1681

Deep Discount Stores (cont.)

Pennsylvania

QVC Network Clearance Center
U. S. Hwy. 30 and Hwy. 896
Lancaster, PA 17601
(717) 293-9595

Bombay Company Clearance Center
Franklin Mills
I-95 and Woodhaven Rd.
Philadelphia, PA 19114
(800 336-6255

J. C. Penney Catalog Outlet
Franklin Mills
I-95 and Woodhaven Rd.
Philadelphia, PA 19114
(800) 336-6255

Spiegel Clearance Center
Franklin Mills
I-95 and Woodhaven Rd.
Philadelphia, PA 19114
(800) 336-6255

Wicker Discount Center
Franklin Mills
I-95 and Woodhaven Rd.
Philadelphia, PA 19114
(800) 336-6255

South Carolina

Stuckey Brothers Furniture
Highway 261 W.
Hemingway, SC 29554
(803) 558-2591

Carolina Furniture
3120 Waccamaw Blvd.
Myrtle Beach, SC 29577
(800) 340-0064

Plaza Furniture
Hwy. 17 Business
Myrtle Beach, SC 29577
(800) 262-9898

South Carolina (cont.)

Triad Furniture Discounters
9770 North Kings Hwy.
Myrtle Beach, SC 29577
(800) 323-8469

Tennessee

Haverty's Direct Clearance Center
3961 Outland Rd.
Memphis, TN 38118
(901) 795-5430

Haverty's Direct Clearance Center
135 River Rock Blvd.
Murfreesboro, TN 37129
(615) 890-7591

Spiegel Clearance Center
2434 Music Valley Dr.
Suite 1310
Nashville, TN 37214
(615) 871-0192

Texas

Dillard's Clearance Center
3000 E. Pioneer Pkwy
Arlington, TX 76010
(817) 649-0782

Baby Company
Infant's and children's furniture only
1700 S. Lamar Blvd., Suite 318
Austin, TX 78704
(512) 442-2418

Haverty's Direct Clearance Center
4207 Simonton Rd.
Dallas, TX 75244
(214) 661-8500

Texas (cont.)

Bombay Company Clearance Center
7519 Grapevine Hwy.
Fort Worth, TX 76180
(817) 485-3151

Finger Furniture Bargain Basement
4001 Gulf Freeway
Houston, TX 77003
(713) 221-4441

Virginia

Brentwood Manor
317 Virginia Ave.
Clarksville, VA 23927
(800) 225-6105

IKEA
Potomac Mills Outlet Center
Exit 156 off I-95
Prince William, VA 22192
(800) VA-MILLS

J. C. Penney Clearance Center
Potomac Mills Outlet Center
Exit 156 off I-95
Prince William, VA 22192
(800) VA-MILLS

Washington

Sears Catalog Clearance Center
8720 S. Tacoma Way
Tacoma, WA 98499
(206) 584-8160

Wisconsin

Odds and Ends
Woodlake Mall
Kohler, WI 53044
(414) 458-2033

Sample Sales

Often, wholesale design centers and even some large furniture stores will hold sample sales to dispose of floor samples, seconds, and returns. Look out for announcements from large furniture stores holding special clearance sales in the home section of your local newspaper.

Estate Sales

Legally, anything that has been previously owned is an "estate piece". You could legally refer to any yard sale as a "estate sale". Bear this in mind when you attend estate sales, and keep things in their proper perspective.

Estate sales can have some great deals. Just remember that many of them are just glorified yard sales, not antique auctions. Buy furniture that is attractive and reasonably priced. Don't gamble on anything you find ever increasing in value.

Unclaimed Freight Stores

Every year, trucking and moving companies lose or damage tens of thousands of packages in transit. Usually the lost packages aren't really lost, they have just been misdirected or become separated from their labels and identifying paperwork. Any damage done to packages is usually minor.

Shipping insurance pays to replace most of these items for the original recipient, but what happens to the lost or damaged items?

Most trucking companies run at least one unclaimed freight store to dispose of these things. Furniture makes up a significant percentage of the stock in these stores because furniture is usually shipped by truck. Most of the furniture is new and has been lost in transit from the factory to a retail store or interior designer.

You can get some incredible bargains in these stores, sometimes as much as 90% off the original price. Call trucking and moving companies in your area to find the unclaimed freight stores closest to you.

Salvage Yards

Salvage yards arrange to take away and restore furnishings from buildings that are being demolished. Some of them also arrange to pick up discards from factories, including furniture factories.

You can find everything imaginable at these places. If you are creative and have always wanted an antique wrought-iron staircase or a real Art Deco fireplace mantel, salvage yards are the place to look. Of course, they do carry more "normal" types of furnishings, too.

You will normally have to pay cash, and everything is usually sold on an "as-is" basis with no returns allowed. Some of the major regional salvage yards are listed on pages 44-45, although there will certainly be others in your area.

The exact selection of types and styles of fixtures will vary widely among different salvage yards.

Where To Find the Most Interesting Salvage Yards

You will usually find more salvage, and more interesting salvage, available in major cities because of the frequency of construction and the demolition of older buildings.

In addition to furniture, you can find all types of fixtures:

fireplace mantels
decorative paneling
staircases
marble
decorative tiles
flooring
plaster mouldings
wood mouldings
windows
mirrors
lighting fixtures
doors
ironwork

Salvage Yards

Alabama

Furniture Salvage Center
5228 Valley Rd.
Fairfield, AL 35064
(205) 744-5236

Arizona

Atwell Salvage and Demolition
3017 W. Pima St.
Phoenix, AZ 85009
(602) 484-7301

Arkansas

Bears Building Salvage
509 Huntsville Rd.
Fayetteville, AR 72701
(501) 443-2327

California

Berkeley Architectural Salvage
722 Folger Ave.
Berkeley, CA 94710
(510) 849-2025

Colorado

Architectural Salvage
504 E. Pikes Peak Ave.
Colorado Springs, CO 80903
(719) 633-9294

Architectural Salvage
1413 S. Broadway
Denver, CO 80210
(303) 777-1922

Queen City Architectural Salvage
4750 Brighton Blvd.
Denver, CO 80216
(303) 296-0925

Connecticut

Connecticut Mill and Salvage
84 Mason St.
Coventry, CT 06238
(203) 742-5740

United House Wrecking
535 Hope St.
Stamford, CT 06906
(203) 348-5371

District of Columbia

Architectural Artifacts
634 North Carolina Ave. SE
Washington, DC 20003
(202) 546-2811

Brass Knob Architectural Antiques
2311 18th St. W
Washington, DC 20009
(202) 332-3370

Urban Artifacts
1918 18th St. NW
Washington, DC 20009
(202) 462-3838

Florida

Architectural Artifacts
1910 W. Kennedy Blvd.
Tampa, FL 33606
(813) 254-1168

Georgia

Architectural Antiques
6450 Roswell Rd. NE
Atlanta, GA 30328
(404) 252-3770

Georgia (cont.)

Metropolitan Artifacts
4783 Peachtree Rd.
Atlanta, GA 30341
(404) 986-0007

The Wrecking Bar
292 Moreland Ave. NE
Atlanta, GA 30307
(404) 525-0468

Illinois

Architectural Artifacts
4325 N. Ravenswood Ave.
Chicago, IL 60613
(312) 348-0622

Salvage One
1524 S. Sangamon St.
Chicago, IL 60608
(312) 733-0098

Urban Artifacts
2928 N. Lincoln Ave.
Chicago, IL 60657
(312) 404-1008

Michigan

Heritage Co. II Architectural Artifacts
2612 N. Woodward Ave.
Royal Oak, MI 48073
(313) 549-8342

Minnesota

Architectural Antiques
801 Washington Ave. N.
Minneapolis, MN 55401
(612) 332-8344

Salvage Yards (cont.)

Nebraska

Conner's Architectural Antiques
701 "P" St.
Lincoln, NE 68508
(402) 435-3338

New Mexico

Architectural Antiques
1125 Canyon Rd.
Santa Fe, NM 87501
(505) 982-0042

New York

Architectural Salvage Warehouse
337 Berry St.
Brooklyn, NY 11211
(718) 388-4527

Irreplaceable Artifacts
14 2nd Ave.
New York, NY 10003
(212) 777-2900

Urban Archaeology
285 Lafayette St.
New York, NY 10012
(212) 431-6969

North Carolina

One Way Architectural Antiques
831 Reynolda Rd.
Winston Salem, NC 27106
(919) 725-6187

Oklahoma

Architectural Antiques
121 E. Sheridan Ave.
Oklahoma City, OK 73104
(405) 232-0759

Pennsylvania

The Antiques Exchange
715 N. 2nd St.
Philadelphia, PA 19123
(215) 922-3669

Urban Artifacts
4700 Wissahickon Ave.
Philadelphia, PA 19144
(215) 844-8330

Architectural Artifacts
3618 Pennsylvania Ave.
Pittsburgh, PA 15201
(412) 621-6726

Texas

Adkins Architectural Antiques
3515 Fannin St.
Houston, TX 77004
(713) 522-6547

The Emporium
2515 Morse St.
Houston, TX 77019
(713) 528-3808

Vermont

Architectural Salvage
212 Battery St.
Burlington, VT 05401
(802) 658-5011

Virginia

Wombles Antiques and Salvage
306 E. Broad Rock Rd.
Richmond, VA 23224
(804) 232-2836

Washington

Captain Sam's Loft
4102 Ave. "D"
Seattle, WA 98104
(206) 624-1478

Seattle Building Salvage
202 Bell St.
Seattle, WA 98121
(206) 448-3453

Antique Malls and Flea Markets

Please see Chapter 17 for a complete discussion of antique malls and flea markets. These can be great sources for new and used furniture (and many other types of furnishings) at great prices, but you must carefully inspect everything to make sure that you are getting quality, well made furniture.

Charity Thrift Stores

Thrift stores run by charities, such as Goodwill and the Salvation Army, often have incredible deals on furniture. Many people arrange to donate furnishings to these organizations when they move, redecorate, or die. These charities usually arrange to pick up furniture at the donor's home, so many people find donating the furniture and taking a tax deduction to be less trouble than arranging to transport it to a flea market and sell it. Much of this furniture is in excellent condition, especially pieces that have been used infrequently, such as those in formal living and dining rooms.

Recently, I found a pair of Chippendale occasional chairs at a Salvation Army store that had nothing wrong with them except faded fabric on the seats. They were made out of beautiful dark cherry wood and had obviously been well taken care of. They were on sale for $120.00 each, but they were comparable to new Chippendale chairs that retail for $1000.00 each. Replacing the fabric on the seats would have taken about ten minutes (this is very easy for anyone to do at home) and about $20.00 worth of fabric. You should be able to find some incredible bargains, too.

Be aware that these furnishings, usually furniture, are normally sold "as-is" with no returns allowed. You may or may not be able to pay with a credit card. Carefully examine all pieces before buying.

Call charities in your area to find thrift stores near you.

Wholesale

If you decide to become your own decorator, as explained in Chapter 19, you will be able to purchase many brands of furniture wholesale (especially from smaller and more specialized manufacturers) at wholesale design centers and independent wholesale showrooms. There are many manufacturers that do sell directly to interior decorators and interior designers. Thousands of manufacturers and showrooms all across the U. S. that sell all types of home furnishings directly to decorators are listed in the _National Directory of Wholesale Home Furnishings Sources and Showrooms_, by William Graham. You may order a copy from this publisher. There is an order form in the back of this book.

These showrooms are where you will find the most unique and unusual furniture: hand-painted French armoires, desks with intricate wood inlay, imported occasional chairs with hand-stitched petit point upholstery, etc. If you are looking for the most gorgeous furniture imported from all over the world, you will definitely want to check out these "to-the-trade-only" showrooms.

If your local wholesale design center has open shopping days, go in and look around. Wholesale design centers that open to the public on certain days are listed on page 328. If you see anything you like, weigh the 40% to 50%

trade discount that decorators and designers usually receive against the cost of becoming your own decorator -- and decide.

If the furniture you are interested in costs at least $300.00, the savings you would enjoy by buying it wholesale should more than cover the cost of getting your business credentials, depending on where you live. If the furniture you want to buy costs more than $300.00, all the better. You can keep the rest of the savings for yourself. Chapter 19 gives complete instructions about how to get your business credentials and shop in all types of wholesale showrooms.

You will also want to check out the periodic sample sales at many design centers and independent wholesale showrooms, usually held in winter and summer. Floor samples and returns are usually sold at about 75% off retail.

These sales are normally restricted to the trade. In fact, most interior decorators and designers in your area know about them long before they occur (because they are on the design center's or showroom's mailing list) and have had their eye on their intended purchases far in advance of the actual sale.

If you decide to become your own decorator, you will want to visit the wholesale design center and independent furniture showrooms in your area as soon as possible, so that you can be added to their mailing lists and receive advance announcements of these special sales to the trade.

Recommendations

1 Consider updating the furniture you already have. You can dramatically change the look of your existing furniture with new finishes, decorative hardware, and other embellishments.

2 Check out unfinished furniture, which can be found at local unfinished furniture stores. Also check out used furniture, which can be found at yard sales, estate sales, charity thrift stores, and salvage yards. These can be terrific bargains, usually about 90% off retail for used furniture, but you will have to invest some effort to fix up many pieces.

3 Contact local retail stores and interior designers. Many have a few customer returns or floor samples that they would like to get rid of. You can usually save up to 75% off retail on these items.

4 The next-best bargains can be found at factory outlet stores and deep discount stores. These sources carry new furniture in a wide variety of current styles and top-quality brands at up to 50% off retail. Many pieces of first-quality furniture, such as irregulars and closeouts, are available at up to 75% off retail.

You can also save up to 75% off retail on second-quality goods with only minor flaws, such as factory seconds, floor samples, and customer returns.

5 Unclaimed freight stores are comparable to outlets and deep discount stores in quality and price, but their selection is usually very limited.

6 The next step up the discount food chain are the telephone ordering services. You will usually save up to 50% off retail from these sources.

Compare prices carefully. Discounts vary from source to source. All furniture is new and first-quality, and most current styles should be available.

7 Consider becoming your own decorator and buying your furniture wholesale. Many smaller furniture manufacturers do sell one piece at a time directly to interior decorators. If you are looking for something a bit more unique or unusual than what is available from major furniture manufacturers, you will likely find it at your local wholesale design center and independent wholesale showrooms.

While the cost of this high-style furniture will run a bit higher than the cost of furniture from major manufacturers, you can save about 40-50% (and occasionally up to 75%) off of the retail price of this furniture if you buy it wholesale instead of through an interior designer.

Details about how you can become your own interior decorator and shop in wholesale showrooms are discussed in Chapter 19. Furniture manufacturers and wholesale furniture showrooms all over the U. S., are listed and cross-referenced in the *National Directory of Wholesale Home Furnishings Sources and Showrooms*, by William Graham. The *Directory* is a complete resource for designers and decorators, listing thousands of wholesale sources and showrooms for all types of home furnishings. It's available from this publisher. There is an order form in the back of this book.

Chapter 3

Fabrics

Fabric costs are a big part of most decorating projects. Saving 50% to 75% off on your fabrics can dramatically reduce the overall cost of your decorating project.

We'll begin with the easiest part of understanding the fabric industry -- choosing the right types of fabrics in the right quantities for your particular decorating job. Later on in the chapter, I'll explain the business aspects of the industry and discuss all of the different ways in which you can buy fabrics. Many low-cost fabric sources -- such as deep discount stores and factory outlets -- are listed here. You'll also learn about several fabric industry scams you need to watch out for.

Will Using Designer Sheets Instead Of Fabric Save You Money?

Yes, but it usually isn't a good idea. In the last few years, sheet manufacturers have pushed the use of sheets to make everything from window treatments to slipcovers. On many major television shows and in many major magazines relating to home furnishings, there have been segments and articles on decorating with sheets. Of course, these segments and articles are usually hosted or written by a paid representative of a sheet manufacturer.

The short-term savings are good, but there are some problems with using sheets instead of decorative fabrics. Home furnishings made from sheets do not last nearly as long as those made from fabrics. They will wear out and have to be replaced more frequently, increasing the long-term cost of your home furnishings. Sheets will not wear well if you use them to make cushions or slipcovers.

Also, no matter what the sheet manufacturers would like you to believe, sheets just don't look as good as decorative fabrics. Sheets are thinner, more transparent, and don't have the attractive glazed finish that decorative chintzes have. Sheets were never meant to be used in window treatments and do not drape well. Some styles of window treatments may show dark shadows of seams through the extremely thin sheeting material. Sheets are also not meant to take constant wear and, therefore, are not a good choice for cushion covers or slipcovers.

Sheets look, frankly, cheap. No amount of sewing skill can ever make sheets look like quality decorative fabrics. It's a mistake to think that by giving sheets to a skilled workroom to be made into elaborate draperies, the end result will look like an expensive window treatment. It won't. Don't waste your money this way.

However, there are times when using sheets will be an acceptable choice. If you can get the sheets at a significant discount, around 50% off retail, you aren't going to spend much on custom sewing, and you plan to use them in a place that won't expose them to very much wear or where the decorations will be changed within a year or two anyway, they will be fine. For instance, you may wish to have a simple window valance made out of a sheet to match a store-bought bedspread. In Chapter 7, I'll tell you which window treatments can be made from sheets, and which can't.

If you do decide to have custom home furnishings made from sheets, be sure to thoroughly pre-shrink them first. Following the manufacturer's instructions, wash and dry the sheets several times on the hottest washer and dryer settings allowed. If you don't, the stitches may pucker when the item is washed, and the furnishings may no longer fit properly.

How To Choose Appropriate Fabrics For Your Custom Furnishings

It is very important to choose the appropriate fabrics for window treatments, upholstery, and other home furnishings. If you choose a fabric that is not designed for the use you have in mind, you will probably find that your custom window treatments don't look very good or that your custom upholstered sofa starts developing worn areas within a year.

Before you spend money (often a lot of money) on custom labor, make sure you have chosen the correct materials. Otherwise, you may just be throwing money away on custom labor that will only have to be redone (with the correct materials) within a very short time.

When you are dealing directly with wholesale workrooms and craftspeople, and acting as your own interior decorator, it is your responsibility to make sure that you choose appropriate fabrics. It is not the responsibility of the seamstress, upholsterer, or workroom to judge the suitability of your fabrics for the custom furnishings you order. They just do the work you hired them to do -- no questions asked. They will not assume any liability for the future performance of the fabrics you choose. We will discuss wholesale workrooms and craftspeople thoroughly in Chapter 18.

As explained in the next three sections, there is a clear and systematic way to choose the right fabrics for your home. You will consider fiber, weave, and weight when making your decision. Each specific aspect of fabric construction is discussed in detail in the following three sections of this chapter.

Use the qualities listed in the next three sections to determine the appropriate fabrics to use for your custom furnishings. For instance, if you are having the family sofa upholstered, you will want to choose a heavyweight fabric (such as a heavy boucle') in a durable weave (such as twill) made from a durable fiber that doesn't have to be dry cleaned (such as wool). If you are having softly flowing draperies made, you will want to choose a lightweight fabric that drapes nicely (such as sateen) in a drapeable weave (such as sateen weave) made from a fading-resistant fiber (such as cotton). And so on.

The recommendations listed in the following three sections of this chapter include only part of the information you need. If you are planning to have custom window treatments, bed treatments, upholstery or other home furnishings made, you should also check the recommendations under the type of home furnishing, which are located in the chapters referring to each specific type of home furnishing. Often, certain window treatments, upholstery styles, and other home furnishings will have additional recommendations for the type of pattern (stripe, plaid, etc.) in addition to more specific recommendations for the type of fabric (crisp fabrics, softly draping fabrics, etc.).

The recommendations here refer to physical suitability only -- resistance to wear, drapability, resistance to fading, etc. You should refer to a book on interior design for advice as to the design suitability of various fabrics -- formality, informality, period, popularity, style, etc.

Design suitability is an entirely different subject, and the rules and guidelines often vary from year to year. This year, velvet might be "in". Next year, you might be embarrassed to have it in your home, depending upon how seriously you take design advice. Ad infinitum.

The design establishment never seems to run out of things to say about what's in and what's out during the current year (or the current week). The physical suitability of fabrics for different types of furnishings never changes. Velvet will always be physically suitable for seat cushions, for example.

Following the recommendations in this chapter and in later chapters will help ensure that your custom home furnishings will look their best and last a long time.

Fiber Types

The fiber content of the fabrics you purchase is a primary factor in the long-term looks and wear of your furnishings. Some fibers hold dyes well and resist fading. Some, particularly silk, fade very quickly. Some fibers, particularly wool, resist wear well. Others, such as polyester, hardly resist wear at all.

Study the list of fiber types on page 52 when shopping for your fabrics. If the fiber content is not clearly marked on the fabric sample or roll, ask a salesperson for the fiber content of any fabrics you are interested in.

Make sure you choose fabrics that resist fading for your custom window treatments. They will often be subjected to strong sunlight and are the furnishings most vulnerable to fading.

Even if you choose a blackout drapery lining that will help block the light, your window treatments will still fade around the hems and edges. So, don't think that you can get away with using a fiber that is very vulnerable to fading, such as silk, for your window treatments as long as you use a good lining. It doesn't work.

Many man-made fibers and fiberglass resist fire well. Many fabrics made of these fibers are marketed as "fire-resistant". This is often a requirement for use in hotels and motels.

Make sure you choose fabrics that resist wear for your upholstery and seat cushions. You don't want your cushions to start developing bald spots just a few months after you have paid the upholstery bill.

Make sure that the recommended cleaning method (dry clean, wash, or hand-wash) fits your lifestyle and the use you have in mind for the fabric. If you are going to upholster the family room couch, and you have small children, don't choose a fabric that must be dry-cleaned.

Choose fabrics that are mildew resistant for use in wet or humid areas, such as bathrooms and around swimming pools.

Bear in mind that surface treatments can be applied that change the durability of the fabric. The qualities listed below refer only to the fiber in its natural state. Application of any surface treatments will change the qualities of the fabric listed here.

Various surface treatments, such as lamination and stain-resistant treatments, are discussed later in this chapter. Lamination can make even the most mildew-prone fabric suitable to use in wet areas, such as around swimming pools. Scotchgarding can make many fabrics much more stain-resistant. A crisp or glazed finish will make any fabric drape poorly.

Also, bear in mind that many fabrics you will encounter are blends of the fibers below. The fabric should contain at least 20% of any fiber in order to realize the benefits associated with that fiber.

For instance, a cotton/polyester blend should contain at least 20% polyester to resist mildew to any appreciable extent. Even so, this fabric will not resist mildew nearly as well as a fabric that is 100% polyester. A cotton/polyester blend that contains only 5% polyester will probably not resist mildew any better than 100% cotton. You get the idea.

Acetate Man-made fiber that can be dry-cleaned or washed. Use a cool iron only. It has good resistance to fire, mildew, pilling, soiling, shrinking, and insect damage. It has poor resistance to wear, wrinkling, and fading.

Acrylic Man-made fiber that can be dry-cleaned or washed. Use a cool iron only. It has good resistance to fire, wear, wrinkling, soiling, insect damage, mildew, and fading. It has poor resistance to pilling.

Cotton Natural fiber that can be dry cleaned or washed. It can be ironed. It has good resistance to wear, fading, pilling, and insect damage. It has poor resistance to mildew, soiling, wrinkling, and fire.

Fiberglass Natural fiber made from glass that must be hand-washed. Do not iron. Hang dry or tumble dry on cool setting. It has good resistance to fire, mildew, fading, wrinkling, soiling, and insect damage. It has poor resistance to wear and pilling.

Hemp Natural fiber made from hemp plants, often used for heavy rope as well. It can be ironed. It has good resistance to wear, fading, wrinkling, pilling, and insect damage. It has poor resistance to mildew, soiling, and fire.

Jute Natural fiber made from jute plants, often used for burlap sacking and upholstery twine. It has good resistance to wear, fading, wrinkling, pilling, and insect damage. It has poor resistance to mildew, soiling, and fire.

Linen Natural fiber made from flax that should be washed. Linen should not be folded for storage as this can bend and break fibers and create weak areas along the folds. Always roll for storage. It can be ironed. It has good resistance to wear, mildew, pilling, fading, and insect damage. It has poor resistance to soiling, wrinkling, and fire.

Nylon Man-made fiber that can be dry-cleaned or washed. Use a cool iron only. It has good resistance to fire, mildew, wrinkling, wear, soiling, and insect damage. It has poor resistance to fading and pilling.

Olefin Man-made fiber that can be washed. Use a cool iron only. It has good resistance to fire, fading, mildew, soiling, wear, wrinkling, pilling, and insect damage. It really doesn't have any resistance problems.

Polyester Man-made fiber that can be dry-cleaned or washed. Use a cool iron only. It has good resistance to fire, fading, mildew, wrinkling, and insect damage. It has poor resistance to pilling, soiling, and wear.

Rayon Man-made fiber that can be dry-cleaned or washed. It can be ironed. It has good resistance to wear, soiling, fading, pilling, and insect damage. It has poor resistance to fire, wrinkling, and mildew.

Silk Natural fiber that must be dry-cleaned or hand-washed. It can be ironed. It has good resistance to mildew, soiling, insect damage, and wrinkling. It has poor resistance to fire, fading, pilling, and wear.

Wool Natural fiber that must be dry-cleaned or hand-washed. Use a cool iron only. It has good resistance to fire, mildew, wear, pilling, fading, wrinkling, and soiling. It has poor resistance to insect damage.

Weaving Methods

The method by which fibers are woven into fabric has a big impact on the fabric's durability and drapability. Crisp or glazed finishes (discussed later) will make fabrics that normally have good drapeability drape poorly, so you have to consider any added finishes as well when you are looking at fabrics. Threads can vary in thickness from fine threads to coarse yarns.

The basic types of fabric weaves are listed on page 54-55. Don't worry about trying to identify these weaves by sight. It isn't necessary. In the next section, we will discuss various types of fabrics and identify the weaving methods used for each. When you shop for fabrics, you will ask about specific fabric types. For instance, you might ask a fabric source if they carry chintz, not a "close plain woven cotton/polyester blend fabric with a crisp shiny finish".

The information given in this chapter about weaving methods and fiber types is designed to prepare you to properly choose the fabric types listed in the following section that are appropriate for your custom furnishings.

Common Fabric Terms

Finish Chemical(s) applied to the surface of the fabric. Effect may be dull or shiny, soft or crisp. A glazed finish is a special kind of finish that is crisp and very shiny.

Many decorative fabric finishes will wash out. Most fabrics with any kind of special finish should be dry-cleaned. However, you should also check the manufacturer's cleaning recommendations for each fabric with your fabric dealer.

Meshes Open areas in lace fabrics.

Monochromatic Having several colors in the same narrow color family -- shades of gray, shades of white, shades of red, etc.

Nubby Yarn that has many very tiny slubs in it.

Slub Irregular thickening of thread or yarn. Varies in size.

Synthetics Man-made fibers.

Close weave Fabric that has no open areas between the threads. Opposite of "open weave". Close woven fabrics have varying degrees of drapeability and durability, depending on the specific weaves and fibers used.

Jacquard weave Fabric that has horizontal and vertical threads interwoven in a wide variety of complex patterns, often forming scenes or designs. These fabrics are close woven. Jacquard weave has varying drapeability and durability, depending on which fibers are used.

Lace weave Fabric that has threads interwoven in a wide variety of complex patterns. These fabrics are open woven. Lace weave has good drapeability and poor durability.

Leno weave Fabric that has pairs of vertical threads twisted one-half turn between each pair of horizontal threads. These fabrics are open woven. Leno weave has good drapeability and poor durability.

Open weave Fabric that has open areas between the threads. Opposite of "close weave". Open weave has good drapeability and poor durability.

Pile weave Plain woven fabric that has an additional horizonal or vertical thread interwoven, looped, and cut to form pile. Velvet is the most common pile weave. These fabrics are close woven. They are normally medium to heavyweight. Pile weave has poor drapeability and good durability.

Plain weave Fabric that has horizontal and vertical threads woven in a simple over-and-under pattern (like a basket is woven) with no variations such as twists or knots. May be open or close woven. Close plain weave has good durability and good drapeability, unless a crisp finish has been applied which would take away its ability to drape well. Open plain weave has good drapeability and poor durability.

Rib weave Fabric that has bundles of horizontal threads plain woven with single vertical threads. These fabrics are close woven. This produces a horizontal ribbed effect. Rib weave has poor drapeability and good durability.

Sateen weave Fabric that has single vertical threads woven over four to eight horizontal threads and under one horizontal thread. This is the same as satin weave with the horizontal and vertical weaving pattern reversed. This weaving method gives the fabric a smooth finish and shows off bright shiny threads (such as silk) very well. These fabrics are close woven.

Sateen weave has good drapeability and relatively poor durability, although medium-weight sateen weave fabrics with a high cotton content are okay to use for seat cushions that don't receive heavy use.

Satin weave Fabric that has single horizontal threads woven over four to eight vertical threads and under one vertical thread. The more threads that are woven over (example: eight rather than four), the smoother the satin is. This weaving method gives the fabric a smooth finish when and shows off bright shiny threads (such as silk) very well. These fabrics are close woven.

Satin weave has good drapeability and relatively poor durability. Most satin woven fabrics are made of fibers that have poor resistance to wear, so there really are no exceptions to the durability problem as there are with sateen woven fabrics.

Twill Fabric that has single threads woven over two-and-under two in a diagonally graduating pattern. These fabrics are close woven. Close woven twill has poor drapeability and good durability.

Fabric Types

The following list of fabric types, categorized by weight, includes all of the fabrics you are likely to find when shopping, with the exception of some the extremely expensive ''fantasy fabrics'' discussed later in this chapter. A few fabrics will appear in more than one weight category -- chintz, for instance.

Weight, in the fabric industry, refers to the thickness of the fabric. Very lightweight fabrics are usually extremely delicate and transparent. Lightweight fabrics are still quite thin but not transparent, like fabrics used for shirts and blouses. Mediumweight fabrics are a bit thicker still, like the fabrics used for pants and trousers. Heavyweight fabrics are the thickest and most durable, like the fabrics used on most family room couches (as opposed to the living room sofa that no one who actually lives in the house dares sit on).

Fiber contents are not discussed in many of the listings below because they can vary widely on many fabrics. For example, a certain chintz fabric might be 20% cotton/80% polyester, 30% cotton/70% polyester, 50% cotton/50% polyester, 100% cotton, or some other combination of fibers. Ask the fabric dealer for the exact fiber content of the specific fabrics you are interested in purchasing. Often, this information is printed on the price tag or showroom sample.

Very lightweight fabrics:

These fabrics are all very lightweight laces and sheers. All are transparent or semi-sheer. They are all well suited for many types of window treatments, particularly those that drape softly. They are not well suited for window treatments that have a highly structured style, such as hobbled Roman shades. These fabrics can be used for some bed treatments, pillow, and tablecloths, if they are properly lined. They should never be used for any kind of upholstery, lined or not, including small seat cushions.

Many of these fabrics contain a combination of nylon, acetate, rayon, glass, and/or polyester. A few contain silk or cotton.

Be careful about color when you buy these fabrics. Many of these fabrics, especially those with pastel tints, can appear to change color dramatically between the showroom and your house. I have seen samples of tinted sheers that look pink in the showroom appear to turn peach in a customer's home, for instance.

This color shift occurs because showroom and retail store lights are usually fluorescent, and the lighting in most homes is a combination of incandescent lighting and daylight. This color shift occurs with some other fabrics, too, but the effect seems to be the most pronounced with the very lightweight fabrics. So always get a sample to try out in your home before you buy.

You should also fold these fabrics several times or bunch them up in your hands when evaluating the color. When these fabrics are made up into your furnishings, they will usually be pleated or ruffled, not stretched out flat. This ruffling of the fabric makes the colors appear darker and more vivid. You should evaluate the colors as they will actually appear when your furnishings are made up, not stretched out flat on a showroom sample.

Batiste Very delicate semi-sheer plain weave, usually made of cotton or polyester. Often has a printed or embroidered design. Available in white, ecru, and a variety of pale pastels.

Bobbinet Fine lace with hexagonal meshes. Available in white, ecru, and pale pastel tints.

Boucle' marquisette Open leno woven fabric with scattered loops. Available in white, ecru, and pale pastels. Pronounced ''*boo-clay*''.

Casements Plain open weaves in a variety of fibers. Relatively thick threads in a variety of colors and color combinations.

Dimity Thin twisted vertical cords woven with plain horizontal threads to form a vertical striped pattern. Sometimes woven with twisted horizontal cords to form a plaid pattern. Available in white, ecru, and pastels.

Dotted Swiss Semi-sheer cotton plain weave with a crisp finish (see ''organdy'' below) embroidered with dots or other patterns. Available in a variety of colors. Dots and embroidery may or may not be in contrasting colors.

Fiberglass Sometimes referred to as ''glass curtains''. Glass fibers in a variety of woven patterns: filet, marquisette, etc. Thickness ranges from sheer to nearly opaque. Available in a variety of solid colors and printed patterns.

Filet Lace with square meshes and knots at each intersecting corner. Available in a variety of colors. Pronounced just like ''*fillet*'' of fish.

French tergal Very delicate sheer silky material. Usually made of silk, rayon, or nylon. It is sometimes also referred to as ''ninon''. Available in a variety of solid colors and tone-on-tone woven vertical stripes. Some ninon fabrics have embroidered borders.

Lace Open woven fabric in a wide variety of decorative patterns. Available in a variety of colors.

Marquisette Open leno woven fabric. Available in white, ecru, and pale pastels.

Muslin Soft plain cotton weave. Thickness ranges from semi-sheer to nearly opaque. Available in a variety of solid colors and printed patterns.

Net Lace with regular meshes of any geometric shape. Bobbinet and filet are both examples of net. Available in a variety of colors.

Ninon Very delicate sheer silky material. Usually made of silk, rayon, or nylon. It is sometimes also referred to as "French tergal". Available in a variety of solid colors and tone-on-tone woven vertical stripes. Some ninon fabrics have embroidered borders. Pronounced "*nee-no*".

Organdy Delicate semi-sheer cotton plain weave, treated to make it slightly crisp. Available in a variety of solid colors and some printed or embroidered patterns.

Osnaburg Open plain weave made from thick coarse nubby cotton yarn. Available in a variety of solid colors and printed patterns.

Point d'esprit Very fine bobbinet with scattered woven dots. Available in white, ecru, and a variety of pastels. Pronounced "*pwaa-de-spree*".

Silk gauze Delicate plain woven silk. Threads usually have slight slubs. Available in a variety of colors.

Theatrical gauze Open weave with a crisp shiny finish. Usually made of cotton or linen. Available in a variety of solid colors and two-tone color combinations.

Voile Plain sheer open weave. May have nubby threads or contrasting vertical threads (for a striped effect) woven into the fabric. Available in a variety of solid colors and color combinations. Pronounced "*voil*" or "*vwall*" -- either is correct.

Lightweight fabrics:

These are all lightweight fabrics suitable for many window treatments, bed treatments, tablecloths, and decorative pillows. They should not be used for any upholstery, including seat cushions. They also should not be used in areas exposed to excessive wear or staining.

These fabrics are made of a variety of natural and man-made fibers in many different combinations. Some of these fabrics are also available in heavier-weight versions, which we will discuss later in the chapter.

Antique satin Satin with horizontal slubs. The name has nothing to do with the age of the fabric. This is just a common name for satin that has horizontal slubs. May be a solid color or have a variety of contrasting color horizontal threads woven in. Available in a variety of colors and color combinations.

Antique taffeta Close plain woven silk with horizontal slubs and a smooth crisp finish. This is just a common name for taffeta that has horizontal slubs -- the term has nothing to do with the age of the fabric. Usually made from wild silk, but some newer fabrics are made from cotton or synthetics. Also referred to as "tussah silk", "pongee", or "doupioni silk". Available in a variety of colors.

Boucle' Close plain woven fabric with many small loops. Usually made from silk, acetate, and/or rayon. Available in a heavyweight version. Pronounced "*boo-clay*".

Broadcloth Close plain woven fabric in a variety of fibers and fiber combinations. Typically has a dull finish. Available in a variety of colors.

Brocade Jacquard woven fabric with intricate raised woven designs, often made with many colors of thread and depicting complex patterns and scenes, and a shiny finish. Usually made from silk and/or rayon. Available in a wide variety of colors and patterns. Pronounced "*broke-ade*".

Calico Cotton broadcloth with tiny printed patterns. Usually brightly colored, although there are also some pastel calicos. Available in a variety of patterns and color combinations.

Challis Close plain woven fabric with a soft finish. Usually made of cotton, wool, or synthetics. Available in a variety of printed patterns and a few solid colors. Pronounced "*shalley*".

Chambray Close plain woven fabric with a white frosted finish. Usually made of cotton or linen. Available in a wide variety of colors. Pronounced "*sham-bray*".

Chintz Close plain woven cotton/polyester blend with a crisp shiny finish. Normally available in solid colors only. Chintzes that have printed patterns are normally mediumweight, although there are a very few, very cheap, very poor-quality lightweight patterned chintzes.

Lightweight chintz is visibly thinner and usually has a much higher polyester content than mediumweight chintz. Chintzes that have 20% cotton/80% polyester or 30% cotton/70% polyester fiber contents are normally lightweight. Chintzes that have at least 50% cotton fiber content are normally mediumweight.

Lightweight chintz is generally a very poor-quality substitute for mediumweight chintz. It looks cheap, too -- hold up samples of light and mediumweight chintz next to each other when you are in a fabric store or showroom and look at the difference. Spend the extra dollar or two per yard and buy a nice mediumweight chintz, especially if you are investing money in custom labor.

Cotton sheeting Close plain woven cotton with a smooth finish. This is the material used in most standard cotton sheets. Available in a variety of solid colors and printed patterns.

Damask Jacquard woven fabric with complex woven patterns, usually florals, and a shiny finish. Usually made from linen, silk, and/or rayon. Similar to brocade, except that the patterns are not raised. Available in a mediumweight version. Many damasks are monochromatic, although some do use contrasting colored threads. Available in a wide variety of colors and patterns.

Doupioni silk Close plain woven silk with horizontal slubs and a smooth crisp finish. Usually made from wild silk, but some newer fabrics are made from cotton or synthetics. Also referred to as "tussah silk", "antique taffeta", or "pongee". Available in a variety of colors. Pronounced "*doop-ee-o-ni*".

Drill Twill woven cotton. Available in a limited variety of colors.

Faille Rib woven fabric with flattened horizontal ribs. Usually made from silk, rayon, or cotton. Available in a wide variety of colors. Pronounced "*file*".

Gingham Close plain woven cotton and/or synthetics in three specific woven patterns -- checks, stripes, or plaids. Available in a variety of bright colors and pastels against a white or ecru background.

Homespun Close plain woven fabric made up of threads in varying thicknesses. Usually made of linen, wool, cotton, or rayon. Has a crude homemade appearance. Available in a variety of colors.

India print Close plain woven cotton fabric printed with ethnic or floral patterns. Dyes are usually primitive vegetable dyes and are prone to fading, although the fabrics are still very attractive in their slightly faded state. Available in a variety of colors.

Indian Head Brand name for a particular close plain woven cotton fabric that has been pre-shrunk and treated to be colorfast (non-fading). Available in a variety of colors.

Jaspe' Plain woven fabric made of thick irregular yarns. Usually made with vertical yarns of contrasting colors to create woven stripes. Available in a variety of color combinations, most monochromatic. Pronounced "*zhaspay*", where the "*zh*" is pronounced like the "*zs*" in "*Zsa Zsa*".

Linen Close plain woven linen fibers. Available in a variety of colors and printed patterns.

Moire' Rib woven fabric with a permanent wavy watermarked pattern and a crisp shiny finish. Usually made of cotton, acetate, silk, and/or rayon. Lightweight moire' tends to have mostly synthetic fibers and silk. Mediumweight moire' generally has a higher cotton content. Available in a wide variety of colors. Pronounced "*moray*".

Oxford cloth Close plain or twill woven cotton fabric. You've probably seen it in oxford shirts. Available in a variety of pastel colors.

Pique' Close plain woven fabric with spaced horizontal ribs. Usually made of cotton, rayon, and/or silk. Available in a variety of colors. Pronounced "*pikay*".

Pongee Close plain woven silk with horizontal slubs and a smooth crisp finish. Usually made from wild silk, but some newer fabrics are made from cotton or synthetics. Also referred to as "tussah silk", "antique taffeta", or "doupioni silk". Available in a variety of colors.

Poplin Close plain woven cotton or synthetic fabric with small rounded horizontal ribs. Available in a variety of colors.

Sateen Sateen woven cotton/polyester blend with a soft finish. Medium-weight sateen is normally 100% cotton. Approximately one-quarter of the fabrics you will find from fabric dealers are light or mediumweight sateen. Available in a wide variety of colors and printed patterns.

Satin Satin woven silk, rayon, and/or acetate with a slippery, shiny finish. Available in a wide variety of colors.

Shantung Close plain woven silk with elongated horizontal slubs and a smooth crisp finish. Available in a wide variety of colors.

Taffeta Close plain woven silk with very few small horizontal slubs and a smooth crisp finish. Available in a wide variety of colors.

Tussah silk Close plain woven silk with horizontal slubs and a smooth crisp finish. Usually made from wild silk, but some newer fabrics are made from cotton or synthetics. Also referred to as "pongee", "antique taffeta", or "doupioni silk". Available in a variety of colors.

Waffle pique' Close plain woven fabric with spaced horizontal and vertical ribs forming a box pattern like on a waffle. Usually made of cotton, rayon, and/or silk. Available in a variety of colors. Pronounced "pikay".

Mediumweight fabrics:

These fabrics are thicker and more durable than the lightweight fabrics and are usually made with more durable fibers: cotton, linen, and wool. Many do contain less durable synthetic fibers, but in smaller quantities. Some are also available in lightweight versions.

These fabrics are suitable for crisp structured window treatments, decorative pillows, some bed treatments, seat cushions, slipcovers, and light upholstery. They are not suitable for window treatments that should drape softly or upholstery that will receive heavy wear.

Bark cloth Close plain woven fabric with a rough texture created by using yarns of irregular thickness. Available in a variety of colors and printed patterns.

Brocade Jacquard woven fabric with intricate raised woven designs, often made with many colors of thread and depicting complex patterns and scenes, and a shiny finish. Usually made from cotton. Available in a wide variety of colors and patterns. Pronounced "*broke-ade*".

Brocatelle Specific type of brocade that has large patterns in high relief. The high relief gives the decorative pattern a puffy appearance, as opposed to most other brocades on which the pattern is not so highly raised. It is normally used on large furnishings, such as sofas and wing chairs. Pronounced "*brock-ah-tell*".

Burlap Open plain woven fabric made from jute or hemp fibers. Also called "hopsacking". It is available in a few colors.

Canvas Close plain woven cotton fabric with relatively large threads. Also referred to as "duck" and "sailcloth". Available in a variety of colors, stripes, and a few printed designs.

Chintz Close plain woven cotton/polyester blend with a crisp shiny finish. Usually has at least 50% cotton. The best chintz is 100% cotton. Available in a wide variety of solid colors and printed patterns. About half of the fabrics you will find from fabric dealers are mediumweight chintzes.

Crash Close plain woven fabric with a rough texture created by using threads of irregular thicknesses. Usually made from linen, rayon, cotton, and/or jute. Available in a variety of colors and printed patterns.

Cretonne Close plain woven cotton fabric very similar to chintz but lacking the crisp shiny finish. Available in a variety of printed patterns.

Crewel Close plain woven cotton or linen fabric with large embroidered patterns. Available in a wide variety of embroidered designs and a limited variety of base fabric colors. Nearly all crewel fabric consists of embroidery on an ecru base fabric.

Damask Jacquard woven fabric with complex woven patterns, usually florals, and a shiny finish. Usually made from cotton. Similar to brocade, except that the patterns are not raised. Available in lightweight versions. Most damasks are monochromatic, although some do use contrasting colored threads. Available in a wide variety of colors and patterns.

Denim Twill woven cotton. Available in a narrow variety of colors. Yes, this is exactly the same fabric used for blue jeans. Denim often costs less in fabric stores that specialize in clothing fabrics than it does in stores that specialize in home decorative fabrics.

Duck Close plain woven cotton fabric with relatively large threads. Also referred to as "canvas" and "sailcloth". Available in a variety of colors, stripes, and a few printed designs.

Gingham Close plain woven cotton in three specific woven patterns -- checks, stripes, or plaids. Available in a variety of bright colors and pastels against a white or ecru background.

Hopsacking Open plain woven fabric made from jute or hemp fibers. Also called "burlap". Available in a few colors.

Moire' Rib woven fabric with a permanent wavy watermarked pattern and a crisp shiny finish. Usually made of cotton and or/acetate. Available in a wide variety of colors. Pronounced "*moray*".

Pique' Close plain woven fabric with spaced horizontal ribs. Usually made of cotton. Available in a variety of colors. Pronounced "*pikay*".

Repp Rib woven fabric with large horizontal ribs. Usually made of cotton, but may also contain synthetics. Available in a variety of colors.

Sailcloth Close plain woven cotton fabric with relatively large threads. Also referred to as "duck" and "canvas". Available in a variety of colors, stripes, and a few printed designs.

Sateen Sateen woven cotton with a soft finish. Approximately one-quarter of the fabrics you will find from fabric dealers are light or mediumweight sateen. Available in a wide variety of colors and printed patterns.

Seersucker Close plain woven cotton with woven puckered stripes. The puckered effect is formed by varying the tension on the threads during the weaving process. Available in a variety of stripe colors against a white or ecru background.

Sunbrella Specific brand of sailcloth that has been treated in a way that makes it highly resistant to sun-fading and mildew. Usually used for patio cushions and awnings. Available in a few colors, stripes, and a limited variety of printed patterns.

Terrycloth Pile woven cotton with loops instead of cut pile. Often used for patio cushions. Available in a few colors.

Textilene Specific brand of open plain woven fabric made from plastic-coated threads. Used for patio furniture cushions because it dries quickly and does not fade. Available in a variety of solid colors and woven striped designs.

Ticking Twill woven cotton or linen with narrow woven stripes. Available in a variety of colors against a white or ecru background.

Waffle pique' Close plain woven fabric with spaced horizontal and vertical ribs forming a box pattern like a waffle. Usually made of cotton. Available in a variety of colors. Pronounced "*pikay*".

Heavyweight fabrics:

These fabrics are primarily used for upholstery, seat cushions, and decorative pillows. They are generally not used for window treatments, although rarely some of these fabrics are used for flat structured window treatments such as pelmets and cornice boards.

Boucle' Close plain or twill woven fabric with many small loops. Usually made from wool and/or synthetics. Available in a lightweight version. Pronounced "*boo-clay*".

Corduroy Pile woven cotton and/or synthetics with raised vertical stripes of pile (called "wales"). Corduroy is also used for clothing, although clothing corduroy usually has narrower stripes and is thinner than upholstery corduroy. Available in a variety of colors.

Cotton moire' Close Jacquard woven cotton fabric with a raised woven pattern that imitates the wavy watermarked pattern of moire'. It is not a true moire'. Available in a wide variety of colors. Pronounced "*moray*".

Frieze Pile woven nylon and/or wool with the pile cut to form stripes or patterns. Available in a variety of colors and woven patterns. Pronounced "*freeze*".

Matelasse' Jacquard woven fabric made of two layers of cotton and/or rayon fabric quilted together. Usually has a raised floral or geometric pattern. Available in a variety of colors and woven patterns. Pronounced "*mad-eh-luh-say*".

Needlepoint Jacquard woven fabric made of wool, cotton, rayon, and/or acetate woven in discrete stitches on an open grid made of hemp or jute. The stitches vary in color to form patterns, usually florals. The Jacquard weaving method allows needlepoint to be mechanically mass-produced -- formerly, all needlepoint was hand-stitched.

Stitches are of equal length and range in size from very tiny (called "petit-point", pronounced "*petty-point*") to quite large (called "gros-point", pronounced "*grow-point*"). Petit-point is much more attractive, and much more expensive, than gros-point. Available in a limited variety of colors and patterns.

There is a less expensive alternative, as explained in the box at right.

Plush Pile woven cotton fabric with long cut pile made from cotton, silk, and/or rayon. Very much like velvet but with longer pile. Pile may be even or have sculptured patterns cut into it. Available in a wide variety of colors.

Repp Rib woven fabric with large horizontal ribs. Usually made of wool, but may also contain synthetics. Available in a variety of colors.

Tapestry Jacquard woven cotton, wool, linen, and/or silk with woven patterns or scenes.

Velvet Pile woven cotton fabric with short cut pile made from cotton, silk, and/or rayon. Very much like plush but with shorter pile. Pile may be even or "crushed" (permanently compressed in places to form a random pattern). A few velvets have woven multicolored patterns or stripes, although this is rare today. Available in a wide variety of colors.

If You Have More Time Than Money...

Mass-produced needlepoint can cost upwards of $75.00 per yard for gros-point patterns, more for petit-point patterns. It can be cost-prohibitive.

If you love the look of needlepoint but you are trying to stay within a budget, there are many inexpensive needlepoint kits at your local crafts store which you can use to make your own small pieces of needlepoint (approximately one to two feet square). These small pieces are fine for upholstering chair backs and seats or making decorative pillows.

There are also a variety of books available at your local library and bookstore that are full of needlepoint patterns and ideas. You will have to buy your own hemp grid and colored thread at your local crafts store, but this is very inexpensive and will allow you to custom match your thread colors to your other furnishings.

Needlepoint is not at all difficult to do. It requires little skill, but a lot of time. If your stitches aren't absolutely perfect, don't worry. Slightly imperfect stitches are one way that antique handmade needlepoint is distinguished from mechanically mass-produced needlepoint. Tiny errors and imperfections will only add to the looks and value of your needlepoint.

If you want to give an elegant and expensive look to your home, at a bargain price, and you don't mind spending a weekend stitching, this is something you should check into.

Moisture Resistant Treatments -- Lamination

Most chintz and sateen fabrics can be laminated with a light plastic coating to ward off stains, spills, and mildew. Modern fabric lamination methods are so sophisticated that you often cannot tell that a fabric has been laminated until you touch it. Modern laminated fabrics do not have the thick, shiny, cheap-looking plastic coatings that existed twenty years ago.

If you are choosing fabrics for outdoor chair cushions, kitchen stools, nurseries, or any other area in which wetness and staining is a major concern, you may wish to invest in lamination. This will also give you the flexibility of choosing from a much wider array of fabrics, rather than being forced to select from only those few fabrics (Textilene and Sunbrella) which are specifically meant to resist moisture.

To be suitable for lamination, a fabric must not have any texture irregularities such as slubs or loops. You will be limited mostly to chintzes, sailcloths, and sateens -- which make up the vast majority of decorative fabrics, anyway. You will normally get better results with light to medium colors than with dark colors.

Most wholesale workrooms can arrange to have fabrics laminated for you. As the equipment used for lamination is quite expensive, this service is available directly only from companies in major cities. All of these companies do accept mail orders.

Of course, if you become your own licensed decorator, you can make your own lamination arrangements and save the workroom's commission -- which is normally 100% over and above the actual cost of the lamination. Companies across the United States that provide lamination services to decorators are listed in the *National Directory of Wholesale Home Furnishings Sources and Showrooms*, which can be ordered from this publisher.

You may be in for a six to eight week wait. You will also usually be required to order no less than six yards. Prices will vary, but the average cost of lamination is about $8.00 to $10.00 per yard, above and beyond the cost of the fabric itself. You will also have to pay to ship the fabric to and from the lamination service. This will probably cost you about $20.00 each way, although the cost will vary according to the amount of fabric you are shipping and how far away you are from the lamination service.

Fabric lamination is an expensive proposition. However, it can greatly lengthen the useful life of furnishings which are exposed to wetness or excessive staining. When you consider the savings from not having to replace these furnishings as often, lamination should more than pay for itself.

Stain Resistant Treatments

You have all heard of Scotchgarding, which is the most widely-known stain resistant treatment used on decorative fabrics. Many fabric manufacturers use their own "house brands" of stain resistant treatments on many of their fabrics. Covington Fabrics calls theirs "Covgard", for instance. You will often see these treatments noted on the selvage of the fabric. All of the various treatment names end in "-gard", so just look for that suffix somewhere on the selvage.

Sateen and chintz fabrics have usually received some type of stain resistant treatment at the factory. Check on the selvage or ask the fabric seller. Many other types of fabrics are not treated and have no printed selvage, so you will have to ask.

How To Be Sure You Are Buying Quality Fabric

Some authors talk about "making sure the fabric has a good hand" and "examining the grain of the fabric". I believe that these vague directions will only confuse most consumers. Part of the purpose of this book is to let you know when you shouldn't waste your time worrying, as well as when you should be concerned about potential problems. This is one of those times.

Problems with the quality of modern fabrics are rare. In many years of manufacturing, during which we processed millions of yards of fabric, we have seldom encountered a fabric that was poorly manufactured. Fabric manufacturing is largely mechanized today. Mechanical looms produce very uniform fabrics.

The simplest way for you to make sure that you are buying quality fabric is to buy only from major fabric manufacturers. The manufacturer's name is printed along the selvage (side edge) of the fabric. Most decorative fabrics have a printed selvage, however, some solid color fabrics do not. However, the vast majority of the solid color fabrics you will find in fabric stores and from telephone ordering services are from reputable manufacturers -- you should have no quality problems with these fabrics.

If you buy decorative fabrics only from the major manufacturers listed in the box at right, you should have no problems with the quality of your fabric. The list also includes the phony brand names discussed later in the chapter, as well as some designer brands. Our workroom and factory never encountered a single quality problem with a fabric produced by any of these companies.

The omission of a fabric manufacturer from this list does not mean that the manufacturer does not produce quality fabric, only that I am not personally familiar with that company's products. There will certainly be quality fabrics from companies not listed in this book. This list is intended only to provide a relatively fail-safe way for you to avoid any problems without the need for you to squint at and handle each fabric, trying to figure out if it is high-quality or not. That would be a waste of your time.

The many small dealers of hand-painted or hand-embroidered fabrics that you will find in wholesale design centers and private studios around the country are not included in this list. They are too numerous to mention here. However, you should have no quality problems buying these fabrics because these companies almost always buy the base fabric from one of the reputable manufacturers listed above and then add their own additional touches.

You should have no quality problems with products purchased from permanent showrooms in wholesale design centers and wholesale trade centers. You don't need to worry unnecessarily when you shop in these places.

Major Fabric Mfrs

ADO
Ambiance Designs
American Silk Mills
Ametex Textiles
Anju-Woodridge Fabrics
Atelier Originals
Barrow Fabrics
Bloomcraft
Braemore
Carolace Embroidery
Charles Barone
Chetley Originals
Cohama-Riverdale
Concord Fabrics
Covington Fabrics
Cyrus Clark
David & Dash
Edgar Fabrics
Fabricut
Fabriyaz
5th Avenue Designs
F. Schumacher Fabrics
Hampshire Printed Fabrics
Hoffman Mills
House 'N Home Fabrics & Draperies
Jablan Fabrics
John Wolf Fabrics
JYD
Kaleidoscope Fabrics
Kenmill Fabrics
Kravet Fabrics
Lanscot-Arlen Fabrics
Margin Designs
Metro Mills
Mill Creek Fabrics
P. Kaufman
Pacific Weavers
Paragon Fabrics
Richloom Fabrics
Roclon Mills
Scalamandre'
Spectrum Fabrics
Springs Mills
Swavelle Fabrics
Taco
Texunion
Tilbury Fabrics
Waverly Fabrics
Western Textile

Buying Fabrics That Coordinate With Wallcoverings

These fabrics are normally sold by the manufacturers who produce the wallpapers. You will usually get the best price on these fabrics by purchasing them as you would purchase a wallcovering, usually from a telephone wallpaper ordering service.

These fabrics are normally not available from the usual fabric sources -- they usually must be purchased from wallpaper sources, instead.

Read the Chapter 4, and follow the advice given for getting the best prices on wallcoverings to find the best sources for these fabrics.

Fabric Repeats

The "repeat" size of a fabric refers to the vertical and horizontal distance covered by each identical pattern block.

The horizontal and vertical repeats on most decorative fabrics range from one inch for tiny patterns to 27 inches for large patterns. The horizontal and vertical repeats on fabrics are usually the same size. The vertical repeat is the measurement you will use to help determine how much yardage you need to buy for window treatments, pillows, upholstery, etc.

Striped fabrics are said to have no vertical repeat because the pattern goes on and on. Solid color fabrics have no repeats at all.

The repeat sizes should be very clearly marked on any fabric samples you see in a wholesale showroom, retail store, or interior design studio. If you are looking at rolls of fabric in a fabric store or factory outlet, the repeat sizes will often be marked on the price tag. If not, you will have to determine the repeat sizes for yourself.

You can find the repeat size for most fabrics by looking at the selvage (the white strips along the edges of most fabrics). There is usually a cross or double-L symbol printed on the selvage at the beginning and end of each repeat. Just measure between two of the symbols to determine the repeat size.

If the repeat symbols are not marked on the selvage or on the price tag, as may happen with some tapestry or woven fabrics, you can determine the repeat size by measuring between two identical elements on the fabric. Just choose something easily identifiable about the fabric, such as a particular flower or leaf, and look further down the fabric until that particular element appears again. Measure between the two identical elements to determine the repeat size.

When choosing fabrics, minimizing the repeat size can help you conserve fabric. Fabrics with large repeats require more yardage to center design elements (flowers, stripes, etc.) and match patterns at the seams. This pattern centering and matching leaves some wasted fabric in most window treatments, upholstery, etc. If you are deciding between two fabrics with differing repeat sizes, choosing the one with the smaller repeat can minimize the wasted fabric and save you money.

Avoid Splitting Pieces of Fabric

Be careful if you buy the fabric you need in two (or more) separate pieces. Whenever possible, buy all of a particular fabric in one unbroken piece. Occasionally, you may find at a fabric store that there isn't enough fabric on a roll to complete your project, and the store may bring out another small length of fabric to make up the difference. Rarely, a telephone order fabric house may ship your order in two separate pieces. There are two problems with this.

You may have a dye lot mismatch in a situation such as this. This means that the dyes for the two pieces of fabric weren't mixed at the same time and may not match. Always compare the two pieces of fabric carefully to be sure that there is no mismatch of any of the dye colors before accepting a split order of fabric.

Also, consult with the seamstress, upholsterer, or workroom who will be making your home furnishings out of this fabric. Most types of home furnishings require certain unbroken lengths of fabric. If the amounts of fabric involved in the split order don't correspond with the needs of your project, you could end up with wasted fabric.

Carefully Check For Flaws

This is a fairly rare problem, but it can be a very expensive problem. You must take time to check your fabric carefully for any flaws before having your custom furnishings made. Otherwise, you could be stuck with hundreds of dollars worth of unusable fabric.

If you are buying fabrics from a fabric store, your order will normally be measured off on a special table that transfers the fabric to a separate roll and measures the yardage. Carefully watch the fabric as the salesperson unrolls it. This way, you can quickly and easily inspect the entire roll.

You must make sure that there are no flaws before you leave the store, because fabrics are ordinarily sold "as is" with no returns allowed. If you find flaws after you get the fabric home, you will probably be stuck.

If you are buying fabrics from a telephone ordering service or wholesale source, you should check them immediately upon receipt. If you find any flaws, notify the fabric company immediately. You should have no problems getting the defective fabric replaced.

However, you must clear up any problems right away, before any work is done with your fabric. Telephone ordering services and wholesale sources generally will not replace defective fabric if the fabric has already been cut or sewn. If you don't do your own inspection, and your workroom calls you in the middle of making your draperies to notify you that there is a large flaw right down the middle of your fabric, you will be out of luck.

You can't rely on seamstresses and workrooms to inspect your fabric for you. It is a well-established custom in the industry that the interior decorator or retail customer is responsible for making sure that fabrics have no flaws and are the correct quantity before delivering them to a workroom or seamstress. These businesses do not inspect fabrics before beginning work -- they just dive right in.

A complete discussion of how to resolve complaints regarding damaged or incorrect merchandise from any source can be found in Chapter 20. Dealing with workrooms and wholesale sources is discussed in Chapters 18 and 19.

Most modern fabrics are mass produced on standardized machines. Human labor and human error are not involved for the most part, so flaws are very rare.

Make Sure You Buy Enough Fabric For Your Entire Decorating Project

Always be sure to get enough fabric for your entire project. If you do not have enough fabric to finish your project and you have to return to buy more, you may have problems with dye lot variations.

Fabrics are manufactured in "dye lots". This means that all of the dye for that particular batch of fabric is mixed at once. It is virtually impossible to mix two different batches of fabric dye to the exact same shade. For this reason, different dye lots of the same fabric often vary slightly in color. Sometimes, they vary a lot.

If you have to buy more fabric to finish your project, the original dye lot you purchased from may have already sold out, and the new dye lot may not match the fabric you already have.

How To Know How Much Fabric You Need To Buy

Whatever you do -- don't pay an interior designer or an interior decorator to tell you. The "Inflated Estimate Scam" (described in the next section) is widespread among these people.

Throughout this book, you will find simple instructions for properly estimating the amount of fabric needed to make all kinds of custom furnishings -- estimating for window treatments is explained in detail in the

"Soft Window Treatments" chapter, estimating for bedspreads is explained in the "Bed Treatments" chapter, etc.

Estimating methods for most basic styles of furnishings are covered in this book, but there will be some unusual styles that are not covered here. If you need a custom fabric estimate for your decorating job, contact the person or business that will actually be making your custom furnishings -- upholsterers, drapery workrooms, home seamstresses, etc.

These sources are very knowledgeable about the proper manufacture of custom furnishings and normally give free estimates of the fabric you will need to purchase.

The Inflated Estimate Scam

Over the years, my family has seen this scam very frequently from interior designers and interior decorators. Many of these people routinely inflate materials estimates to provide "insurance" against their own mistakes in measuring and estimating quantities of materials needed to decorate their clients' homes -- fabrics, wallpaper, trimmings, carpeting, etc. This is the standard procedure for many businesses in the trade. Upholsterers and wallpaper installers we have known over the years have told us that they see this scam frequently from designers and decorators, too.

We have returned tens of thousands of yards of extra, unneeded, wasted fabric to interior designers and interior decorators over the years. Most of the custom orders we received in our factory and custom workroom over the years were submitted with far more fabric than was necessary to do the work. We routinely returned 1 to 3 yards of wasted fabric to designers and decorators on small jobs (such as a pair of pillows or a small window valance) and even small ROLLS of fabric on larger jobs (such as a large pair of draperies).

Guess who paid for all of the yards and yards of wasted fabric? Hint: It wasn't the designers and decorators. In fact, most of them actually enjoyed a bigger commission on the job because of the excess fabric they persuaded their clients to purchase.

The vast majority of interior designers and interior decorators have no more training, knowledge, or experience in the manufacturing and installation of custom home furnishings than you do. Wallpapering, sewing, and upholstery are generally not taught in interior design schools. I have never seen a single interior design school course catalog that listed any classes that teach designers how to sew window treatments, put up wallpaper, or do any other type of custom manufacturing or installation. It is extremely rare for an interior designer or interior decorator to have any prior experience in manufacturing or installation. I have certainly never met one who did.

If you don't understand how custom furnishings are made well enough to make a correct materials estimate, you have two choices -- you can guess too much, or you can guess too little. One has expensive consequences for the designer or decorator. The other does not and can even help the designer or decorator turn a little extra profit on the job.

Guessing too little will cause major problems for any interior designer or decorator. If there isn't enough fabric to make the draperies or enough wallpaper to cover the room, the designer or decorator is going to have to buy more materials at her own expense to make up the shortage. She might also have to pay an installer to make a return visit and finish the installation. She might even run into dye-lot mismatch problems. Guessing too low on an estimate is a very embarrassing and expensive mistake. Most interior designers and interior decorators only have to have this happen once before they learn not to ever let it happen again.

Guessing too much is usually undetectable to clients. If the designer or decorator always intentionally makes her estimates a little too high, adding in a few extra yards of fabric or a few extra rolls of wallpaper here and there, she probably won't ever get caught short. Even if she doesn't know the first thing about manufacturing or installation, she can breathe a sigh of relief knowing that it is highly unlikely that she will ever have to pay for any extra materials out of her own pocket or suffer any embarrassment in front of her client. She can even boost her commission a little bit because she will usually be paid a straight percentage of what the labor and materials cost on a decorating job. She can't lose.

Her clients lose big, however. They're the ones who have to pay for the wasted fabric and wallpaper -- not the designer or decorator. The clients usually never even know that they have been ripped off. Most of them don't know how to make correct estimates either. After all, that's why they hired a designer or decorator in the first place and trusted them to do the job right.

We estimate that most of the consumers served by the designers and decorators we have made custom window treatments for lost between $50.00 and $250.00 on wasted fabrics, depending upon the size of the decorating job that was done. This is just the waste from the work we did. Undoubtedly, many of these consumers also lost money on wasted upholstery fabrics and wallpapers. At an average of $22.00 per yard for fabrics sold through designers and decorators, wasted money adds up fast.

Only a little more than two wasted yards of an average decorative fabric, an amount we saw wasted routinely on a single window treatment, would result in $50.00 down the drain. The consumer might as well have taken a $50.00 bill out and burned it. Of course, the designer or decorator would lose out on her $25.00 commission on the sale of the fabric if that happened.

Most consumers who have custom home furnishings made through interior designers and interior decorators fall victim to this scam -- usually without ever realizing it. Don't be one of them. It is completely unnecessary for you to ever risk getting ripped off this way.

Always make your own materials estimates. Use the guidelines in the chapters throughout Part I of this book to estimate the amount of fabric, wallpaper, carpet, trimmings, and other materials you need to decorate your home.

Where Does All Of the Wasted Fabric Go?

What happens to all of the tens of thousands of yards of fabric that interior designers and interior decorators all over the United States waste every year? We're talking about hundreds of thousands of dollars worth of fabric here. Where does it all disappear to? Who is getting all of this "free" fabric?

The designer or decorator? Sometimes. Once, I went out to a designer's own home to measure her windows for draperies, and she showed me a chair upholstered in leftover fabric we had recently returned to her on a custom drapery job. She even commented that she had gotten the fabric free because it was left over from one of her clients' homes. She was quite pleased with herself about the great bargain she had gotten.

I wonder what her client would have thought if she had ever found out about this -- which, of course, she never will. She helped pay for the designer's new chair. It only seems fair that she should have an opportunity to express her opinion about it.

Over the years, a number of designers and decorators brought in pieces of fabric that were left over from their clients' jobs to have small items, such as pillows and small window treatments, made for themselves. This is a fairly common occurrence.

The workroom? Sometimes. Usually, the designers and decorators didn't ask us for the wasted fabric, because they didn't have to pay for it. They did usually ask us for a few small scraps of fabric to present to their clients as the total leftovers. This has been the standard procedure for many, many years.

Some workrooms sell the leftover fabrics, as discussed later in this chapter.

The client who actually foots the bill for the fabric? Virtually never. I have never heard of one single designer or decorator returning the wasted fabric to her client.

After all, what would the client say? In all likelihood, the client would expect to be reimbursed for the wasted materials because they never should have been ordered in the first place.

The Phony Brand Name Scam

Some fabric manufacturers print phony brand names on the selvages (white strips along each side) of their fabrics. This helps prevent customers from comparison shopping to get the best price because they have no practical way of knowing who really manufactured the fabric.

When customers call telephone information to locate the manufacturer of the fabric to find a factory outlet or discounter or even to purchase it directly, they can't because there are no telephone listings for these phony company names. I have been unable to locate telephone listings for any of these phony company names in the cities in which each fabric manufacturer is based, despite repeated attempts.

Interior designers and store owners have a decoding key to these phony brand names. They have no difficulty tracking down the true sources of these fabrics because they have the correct business names and phone numbers.

Consumers don't have a decoding key, of course, which allows the interior designer or store owner to charge them more for the fabric, usually at least double what they would have to pay if they could decode the phony brand name and order the fabric from a telephone ordering service or buy it at a factory outlet. This phony brand name system helps support a level of middlemen who do little more than relay the order to the manufacturer, usually doubling the cost of the fabric to the consumer.

This doesn't have to happen to you, however. Now you have a decoding key, too. All of the major fabric manufacturers who print phony brand names on some or all of their fabrics are listed below, along with each manufacturer's true identity.

Phony Brand Name	***Mfr's True Identity***
Ambiance Designs	*Western Textile*
Atelier Originals	*Spectrum Fabrics*
Chetley Originals	*Richloom Fabrics*
Fabriyaz	*Braemore*
5th Avenue Designs	*Covington Fabrics*
House 'N Home Fabrics & Draperies	*John Wolf Fabrics*
Interior Fabric Design	*Ametex Fabrics*
Margin Designs	*Anju-Woodridge Fabrics*

Now when you find an attractive fabric that is labeled with a phony brand name, you will be able to identify its true source and contact a manufacturers' outlet store (for those manufacturers who use outlet stores) or a telephone fabric ordering service to get a much better deal, usually up to 50% off retail.

If you decide to become your own decorator and you need a large quantity of a fabric (usually at least 50 yards), you may be able to purchase it directly from the manufacturer. Even if you only need 25 yards or more for your decorating job, you will usually come out ahead to order 50 yards at 75% off retail instead of ordering the exact amount you need at only 50% off retail. We will discuss this buying strategy in detail on pages 79-82.

How To Buy Many "To the Trade Only" Fabrics At the Same Prices Interior Decorators Pay

You might think that the "to-the-trade-only" fabric showrooms in exclusive wholesale design centers and wholesale trade centers around the country are full of unique, one-of-a-kind fabrics that you could never purchase unless you paid an interior decorator or interior designer a big commission to buy them for you.

You would be wrong on both counts. Many of these fabrics are available from many different sources (most of which are open to the general public), and you do not need the services of a designer or decorator to buy the most of them.

Many of the fabrics found in exclusive trade showrooms are also available from telephone order fabric houses and local fabric discounters at 50% to 65% less than what a decorator or designer would normally charge you for the very same fabrics.

Please be aware that the fabrics sold by these discounters are NOT cheap knockoffs of the fabrics available in the design centers, but are the very same high-quality fabrics from the very same manufacturers. The fabric discounters just buy fabrics in large quantities and don't mark their prices up nearly as much as the fancy "to-the-trade-only" showrooms in the high rent district.

The trick is to identify the fabric's manufacturer and the correct fabric name or number. This can be done with a "cross-over" book, as explained later in this chapter. You normally cannot read the manufacturer's name off of the selvage in these showrooms, because the selvage will almost always have been removed from showroom fabric samples.

After you correctly identify the fabric, you can often order it through a telephone order fabric house at the same price interior decorators and interior designers pay for that fabric when they buy it at the "to-the-trade-only" showroom.

Many of the fabrics in these trade showrooms that truly are one-of-a-kind exclusives can be purchased by the public at a discount on special shopping days at the wholesale design centers. Many design centers have certain days each month when they are open to the public. You should contact the design center directly for a current schedule.

Please see page 328 for a list of wholesale design centers in the United States that have open shopping days. The typical discount you would receive off of the usual retail price on these fabrics is about 20%.

If you decide to become your own licensed interior decorator as discussed in Chapter 19, you can almost always get the same 40% to 50% discount that decorators and designers receive on these exclusive fabrics, and you can shop at the design centers and wholesale showrooms whenever you want.

If you are interested in buying a fabric you have seen in a "to-the-trade-only" showroom or in a magazine with a notation that it is available only to the trade, follow the steps listed at the end of this chapter to determine if it can be purchased directly at a lower price. Many of these fabrics can be purchased for up to 50% (or more) off the standard retail price.

Exclusive vs. Non-Exclusive Fabrics

On some fabric samples and swatches, you will see a notation that the fabric is "exclusive". When a company offers an exclusive fabric, they tend to shout it from the rooftops. You needn't worry about accidentally missing this notice. If you don't see a prominent notice of exclusivity, you can safely assume that the fabric is "non-exclusive".

"Non-exclusive" in the fabric business means that a fabric is available from many different sources at a wide range of prices, from interior designers all the way down to telephone fabric discounters and factory outlets. In other words, the manufacturer is willing to sell it to any and every wholesale buyer who wishes to purchase it in an appropriate quantity.

"Exclusive" is supposed to mean that the manufacturer only sells the fabric to certain wholesale customers who can then command a higher price for it from other wholesale customers and retail consumers because open price competition has been eliminated, but this is sometimes not really the case. Some so-called "exclusive" fabrics are available from other sources at greatly reduced prices.

There is also the question of whether exclusive fabrics are really worth the high prices that are charged for them. Almost all exclusive fabrics have very similar patterns available on a non-exclusive basis at much cheaper prices, sometimes from the very same manufacturer.

For every exclusive fabric with a certain pattern on it, you can find at least ten lovely, high-quality, non-exclusive fabrics with very similar patterns on them for half the price or less. Many times, similar non-exclusive fabrics will be made by the very same manufacturer that is selling the high-priced exclusive fabric. Instead of waiting for a competitor to knock-off their exclusive fabrics, manufacturers will often go ahead and do this themselves.

If an exclusive fabric has a pattern you like, you usually won't have to look far to find a non-exclusive fabric with a similar pattern, sometimes from the same manufacturer. There is really no practical reason to ever pay high prices -- usually double the prices of non-exclusive fabrics with comparable patterns -- for exclusive fabrics.

Exclusivity is the main factor in determining prices on most fabrics. Exclusive fabrics are almost always more expensive than comparably designed and manufactured non-exclusive fabrics. However, they are generally not of any higher quality. In fact, most of these high-priced exclusive fabrics are manufactured by the very same fabric manufacturers who supply fabrics to telephone order fabric houses and fabric discounters.

These exclusive agreements serve to protect, and profit, one or more levels of middlemen between the manufacturer and the retail consumer by eliminating open price competition and creating monopolies on certain products. Everyone involved benefits at the expense of the retail consumer.

If there is an exclusive fabric which you simply must have, you may wish to become your own decorator as discussed in Chapter 19. Buying these fabrics wholesale at direct interior decorator prices can make them almost as affordable as non-exclusive fabrics. Wholesale fabric showrooms across the U. S. are listed in the *National Directory Of Wholesale Home Furnishings Sources and Showrooms*.

Time is On Your Side

Sometimes, fabrics which are marked "exclusive" can be ordered over the phone or purchased at a local fabric warehouse for about half-price because the exclusivity period has run out.

Usually, exclusive fabrics are only exclusive for a limited period of time. After six months to a year, many revert to non-exclusive status and can be purchased from discounters.

It is possible that the fabric sample on which you saw the exclusivity notice is out of date. There aren't any sample police who visit interior designers and retail stores to make sure that all of their samples are up to date. I see out of date and improperly marked samples all the time in retail stores and interior design studios. It's worth double-checking.

How Do You Know If a Product Is Ultra-Exclusive?

Ultra-exclusive products aren't labeled "ultra-exclusive".

The only way to find out if a product is ultra-exclusive is to shop around for it. It's a process of elimination.

If you can't find it at any discount source, such as a telephone ordering service, or from most of the decorators and designers in your area -- it's likely that the product is ultra-exclusive.

Call the manufacturer. If they refer you to a very few "approved" designers in your area that sell the product, then you can be pretty sure that it is ultra-exclusive.

Don't forget -- there is no way that you can have direct access to ultra-exclusive products, even if you become your own decorator. If you are thinking of getting being your own decorator to buy one particular product, make sure that the manufacturer will sell to decorators, first.

We'll discuss this topic in more detail in Chapter 19.

Ultra-Exclusive Fabrics

A few fabric manufacturers and distributors have taken steps to severely limit the availability of some of their fabrics, thereby allowing them to charge higher prices. These ultra-exclusive fabrics are not available to interior decorators or retail stores. Even if you become your own licensed interior decorator, you will not be able to buy these fabrics directly.

They are available only to selected interior designers who have well established businesses. If you want to buy any of these fabrics, you must purchase them through certain interior designers and pay a hefty commission.

There are very few ultra-exclusive high-priced fabrics that are more durable or higher-quality than the fabrics you can buy from your local fabric discounter or over the phone, although I have often heard interior designers try to justify the high prices of these ultra-exclusive fabrics by making such claims.

Very few of these ultra-exclusive fabrics are worth the greatly inflated prices charged for them. When you buy these fabrics, you are paying primarily for snob appeal and perhaps a famous designer's name. If that is important to you, fine. Don't be fooled, however, into believing that most of these fabrics are of any higher quality than the majority of fabrics which can be purchased directly by consumers.

In almost all cases, the fiber contents, weights, weaving methods, types of dye used, and methods of production of these fabrics are identical to those of the fabrics you can buy in your local fabric warehouse or over the phone. In fact, many of these ultra-exclusive fabrics are made by the very same manufacturers that supply non-exclusive fabrics to telephone ordering services and fabric stores.

Usually, when a manufacturer makes ultra-exclusive and non-exclusive fabrics, each type of fabric has a very similar fiber content, look, feel, weight, and texture. I have worked around fabrics all of my life, and I usually can't tell a given manufacturer's ultra-exclusive and non-exclusive fabrics apart unless I look at the description on the manufacturer's product tag -- or the price tag. So, why pay twice as much for the exclusive fabric?

No matter what an interior designer may try to tell you, the vast majority of these ultra-exclusive high-priced fabrics do not last longer, wear better, drape better, or look better than the fabrics you will find at your local fabric discounter or from a telephone fabric ordering service.

For the most part, ultra-exclusive fabrics are a big waste of money. Don't throw your money away on them.

Fantasy Fabrics

There are, of course, a few exceptions. There are some ultra-exclusive fabrics that are hand-woven, hand-embroidered, embellished with tassels or metallic trinkets, or hand-painted, and are truly lovely and unique. The prices of these few fabrics reflect a tremendous amount of effort and, although high, are entirely reasonable when you consider what you are getting for your money.

You certainly don't have to buy these extremely expensive fabrics in order to have a beautiful home, but you might want to buy a couple of yards for small touches such as decorative pillows.

Many of these fabrics can be purchased directly by consumers at 20% off retail on special public buying days at the wholesale interior design centers or at 40% to 50% off retail any day if you become your own licensed interior decorator. Some of these fabrics are shown at the artist's private studio, which should be identified in the interior design magazines where they are often featured.

Some of the artists who produce these fabrics choose to make them available only through selected interior designers. There is no way for you to avoid paying a hefty commission to an interior designer if you wish to buy these particular fabrics. However, many of these artists will sell to interior decorators and to the public on certain buying days if the artist has a showroom in a wholesale interior design center.

If you are considering becoming your own licensed interior decorator only for the purpose of buying these ultra-exclusive fabrics, you should first verify that the fabric you want is available to interior decorators.

The Phony Product Information Scam

There is a widespread and firmly entrenched scam that many wholesale fabric distributors use to keep their prices high, thereby making many fabrics cost much more for interior designers and consumers. Many of these distributors hide the manufacturer's identity on their fabric samples and change the original names or numbers used by manufacturers to identify their fabrics, replacing the original product information with their own phony fabric names and numbers. They use secret codes to hide the real product information from interior designers and consumers.

This practice helps prevent interior designers and consumers from comparison shopping among different fabric distributors to get the best price on identical fabrics. It also helps prevent designers and consumers from knowing who manufactured these fabrics. This scam doubles the average price to consumers on most fabrics that are sold through distributors. Sometimes, this scam costs consumers even more.

To get an idea of how difficult this extremely unethical practice makes it for designers and consumers to comparison shop for the best prices on fabrics, try to imagine what it would be like if car dealerships did the same thing. What if car dealers tore all of the manufacturer's identifying information off of the cars and falsified the names of the car models? How could you ever call around for the best price on a car when each dealer calls the same model by a different phony name and hides the manufacturer's identity from you?

How could you call around to different dealerships to get the best price on a car if dealership "A" calls it a "Falcon", and dealership "B" calls the same car a "Cardinal", and dealership "C" calls the same car a "Bluebird", and none of the dealerships will tell you who manufactured the car and what the real name of the car is according to the manufacturer? You can certainly see how confusing it would be and how difficult it would be to narrow down the best price.

You'd probably give up price shopping pretty quickly and settle for paying a relatively high price. That's exactly what happens to designers and consumers when they run into this scam on a daily basis while trying to compare prices on fabric. Trying to sort out all of these phony names every time you need to buy fabric is so difficult that it is actually simpler and more cost-effective for most designers and consumers to just give up and pay twice as much for the fabric -- unless they have a "cross-over" book that decodes the phony names. We'll talk about that in a few minutes.

It's outrageous, isn't it? You'd be furious if a car dealer, or any other type of business, actually tried to pull such a scam on you. I can't think of a single product, other than fabric, that undergoes all of these phony name changes on its way from the manufacturer to the consumer.

Unfortunately, this scam is so widespread and entrenched in the wholesale fabric industry that many designers and decorators just accept it. Of course, the designers and decorators don't suffer from it -- consumers do. Designers and decorators just pass the inflated costs along to their clients, and pick up a bigger commission check in the process. You all end up paying for this scam, ultimately, by being charged twice as much as you should be for many fabrics.

In addition to this book, I also research and write a reference book for interior designers and interior decorators that decodes some of this phony product information spread by fabric distributors. I dig through thousands of fabric samples from various distributors and match them up with each other and with the real product information and manufacturer identity.

Designers and decorators all over the United States use my cross-over book to find out what the real product information and sources are for over 10,000 fabric distributor samples, so they can save up to 50% off the prices they usually pay for fabrics.

In the following section, I'll show you how you can use a cross-over book to save 50% to 75% off retail on thousands of fabrics from over seventy major fabric distributors. You'll be able to save more money than designers and decorators do off of the prices you would normally pay because you will also be eliminating the designer's or decorator's commission.

You don't have to pay high prices because of this scam anymore. You will be able to skip over this entire mess and buy your fabrics directly from telephone ordering services (which have great prices and don't falsify product information) and factory outlets at up to 50% off retail. If you decide to become your own licensed decorator, you will be able to buy many fabrics from wholesale showrooms at 40% to 50% off retail and directly from the manufacturer (in larger quantities) at about 75% off retail.

Cross-over Books -- How They Can Save You 50% (Or More) On Fabrics

Cross-over books have been used for many years by designers and decorators to get the best possible prices on fabrics. Essentially, a cross-over book decodes the phony fabric names and numbers and hidden manufacturer names that you will find in many fabric distributor sample books. Consumers can also use a cross-over book to find much cheaper prices for many fabrics -- 50% to 75% off retail. First, however, you need to understand how the fabric business works and how interior designers use cross-over books to save money.

Fabric distributors purchase large quantities of fabrics directly from the fabric manufacturers and then sell them in small quantities directly to decorators and designers. Distributors usually provide books of cut samples of fabric, on which the manufacturer's name (which is normally printed on the selvage) has been cut off and the original manufacturer's fabric name or number has been often been falsified. This helps prevent decorators and designers from knowing which manufacturer made the fabric and buying it directly from the manufacturer (in larger quantities).

This practice also prevents price comparisons between fabric distributors. Often, a particular fabric may be carried by many different distributors under many different phony names and numbers, and at a variety of prices. By using a cross-over book to decode all of this phony product information, decorators and designers can determine which other fabric distributors carry a specific fabric they wish to purchase and can compare the other distributors' prices.

If the cross-over book also identifies the manufacturer of the fabric, and a large quantity is needed, the decorator or designer can sometimes order the fabric directly from the manufacturer. This cuts out the distributor's commission entirely and usually results in a 50% savings off of the wholesale price (for a total savings of 75% off retail) to the decorator or designer.

In the excerpt at top right, taken from page 76 of the *1995 Decorative Fabrics Cross-Reference Guide* (the entire page from the cross-over book is shown on the next page), we see that the distributor Kasmir Fabrics sells a fabric to which it has assigned the phony name "Aztec". We also see that the manufacturer of the fabric (listed in bold italics right below Kasmir's name for this fabric) is the Cohama-Riverdale fabric mill and that the real name of the fabric is "Apache". Don't forget that you usually can't see from the fabric distributor's sample who manufactured the fabric because the selvage has almost always been cut off.

The cross-over book also shows that the fabric is also sold by sixteen other distributors, most of which have also falsified the original manufacturer's fabric name. The distributor Kravet Fabrics refers to this fabric by the phony name "Silent", Duralee Fabrics uses the phony name "Hartford", etc.

All of these names in this long list describe the very same fabric. One fabric -- one real manufacturer's name -- thirteen phony names. No wonder designers and decorators have problems sorting out all of this phony product information.

To get the best prices on fabric, designers and decorators have to cut through all of the phony product information to make honest comparisons between distributors on identical fabrics. You can do the same thing to reduce the prices you pay for fabric by 50% or more.

Getting back to our example -- if a decorator or designer is considering purchasing a quantity of "Aztec" from Kasmir Fabrics, he or she can first call the other distributors listed to see if a better price is available. The cross-reference book also lists addresses and phone numbers for all of the cross-referenced fabric distributors in the back. If the interior decorator or interior designer needed a large quantity of fabric, he or she might be able to order it directly from the manufacturer, which in this case is Cohama-Riverdale.

You can use cross-over books to save money, too. If the selvage showing the manufacturer's name has been removed from the sample you are interested in, as will usually be the case with fabric distributor samples, you

Excerpt From the 1995 Decorative Fabrics Cross-Reference Guide

AZTEC
COHAMA-RIVERDALE: APACHE
AWARD: 1451
CARO/UPRIGHT: APACHE
DAVIS: AZTEC
DOGWOOD: P603
DURALEE: HARTFORD
FABRICUT: MESA
KAS-TEX: NUEVO
KRAVET: SILENT
LADY ANN: APACHE
LAFAYETTE: APACHE
NORBAR: ANKARA
R&M: SELLICK
S&S: BACALL
SOUTHLAND: KEN APACHE
STOUT: DODGE
TEMPO: RAFFIA

Note:

The *1995 Decorative Fabrics Cross-Reference Guide* is the only cross-over book currently available in the U. S.

There is an order form in the back of this book.

Page 76 -- 1995 Decorative Fabrics Cross-Reference Guide

76

KASMIR FABRICS

ABIGAIL
DELTA: 8285

ACCENT
DELTA: 8284
KASMIR: FABLE
LAFAYETTE: DEBONAIR

ACE
DOGWOOD: P604
DURALEE: HOME
FABRICUT: MAVERICK
KAS-TEX: NATIONAL
NORBAR: DOMINO
R&M: GIBSON
STOUT: REDBAY
TEMPO: ROBIN

ACOSTA
COVINGTON: MOJAVE
KRAVET: VASSAR
LADY ANN: MOJAVE
NORBAR: DURANGO
S&S: KELLY

ADAIR
KAS-TEX: FAIRHAVEN

ADLER
ANJU-WOODRIDGE: ALLIANCE
ASHBOURNE: FUSION
BARROW: LASTING
LADY ANN: ALLIANCE
TEMPO: VISTA P8500
P COLLINS: 3436

AGNEW
COVINGTON: TIRICA
CAROLE: SWIRLS
KAS-TEX: BRIGGS

ALAMO
KAS-TEX: FOWLER

ALBA
COHAMA-RIVERDALE: CASCADE
DAVIS: CARSON
DOGWOOD: P606
KAS-TEX: NORWOOD
NORBAR: CASINO
SOUTHLAND: KEN CASCADE
STOUT: NARBETH
TEMPO: RALEIGH

ALBANY
BLOOMCRAFT: FIRESIDE

ALBERTA
CAROLACE: 21793
CAROLE: FIFI
LADY ANN: ELITE

ALCOT
KAS-TEX: CAMINO
SIERRA: WALDORF
SOUTHLAND: ILLUMINATE

ALLISON
COCO: G17
FABRICUT: INDRA
LADY ANN: BIANCA

ALPHA
BISHOPS: RUBY

ALTO
COHAMA-RIVERDALE: DESIREE
ARTMARK: COUNTERPOINT
AWARD: 1454
CARO/UPRIGHT: DESIREE
DAVIS: DURANGO
DOGWOOD: P605
DURALEE: HALL
FABRICUT: HIDEAWAY
KAS-TEX: NASSAU
LADY ANN: PALISADES
LAFAYETTE: DESIREE
NORBAR: PARADISE
R&M: BRONSON
S&S: GARSON
SOUTHLAND: KEN DESIREE
STOUT: TEATIME
TEMPO: REJOICE

AMBIANCE
CAROLE: DANIELLE

AMHERST
BLOOMCRAFT: TRADITIONS

ANDES
ANJU-WOODRIDGE: ALLUSION
ASHBOURNE: WINDSWEPT
AWARD: ALLUSION
BARROW: MEMORY
COCO: H21
LADY ANN: ALLUSION
P COLLINS: 3435
TEMPO: PRO 112-114
TEMPO: VISTA T8000
WESCO: AMBROSIA

ARAPAHO
COHAMA-RIVERDALE: ALGONKIN
AWARD: 1450
CARO/UPRIGHT: ALGONKIN
DAVIS: ARROYO
DURALEE: HURON
FABRICUT: MOHAWK
KAS-TEX: NEEDLES
KRAVET: SYSTEM
LADY ANN: ALGONKIN
LAFAYETTE: ALGONKIN
NORBAR: ANTIOCH
R&M: EASTWOOD
SOUTHLAND: KEN ALGONKIN
STOUT: FILLMORE
TEMPO: RAINTREE

ARRAY
BLAUTEX: DIGITS

ASBURY
BLOOMCRAFT: TREASURES

ATWOOD
SPECTRUM: FIESTA

AUBURN
BLOOMCRAFT: TEA TIME

AWARD
ANJU-WOODRIDGE: ALHAMBRA
ASHBOURNE: MIRAMAR
BARROW: PARAMOUNT
COCO: H20
LADY ANN: ALHAMBRA
P COLLINS: 3434
TEMPO: PRO 115-117
TEMPO: VISTA V9000
WESCO: ANISETTE

AZTEC
COHAMA-RIVERDALE: APACHE
AWARD: 1451
CARO/UPRIGHT: APACHE
DAVIS: AZTEC
DOGWOOD: P603
DURALEE: HARTFORD
FABRICUT: MESA
KAS-TEX: NUEVO
KRAVET: SILENT
LADY ANN: APACHE
LAFAYETTE: APACHE
NORBAR: ANKARA
R&M: SELLICK
S&S: BACALL
SOUTHLAND: KEN APACHE
STOUT: DODGE
TEMPO: RAFFIA

B-LINE
ROCLON: ECONOSHEEN
LADY ANN: DACROLINE

BACH
BLAUTEX: FLASH

BAKER
KAS-TEX: CHANNEY
LORD JAY: FLORI
MARSHALL: ILLUSION
SIERRA: WHISPER
SOUTHLAND: ILLUSIONS
TEMPO: MOMENTO
THOMAS: PARADISE

BALTIC
KAST: ADOBE
SIERRA: OVATION
WESTFIELD: DEXTER

BARCELONA
EMMESS: PASEO
O KRENT: KITE
P COLLINS: 3112
WESCO: WES PROVINCE
WESTFIELD: DUDASH

BARON
EMMESS: ESTRADA
FABRICS 21: EMBASSY
KAS-TEX: LOMAX
S&S: EBSON
SALCO: SANTA ROSA
WESCO: WES EVEREST
WESTFIELD: ADNEY
WYMAN: EDEN

BASCOM
MICHAELS: SHERBET
PINDLER: WINDWARD

BASSETT
BLAUTEX: DRIZZLE

BEABES
WESTFIELD: HILLTOP

BECKET
BELCO: BELLE
FABRICUT: TANYA
NORMANS: GYPSY
SALCO: PRINCESS
SIERRA: OLYMPIA
WESTFIELD: HAYDEN

BENTLEY
WESTFIELD: APRIL FLOWERS

BISHOP
CAROLE: DOVER

BOLDEN
WESCO: NEXUS

BONNIWELL
FABRICADE: 4968
WIN-TEX: APOLLO

BORDEN
BLAUTEX: LIGHTNING

BORLING
FABRICADE: 4962
WIN-TEX: AMANDA

BRAVO
KAST: COMET
SIERRA: OAKLAND
WESTFIELD: GIRARD

BURG
CAROLE: TARTAN
FABRICADE: 4964
WIN-TEX: ADAMS

BURTON
WESCO: QUICKSILVER

CALHOUN
CAROLE: ARIZONA
EMMESS: ASTROID
KRAVET: CALHOUN
MICHAELS: VOLCANO
STEVEN: YELLOWSTONE
WESTFIELD: LABELLE
WIN-TEX: HUTCHINSON

CALVIN
DURALEE: FLEET

CAREY
A FOLTYN: ROVER
BLAUTEX: WHITING
LADY ANN: ROVER

may be able to identify the manufacturer and the correct manufacturer's fabric name or number through a cross-over book.

With the correct manufacturer and the correct fabric name or number, you can contact a factory outlet to save 50% or more off of the fabric's retail price if the outlet carries the particular fabric you are looking for. If there is no factory outlet, you can contact a telephone ordering service and order most fabrics at up to 50% off of the retail price.

If you decide to become your own licensed interior decorator, you will be able to purchase many fabrics directly at the fabric distributor's wholesale showrooms for 40% to 50% off of retail. If you need a sufficient quantity of the fabric, you may be able to save as much as 75% off retail by purchasing the fabric directly from the fabric manufacturer, as discussed in the next section.

How You Can Save 75% Off of Retail On Some Fabrics

If you decide to become your own licensed interior decorator, and you need a large quantity of fabric (about 50 yards of a single fabric), you may be able to order it directly from the fabric manufacturer just as many professional interior decorators and interior designers do. If you can order this way, you will normally save 75% off of retail. It will usually be cheaper overall to order about 50 yards directly from the manufacturer even if you only need at least 26 yards of fabric for your project.

It is not uncommon for a consumer to need at least 26 yards of a single fabric. We often saw this occur in situations where the consumer is having a bedspread and matching window treatments made for a bedroom or having a sofa custom-upholstered and matching window treatments made for a living room. At our workroom, we saw many interior designers and interior decorators use this buying method to order fabrics at 75% off retail directly from the manufacturer in decorating situations such as these.

Minimum order quantity You must normally order at least one full "piece" ("piece" refers to a roll of fabric) of each fabric you wish to purchase. Do not try to mix patterns, such as ordering 20 yards of one fabric and 30 yards of another fabric from the same manufacturer to make up the 50 yard minimum order. The manufacturers simply will not allow that.

You normally cannot order a fraction of a piece, even if you are ordering at least one full piece. For example, you normally cannot order 75 yards of a fabric -- you must order either one piece (approximately 50 yards) or two pieces (approximately 100 yards), nothing in-between.

Dealing with manufacturers Your ability to order fabrics directly from the manufacturer will depend upon the attitude and sales policy of the particular fabric manufacturer you are approaching. Richloom Fabrics (plus its various divisions and brand names), Concord Fabrics, Western Textile, and Ametex Fabrics are reputed in the trade to be some of the easiest manufacturers for decorators and designers to buy from directly.

They all have stated policies allowing decorators and designers to order one "piece" at a time (approximately 50 yards), which is an appropriate quantity for some home decorating jobs. I have heard many interior decorators and interior designers praise their pleasant and cooperative

Should You Buy Your Fabric Directly From the Manufacturer?

This might be the best option for you if you need more than 25 yards of a single fabric.

It is usually cheaper to order 50 yards directly from a manufacturer at about 75% off retail than it is to order any amount over 25 yards from another type of discount source at only about 50% off retail.

For example, you might need a total of 35 yards of a particular fabric in order to have a custom bedspread and two matching window treatments made. Let's assume that this fabric is an average patterned chintz and that you can order it for $12.00 per yard from a telephone ordering service (about 50% off the usual retail price for such a fabric). If you ordered exactly 35 yards of this fabric over the phone, you would pay $420.00.

However, if you were able to identify the manufacturer of the fabric and order a full piece (about 50 yards) at a usual manufacturer's price of $6.00 per yard for this type of fabric, you would only pay $300.00! You save $120.00 off of the total cost you would have paid through a telephone ordering service. Plus, you have 50 yards of fabric instead of only 35. You could use the other 15 yards somewhere else in your home.

If you need to order more than 25 yards of a single fabric, find out if you can order it from the manufacturer and consider ordering a full piece. Usually, this is the least expensive option.

attitudes.

Some fabric manufacturers are very difficult for decorators and designers to buy from directly, primarily because they often require a large opening order from new customers. These companies generally require new customers to order at least 200 yards of fabric (or more) on their first order. These huge quantities of fabric are almost never practical for an decorator or designer to order, and almost certainly will not be practical for you when you are decorating your home. These policies tend to discourage business from decorators and designers.

Please be aware that some fabric manufacturers do not wish to be "bothered" with small orders from decorators and designers. There will certainly be a few fabric manufacturers who respond rudely when you try to place an order. I have spoken with several of them personally, and they made it very clear that they did not want to "accommodate" decorators by accepting the "tiny" orders that they usually place.

If this should happen to you, select another fabric from a more accommodating manufacturer. There are many other fabric manufacturers who are more agreeable to selling directly to decorators and designers.

Your best bet will be to contact Richloom Fabrics (and its various divisions), Ametex Fabrics, Concord Fabrics, and Western Textile. Each of these companies has a stated policy of selling one piece at a time to decorators. Many designers and decorators have told me that they have been pleased with the service given by these companies.

There will certainly be other manufacturers whom I have not dealt with who will also welcome orders from decorators. I am not personally acquainted with every single fabric manufacturer in the industry. If you are interested in a fabric that is not from the above four companies -- by all means, call the manufacturer and ask if they work with decorators. You may or may not be able to purchase directly from them, but it is certainly worth your time to ask.

Attitudes do change over time. Maybe some of the companies who do not currently welcome orders from decorators will change their minds when they see their more accommodating competitors getting all of your business. At some later date, you might find that they would be very happy to take your order. In fact, one of the four companies listed above had more restrictive ordering requirements only a few short years ago.

Smaller quantities of fabric If you need more than 25 yards of a single fabric, you will probably also come out ahead to buy a 50 yard (approximately) piece from the manufacturer, unless you can get a great deal at a factory outlet. Twenty-five yards purchased at standard wholesale through a distributor or telephone ordering service (at an average $12.00 per yard) usually costs exactly the same as 50 yards of the same fabric purchased directly from the manufacturer (at an average $6.00 per yard).

If you need more than 25 yards of a fabric, purchasing 50 yards directly from the manufacturer is normally cheaper than purchasing just the amount you need from a fabric distributor or telephone ordering service. In addition, you will also have the extra fabric, "free". You might decide to use it somewhere else in your home or sell it to a friend for even greater savings.

The box at left explains how you might approach just such a situation, and how the prices normally compare between manufacturers and fabric discounters.

Individual cases will vary, so you should consider the actual cost of the particular fabric you want when deciding whether you should buy it from a retail source, such as a telephone ordering service or factory outlet, or directly from the manufacturer.

Note: Please note clearly that some manufacturers will not sell you only 25 yards (or any other amount less than a full piece). Some manufacturers occasionally allow customers to purchase (approximately) 25 yard half-pieces of patterned chintzes and sateens, but will only allow customers to order full 50 yard pieces of their other fabrics. Some other manufacturers require minimum orders of one piece (approximately 50 yards) on all of their fabrics.

Half-pieces Our workroom and factory purchased many half-pieces from fabric manufacturers over the years, and I have spoken with many decorators and designers who have done the same. Chintzes and sateens with printed patterns are the most likely types of fabrics to be available in half-pieces.

It is highly unlikely that you will be permitted to order half-pieces of solid-color fabrics (antique satins, sateens, chintzes, etc.), sheers, linings, or upholstery fabrics. You will also find that many solid color fabrics are packaged in larger pieces than other fabrics -- sometimes as much as 80 to 100 yards. The normal requirement for most fabric manufacturers that only full pieces be purchased.

These policies vary, even within the same manufacturing company. My family has occasionally purchased half-pieces of fabrics from companies that ordinarily do not sell them. So have many designers and decorators I have spoken with on this subject. Exceptions are sometimes made -- especially if the fabric you want has been discontinued, is overstocked, or is selling slowly. It certainly doesn't hurt to ask.

Placing your order When you buy fabric directly from a manufacturer, you will order either a "piece", which is approximately equal to 50 yards for most fabrics, or a "half-piece" (if this is allowed), which is approximately equal to 25 yards for most fabrics. The roll of fabric you receive will often be slightly more or less than the usual size, usually somewhere between 45 and 60 yards for a full piece and between 20 and 30 yards for a half piece.

If you order a piece of fabric expecting to receive 50 yards, and instead you receive 55 yards or 47 yards, the factory didn't make a mistake. That's just the established system. You are expected to accept and pay for the extra yards, or live with the shortage. If your decorating job absolutely requires a certain minimum quantity, 49 yards for instance, say so when you place your order. The manufacturer will usually note this on your order and accommodate it if possible.

The manufacturer will not be able to tell you in advance the exact size of the roll of fabric you will receive, and you should not ask. Never forget that decorators and designers represent the very tiniest sales to a fabric manufacturer. Many of them consider that they are doing you a favor to take your order at all.

Final note If you decide to become your own licensed decorator and you need to purchase at least 50 yards (or even as little as 26 yards) of a single fabric, you should at least try to order it directly. If the fabric you want isn't available this way, look for a similar one that is. There are thousands of fabrics available to you directly from the manufacturer.

The more fabric you need, the more money you can save. Seventy-five percent off retail on 50 yards of an average decorative fabric would result in a total savings of $900.00. Savings like that are definitely worth checking out.

Please note that this method of savings, as with many other wholesale buying methods listed in Chapter 19 and throughout this book, will not work with every manufacturer or with every fabric. The savings can indeed be huge, but there will be many fabrics that will not be available to you this way. Some manufacturers do not wish to sell directly to interior decorators and actively discourage these sales.

However, even the most resistant manufacturer may welcome an opportunity to sell a fabric that is overstocked, about to be discontinued from sale because it is too old, or just not selling very well. You will not always be able to work directly with a given fabric manufacturer, but the huge savings you may realize make it well worth the attempt. There are thousands of fabrics that are available from manufacturers that do work directly with interior decorators -- enough to keep you redecorating for years.

Please read all of Chapter 19 carefully before attempting to deal directly with a fabric manufacturer. Chapter 19 also contains complete instructions on how you can easily become a licensed interior decorator and buy your furnishings at wholesale.

Fabric Stores

Local fabric stores often have great prices on fabrics. Many stores have prices ranging from $8.95 to $11.95 on decorative chintz and sateen fabrics, which is approximately 50% to 62% off of the usual retail price. Also, many fabric stores have remnants and roll ends available, which are usually marked down an additional 50% for a total savings of about 75% off retail. Remnants and roll ends are usually very small pieces of fabric, only about 1 to 3 yards, but that is more than enough for a small valance or a pair of pillows.

Don't forget to check fabric stores that carry primarily clothing fabrics. These stores often have smaller sections devoted to home furnishings fabrics, and they have great prices.

If you are a careful shopper, you can get a great deal on fabrics at local fabric stores. Shop carefully, and compare prices. Prices can vary widely between stores, even on identical fabrics.

Irregulars vs. Seconds vs. Closeouts

You can save up to 75% off of retail when you buy fabrics that are irregulars, seconds, or closeouts. Irregulars and closeouts are first quality goods that are not damaged or flawed in any way. They represent the best bargains in fabrics. Seconds are fabrics which are flawed in some way. However, since the law requires that even fabrics with very tiny flaws must be sold as seconds, you will be able to find many second-quality fabrics which have flaws that can be trimmed out or will be completely unnoticable when your home furnishings are completed.

Irregulars These are products which are in new condition and are not damaged in any way, but do not match the samples which are on display in stores or shown by salespeople. For instance, a fabric manufacturer may make up a batch of fabric which comes out in a darker shade than the sample. It cannot be shipped to customers because it does not match the sample they ordered from. However, there is nothing wrong with the fabric itself. Irregulars are usually available at half price (75% off retail).

You will normally find irregulars at factory outlets.

Seconds These are second-quality goods that are flawed in some way. There may be a tiny hole or snag on the fabric, or there may be a small patch on which the dye did not adhere properly. These flaws are usually very small, and may be completely unnoticable when your home furnishings have been made up.

If you are having pillows or other small items made, the workroom may be able to cut around the flaw. If you are having upholstery done, the upholsterer may be able to place the flaw on the back side of the furniture. Do be sure to consult with your workroom or upholsterer before purchasing second quality fabrics to make sure that the flaws can be cut out or hidden.

Often, these flaws can be prevented from detracting from the appearance of your home furnishings in any way, but you can still enjoy the savings (normally 50% off of the discounted price, or 75% off of retail). You will normally find seconds at factory outlets.

Closeouts These fabrics are leftovers from the previous season which are no longer worth advertising. Sometimes, these are referred to as ''discontinued''. Almost every fabric manufacturer has closeout fabrics. These are in new condition, but are not worth advertising because only a small quantity remains and because most manufacturers do not want to be seen advertising last year's products.

You will normally find closeouts at factory outlets. These are also usually marked down to half price (75% off retail).

Wholesale Drapery and Upholstery Workrooms

All drapery and upholstery workrooms accumulate small pieces of fabric, usually anywhere from one to five yards each. Occasionally, on bigger jobs, they may have small rolls of fabric left over. Decorators and designers usually order too much fabric for the draperies or upholstery they are having made for their clients as insurance against the possibility that they have not correctly figured the fabric amounts needed for the particular type of furnishings being made.

Some drapery and upholstery workrooms return the excess fabric to the decorator or designer, but many do not. Often, the decorator or designer does not ask for the fabric back. After all, she isn't the one paying for it -- her client is.

The clients usually never ask for the extra fabric back, either, because they don't know how to figure their own yardage requirements. They usually never know that they have been ripped off by the designers and decorators they hired and trusted to make accurate estimates for them.

If you need fabric for a small project, such as decorative pillows or chair cushions, you may wish to ask around at these workrooms to see what they might have laying around. Most of these fabric pieces are virtually given away because the workroom paid nothing for them. You might pay $10.00 at the most for a two or three yard piece of a nice fabric. The very same piece of fabric would cost you a minimum of $20.00 to $30.00 from most other sources.

Telephone Fabric Ordering Services

The usual discount on fabric from telephone fabric ordering services is up to 50% off retail. Please read Chapter 16 for general tips and instructions on buying all types of merchandise from telephone order companies.

These companies are generally very reputable. Most will ship your fabric order within two weeks. If you are quoted a longer shipment time, it is probably because that particular service is out of stock in that fabric. Try another service -- you can usually find at least one service that has the fabric you want in stock and can ship it out much more quickly.

Before you call, you should know the correct name of the fabric manufacturer, the correct fabric name or number, and the yardage you require. Shop in your neighborhood, like the ads say, and write down the fabric information. You will usually find fabric distributor sample books in interior design studios, bed and bath shops, furniture stores, and (on days when some of them are open to the public) wholesale design centers. Please see page 328 for a list of wholesale design centers that have open shopping days.

The manufacturer names and fabric names and numbers on these distributor samples will almost always have been altered or removed, but they can often be deciphered. Write down the fabric distributor's name and the fabric name or number as it appears on the sample, and then use a cross-over book to decode the altered information.

Not all distributor fabric samples can be decoded back to their original source and product information, but about 10,000 can with the _1995 Decorative Fabrics Cross-Reference Guide_. If you can't decipher one fabric, consider choosing another. There are a wide variety of fabrics that can be decoded and purchased at great discounts.

Telephone Ordering Services

ABC Decorative Fabrics
2410 298th Ave. N
Clearwater, FL 34621
(800) 548-3454

American Discount Wall
and Window Coverings
1411 Fifth Ave.
Pittsburgh, PA 15219
(800) 777-2737

Benington's
1271 Manheim Pike
Lancaster, PA 17601
(800) 252-5060

Custom Windows and Walls
32525 Stephenson Hwy.
Madison Heights, MI 48071
(800) 772-1947

The Decorator's Edge
509 Randolph St.
Thomasville, NC 27360
(800) 289-5589

Designer Secrets
P. O. Box 529
Fremont, NE 68025
(800) 955-2559

Dorothy's Ruffled Originals
6721 Market St.
Wilmington, NC 28405
(800) 334-2593

Edgar B.
P. O. Box 849
Clemmons, NC 27012
(800) 255-6589

The Fabric Center
485 Electric Ave.
Fitchburg, MA 01420
(508) 343-4402

Fabrics By Phone
P. O. Box 234
Walnut Bottom, PA 17266
(800) 233-7012

Fabric Outlet
30 Airport Rd.
West Lebanon, NH 03784
(800) 635-9715

Home Fabric Mills
882 S. Main St.
Cheshire, CT 06410
(203) 272-3529

Marlene's Decorator Fabrics
301 Beech St., Dept 2J
Hackensack, NJ 07601
(800) 992-7325

P. and J. Home Furnishings
and Fabric Outlet
4114 Hwy. 70 S.
Hickory, NC 28602
(704) 326-9755

Quality Furniture Market
2034 Hickory Blvd. SE
Lenoir, NC 28645
(704) 728-2946

Resource Designs
Hickory Furniture Mart
Hickory, NC 28602
(704) 322-3161

Sanz International
1183 E. Lexington Ave.
High Point, NC 27262
(910) 883-4622

Wallpaper Xpress
1723 Jericho Rd.
Aurora, IL 60506
(800) 288-9979

Factory Outlets

Fabric manufacturers generally do not operate their own company-owned factory outlets (except for Waverly, Fabricut, and Scalamandre'). Fabric manufacturers normally sell their irregulars and seconds to one or more of the consolidated outlets listed below. Each of these stores carries fabrics from many different manufacturers.

Often, any flaws in second-quality fabrics will not interfere with the project you have in mind. Workrooms can cut around many types of flaws. However, occasionally a fabric will be too flawed to be usable.

Always discuss your project with your workroom before going to a fabric outlet so that you will know what flaws they can and cannot work with, and always go to the outlet personally and inspect the fabrics yourself.

Some of the stores listed below also carry first-quality fabrics. Occasionally, these stores keep second-quality fabrics in a back room or basement. You may have to ask where the bargains are kept.

Factory Outlets

Alabama

Discount Fabric Outlet
Highway 431 North
Boaz, AL 35957
(205) 593-6501

The Interior Alternative
601 Elizabeth St.
Boaz, AL 35957
(205) 593-8887

Connecticut

By the Yard
Exit 16 off I-95
Norwalk, CT 06855
(203) 855-1747

Fabric Remnant Annex
Exit 16 off I-95
Norwalk, CT 06855
(203) 866-2712

Delaware

Kentmere Fine Fabrics
117 Schley Ave.
Lewes, DE 19958
(302) 645-0787

Delaware (cont.)

The Interior Alternative
Bellvue Ave.
Newark, DE 19713
(302) 454-3232

Georgia

Designer Fabrics/Curran Associates
737 Miami Circle NE
Atlanta, GA 30324
(404) 237-4246

Decorator's Outlet
615 Frontage Rd. NW
Augusta, GA 30907
(706) 855-5070

The Interior Alternative
3004-B Parquet Rd.
Dalton, GA 30720
(706) 217-6544

Massachusetts

The Interior Alternative
5 Hoosac St.
Adams, MA 01220
(413) 743-1986

Factory Outlets (cont.)

Massachusetts (cont.)

Designer Fabrics
Wampanoag Mill Factory
Outlet Center
Alden St. and Quequechan St.
Fall River, MA 02721
(508) 678-5242

New York

Silk Surplus (Scalamandre')
1215 Northern Blvd.
Manhasset, NY 11030
(516) 627-3737

Intercoastal Textile Co.
480 Broadway
New York, NY 10013
(212) 925-9235

Silk Surplus (Scalamandre')
235 E. 58th St.
New York, NY 10022
(212) 753-6511

Silk Surplus (Scalamandre')
449 Old Country Rd.
Westbury, NY 11590
(516) 997-7469

Silk Surplus (Scalamandre')
281 Mamaroneck Ave.
White Plains, NY 10605
(914) 684-0041

North Carolina

Textile Sales Room
Hwy. 70 W.
Burlington, NC 27216
(910) 584-7451

Home Outfitters Factory Outlet
Hickory Furniture Mart
Hickory, NC 28602
(704) 324-2220

North Carolina (cont.)

P. & J. Home Furnishings
and Fabric Outlet
4114 Highway 70 S.
Hickory, NC 28602
(704) 326-9755

Resource Designs
Hickory Furniture Mart
Hickory, NC 28602
(704) 322-3161

Waverly Factory Outlet
Hickory Furniture Mart
Hickory, NC 28602
(704) 326-1740

Piece Goods Shop
Exit 20 off I-95
Lumberton, NC 28358
(919) 738-9454

Foam and Fabrics Outlet
17 S. Logan St.
Marion, NC 28752
(704) 652-6121

Printer's Alley
4112 Pleasant Valley Rd.
Suite 13
Raleigh, NC 27612
(919) 781-1777

The Fabric Outlet Store
141 S. Main St.
Warrenton, NC 27589
(919) 257-1337

Designer Fabric Outlet
3445 Robin Hood Rd.
Winston Salem, NC 27106
(910) 765-3577

Oklahoma

Fabricut/S. Harris Outlet
Midamerica Industrial Park
Pryor, OK 74362
(918) 825-4400

South Carolina

The Interior Alternative
1 Frederick Dr.
Richburg, SC 29729
(803) 789-6655

All American Fabrics
I-85 at Bryant Rd.
Spartanburg, SC 29303
(803) 578-8513

Texas

The Interior Alternative
2626 Northhaven Rd.
Dallas, TX 75229
(214) 241-5422

Virginia

Printer's Alley
2133 Coliseum Dr.
Hampton, VA 23666
(804) 827-1404

Printer's Alley
6006 W. Broad St.
Richmond, VA 23230
(804) 285-9591

Printer's Alley
4369 Starkey Rd.
Roanoke, VA 24014
(703) 774-0966

Deep Discount Stores

These discount stores are not true outlets. They keep prices low by buying in very large quantities directly from the manufacturer. Most carry fabrics from many different manufacturers. Some also carry other types of furnishings.

These stores all have great deals on fabric. Their prices are nearly as low as those you will find in true factory outlets, and the selection is often broader. In fact, one of the stores listed -- Herschell's in Atlanta -- was a "to-the-trade-only" wholesale fabric showroom until very recently.

Many of you will find that the discount stores are much more convenient to you than the outlet stores listed above. You may find that the convenience of shopping closer to your home outweighs the small added savings of shopping at a true outlet.

Deep Discount Stores

Connecticut

Home Fabric Mills
882 S. Main St.
Cheshire, CT 06410
(203) 272-3529

Georgia

Herschell's
1255 Williams St.
Atlanta, GA 30309
(404) 875-8133

Kentucky

Bolts
407 Lyndonwood Circle
Louisville, KY 40222
(502) 267-1111

New Hampshire

Fabric Outlet
30 Airport Rd.
West Lebanon, NH 03784
(800) 635-9715

New York

Beckenstein Home Fabrics
130 Orchard St.
New York, NY 10002
(212) 475-6666

Harry Zarin Fabric Warehouse
72 Allen St.
New York, NY 10002
(212) 226-3492

Interiors By Royale
289 Grand St.
New York, NY 10002
(212) 966-3053

New York (cont.)

Richard's Interior Design
1325 Madison Ave.
New York, NY 10128
(212) 831-9000

Rubin and Green
290 Grand St.
New York, NY 10002
(212) 226-0313

Home Fabric Mills
443 Saratoga Rd.
Schenectady, NY 12302
(518) 399-6325

North Carolina

The Furniture Patch
10283 Beach Dr. SW
Calabash, NC 28467
(910) 579-2001

Priba Furniture Sales
5-A Wendy Ct.
Greensboro, NC 27409
(910) 855-9034

Resource Design
Hickory Furniture Mart
Hickory, NC 28602
(704) 322-3161

A. Windsor Furniture Galleries
607 Idol St.
High Point, NC 27262
(910) 883-9000

North Carolina Textile Sales
of High Point
108 Renay Dr.
High Point, NC 27263
(910) 431-3238

North Carolina (cont.)

Rose Furniture
916 Finch Ave.
High Point, NC 27263
(910) 886-6050

Rose Furniture Clearance Center
1813 S. Main St.
High Point, NC 27260
(910) 886-8525

Sanz International
1183 E. Lexington Ave.
High Point, NC 27262
(910) 883-4622

Furnitureland South
5635 Riverdale Rd.
Jamestown, NC 27282
(910) 841-4328

Quality Furniture Market
2034 Hickory Blvd. SE
Lenoir, NC 28645
(704) 728-2946

Turner Tolson Furniture
U. S. Hwy. 17 S
New Bern, NC 28562
(919) 638-2121

Murrow Furniture
3514 S. College Rd.
Wilmington, NC 28412
(910) 799-4010

Pennsylvania

Fabrics By Phone
120 N. Seneca St.
Shippenburg, PA 17257
(800) 233-7012

4 Places You Should Never Buy Fabrics

Blinds stores
Furniture stores
Interior Designers and Interior Decorators
Wallpaper stores

All of these places normally sell fabric from sample books provided by fabric distributors. This means that you are paying two levels of middlemen in addition to paying the manufacturer. At all of these places you will normally pay full retail, which is two to four times as much than you would pay by following the advice in this book.

You can do much better. Follow the recommendations below to buy fabrics without paying middleman markups.

Recommendations

First, consult the yardage charts and recommendations in the chapters which refer to the specific type of home furnishing you plan to have made out of the fabric -- window treatments, bed treatments, pillow, etc. Make a note of the type of fabric, yardage, and repeat size you are looking for. You will find a wide variety of fabrics to choose from for almost any combination of requirements. You should have no difficulty getting a great price on fabric, no matter what type or repeat size you need.

When you find a suitable and attractive fabric from any source -- fabric stores, trade showrooms, magazines, interior designers, interior decorators, retail stores, furniture stores, etc. -- you should follow these steps to locate the very best price available on that fabric:

1 Identify the manufacturer of the fabric. If there is a printed selvage on the fabric, you can usually read the manufacturer's name right there. Check the list of phony brand names on page 71 to make sure that the name on the selvage is the real name of the fabric manufacturer.

If there is no printed selvage or the selvage has been removed (as many stores and fabric distributors do) use a cross-over book to determine the manufacturer's identity and the correct fabric name or number.

If you find that the fabric is an exclusive or the manufacturer cannot be identified, consider changing to another fabric at this point. There are thousands of beautiful fabrics which can be purchased at rock-bottom prices from factory outlets and telephone order fabric houses or directly from the manufacturer, if you can identify the correct manufacturer and the correct fabric name or number.

However, if you decide that you do want to purchase an exclusive fabric, you will get the best possible price available to the general public (usually 20% off retail) by shopping at the fabric distributor's wholesale showroom at a design center in your area on the days when it is open to the public. Design centers that are open to the public on certain days are listed on page 328.

If you decide to become your own decorator, you will be able to purchase many exclusive fabrics at 40% to 50% off retail at design centers and wholesale showrooms.

If you need at least 26 yards of a single fabric, consider attempting to buy it directly from the manufacturer as stated in step 5. Otherwise:

2 Contact a factory outlet: Usually you will save at least 50% off of the standard retail price. Be sure to ask about the availability of irregulars, seconds, and closeouts in the pattern you want. If available, these fabrics are generally discounted even further, sometimes as much as 75% off retail.

3 Try a discount store: Discount fabric stores have great prices on fabrics -- usually about 50% off retail. The selection may be somewhat limited.

4 If there is no factory outlet or discount store near you, contact a telephone fabric ordering service. These sources usually offer up to 50% off of retail prices on fabrics from most manufacturers. However, if you can't get a 50% discount on the fabric you want from any of these sources, either make another fabric choice or consider going on to step 5.

5 Buy it wholesale. If you become your own interior decorator (as discussed in Chapter 19), you can buy most fabrics wholesale at 40% to 75% off the standard retail price, depending upon the quantity you wish to purchase. This method will usually get you the best possible price on fabrics outside of a factory outlet and also gives you the largest selection of bargain-priced fabrics to choose from.

Details about how you can become your own interior decorator and shop in wholesale showrooms are discussed in Chapter 19. Wholesale fabric distributors, fabric manufacturers, and wholesale fabric showrooms all over the U. S., are listed and cross-referenced in the *National Directory of Wholesale Home Furnishings Sources and Showrooms*. The *Directory* is a complete resource for designers and decorators, listing thousands of wholesale sources and showrooms for all types of home furnishings. It's available from this publisher. There is an order form in the back of this book.

Be sure to use a cross-over book to identify the fabric distributor who has the lowest price on a particular fabric before you buy it. Often, a certain fabric may be carried by more than one distributor (sometimes as many as ten or fifteen) each of whom sets their own price. A cross-over book can help you determine the lowest possible price available before you buy.

The only cross-over book currently available in the U. S. is the *1995 Decorative Fabrics Cross-Reference Guide*. It cross-references over 10,000 fabric distributor samples. Thousands of interior decorators and interior designers all over the U. S. and Canada use my cross-reference system to save money on fabrics. So can you, whether you are shopping from retail or wholesale fabric sources. There is an order form in the back of this book.

You can usually save 40% to 50% off the retail price on exclusive fabrics if you decide to become your own licensed interior decorator and buy them directly at the fabric distributor's or small manufacturer's wholesale showroom. This is by far the best way for most consumers to buy exclusive fabrics. Buying them wholesale will bring the price down almost as low as non-exclusive fabric prices.

If you need a larger quantity of fabric, at least 50 yards of a single fabric, you may be able to purchase it directly from the manufacturer at approximately 75% off of retail.

If you need at least 25 yards of a single fabric, it will usually be cheaper for you to order 50 yards directly from the manufacturer (at about 75% off retail) than to order the exact yardage you need from a distributor, factory outlet, or telephone ordering service at straight wholesale (at about 50% off retail).

Chapter 4

Wallcoverings

Sometimes, it seems cheaper just to paste dollar bills all over the walls. It costs about $300.00 at retail to professionally paper just one 10 X 10 foot room with attractive high-quality standard wallpaper, more if you choose a fancier type of wallpaper.

You can cut the cost in half by shopping at a wallpaper factory outlet, telephone ordering service, deep discount store, or wholesale showroom -- and still have access to most of the very same brands that high-priced interior designers sell to their clients.

You can cut the cost even further, up to about 75% off the retail cost, if you measure the room and install the wallpaper yourself. It's easy. All of the instructions and charts you need to properly estimate how much wallpaper you need are right here. You'll also learn how to get free information about installing your own wallpaper.

There really aren't any scams to watch out for when you are buying wallpaper, except for the usual overestimating by designers and decorators and the usual exclusive and ultra-exclusive products that aren't worth their prices. You won't have to worry about inflated estimates because you can easily do your own estimating with the instructions in this chapter. You won't have to worry about over-priced exclusive and ultra-exclusive wallpapers because you will learn how to find very similar patterns for much, much, less.

This chapter will teach you how to wallpaper a room beautifully without wasting a penny on middlemen or unnecessary professional installation services. There are extensive resource listings later in the chapter that you can use to cut wallpaper prices by at least half without sacrificing quality or style. You'll learn which types of wallpaper you can easily install yourself, and save even more money. You'll also learn how to avoid common pitfalls and scams that cost consumers money every year.

Matching the Right Wallpaper To the Right Room

Bathrooms
Metallic foils
Vinyls

Bedrooms
Embossed wallpapers
Flocked wallpapers
Hand-printed wallpapers
High-relief wallpapers
Murals
Silks
Standard wallpapers

Children's rooms
Vinyls

Dining rooms
Burlap
Embossed wallpapers
Flocked wallpapers
Grasscloth
Hand-printed wallpapers
High-relief wallpapers
Murals
Silks
Standard wallpapers

Hallways
Embossed wallpapers
High-relief wallpapers
Standard wallpapers
Vinyls

Kitchens
Metallic foils
Vinyls

Living rooms
Embossed wallpapers
Burlap
Flocked wallpapers
Grasscloth
Hand-printed wallpapers
High-relief wallpapers
Murals
Silks
Standard wallpapers

Wallpaper Types

To get the best value for your money, you must choose the correct type of wallpaper for the area in your home where it will be used. Kitchens and children's rooms need durable wallpaper than can be easily cleaned. Bathrooms and kitchens need wallpaper that will still adhere to the wall when exposed to steam or water.

You should also consider ease of installation. Hiring a professional to install your wallpaper is expensive. If you choose a standard wallpaper, you should be able to do your own installation.

You should always look for pre-pasted and pre-trimmed wallpapers. These are much easier to install if you decide to do it yourself and considerably cheaper to have installed if you hire a professional to do it. "Pre-pasted" means that dry glue has been applied and will activate automatically when the paper is soaked in water. "Pre-trimmed" means that the side edges of each roll have been trimmed so that the pattern at the edge of each strip will exactly match the pattern at the edge of the next strip when the wallpaper strips are put up. Pre-pasting and pre-trimming each eliminate an enormous amount of work, for you or for the professional installer.

If you choose a more unusual or delicate type of wallpaper, you will almost certainly have to hire a professional installer. Many of these papers do not come pre-pasted or pre-trimmed. They often require special care in handling and are very easy to accidentally ruin. When you are considering the prices of the more expensive and unusual types of wallpapers, don't forget to also consider the installation charges when you make your decision.

Charges start at about $10.00 per roll for standard pre-pasted pre-trimmed wallpaper and increase for wallpapers that require more work and special care. Charges can run as high as several hundred dollars PER ROOM. Call several installers to get an estimate on professional installation before you buy anything other than standard pre-pasted pre-trimmed wallpaper.

Burlap This is burlap fabric with a special paper backing that keeps the grain of the fabric straight and allows it to be applied to walls. It is moderately expensive and usually must be professionally installed. It is also difficult to keep clean. You should be able to find burlap wallpapers at wallpaper stores and wholesale design centers.

Embossed Wallpapers These are plain wallpapers which have been stamped with different three-dimensional patterns, from simple squares and basketweaves to complex floral designs. They are designed to be painted after they are installed. Installation is fairly easy -- you should be able to do this yourself. The expense is moderate. These wallpapers are often available at wallpaper stores, home centers, and a few telephone wallpaper ordering services.

These wallpapers are usually pre-trimmed, but they are usually not pre-pasted. However, they are relatively heavy and durable, which makes them a lot easier to install. You might consider installing this particular type yourself, even though you will have to do your own pasting. Get a book on wallpaper installation from you library and give some serious thought to doing your own installation if you choose embossed wallpaper.

Flocked Wallpapers These are solid-colored standard or vinyl wallpapers with large fuzzy floral patterns. They are moderately expensive and difficult to find, install, and keep clean.

You must have these papers professionally installed because they generally do not come pre-pasted. Paste must be applied by hand -- very carefully. If any paste gets on the decorative side of the wallpaper, especially in the fuzzy portions, the wallpaper will usually be ruined.

Wallpaper stores can usually special-order flocked wallpapers.

Grasscloth This is very similar to burlap wallpaper, except that grasscloth normally has irregular horizontal slubs. Like burlap wallpapers, grasscloth has a special paper backing that keeps the grain of the fabric straight and allows it to be applied to walls. It is moderately expensive and usually must be professionally installed. It is also difficult to keep clean. You should be able to find grasscloth at wallpaper stores and wholesale design centers.

Hand-printed Wallpapers These wallpapers are hand-printed using stamped block designs or screen printing. They are very expensive and are usually only available through decorators and designers, which adds yet another level of expense.

Of course, if you become your own decorator, you can eliminate the designer's commission and buy directly from the manufacturer. This will cut the cost dramatically, but even at wholesale, hand-printed wallpapers are usually far more expensive than standard wallpapers.

Installation can be very difficult. These wallpapers are usually less durable than standard wallpaper, which can make them easy to tear or stretch during installation. The widths of the rolls may not be uniform, and the patterns may not match correctly at the seams. These wallpapers are virtually never available pre-pasted or pre-trimmed. You will almost certainly need to hire professional help for installation, which will increase the expense even more.

These wallpapers do have the advantage of custom coloration, and occasionally custom pattern design. If you wanted a wallpaper made to match a certain lamp, rug, or even a design out of a book, you would go to a hand-printed wallpaper manufacturer in your local area. <u>The National Directory of Wholesale Home Furnishings Sources and Showrooms</u> lists many such small manufacturers all over the U. S.

High-relief Wallpapers These wallpapers are designed to imitate the texture of stucco, stone, tile, or other three-dimensional surfaces. They are meant to be painted over after installation. Installation is fairly easy -- you should be able to do this yourself. The expense is moderate. Most wallpaper stores, home centers, and telephone wallpaper ordering services carry this type of wallpaper.

These wallpapers are ideal for covering up walls that have lumps, large cracks, or other irregularities.

Metallic Foils These wallpapers are made from very thin sheets of foil applied to a paper backing. They are ideal for bathroom and kitchen use because they are almost impervious to steam. They work well in dark rooms because they can help brighten the room, but they are unsuitable for sunny rooms because the glare can be uncomfortably bright.

You should hire professonal help to install these wallpapers. They are moderately expensive and relatively easy to tear. They also require an absolutely perfect surface. Any imperfections in the wall underneath will be greatly emphasized when covered with shiny paper. The installer may need to do some extra surface preparation on your walls before installing the wallpaper. Foils are usually not pre-pasted or pre-trimmed.

If you should decide to do your own installation, be very careful. Many styles can conduct electricity. Be absolutely sure that the current is turned off to the room before you begin installing. If the wallpaper came too close to a live electical outlet, you could be electrocuted.

Metallic foils are available at most wallpaper stores, some telephone wallpaper ordering services, and a very few wholesale design center showrooms.

Murals These are wallpapers that depict a large scene that will stretch across a wall or around your entire room. They can be very expensive, plus you may need help to evaluate which patterns can be installed in the particular room you have in mind. The size and arrangement of the scene depicted in the mural has to harmonize well with the size and architecture of your room.

Depending on the expense and complexity of the particular mural you plan to purchase, you may need to hire a professional installer to help you determine if the mural will work well in your home and how it should be placed.

These wallpapers are generally not pre-pasted or pre-trimmed. Alignment is crucial, not only with the next strip but with the entire rest of the scene. Installing a mural is like putting a big puzzle together, but every piece is permanently mounted. You won't get any second chances to position things properly. You will definitely need to hire a professional installer to put this kind of wallpaper up.

The effect can be striking. I have seen some beautiful rooms that were papered this way. However, this is a complex and expensive project. Only go this route if you aren't on a budget. These wallpapers are normally only available in wholesale design centers.

Silks Silk wallpapers are simply plain or patterned silk fabrics that have been applied to a paper backing. They are extremely expensive and delicate. You must hire a professional installer and be prepared to pay a high installation fee. Silk wallpapers are also very difficult to keep clean.

Silk wallpapers give a very luxurious look to a room, but they are definitely not for the budget-conscious. They can usually be found at wholesale design centers.

Also, Shibui Wallcoverings (listed under "Telephone Wallpaper Ordering Services on page 107), sells several faux silk wallpapers that look very close to the real thing -- at a fraction of the cost. Contact Shibui to receive samples by mail.

Standard wallpapers These wallpapers are by far the most common, and the least expensive. You will find the widest variety of patterns in standard wallpapers. They make up 75% to 90% of the wallpapers stocked in wallpaper stores and home centers and much of the wallpapers sold in wholesale design centers and through telephone order shopping services.

These wallpapers are well suited for every room in your home except the bathrooms and some parts of your kitchen. It would be fine to use these wallpapers in a breakfast nook or other eating area in your kitchen, but they will not hold up well to exposure to steam from pots on your stove. As long as you don't use standard wallpapers within a few feet of the stove-top, they should be just fine.

You may also wish to avoid using standard wallpaper in children's rooms. Vinyl, or certain kinds of paint, is generally a better choice because it can be washed if your little artist decides to "redecorate" on his own.

You can get the best bargains on these wallpapers. Most are prepasted and pretrimmed, which makes doing your own installation very easy. If you need to keep costs down, choose standard wallpaper.

Vinyls Vinyl wallcoverings are simply plain or patterned vinyl fabrics applied to a paper backing. They are often available pre-pasted and pre-trimmed. They aren't quite as inexpensive as standard wallpapers, but they are still available at a very good price. Most wallpaper stores, home centers, and telephone wallpaper ordering services sell them.

Installation is easy, provided that you choose wallpapers that are pre-pasted and pre-trimmed. These wallpapers are ideal for areas that are exposed to steam and/or must be cleaned often, such as kitchens, bathrooms, and children's rooms.

Using Fabrics As Wallcoverings

Theoretically, a good wallpaper installer can attach virtually any fabric to your walls. In practice, however, fabrics are sometimes ruined (at your expense, not the installer's) and installation fees are sky-high.

If you want to use fabrics on your walls, check out silk, grasscloth, and burlap fabrics that have already been attached to paper backings and are meant to be used as wallpaper. This eliminates many problems and will save you some money on installation. You can find these fabric wallcoverings at wholesale design centers, telephone wallpaper ordering services, and a few wallpaper stores.

Also, contact Shibui Wallcoverings at (800) 824-3030. They carry a nice variety of fabric wallcoverings at good prices. For $4.00 they will send you a sample kit.

If you find that none of these sources have any fabric wallcoverings that you like, your only other option is to consult with a wallpaper installer (for a fee) to help you choose a fabric that can be attached to your walls reasonably well (at a sky-high charge per yard). This is a very expensive and problematic way to go. Take another look at the samples from Shibui or the local wholesale design center before you take this step.

American Rolls vs. Metric (European) Rolls

In order to properly compare prices between different wallpapers, you need to know if the pattern you are interested in comes in American rolls or metric rolls. Metric rolls are often referred to as European rolls.

These common names have nothing to do with where the wallpaper was manufactured. Many American manufacturers use the metric system, and some European manufacturers (particulary British ones) use the "American" system of measuring. Look at the measurements printed on the label to determine which type you have.

American rolls use the "American" measurement system and are measured in square yards. European rolls use the metric system and are measured in square meters. Most manufacturers use one system or the other, not both.

European rolls are the smaller of the two, having only about three-quarters of the amount of wallpaper contained in American rolls. If you are comparing two different wallpapers, one available in European rolls and one available in American rolls, and the wallpaper that comes in European rolls costs less per roll, the wallpaper that comes in European rolls might actually cost MORE to cover your room because you don't get as much wallpaper for your money.

If you are comparing prices between a wallpaper that comes in European rolls and a wallpaper that comes in American rolls, multiply the price of the wallpaper that comes in American rolls by 0.75 to arrive at an adjusted price that you can compare to the price of the wallpaper that comes in European rolls. This way, you can make a fair comparison of the prices.

For instance, if you are deciding between a wallpaper that is priced at $20.00 per single American roll and another wallpaper that is priced at $18.00 per single European roll, you need to recalculate the price of the American roll so that you can make an accurate comparison. Multiply the price of the American roll by 0.75 to arrive at an adjusted price of $15.00. This adjusted price represents how much you would have to pay for an amount of wallpaper that is equal to the amount of wallpaper that is contained in the European roll.

As you can see, the wallpaper that comes in American rolls is actually cheaper than the wallpaper that comes in European rolls -- in this particular example. In another case, the European roll might be the better bargain. You should always do your own price calculations before making a decision.

Don't be misled by the sticker price. Always make sure that you are making accurate price comparisons between different wallpapers when you go shopping.

Buy a Little Extra Wallpaper For Future Repairs

You never know. You may have to tear out part of your bathroom wall to repair a leaky pipe. Your child may decide to add his own artistic touch to your living room walls. You may have a roof leak which also damages your walls.

Any problem which damages a wall will require you to replace the existing wallpaper. However, wallpapers are manufactured in dye lots, just as fabrics are. If you need to purchase more wallpaper at a later date for repairs, it will almost certainly be from a different dye lot as your original wallpaper and the colors probably will not match.

In fact, the pattern you need might not be available at all. Wallpaper patterns are usually discontinued after about three years on the market to make room for new styles. Even popular styles that have sold well usually do not stay on the market for more than a few years.

If you have a little extra wallpaper set aside, you can make the repairs with no problem. If not, you are likely to end up with two different shades of wallpaper from a dye lot mismatch. If your pattern is no longer available, you will have to rip everything out and start over, which will be at least several hundred dollars more expensive than simply buying a little extra in the first place.

A good rule of thumb is to set aside about 5% of the amount you actually need to wallpaper the room as "insurance" against future problems.

Another Way To Cut Costs In Half

If you install a chair rail and wallpaper only above the rail, you will need only about half as much wallpaper. The look of the room, however, will be very similar. Chair rail molding can be purchased for only a few pennies per foot at most home centers and lumber yards, and it is very easy to install.

If you paint below the chair rail, as you almost certainly will, wait to purchase the paint until actually receive your wallpaper. The wallpaper you actually receive will probably vary slightly in color from the store sample or magazine picture that you ordered from. This is due to dye lot differences and the effects of photographic lighting and reproduction.

Wait until you actually receive your wallpaper, and take a small piece of it to match colors when you are buying paint. Many paint and hardware stores now have equipment that can analyze your wallpaper swatch and custom mix the paint to exactly match it.

Estimating How Much Wallpaper You Need

Now that you have selected your wallpaper, you need to determine how much you should buy. This is not very difficult. Just follow the steps below.

Bear in mind that the steps listed here do not apply to fabrics or murals. You should hire a professional installer to make these more complex estimates for you. Also, if you are papering an unusual room, such as a room with a very high ceiling (over nine feet) or an attic room with sloping walls and dormer windows, you should consult a book on wallpaper installation for more specific measuring instructions that apply to odd-sized or shaped rooms.

The instructions given here will show you how to calculate the number of single rolls you need to buy. If you find that the wallpaper you want to buy is packaged in double or triple rolls, you will need to make an adjustment, as explained on pages 101-102.

Step 1: Measure the total area of the walls.

Don't worry about doors and windows right now, we'll make adjustments for those later. Right now, you just want to measure your room as though it were a big box, and get the overall surface area of the walls.

Always use a steel tape measure. Never use a cloth or plastic tape measure, as these often stretch and give inaccurate measurements. Steel tape measures are very inexpensive and can be purchased at any hardware store or home center. Always measure in feet, and round up to the next half foot or foot.

First, measure the height of your room. Choose a wall and measure the height between from the floor to the ceiling, leaving out any baseboards or mouldings. If you are only going to wallpaper the upper portion of the wall above a chair rail, only measure the height between the top of the chair rail and the ceiling.

Then, measure the width of that wall from corner to corner. Multiply the width by the height to get the area of the first wall. Then, measure the widths of the other walls and calculate the area of each wall.

Add the areas of all of the walls to get the total area. This will give you the total square footage of the walls.

Step 2: Determine the net area to be wallpapered.

Now you need to subtract areas, such as doors and windows, that will not be covered. Measure the length and width of each door and window and calculate its area as explained above. Subtract the area of each door and window from the total square footage. This will give you the net area of the room that will actually be wallpapered.

Step 3: Determine the usable yield of each single roll of wallpaper.

Now, you need to set aside your area calculation and turn your attention to the wallpaper rolls themselves. The number of single rolls you need to buy will depend upon the usable yield of each single roll. If the wallpaper you have chosen has a low usable yield per single roll, you will have to buy more rolls to compensate. If the wallpaper has a high usable yield per single roll, you won't need to buy as many rolls.

Wallpapers that have large repeats will have a lower usable yield per single roll. Wallpapers that have no repeats (referred to as a repeat of zero inches), such as solid-colored wallpapers, will have the largest possible usable yield per single roll.

Minimizing the repeat size of your wallpaper can help you save money by preventing wasted wallpaper. The repeat size refers to the vertical distance between identical pattern elements, just as it does with fabrics. If your wallpaper has any pattern at all, some wallpaper will be wasted when the strips of wallpaper are aligned with each other so that the patterns match at the seams. The smaller the repeat size is, the less waste there will be. You should keep this in mind when you are choosing patterns.

The repeat size is normally marked on the roll label or wallpaper sample. If you don't see it right away, ask the wallpaper dealer for help.

Use the charts at left to determine the usable yield per single roll of the wallpaper you have selected.

These charts are appropriate for most rooms. However, if the area you are wallpapering is unusually short (under three feet) or tall (over nine feet), you will want to refer to a book about wallpaper installation to make your estimates rather than using these charts and the method explained here.

American Rolls

Repeat Size	*Usable Yield*
0" to 6"	32 sq. ft.
7" to 12"	30 sq. ft.
13" to 18"	27 sq. ft.
19" to 23"	25 sq. ft.

European (Metric) Rolls

Repeat Size	*Usable Yield*
0" to 6"	25 sq. ft.
7" to 12"	22 sq. ft.
13" to 18"	20 sq. ft.
19" to 23"	18 sq. ft.

Step 4: Determine the number of rolls you need to buy.

Divide the net area determined in Step 2 by the usable yield per single roll determined in Step 3, and round up to the next whole roll. For instance, if the net area of the room is 300 sq. ft. and the usable yield per single roll is 30 sq. ft., you will need to buy exactly ten single rolls of wallpaper.

Of course, you should always add in a little extra in case of installation problems, especially if you are going to be doing your own installation. It's bad enough to accidentally ruin a roll when you are papering the room, but it's even worse to find out that you can't buy a replacement roll in the same dye lot. You will also want to keep some extra wallpaper around in case you ever need to make any repairs later on.

Don't skimp here. If you make any mistakes and come up short, you will have to go back and order more wallpaper. The new wallpaper will almost certainly be from a different dye lot and will probably not match the wallpaper that is already up. Also, if you are using a professional installer, you will have to pay the installer to make an extra trip out to your house, which will usually cost much more than simply buying an extra roll of wallpaper in the first place.

Always buy at least 5% more wallpaper than your final estimate indicates. In the example above, 5% extra would be an extra half roll. You can't buy half rolls, so you would have to buy an extra single roll. It's very cheap insurance and well worth the small expense.

Also, read the next section carefully before placing your order. Some wallpapers aren't available in single rolls -- only double or triple rolls. The confusion created by this system could cause you to make an expensive error.

Singles, Doubles, and Triples

Wallpaper manufacturers usually *price* their wallpapers by the single roll, but many manufacturers *package* their wallpapers by the double roll, or occasionally even by the triple roll. This unwieldy system can create a lot of confusion for consumers and sometimes results in the consumer ordering much more unreturnable wallpaper than they intended to.

Use the charts at right to decide if a wallpaper roll is a single, double, or triple. For example, if the label says that a wallpaper roll is 56 sq. ft. in area, it's a double roll. If the label says the roll is 29 sq. ft. in area, it's a single roll. And so on. European rolls usually list the equivalent area in square feet on the manufacturer's label.

Please note that the instructions given in this book will help you determine the number of single rolls you need to buy. You will have to adjust this figure if the wallpaper is packaged in double or triple rolls.

For instance, in the example given in the previous section, we determined that you should buy 10 single rolls of wallpaper. If you then find that the wallpaper only comes in double rolls, you would need to buy only five double rolls. If the wallpaper only comes in triple rolls, you would have no choice but to buy four triple rolls because three triple rolls would only equal nine single rolls.

Be sure to clarify this point with the wallpaper source. Don't just tell the

American Rolls

Roll Type	Total Area
Single	32 to 36 sq. ft.
Double	64 to 72 sq. ft.
Triple	96 to 108 sq. ft.

European (Metric) Rolls

Roll Type	Total Area
Single	27 to 29 sq. ft.
Double	54 to 68 sq. ft.
Triple	81 to 87 sq. ft.

wallpaper source how many single rolls you need and rely on the salesperson to make the proper adjustments. Ask the salesperson if the wallpaper comes in single, double, or triple rolls and make your own calculations. If you don't, you might end up buying much more wallpaper than you actually need, and you usually won't be able to return the excess.

Make Sure Your Entire Order Is From the Same Dye Lot

When you buy wallpaper, verify that all of the rolls come from the same dye lot. If you are buying wallpaper from a store, the bin you select from may have rolls from more than one dye lot mixed in. If you are custom ordering wallpaper, whether from a store or from a telephone ordering service, your order may have been packed incorrectly. You are responsible for making sure that your order is correct.

Each roll of wallpaper will have a code to indicate the particular dye lot it belongs to. The code is usually stamped on the manufacturer's label. Look for a notation that says "lot" or "lot number" followed by a series of numbers and/or letters. Make sure that the codes on all of the rolls match.

If your custom order is incorrect, insist that the store correct the problem BEFORE you accept any wallpaper and pay the balance due. If you have ordered the wallpaper from a telephone ordering service, call them immediately to insist that your order be corrected. The service should send you however many rolls from the correct dye lot that you need and arrange to pick up the incorrect rolls at no charge to you.

Check your credit card bill over the next couple of months to make certain that you are not billed a "re-stocking" fee (usually 10% to 15% of the bill) for the returned rolls. Re-stocking fees are sometimes charged automatically when a customer returns a custom order and the wallpaper ordering service is not at fault. However, in this situation, the service is at fault and should not bill you for this fee.

If this should happen, don't worry. The added billing is probably just a simple clerical error that can be quickly cleared up. Just call the service.

Murphy's Law Of Wallpapering

Never begin wallpapering until you receive your entire order correctly. If your order is a few rolls short or has a few rolls from the wrong dye lot, you may be tempted to go ahead and install the correct rolls while you are waiting for the rest.

Big mistake. *Murphy's Law of Wallpapering* clearly states that if you do this, you will promptly hear that there are no more rolls available in the dye lot you need. It never fails.

If no more wallpaper is available in the dye lot you need, and the rolls you have are unopened, you should have no problem returning them and getting your entire order from a different dye lot. However, if you have already installed the wallpaper, you will almost certainly not get your money back, even if the short order or dye lot mismatch was the store's fault.

It is best not to accept and pay for your order until the whole order is correct. If you accept the correct portion of your order and pay the balance due, even a reputable company may not move very quickly to complete your order. A dishonest store may not correct the mistake at all if they already have your money. If you refuse to pay until the entire order is correct, the store will have a financial incentive to get the problem corrected as quickly as possible and you can avoid being ripped off.

Should You Install Your Own Wallpaper?

If you are using pre-pasted and pre-trimmed standard, embossed, high-relief, or vinyl wallpapers, you should have no difficulty installing it yourself. When you consider that an average room costs at least $150.00 to have professionally wallpapered, doing your own installation is definitely worth the effort.

There are many well-written guides to installing wallpaper available at your local bookstore and library. There is also an excellent guide called "*How To Hang Wallcoverings*" which is published by the National Decorating Products Association. The cover price is 75 cents, but many wallpaper dealers routinely give out free copies. Call your local wallpaper store or telephone order wallpaper service for a copy.

Many Home Depot stores all over the United States offer free classes in many subjects, including wallpaper installation. Call the Home Depot store in your area for information about any upcoming classes. You can also contact community colleges and technical schools in your area. Many offer low-cost classes on a wide variety of home furnishings topics.

Finding A Reputable Installer

Many wallpaper installers now advertise in the Yellow Pages. They comprise the same pool of workers that interior designers use. There are no wholesale wallpaper installers. Everyone is charged the same basic price.

Read Chapter 18 for complete information about dealing with installers.

Typical Charges For Professional Installation

The average charge is $10.00 per pre-pasted pre-trimmed single roll of standard wallpaper. Keep in mind that many wallpapers are packaged as double (or even triple) rolls, which would cost more to have installed. If the installer charges $10.00 to install a single roll, double rolls would normally cost $20.00 and triple rolls would normally cost $30.00 to install. The charges are usually higher for wallpapers that require pasting or trimming.

Charges are often very high for delicate wallpapers such as silks and hand-printed wallpapers. When you are considering purchasing any wallpaper other than the standard pre-pasted pre-trimmed kind, you should contact several installers and find out about installation fees before you make your purchase. You might find that the sky-high fees that are charged for installing some of the more delicate types of wallpaper put them out of your budget range.

These fees vary widely according to the specifics of your particular wallpaper and your home. Write down all of the information on the wallpaper label or sample -- wallpaper type (embossed, vinyl, etc.), repeat size, width, pre-trimmed or not, pre-pasted or not, roll length, sq. yards or

Help For the Wallpapering Impaired

It's after midnight. You've got wallpaper paste in your hair, your cat is turning the last of your $50.00 per roll silk wallpaper into the world's most expensive confetti, and you have just realized that the only strip of wallpaper that isn't peeling off the wall is on upside down. Who you gonna call?

GenCorp Wallcoverings. This company has been kind enough to set up a toll-free information line for the wallpapering impaired:

(800) 925-5825

If you have a touch-tone phone, you can access recorded information on three wallpapering topics:

"*Before You Begin*"
"*Installation Basics*"
"*Special Techniques*".

There is no charge of any kind, although they do ask (and this is not at all compulsory) that you add your name to their mailing list.

They won't be able to help you much with wallpaper that has already been put up incorrectly, but at least they can help you get it right the next time.

sq. meters per roll, and anything else that looks important -- and call several installers to get the going rate for installing that particular wallpaper.

It is unlikely that you could save the high fees charged for delicate wallpapers by doing your own installation. You really shouldn't attempt to install any of the more unusual or delicate types of wallpaper by yourself. This type of work requires skill and experience, and you usually won't have a second chance to get things right. If you make any mistakes, your $50.00 per roll hand-screened wallpaper is going to be in a big sticky wad on the floor instead of on your walls. This is not a good place to cut corners.

Study the list of wallpaper types given earlier in the chapter to determine which types you can and cannot install yourself. If you choose a wallpaper that needs to be professionally installed and this is out of your budget, you should choose a different wallpaper.

Exclusive vs. Non-Exclusive Wallpapers

Just as with fabrics, there is a two-tiered marketing system for wallpapers. Non-exclusive wallpapers are sold to anyone wholesale buyer, including discounters, that can purchase a sufficient quantity. This open competition helps keep prices low. Non-exclusive wallpapers typically cost about half as much as exclusive wallpapers that are comparable in style and quality.

Exclusive wallpapers are normally only sold through interior designers and interior decorators and are never sold to discounters. This allows designers and decorators to command high retail prices for these wallpapers because open competition has been eliminated.

There is typically no real difference between exclusive and non-exclusive wallpapers as to their quality, style, or durability. If a decorator or designer tries to tell you that an exclusive wallpaper will wear better than non-exclusive wallpapers, don't buy it. Decorators and designers heavily promote exclusive wallpapers and other exclusive furnishings because they can make much higher commissions on them.

If you see a wallpaper sample that is marked "exclusive", call a telephone wallpaper ordering service to check if it might be available. Exclusivity is usually granted by manufacturers for a specific length of time, after which any wholesale buyer is allowed to buy the wallpaper. Maybe the sample you saw is out of date and the wallpaper is no longer exclusive. I see out of date samples in stores and design studios all the time.

However, if you find that the wallpaper is still exclusive (because none of the telephone ordering services carry it), consider changing to a different wallpaper. You won't have to look far to find many non-exclusive wallpapers that look very similar and cost about half as much. Sometimes, these "knockoffs" of exclusive patterns are made by the very same manufacturer, which means that the quality should be about the same. Shop around in local wallpaper stores and interior design studios. You'll almost certainly find what you're looking for before long.

Exclusive wallpapers are almost always a big waste of money. They are designed to appeal to consumers who want to be sure that they are the only people they know who have that particular pattern.

If they only knew. There are thousands and thousands of wallpaper patterns. It is unlikely that any of their neighbors would ever choose the same wallpaper they did, whether they paid a high price for an exclusive product or not. They could have saved a lot of money.

Ultra-Exclusive Wallpapers

As with fabrics, there are also ultra-exclusive wallpapers. These wallpapers are a cut above exclusive wallpapers (in price). Instead of just being restricted to interior designers and interior decorators, ultra-exclusive products are restricted to a few selected interior designers. Naturally, this boosts the prices even more.

Some of these wallpapers are lovely. Most hand-printed wallpapers, many silks, and many murals are marketed this way. Most ultra-exclusive wallpapers, however, really aren't worth the much higher prices that are charged for them.

The quality and durability of these wallpapers is generally no better than that of non-exclusive wallpapers. In fact, ultra-exclusive wallpapers are usually very delicate and difficult to keep clean. And don't forget those sky-high professional installation charges on top of the ridiculously high prices for the wallpaper itself.

Like exclusive products, the main reason ultra-exclusive products exist is to pad designers' commissions and provide a way for certain consumers to outdo their friends. There really is no other reason to buy these ultra-exclusive products. There are many better ways to splurge.

If you see a pattern that you just love and it is totally dissimilar to any non-exclusive wallpaper (which is highly unlikely), and you don't mind spending a fortune, you will have to pay one of the favored few interior designers a hefty commission to process your order. Call the wallpaper manufacturer to locate an approved designer in your area. Even if you become your own decorator, you won't be able to buy ultra-exclusive wallpapers on your own.

How Do You Know If a Product Is Ultra-Exclusive?

Ultra-exclusive products aren't labeled "ultra-exclusive".

The only way to find out if a product is ultra-exclusive is to shop around for it. It's a process of elimination.

If you can't find it at any discount source, such as a telephone ordering service, or from most of the decorators and designers in your area -- it's likely that the product is ultra-exclusive.

Call the manufacturer. If they refer you to a very few "approved" designers in your area that sell the product, then you can be pretty sure that it is ultra-exclusive.

Don't forget -- there is no way that you can have direct access to ultra-exclusive products, even if you become your own decorator. If you are thinking of getting being your own decorator to buy one particular product, make sure that the manufacturer will sell to decorators, first.

We'll discuss this topic in more detail in Chapter 19.

Irregulars vs. Seconds vs. Closeouts

You can save up to 75% off of retail when you buy wallpapers that are irregulars or closeouts. These are first quality goods that are not damaged or flawed in any way. They represent the best bargains in wallpapers. You can find these products at factory outlets and some deep discount stores, which are listed later in this chapter.

Irregulars are wallpapers that are in new condition and are not flawed in any way, but do not match the samples which are on display in stores or shown by salespeople.

For instance, if a wallpaper manufacturer makes up a batch of wallpaper and one of the colors varies greatly from the sample, it will normally sell off the bad batch in a factory outlet or deep discount store as an irregular product. There is nothing wrong with the wallpaper itself, but it doesn't match the samples that the manufacturer's customers are ordering from.

Closeouts are wallpapers that are left over from the previous season. Typically, there are such small quantities left that they are not worth the expense of advertising. Also, many manufacturers do not wish to be seen advertising last season's products. It creates an image that the manufacturer's products aren't fashionable or stylish.

Seconds are wallpapers which are flawed in some way. Although seconds can be great bargains in fabrics, they are not a good buy in wallpapers. You should avoid buying second-quality wallpapers because you cannot cut around the flaws as you can with many second-quality fabrics.

Seconds are occasionally sold at factory outlets and deep discount stores. Carefully examine any discounted products you find at these places to be sure that they have no flaws.

Wallpaper Stores

Wallpaper stores usually have good prices on in-stock wallpapers that you can buy and take home that day. However, you should avoid special-ordering wallpapers here. These stores typically charge relatively high prices on anything that they don't stock. You can usually get a much better price from a telephone wallpaper ordering service.

If you do buy your wallpaper here, be sure that the dye lots on all of the rolls match. Dye lots often get mixed up with so many customers looking through the wallpaper bins.

Telephone Wallpaper Ordering Services

You will usually find the best bargains -- outside of a factory outlet, deep discount store, or wholesale showroom -- from these services. Unless there is a factory outlet or deep discount store within a reasonable driving distance from your home, or you decide to be your own decorator and shop wholesale, this will usually be your best source for wallpapers.

The wallpapers are first-quality, not cheap knockoffs of designer brands. These services carry most of the very same brands that interior designers and interior decorators sell. They even carry many of the same wallpapers found at your local wholesale design center, and are much less expensive.

Like the ads say, shop in your neighborhood and write down all of the product information before you call to place your order. Write down all of the information on the wallpaper label or sample -- wallpaper type (embossed, vinyl, etc.), repeat size, width, pre-trimmed or not, pre-pasted or not, roll length, sq. yards or sq. meters per roll, and anything else that looks important. You can find wallpaper samples in interior design studios, wallpaper stores, and many furniture stores.

Don't worry about phony pattern names. Wallpaper distributors don't perpetrate this scam like fabric distributors do. Just write down the manufacturer or distributor name on the wallpaper sample and the pattern name or number. The telephone ordering service should have no difficulty filling your order, unless the wallpaper is exclusive or ultra-exclusive.

Use the information given earlier in the chapter to determine how much wallpaper you should order. Be sure to read Chapter 16 for general tips on dealing with any telephone ordering service. These services are generally quite reputable. You shouldn't have any problems with your order, but always use a credit card just in case. Most wallpaper orders from these companies are shipped within a very few days of placing your order.

Most of the services listed below and on the next page carry most types of wallcoverings from a wide variety of manufacturers, but a few specialize in only one type. The specialities of these sources are noted in italics after the company name. Most of these specialized sources offer a free catalog. You may not be able to view some of their products in local stores.

Telephone Ordering Services

American Blind and Wallpaper Factory
28237 Orchard Lake Rd.
Farmington Hills, MI 48334
(800) 735-5300

American Discount Wall and Window Coverings
1411 Fifth Ave.
Pittsburgh, PA 15219
(800) 777-2737

Antique Hardware Store
Embossed wallpapers only
9730 Easton Rd.
Kintnersville, PA 18930
(800) 422-9982

Benington's
1271 Manheim Pike
Lancaster, PA 17601
(800) 252-5060

Custom Windows and Walls
32525 Stephenson Hwy.
Madison Heights, MI 48071
(800) 772-1947

The Decorator's Edge
509 Randolph St.
Thomasville, NC 27360
(800) 289-5589

Designer Secrets
P. O. Box 529
Fremont, NE 68025
(800) 955-2559

East Carolina Wallpaper Market
1106 Pink Hill Rd.
Kinston, NC 28501
(800) 848-7283

Hang It Now Wallpaper
10517 N. Main St.
Suite F
Archdale, NC 27263
(800) 325-9494

Harmony Supply Co.
P. O. Box 313
Medford, MA 02155
(617) 395-2600

Headquarters Window and Walls
8 Clinton Place
Morristown, NJ 07960
(800) 338-4882

Interiors Guild
P. O. Box 99352
Cleveland, OH 44199
(800) 805-8081

Mary's Wallcoverings
400 Galleria, Suite 400
Southfield, MI 48038
(800) 521-3393

National Blind and Wallpaper Factory
400 Galleria, Suite 400
Southfield, MI 48038
(800) 477-8000

The Old Wagon Factory
Embossed wallpapers only
103 Russell St.
Clarksville, VA 23927
(800) 874-9358

Peerless Wallpaper and Blind Depot
39500 14 Mile Rd.
Walled Lake, MI 48390
(800) 999-0898

Post Wallcoverings
333 Skokie Blvd.
Northbrook, IL 60062
(800) 322-5400

The Renovator's Supply
Embossed wallpapers only
Renovator's Old Mill
Millers Falls, MA 01349
(800) 659-2211

Robinson's Wallcoverings
225 W. Spring St.
Titusville, PA 16354
(800) 458-2426

Sanz International
1183 E. Lexington Ave.
High Point, NC 27262
(910) 883-4622

Shibui Wallcoverings
Grasscloth and woven wallcoverings only
P. O. Box 1268
Santa Rosa, CA 95402
(800) 824-3030

Telephone Ordering Services (cont.)

Shriber's Discount
Wallcoverings and Blinds
3222 Brighton Rd.
Pittsburgh, PA 15212
(800) 245-6676

Silver's Wholesale Club
3001-15 Kensington Ave.
Philadelphia, PA 19134
(800) 426-6600

Smart Wallcoverings
400 Galleria, Suite 400
Southfield, MI 48038
(800) 677-0200

Style Wallcoverings and Blinds
400 Galleria, Suite 400
Southfield, MI 48038
(800) 627-0400

Wallpaper Xpress
1723 Jericho Rd.
Aurora, IL 60506
(800) 288-9979

Wholesale Wallcovering Depot
1583 N. Military Trail
West Palm Beach, FL 33409
(800) 221-5559

Worldwide Wallcoverings
and Blinds
333 Skokie Blvd.
Northbrook, IL 60062
(800) 322-5400

Yankee Wallcoverings
109 Accord Park Dr.
Norwell, MA 02061
(800) 624-7711

Factory Outlets

Wallpaper manufacturers usually don't operate their own company-owned factory outlets (except for Waverly, Warner, and Seabrook). Manufacturers normally sell their irregulars, closeouts, and seconds to one or more of the consolidated outlets listed below. Each of these stores carries wallpapers from many different manufacturers.

Those outlets that specialize in a particular brand have the brand listed in italics below the outlet name. All four of the Seabrook stores are factory-owned retail stores. Each carries a limited supply of Seabrook closeouts and irregulars in addition to its first-quality stock.

All of the other outlets carry irregular and closeout wallpapers from a wide variety of manufacturers.

Factory Outlets

Kentucky

Gardner Wallcoverings
Warner
3300 Canton Pike
Hopskinsville, KY 42240
(502) 885-0897

North Carolina

Waverly Outlet
Waverly
Hickory Furniture Mart
Hickory, NC 28602
(704) 326-1740

Tennessee

Dan's Factory Surplus
114 N. 14th Ave.
Humboldt, TN 38343
(901) 784-3883

Seabrook Wallcoverings
Seabrook
601 S. Mendenhall
Memphis, TN 38117
(901) 683-7369

Tennessee (cont.)

Seabrook Wallcoverings
6326 Winchester
Memphis, TN 38118
(901) 795-7250

Seabrook Wallcoverings
2031 S. Germantown
Memphis, TN 38138
(901) 755-5797

Seabrook Wallcoverings
4354 Stage Rd.
Memphis, TN 38128
(901) 388-5165

Wisconsin

Wallpaper Plus
Factory Outlet Center
I-94 and Highway 50
Kenosha, WI 53142
(414) 857-7792

Deep Discount Stores

These stores have prices comparable to telephone ordering services. They buy in very large quantities and have low overhead costs. If you want to browse, these stores are a great place to shop. Each has a good variety of closeouts and irregulars.

However, if you have shopped in your neighborhood and already know what you want, telephone wallpaper ordering services will usually be the cheapest and most convenient source for you.

Deep Discount Stores

Alabama

The Interior Alternative
601 Elizabeth St.
Boaz, AL 35957
(205) 593-8887

Delaware

The Interior Alternative
Bellvue Ave.
Newark, DE 19713
(302) 454-3232

Georgia

The Interior Alternative
3004-B Parquet Rd.
Dalton, GA 30720
(706) 217-6544

Massachusetts

The Interior Alternative
5 Hoosac St.
Adams, MA 01220
(413) 743-1986

North Carolina

The Furniture Patch
10283 Beach Dr. SW
Calabash, NC 28467
(910) 579-2001

Priba Furniture Sales
5-A Wendy Ct.
Greensboro, NC 27409
(910) 855-9034

Resource Design
Hickory Furniture Mart
Hickory, NC 28602
(704) 322-3161

South Carolina

The Interior Alternative
1 Frederick Dr.
Richburg, SC 29729
(803) 789-6655

Texas

The Interior Alternative
2626 Northhaven Rd.
Dallas, TX 75229
(214) 241-5422

Wholesale Wallpapers

You will usually get the best prices on major wallpaper brands from telephone wallpaper ordering services, occasionally even lower prices than designers pay their wholesale suppliers for the very same wallpapers. Telephone ordering services will be your best source for wallpapers in most cases.

However, if you are looking for unusual wallpapers, such as hand-printed wallpapers, silks, and murals, you may wish to check out wholesale showrooms in your local area. You can usually save at least 50% off of the retail price on these very expensive wallpapers if you become your own decorator and buy them wholesale.

Hundreds of wholesale wallpaper manufacturers and showrooms are listed in the National Directory of Wholesale Home Furnishings Sources and Showrooms, which can be ordered from this publisher. Chapter 19 discusses exactly how to be your own decorator and buy home furnishings from wholesale sources.

It is not practical for you to attempt to purchase wallpapers directly from any major manufacturer, as you might do with many fabrics. The minimum quantities required are just too huge to be practical for you to buy. Even professional designers and decorators almost never buy wallpapers this way. You will have to stick with the small manufacturer and distributor showrooms in your area if you wish to shop wholesale.

2 Places You Should Never Buy Wallpaper

Furniture stores
Interior Designers and Interior Decorators

These businesses usually buy their wallpapers through wholesale distributors, which means that there are two levels of middlemen between the manufacturer and you. The end retail price of the wallpaper can be as much as four times the original cost from the manufacturer on major brands, more on exclusive and ultra-exclusive wallpapers. You can do much better.

Recommendations

1 Decide which type of wallpaper you wish to purchase, keeping in mind your budget restraints and willingness to do your own installation. Don't forget to include professional installation charges, if applicable, when you are deciding whether a certain wallpaper fits your budget.

2 Determine how much wallpaper you need. Don't skimp. There is no such thing as an estimate that is exact down to the last square inch. Remember also that mistakes do happen in installation, whether you do it yourself or hire a professional. It is much better to overestimate a little than to underestimate.

3 When you are ready to buy, check out a factory outlet if there is one close by. A few accept phone orders, although these policies change fre-

quently. You will need to call the outlet directly to find out if you can do this.

4 If you can't shop at an outlet, a telephone wallpaper ordering service will normally be your next best choice. Compare prices carefully and read Chapter 16 carefully for tips on dealing with any telephone ordering service.

5 If you still haven't found anything you like, or if you are looking for murals or hand-printed wallpapers, wholesale showrooms should be your next stop. It's well worth becoming your own decorator to buy these high-style wallpapers wholesale. You could save several hundred dollars on your purchase, depending on which wallpaper and what quantity you are buying.

If you do decide to be your own decorator, read Chapter 19 thoroughly for instructions on how to buy from wholesale sources. Order a copy of the *National Directory of Wholesale Home Furnishings Sources and Showrooms*, by William Graham, to locate wholesale showrooms and wallpaper manufacturers in your area that carry the specific type of wallpaper you want.

Chapter 5

Carpeting

It costs approximately $3,500.00 (at retail prices) to carpet an average home with even the most basic and inexpensive beige carpeting, more if you want a higher quality grade of carpeting.

Fortunately, the carpet manufacturing industry has a very well established system to sell directly to the public. There are a wide variety of factory outlets that will sell most major brands directly to you at about 50% off retail, and they can ship anywhere.

Of course, you have to know how much carpeting you need and which type is best for your home. You will also have to find your own installer and make sure he does the job properly if you don't buy your carpet from a retail store. Everything you need to know to choose the proper type and quantity of carpeting for your home and have it properly installed is right here in this chapter.

How To Recognize High-Quality Carpeting

Your carpet installer is the best person to consult with to determine the right carpet for your home. The best choice will depend on many factors, including your lifestyle, areas of heaviest traffic, etc. Later in this chapter, we will discuss carpet installers in detail. Their consultations are normally free.

No matter what carpet you decide upon, there are some quality checks that you can use to make sure that your carpet is well made.

Fiber content The best fiber choice will depend upon your family's needs. Generally, nylon is the best choice for most homes. It has the best value for the money.

The only exception is if you plan to use carpeting in your kitchen or bathroom. Polyester, while less durable, is much more water-resistant than nylon. That makes it a better choice for these rooms.

Often, you find that carpeting contains a combination of different fibers. For instance, wool/nylon carpeting comes close to the quality of pure wool carpeting but at a cheaper price. Nylon/polyester carpeting is more water-resistant than plain nylon carpeting. And so on. Evaluate these fiber combinations according to the list below.

Also, bear in mind that there should be at least 20% or so of a particular fiber in the carpeting to realize the benefits of using that fiber. Adding 5% polyester to a carpet won't significantly increase its water-resistance, for example.

These are the five most common fibers used in carpeting today:

Wool is a very high-quality fiber for carpeting. Its only real drawback is the possibility of allergic reactions.

Nylon is also very good. It tends to be less expensive than wool while still providing excellent value for your money. As a synthetic fiber, it cannot cause or exacerbate allergies.

Polyester is not as long-lasting as nylon, but it has a special advantage. It is water resistant, which makes it a better choice for bathrooms and kitchens.

Acrylic looks and feels like wool, but cannot cause allergic reactions. It is also a good bit cheaper than wool or nylon. However, it does not wear as well, so it is not as good a choice over the long term as nylon.

Olefin is also a cheaper, and less-durable, alternative to nylon. Again, it makes little sense to shave years off the useful life of your carpeting just to save a few dollars right now. Nylon is a better choice.

Weight Weight refers to the amount of fibers per square foot of carpeting. This should be noted on the sample label. Generally, the higher the weight, the better the carpet will wear.

Density Do the tufts of yarn seem sparse and separate into obvious rows, or are they very closely bunched together? Generally, the denser the tufts, the better the carpet.

Twists Check the cut ends of the yarn itself. Do the ends seem tightly twisted, or are they already beginning to unravel and fray? If you see frayed, puffy fibers, don't buy the carpet.

Heat set You want to make sure that the tufts of yarn have been heat set. They will retain their tight twists and wear much better than carpets that have not been heat set. This information should be on the sample label.

If there is no label, and there may not be on a carpet remnant or second, you can check this by untwisting a strand of yarn with your fingers. If it springs back very quickly and very tightly, the carpet has probably been heat set. If it sort of half-heartedly twists back to its original state, or something approaching its original state, the carpet has probably not been heat set and you shouldn't buy it.

This only applies to cut-pile carpeting. Looped carpeting is usually not heat set because it cannot untwist, as the yarn is attached on both ends.

Tightness Turn the carpet, or the sample, over to look at the backing. The yarn tufts should be very tightly woven to the backing. If they appear loose or frayed on the back, don't buy the carpet.

Don't Forget Allergies When Choosing Your Carpet

Wool is the only allergenic fiber commonly used in modern carpeting. All other fibers commonly used are synthetic and, therefore, do not cause allergies. Never buy carpeting that contains any wool unless you are certain that no one in your family will be allergic to it.

If you have small children, or plan to, you may wish to avoid buying carpeting that contains any wool. Some doctors believe that exposure to common allergens early in life can actually cause or exacerbate life-long allergies. Ask your pediatrician or family physician.

Most modern carpeting is manufactured from synthetic fibers. They provide good value for your money and are reasonably priced. In view of this, you may wish to avoid wool carpeting altogether to prevent any possibility of future allergy problems.

Federal Trade Commission regulations require that the complete fiber content of all carpets be labeled on the carpet sample. Do your own checking.

Carpet Warranties

Nearly all carpeting comes with a five year warranty from the manufacturer. Double-check just in case. Never just assume anything when you are dealing with a business.

Most carpet warranties also cover the cost of replacement carpet padding if it should wear out before the carpeting does. Most warranties do not cover the cost of having the replacement padding installed. Again, verify this for yourself. Also, most warranties specifically exclude carpeting used on stairs.

Most warranties will also cover the cost of correcting stretching and buckling of your carpeting for at least one year after installation. These problems can be caused by improper installation, defects in the carpeting itself, high humidity, dragging furniture across the carpet, or even the house settling on its foundation.

Stretching and buckling are relatively rare in modern carpeting and should not occur as long as you use a reputable installer, treat your carpeting with a reasonable amount of care, and have a properly built home. Still, this warranty protection is free and available from most manufacturers, so you should make sure that you have it.

Most warranties state that they are null and void if you do not have the carpet installed by a professional installer. When you have your carpet installed, make sure that you retain a copy of the installer's bill or invoice to certify that you did hire a professional. Keep this copy with your warranty papers throughout the entire warranty period, just in case you are ever called upon to prove that you did hire professional help in order to have the manufacturer honor your warranty.

Most major carpeting manufacturers are very reputable and honor their warranties without any hassle. However, it never hurts to be prepared.

Don't Panic

If you notice that your vacuum cleaner is picking up a lot of fibers from your new carpet, don't panic. This is perfectly normal for the first three months after a new carpet is installed.

The loose fibers usually have not pulled loose from the carpet backing. They are much more likely to be small cut pieces that are left in the carpet during the manufacturing process. This is normal and commonplace.

Some carpets will still shed very slightly months or years after installation. However, if the shedding still seems excessive after three months have gone by, there might be a more serious problem. Call the manufacturer.

Carpet Padding

Don't skimp on good carpet padding. This is not a good place to cut corners or pinch pennies. Good carpet padding can greatly enhance your carpeting's appearance and lengthen its useful life. Sometimes, good padding can even double the life of your carpet.

Good carpet padding will reduce wear on your carpeting by absorbing much of the impact of footsteps and furniture. It also reduces friction and wear on the backing of your carpeting, which is part of what is holding your carpeting together.

Good carpet padding can help insulate your home. It can also reduce drafts around baseboards. This can result in substantial savings on your heating or cooling bill, depending upon where you live.

Carpet padding is also a good investment. Many carpet manufacturers will guarantee their padding for the life of your carpet. If the padding should ever wear out before the carpet does, most manufacturers will replace it at no cost to you, although the cost of taking up the old padding and installing new padding will normally be your responsibility. Still, this is a lot cheaper than having to replace the carpet as well.

It makes good financial sense to buy the best quality padding available and let the padding absorb the wear and tear of everyday life rather than letting your carpeting take the brunt of it.

You will usually purchase your carpet padding from the same source where you buy your carpet. Prices and quality of the various types of carpet padding vary little among different manufacturers. It is a usually a waste of time to comparison shop separately for your carpet padding.

How will you know what kind of padding to order? Different types of carpeting, and different lifestyles, require different types of padding. This is a complicated topic. How can you know what will be the best choice for your home?

There is an easy way to resolve this. Ask your carpet installer when he or she measures your home. The installer will not be making any commission on the sale of your carpet or carpet padding and, therefore, has no financial incentive to give you a biased answer. Also, installers are often more knowledgeable than carpeting salespeople about the long term wear of carpet padding because they see it every day when they take up or repair existing carpeting.

The carpet installer will also tell you how much carpet padding should be ordered along when your home is measured.

Should You Install Your Own Carpeting?

No. Quality installation is an integral part of quality carpeting. A good installer's skill can add years to the useful life of your carpeting. Likewise, a poor installation job can make a high-quality carpet look and wear like a low-quality one.

In fact, most carpet manufacturers specifically state that their warranties are null and void if the carpeting is not installed by a professional. That's a pretty good indicator of the importance of professional installation.

Saving money by doing your own installation is not a bargain if you are setting yourself up to have to replace your carpet much sooner than would otherwise have been necessary. It's not always a good idea to "do-it-yourself".

If you absolutely insist on installing your own carpeting, there are a few books on the subject available at your local library and bookstore. Read them carefully before you begin.

How To Find a Reputable Installer

Just look in the Yellow Pages under "*Carpet and Rug Repair*". Most phone books don't have a separate category for carpet installation, but you will find that many of the companies that advertise carpet repair and replacement will also install new carpeting.

You can also look in the Yellow Pages under "*Contractors-Home*" to get referrals to reputable local installers. Contractors almost always arrange the carpet installation in new homes. The contractors I called when researching this book didn't mind getting this information for me at all and seemed genuinely pleased to refer installers who had done excellent work for them in the past.

Contractors usually know who the best professional installers in the local area are because they arrange so many carpet installations. They've already gone through all of the trial and error screening necessary to determine which installers do a good job, and which don't. If the new homeowners have a problem with the carpet after moving in, the contractor will usually be the first person to hear of it. You can feel reasonably certain that any carpet installer who is recommended by a local contractor will do a satisfactory job for you.

Be sure to get references from any installer before hiring him or her. Get a minimum of three references, preferably more. The trouble of calling the references is small compared to the trouble and expense caused by having to replace poorly installed carpeting.

Make sure that some of the references are at least six months old. Often, problems associated with shoddy carpeting installation don't show up immediately. However, if the customer is still happy with the job after six months have gone by, you can feel pretty safe trusting that installer.

Call the local Chamber of Commerce and the local Better Business Bureau to make sure that the installer has no unresolved complaints on record.

Don't feel insecure about hiring a local installer yourself instead of having a carpeting store or interior designer arrange installation for you. Usually, carpeting stores and interior designers hire installations out to professional installers and collect a hefty commission just for making a simple telephone call.

So, don't worry that you may be settling for less qualified help by making these arrangements yourself. You will be hiring an installer from the same local pool of workers either way, but by making that call yourself you can cut out the middleman's big commission check.

Look for an installer who works with several helpers. These crews of workers can usually complete an average home in a single day, which will mean that you can sleep there that night. If your installation runs more than one day, you may have to go to a hotel because all of your furniture might have been moved into a big pile in one corner of your house. Installers who work alone can seldom complete an average house in only one day.

How To Work With a Professional Installer

You should also read Chapter 18 for general tips and information on dealing with local workrooms and installers, but there are also some special considerations that only apply to carpeting installers.

Measuring After deciding which installer to hire, the first step is to have your home professionally measured. Measuring for carpeting is much more complicated than just calculating the square footage of your home. The carpeting will have to be cut and pieced together in many places to work around closets, narrow hallways, etc. Measuring for carpeting isn't as simple as it might seem on the surface.

You shouldn't just blindly trust the installer's estimate either, though. Installers are normally paid according to the number of square yards they install. Most installers are honest, but a few aren't.

Rarely, a dishonest installer will inflate your carpet estimate (after all, the installer isn't paying for the carpet -- you are) and then stash the excess carpeting in his truck during the installation when you aren't paying attention. You will almost certainly be paying the installer according to the yardage quoted in the estimate. This way the installer gets paid for more work than was actually done and keeps the extra carpet to sell to someone else.

If you check references carefully, you shouldn't get stuck with a dishonest installer, but, just in case you do, there is a simple way to avoid being ripped off with an inflated yardage estimate. Carefully measure your own home to determine the square yardage of your floor. Measure the length and width of each room in feet and multiply them to get the area. Add up the areas of each room to determine the total area of your home. Divide the total area of your home by nine to arrive at the square yardage necessary to carpet your home. If you plan to carpet any stairs, you will need to add 3/4 of a square yard for each stair.

The installer's yardage estimate will almost certainly be a bit higher than yours. Extra carpeting will be necessary to handle odd spaces, such as closets. However, if there is a big discrepancy between your estimate and the installer's, more than 10% difference, ask the installer for an explanation. If his explanation doesn't seem reasonable, get a different installer.

You should already have decided what type of carpeting you will be purchasing. Have all of the product information ready to show the installer. This information can sometimes affect the amount of carpeting needed.

The installer should also give you an estimate of how much carpet padding you will need to order, as well as the specific type of padding that should be ordered. Be sure to tell the installer that you want any stair steps double-padded -- this will affect the amount of padding needed. Double-padding your stairs will help offset the excess wear and tear stairs go through and extend the useful life of the carpeting on your stairs. Don't forget that stair carpeting is specifically excluded from many manufacturers warranties -- if it has to be replaced early, it will be at your expense.

Most installers will measure your home at no charge, if you hire them to do the installation. Typically, the installer will not bill you at the time he or she makes the measurements. However, if you do not hire the installer within a reasonable period of time, you will receive a bill for the measuring.

The typical cost of measuring, when it is billed separately, is between $20.00 and $50.00, depending on how far the installer has to travel to get to your home and how large your home is. If you hire the installer to install your carpet, this charge is usually waived.

The advice is generally free, so you should make good use of it. Carpeting installers don't receive any commissions on your carpeting purchase, so they are excellent sources for unbiased advice on the types of carpet and carpet padding you should purchase.

Carpeting installers are almost always self-employed or members of a small family business. These businesses are hurting severely during the current bad economy. You are in a very strong buyer's market when you are dealing with these people. They will want very much to please you in order to get your business. Let them.

Determining the fee Most installers charge according to the square yard of carpeting installed. The typical fee ranges between $2.50 and $3.50 per square yard, depending upon many factors -- the size of your home, what type of padding you are using, what type of carpeting you are having installed, etc.

Most installers charge for stairs separately, usually about $5.00 per stair for a standard straight staircase. Spiral staircases usually cost a bit more per stair.

Some installers will charge you a higher fee per square yard of carpeting if they are expected to move your furniture, dispose of your carpet, or provide any other extra service. Don't let them figure the price of these services this way. It is confusing, and you will probably end up paying too much.

Charging you an extra fifty cents per square yard to move your furniture, for instance, doesn't sound like much until you realize that this amounts to $100.00 for an 1800 square foot home.

Price out any extra services, such as moving furniture or disposing of your old carpeting, separately on a flat fee basis. In the later stages of your negotiations, it will be easier to get the installer to waive fees for extra services to get your business if you already have them priced out separately from the installation charge.

Do compare prices among several installers and let them bid against each other for your business. It's a buyer's market out there. Workers in all parts of the home furnishings industry are hurting for business. Don't be afraid to haggle.

You will usually get the best prices during summer and winter. Don't shop for an installer during spring and fall if you can possibly help it. These are the busiest seasons in the industry when the installers will be in the highest demand, and much less inclined to give you a bargain price.

Moving furniture Most installers will move your furniture for a fee. However, if you possibly can, you will be better off to arrange this yourself. If you don't have family members or friends who can help, you can contact a local high school. School administrators will usually be able to refer you to several dependable students who want to make some extra money.

If you do decide to arrange with the installer to move your furniture, insist upon a clear flat fee for moving your furniture -- before and after the carpeting

Plan Ahead

Carpeting isn't very difficult to repair if it becomes damaged by spills, burns, or other mishaps. However, most repairs involve removing the damaged section and replacing it with new carpeting. For this reason, you should order a little extra carpet, just in case.

If you were to try to buy a small piece of carpet months or years after the original installation to perform repairs, you would be likely to find that your carpet was no longer available. Manufacturers change colors, shades, and textures seasonally. Your original carpet might not be in production anymore.

Even if you could order more carpet in your original style and color, it will certainly be from a different dye lot, which can also cause matching problems.

Plan ahead, and set aside a little extra carpeting for any future emergencies. Five percent extra is plenty.

Store the carpet carefully. Seal it in a plastic bag to make sure that moisture and insects don't get into it, especially if your carpeting contains any natural fibers, such as wool.

is installed. Sometimes, people forget to specify in the contract that the furniture has to be put back again after the carpet has been installed. You aren't in a very good bargaining position when it's 8:00 at night and all of your furniture is stacked in one corner of your home.

If you are hiring an installer during the slow business seasons, you might be able to get your furniture moved free just to get your business. Ask.

Disposing of your old carpeting Many installers will do this for you for a small fee, usually around $25.00. If you are hiring an installer during a slow business period, you may be able to get the installer to throw this service in at no charge to get your business. Ask.

The contract Get everything in writing, as always. Specify all details, such as double-padding on stairs or free disposal of your old carpet.

The warranty The installer should warranty the work for at least one year, but probably won't unless you ask. Make sure that your carpeting is guaranteed against any defects in installation for a minimum of one year.

This warranty is very important. Defects in installation often do not become apparent for several months, or longer. If the installer refuses to guarantee the quality of the work, hire someone else.

Payment The vast majority of professional installers do not accept credit cards. They aren't set up to process them. This is simply not expected of people and businesses that normally work on a wholesale basis. If you are going to deal directly with wholesale workers, you will just have to get used to this.

Always pay by check, never by cash. Cash receipts don't always hold up in court, if you ever need to take the installer to court.

It is customary to pay the installer in full when the job has been completed.

Start early When the day arrives, arrange to start work as early in the day as possible. If your installation can't be completed in one day, you may run into extra expenses to stay in a hotel overnight.

Retail Stores and Interior Designers

Avoid buying carpeting here. These businesses usually charge the highest prices and middleman markups. Carpet manufacturers have a well established system to sell directly to the public. You should take advantage of it.

Specialty Carpeting Stores

Usually, these stores won't be able to beat the prices offered by factory outlets and telephone ordering services. You might be able to get a bargain at these stores during a sale, which normally are held in late summer and winter.

You might also be able to purchase carpet that another customer didn't or couldn't pay for. Most businesses get stuck with merchandise that a customer has returned or defaulted on paying for sooner or later. Sometimes, there is a genuine defect in the carpet, so you must carefully check it over.

However, there are also cases where the carpet is fine but the customer has had a change of heart, taste, or financial condition. These carpets can be discounted as much as 90% off retail. It's worth checking out.

Telephone Ordering Services

All telephone carpeting ordering services are based in the Dalton, Georgia area -- the center of the carpeting industry. Many of these are run by the various factory outlets themselves. Ordering from these services isn't quite as cheap as going directly to the outlet, but it is very, very close.

Considering the time and trouble that almost all of you would expend in traveling to the outlets themselves, the vast majority of you would be much better off just to use a telephone ordering service.

Prices and Payment The typical discount offered by these services is 50% to 80% off retail, depending upon the brand and style you choose. Most major brands are available. All of the services listed at right accept credit cards and will arrange shipment of your carpeting.

Ordering You should make sure that you have all of the necessary product information at the ready before you call the service. You will need to know the brand of carpet you want, the color, and the square yardage needed. Have the installer's advice about carpet padding written down to discuss with the service.

Like the ads say, you should shop in your neighborhood and write down the product information for the carpet you wish to buy: manufacturer name, style, color, special finishes such as Scotchgarding, and any other details that seem important.

Delivery The typical delivery time is anywhere from one day to two weeks. If the carpet you want is in stock, it will usually be shipped the same day you place your order. If the carpet has to be manufactured for you, you may have to wait up to two weeks for shipment. It will also take one to five days for the carpet to reach you by truck, depending on where you live. Customers on the West Coast will have the longest wait.

Due to size constraints, your carpeting will usually be shipped via a commercial truck line. Commercial truck drivers do not carry your packages inside for you. You will want to have help available when the carpeting arrives. Rolls of carpet are quite heavy and awkward to carry. You will need at least one other person to help you.

These services are accustomed to making truck deliveries as simple as possible for their customers. They have a well established routine. Usually, you will leave a daytime phone number with the telephone ordering service when you place your order. When your order is shipped, the service will call you with the name and phone number of the specific truck line that will be delivering your order and a "tracking number" that identifies your packages to the trucking company.

Telephone Ordering Services

Bearden Brothers Carpet
& Textile Corp.
3200 Dug Gap Rd. SW
Exit 135, off I-75
Dalton, GA 30720
(800) 433-0074

Dalton Paradise Carpets
2601 Chattanooga Rd.
Exit 137, off I-75
Dalton, GA 30721
(800) 338-7811

Gold Label Carpet Whse
3744 Lake Catherine Rd.
Tunnel Hill, GA 30755
(800) 346-4531

Johnson's Carpets
3239 S. Dixie Rd.
Dalton, GA 30720
(800) 235-1079

Long's Carpets
2625 S. Dixie Hwy.
Exit 135, off I-75
Dalton, GA 30720
(800) 545-5664

Owen Carpet Company
2752 Dug Gap Rd.
Exit 135, off I-75
Dalton, GA 30720
(800) 626-6936

Parker's Carpet
3200 Dug Gap Rd.
Dalton, GA 30720
(800) 442-2013

S & S Mills
2650 Lakeland Rd. SE
Dalton, GA 30721
(800) 241-4013

Warehouse Carpets
2225 E. Walnut Ave.
Exit 136, off I-75
Dalton, GA 30721
(800) 526-2229

You should then call the trucking company and give them your tracking number to determine when your order should arrive. This may be any time from the next day to the next week, depending upon how far away from Georgia you are located. The trucking company will usually be able to give you a specific day and a rough idea of the time of your delivery. Most trucking companies will also call you, at your request, when the driver is actually on the way to your home.

You must be home when the carpet arrives. Commercial truck drivers will not wait, nor will they come back at a later time. If you miss the delivery, you will have to pay the freight charges to bring the carpet to you, take it back to Georgia, and then bring it back to you again. This can get extremely expensive. Be absolutely sure that you, and your helper, will be there when your carpet arrives.

Residential deliveries are usually made between 9:00 AM and 2:00 PM, Monday through Friday. Trucking companies generally do not make weekend or evening deliveries.

You may choose to pay the trucking company for the freight charges when the carpet arrives, or you may ask the telephone ordering service to include these charges when you pay for your carpet. The charges will be the same either way.

You should arrange to pay the freight charges when you order your carpet. Truck drivers are unable to process credit card payments. If you pay the freight charges to the telephone ordering service, you will be able to use your credit card. This way, if there should be any future discrepancies or problems with your freight charges, you will have much more leverage to get the problems resolved.

Please read pages 316-319 for more information on dealing with any problems that may occur with commercial truck shipments and merchandise shipped directly from a manufacturer to you.

Factory Outlets

Ninety percent of all carpeting is manufactured in and around Dalton, Georgia. Consequently, this is where all of the carpeting factory outlets in the United States are located.

Dalton, Georgia is approximately one hour's drive northwest of Atlanta on I-75. Exits 135 through 138 will all take you into the Dalton/Tunnel Hill area. Most of the outlets are clustered at these exits, very close to the interstate. A list of the major factory outlets in the Dalton area can be found on pages 123-124.

If you have access to a truck and live nearby, a trip to Dalton might be worth your while. These factory outlets sell seconds, roll ends, and irregulars at up to 75% off retail, and first quality merchandise at up to 50% off retail. You could get a terrific deal.

However, chances are relatively small that these heavily discounted pieces of carpeting would be large enough for your home, or have the color and texture you want. You usually will not be able to transport any but the very smallest pieces of carpeting in a car. Usually, you must own, or rent, a truck. You will also need someone to help you -- carpeting is very heavy and awkward for one person to carry.

Even though you will miss out on the few spectacular deals that are available at factory outlets, the vast majority of you would be much better off to buy your carpeting through a telephone ordering service. All of them are based in Dalton and offer prices as low or almost as low as the factory outlets. In fact, most of them ARE factory outlets. All of their carpeting is first-quality, and you can order any color or texture you want.

If you do decide to shop directly at the outlet, bring your credit card. Most of the outlets accept them. Please read pages 344-346 for complete information about credit card transactions.

Examine all carpets thoroughly. Most seconds and irregulars don't have significant defects, but some do. Seconds, irregulars, and closeouts are normally sold "as-is" and are not returnable. Read the quality checks in this chapter carefully and discuss your decorating job with a carpet installer before you head out for Dalton.

Factory Outlets

A & W Carpet Sales
550 Conway St.
Dalton, GA 30720
(706) 278-7660

Access Carpet
3068 N. Dug Gap Rd. SW
Exit 135, off I-75
Dalton, GA 30721
(800) 334-0735

Baker's Carpet Gallery
693 N. Varnell Rd.
Tunnel Hill, GA 30755
(706) 673-2343

Barrett Carpet Mills
3004 Parquet Rd.
Exit 135, off I-75
Dalton, GA 30720
(706) 277-2114

Bearden Brothers Carpet
& Textile Corp.
3200 Dug Gap Rd. SW
Exit 135, off I-75
Dalton, GA 30720
(800) 433-0074

Beckler's Carpet Outlet
3051 N. Dug Gap Rd. SW
Exit 135, off I-75
Dalton, GA 30720
(800) BECKLER

Blue Circle Carpetown
1706 Hwy. 41 S.
Dalton, GA 30720
(800) 622-7561

Britton Carpet Alley
3198 N. Dug Gap Rd.
Exit 135, off I-75
Dalton, GA 30722
(800) 232-3913

Broadacre Carpet
and Orientals
703 N. Varnell Rd.
Exit 138, off I-75
Tunnel Hill, GA 30755
(706) 673-6588

Brown Carpet
2514 E. Walnut St.
Exit 136, off I-75
Dalton, GA 30721
(706) 278-5411

Carpet Express
915 Market St.
Dalton, GA 30720
(706) 278-8507

Carpets American Made
3056 N. Dug Gap Rd.
Exit 135, off I-75
Dalton, GA 30722
(800) 243-7998

Carpets by Sarah Ruth
2804 E. Walnut Ave.
Exit 138, off I-75
Dalton, GA 30722
(800) 847-3476

Carpets of Dalton
3010 Old Dug Gap Rd.
Exit 135, off I-75
Dalton, GA 30722
(800) 262-3132

Carpet Values
800 Abutment Rd.
Dalton, GA 30721
(706) 275-1334

Carpet Wholesale Outlet
690 N. Varnell Rd.
Tunnel Hill, GA 30755
(706) 673-2112

Factory Outlets (cont.)

Crown Carpet
Highway 76 West
Chatsworth, GA 30705
(706) 695-1440

Dalton Carpet Master
3060 N. Dug Gap Rd. SW
Exit 135, off I-75
Dalton, GA 30720
(706) 277-2700

Dalton Paradise Carpets
2601 Chattanooga Rd.
Exit 137, off I-75
Dalton, GA 30721
(706) 226-9064
(800) 338-7811

Dalyn Oriental Rugs
2942 N. Dug Gap Rd. SW
Dalton, GA 30720
(706) 277-2909

Dennard Brothers Carpet Barn
3054 N. Dug Gap Rd. SW
Exit 135, off I-75
Dalton, GA 30720
(800) 345-0478

Eastside Carpet Mills
1804 Hwy. 41 S
Exit 136, off I-75
Dalton, GA 30720
(800) 654-6123

The Floor Group
418 W. Hawthorne St.
Exit 136, off I-75
Dalton, GA 30720
(706) 278-7299

Floor Trends
919 S. Thornton Ave.
Exit 136, off I-75
Dalton, GA 30720
(800) 462-6210

Gold Label Carpet Warehouse
3744 Lake Catherine Rd.
Tunnel Hill, GA 30755
(800) 346-4531

Hanks Carpet
691 N. Varnell Rd.
Exit 138, off I-75
Tunnel Hill, GA 30755
(706) 673-2410

I-75 Carpets
3002 N. Dug Gap Rd. SW
Exit 135, off I-75
Dalton, GA 30720
(800) 233-6286

Johnson's Carpets
3239 S. Dixie Rd.
Dalton, GA 30720
(800) 235-1079

Kinnaird & Francke Wholesale Carpets
3021 S. Dug Gap Rd.
Exit 135, off I-75
Dalton, GA 30720
(800) 423-1823

Michael's Carpets of Dalton
920 Market St.
Exit 138, off I-75
Dalton, GA 30722
(800) 634-9509

Owen Carpet Company
2752 Dug Gap Rd.
Exit 135, off I-75
Dalton, GA 30720
(800) 626-6936

Parker's Carpets
3200 Dug Gap Rd.
Exit 135, off I-75
Dalton, GA 30720
(800) 442-2013

Peanut's Carpet House
3358 Chatsworth Rd. SE
Exit 136, off I-75
Dalton, GA 30721
(706) 278-8120

Quality Discount Carpets
1207 W. Walnut Ave.
Exit 136, off I-75
Dalton, GA 30720
(800) 233-0993

Rave Carpet
2875 Cleveland Rd.
Exit 137, off I-75
Dalton, GA 30721
(800) 942-6969

Tailor Made Carpets
1526 W. Walnut Ave.
Exit 136, off I-75
Dalton, GA 30720
(706) 226-4411

Varsity Rug Company
2000 S. Dixie Hwy.
Exit 136, off I-75
Dalton, GA 30722
(706) 226-7300

Warehouse Carpets
2225 E. Walnut Ave.
Exit 136, off I-75
Dalton, GA 30721
(800) 526-2229

Whaley Carpet Outlet
109 Bryant Ave.
Exit 136, off I-75
Dalton, GA 30722
(800) 422-2730

Wholesale

Unless you are buying tremendous quantities of carpeting, far more than you would need for an average home, it is very difficult to buy standard carpeting at the wholesale prices carpeting stores enjoy. The carpet industry has already established a very effective system of selling directly to the public at rock-bottom prices through factory outlets and telephone ordering services.

You should not become your own decorator solely for the purpose of buying standard household carpeting wholesale. The small savings you might realize are not worth the trouble.

There are some extremely expensive, high-quality, designer carpets available through interior designers and retail stores, as well as through wholesale design centers. These carpets are lovely. Some are even handmade, with intricate needlework and embroidery. If this is what you want, you will benefit greatly by becoming your own decorator and shopping for them directly at the local wholesale design center or independent wholesale showroom.

Hundreds of wholesale rug and carpeting showrooms all over the U. S. are listed in the *National Directory of Wholesale Home Furnishings Sources and Showrooms*, by William Graham. The *Directory* is a complete resource for designers and decorators, listing thousands of wholesale sources and showrooms for all types of home furnishings. It can be ordered from this publisher. There is an order form in the back of this book.

These high-style carpets are a world apart from the standard carpeting in most homes that we have been discussing in this chapter. These exclusive carpets should be considered for design value only. There is no significant difference between the quality and durability of these ultra-expensive carpets and those of standard carpets available through factory outlets and telephone ordering services.

Recommendations

1 Scout out local carpeting stores to decide what carpeting you want, using the quality checks given in this chapter to determine the most appropriate carpet for you. Choose at least three different brands of carpets that would be acceptable to you so that you can then compare prices among them. Be sure to write down all product information needed to place your order from the carpeting samples. Check out any special sales or returned carpeting that the store may have.

2 Call a local home contractor or carpet repair service to get installer referrals. Check out several installers, and their references, before settling on one. Quality installation is as important to the looks and wear of your carpet as quality manufacturing.

3 Discuss your carpet choices with the installer to make sure that they are indeed appropriate for your home and your family's lifestyle. Have the installer measure your home for carpeting and padding. Double-check the installer's square yardage estimate against your own calculations to make

sure that you aren't being ripped off.

4 Call a telephone ordering service to order your carpet. It will not be practical for the vast majority of you to shop directly at the carpeting factory outlets in Dalton, Georgia. Telephone ordering services run a very close second in price and quality to factory outlets.

5 If you are within a reasonable driving distance to Dalton, you may want to investigate the factory outlets. If you shop there in person, you will be able to select from irregulars and seconds, which can be incredible values.

Be prepared to choose from a smaller range of choices in colors and textures. If you have a truck, or can borrow one, and a friend to help you load your carpet on and off the truck, you can save the freight expenses by bringing your own carpet and padding home.

6 Now, you are ready to call the installer back and arrange the installation, making sure that you get all details in writing and a warranty for at least one year on the installation.

Chapter 6

Quality Sewing

There are many little details that show whether or not your furnishings are well made -- the ruffles, the welting, the seams, the hems, and many other little touches that often go unnoticed to retail consumers. That is, until they start to ravel or come apart.

After many years of working in the industry, I can look at a bedspread or drapery and know if it will fall apart after a year of normal use or last twenty years and still look wonderful. There are many tell-tale signs of good sewing and quality manufacturing methods.

This chapter is your crash course in quality sewing. Study this chapter carefully, and you will know how to spot high quality (and inferior quality) furnishings, just like I do.

In the next three chapters we will be discussing soft window treatments, bed treatments, and various soft furnishings such as tablecloths, pillows, and cushions. Before having any of these types of furnishings custom made, you need a primer in sewing details. You need to be able to evaluate a workroom's or seamstress' skill before you entrust them with your money and your expensive fabrics.

Before contracting with any custom workroom or seamstress, ask to see samples of their work. Look them over carefully and evaluate them according to the standards listed below. This is the best way to make sure that a workroom is truly qualified to make your custom furnishings.

Thread

Always make sure that your furnishings are sewn with cotton/polyester thread, never monofilament. They are very easy to tell apart. Monofilament is clear and tough and looks like fishing line. If the thread doesn't look like monofilament, then you can be sure that it is cotton/polyester and that it's fine to use.

Monofilament is cheap, and it is very strong. It almost never breaks, which reduces production problems for the manufacturer. It is clear, which eliminates the need to stock hundreds of different colors of thread to match

No samples?

If the workroom or seamstress says that they have no samples or work in progress to show you, don't place your order there.

All competent workrooms and seamstresses should have at least one or two jobs in progress that they could show you. Most competent workrooms also keep samples of various types of furnishings to show to customers, although most home seamstresses do not because of the expense involved.

If you aren't allowed to see any samples, then the workroom or seamstress either has no jobs in progress or doesn't want you to see the quality of their work. Either way, this is a bad sign. Shop somewhere else.

many different fabrics. Monofilament is the usual choice of large companies that manufacture cheap, ready-made, sewn products.

It's all right for ready-made products (which aren't meant to last for many years), buy you don't want monofilament for your custom furnishings. Fine custom furnishings should last a long, long time, but they probably won't if you have them made with monofilament thread. Its toughness can be a big disadvantage.

Over time, there will be friction between the thread and the fabric on many of your custom furnishings, especially in quilted areas and on hems. Sooner or later, one of them will give way.

If the fabric is stronger than the thread, as will be the case if you use cotton/polyester thread, then a few threads may break as the furnishings get old and begin to wear out. This is not a big deal. Fixing broken threads and restitching small areas of your furnishings is very easy. Any home seamstress, or you for that matter, can easily make these repairs.

However, if the thread is stronger than the fabric, as will be the case if you use monofilament, the fabric will give way under the friction of the threads. As the furnishings begin to wear out, you will start to see little cuts in the fabric right underneath the threads, especially in quilted areas. Repairing fabric that has been cut this way is virtually impossible. You won't be able to have this fixed, even by a highly-skilled workroom. When the cuts become too noticable, you will just have to throw the item away and buy something new.

With only one exception -- multi-needle or hand-guided quilted bedspreads -- quality home furnishings workrooms and seamstresses do not use monofilament thread. Bedspreads that are quilted with monofilament thread do not last nearly as long as those that are quilted with cotton/polyester thread. However, the automated machinery that makes these less expensive bedspreads can only use monofilament. You may wish to go to the extra expense of having your custom bedspreads outline-quilted so that cotton/polyester thread can be used. You will have to weigh the expenses and decide.

Aside from this special case, do not buy from a seamstress or workroom that uses monofilament.

Seams

Look at the seams on the front of any bedspreads or window treatments. This is where the widths of decorative fabric are sewn together. Decorative fabrics are only 54" wide at the most, so they must be joined together in panels to make furnishings that are wider than that.

Look at how the fabric pattern matches at the seam. Is the pattern lined up perfectly? It should be. This isn't difficult to do.

Any competent seamstress or workroom should be able to make the patterns blend together perfectly. If the patterns are out of alignment at the seam, have your work done elsewhere. Poorly matched patterns are a sure sign of a sloppy workroom or seamstress.

Welting

The fabric covering on plain welting should lie smoothly with no wrinkles. This is accomplished by cutting the fabric diagonally to the grain of the fabric. Of the seamstress or workroom simply cuts strips of fabric to make the welting without paying attention to the grain (as inexperienced seamstresses often do) the resulting welting will look terrible.

Banding

Banding should always be sewn, never glued. Look at the edges. You should see a small seam at each edge, like the ones shown below, where the banding has been sewn. If there are no seams, then the banding must have been glued.

Also, check to make sure that the banding lies flat and smooth. It should not wrinkle or ruffle up at the seams.

Fringes and Trims

Never use a workroom or seamstress who glues on fringes and decorative trims. These should always be sewn. Look at the base of the fringe or trim for tell-tale dried lumps of glue.

Look closely at fringes and trims on any window treatments, tablecloths, bedspreads, or other furnishings. Are they straight? Are the neatly attached with small, barely visible stitches? Do they feel firmly attached when you tug lightly on them? Or do they feel like they might fall off any minute?

If fringes or trims look sloppily or loosely applied, find another seamstress or workroom.

Tassels

Like fringes and trims, tassels should always be sewn on, never glued. Also, lightly tug on them to make sure that they are firmly attached.

Buttons

You will usually find buttons on seat cushions, bolsters, neckrolls, and some pillows. Gently tug on the buttons to make sure that they are firmly attached. Some seamstresses and workrooms attach buttons so insecurely that they soon pop right off.

Zippers

Zippers, which are normally used on pillows, cushions, pillow shams, and duvet covers, should not be noticable. Quality made furnishings will have a fabric placket covering the zipper.

The fabric placket should lie flat, completely covering the zipper. It shouldn't gap open, making the zipper obvious. You shouldn't even be able to see the zipper on well made furnishings without pulling back the placket.

You should always make sure that any stuffed furnishings, such as pillows and cushions, have zippers. Don't settle for having these furnishings permanently sewn shut. This greatly shortens the useful life of your furnishings.

If your pillows and cushions have zip-off covers, they can be dry-cleaned. You should never wash most custom furnishings. You have to remove the inner stuffing, which will be encased in its own separate plain cover, in order to dry-clean the decorative top cover. If you can't remove the stuffing, and you stain the pillow or cushion, it will probably be ruined.

Pattern Centering

Carefully evaluate the pattern placement on any samples you see according to these guidelines:

1 Are main pattern elements, such as bouquets, kept whole in most places, or are they routinely cut in half? Is everything lined up evenly?

2 Are patterns centered nicely on pillows and cushions? Main pattern elements, such as flowers or bouquets, should be centered attractively.

3 Some patterns, such as many florals, ramble all over the fabric and can't be matched at the edges of pillows and cushions, but patterns with stripes or plaids should always match at the edges.

4 Look at the front edges of boxed seat cushions. The pattern on the top of a boxed-edge seat cushion should match the pattern on the front side. If the cushion (or pillow) is knife-edged, the top and bottom patterns should match at the seam.

5 On window treatments with many identical segments, such as balloon valances and swags, the fabric pattern should match on each segment. If you are having a balloon valance made from a fabric that has a floral bouquet pattern on it, for instance, there should be a bouquet centered on each balloon segment all the way across the treatment.

6 On all types of furnishings, is the fabric pattern arranged in an appealing way? Does it look as though some care went into the pattern placement, or does it seem that the fabric was cut haphazardly with no thought to the end results? Make sure that the workroom or seamstress you choose pays attention to these details.

Valance Boards

Many window treatments and valances are attached to boards which are then hung over the window, instead of using drapery or curtain rods. These boards should always be wrapped on all sides in white drapery lining before the window treatment is attached. Look underneath the window treatment or valance to check.

After the window treatment has been attached to the board, the top of the board should always be neatly covered with a "cap". A "cap" is a piece of the decorative fabric cut to the size of the board that covers the staples that are used to attach the window treatment to the board. The staples and raw edges of fabric should never be left showing.

Neatness

By this, I mean the neatness of the furnishings, not the neatness of the workroom. Good workrooms are always messy. You just can't sew anything without little piles of scraps and threads and stuffing material congregating all over the floor. There just isn't time enough in the day to clean up every two minutes.

So, if the workroom looks like a fabric tornado has just blown through, don't hold it against them. The busiest, and many of the best, workrooms usually look this way.

However, if the furnishings themselves look sloppy, watch out. Look at the samples carefully. Does everything look neat and symmetrical? Do pillows and cushions look square at the corners? Do round pillow and cushions look round, or sort of squashed?

Carefully examine any window treatments. If you are looking at a swag treatment, are all of the individual swags even and of the same length and width? If you are looking at a balloon treatment, are all of the individual balloons of the same length and width?

Overall, do the furnishings look like they were carefully planned and executed, or do they look like they were just thrown together? If the workroom or seamstress appears to be sloppy in the way that they put furnishings together, you can bet that they are sloppy in other areas too, such as making sure that furnishings conform to the proper measurements and are made exactly according to the details of the order.

Don't mind sloppy workrooms, but do avoid sloppy workmanship.

Recommendations

When you are selecting a workroom or seamstress, make sure that the businesses you consider pay proper attention to all of the details described above.

To avoid duplication and wasted pages, these fine points of sewing won't be repeated constantly throughout the next three chapters on custom soft furnishings. However, you should bear in mind that many of these details are applicable to each type of furnishing.

Chapter 7

Soft Window Treatments

Having custom soft window treatments made isn't complicated at all. All you have to do is choose styles that are right for your home, make the proper measurements, and select appropriate fabrics for the particular window treatment styles you wish to order. Then, just place your order directly with a wholesale workroom or seamstress in your area.

You can easily do this for yourself with the right instructions. It's unnecessary to hire a professional interior decorator or interior designer to help you. All of the information you need to prepare your own window treatment order for basic window treatments is right here.

If you need information about more complex custom window treatments, like swags or elaborate valances, you should do your own research. Hiring a designer or decorator to help you is usually a complete waste of money because these professionals rarely ever have any training in how soft window treatments are manufactured.

You should always have your soft window treatments made by a local wholesale workroom or seamstress, and keep the decorator's or designer's usual 100% commission in your own pocket.

Don't forget to read over the quality checks in Chapter 6 when you are evaluating any custom workroom or seamstress. Chapter 18 discusses local workrooms and craftspeople: how to locate them, evaluate them, and get the best work from them at the best price.

There are also a few factory outlets and deep discount sources for ready-made window treatments. We'll discuss those later in the chapter.

Measuring Specific Types of Windows

There are six basic categories to consider: standard windows, bay windows, palladian windows, corner windows, sliding glass doors, and French doors. Each has special considerations that need to be taken into account, so each has its own special chart for you to use.

You may make photocopies of these charts. Fill in the measurements and give the charts to the workroom or seamstress stapled to your custom window treatment orders. This will eliminate a lot of the confusion that can occur with window treatment orders.

Standard Windows

Most of the windows in your home are considered to be standard windows. It doesn't matter how wide or narrow they are or how many segments they have.

You should note any features of the window (sill, apron, crank, etc.) in the blank marked Window description, as well as the location of the window in the room (near bed, by piano, etc.).

Standard windows:

Measurements A and B are very simple: the inside width and length of the window. Take these measurements inside the smallest area of the window frame. These are the measurements that will be used to order inside-mounted blinds, shades, and valances.

Measurements C and D are the outside width and length of the window. Take these measurements from the outside edges of any mouldings around the window. These are the measurements that will be used to determine the final width of most of your custom window treatments.

Normally, you will measure the outside length of the window to the bottom edge of any mouldings or apron. However, if you are ordering outside-mounted shades or mini-blinds, your measurement will only go down to the top of the sill (if any). Custom soft shades, pleated shades, and mini-blinds should end right at the sill when they are closed.

Measurement E is the measurement from the top of the window to the ceiling. This is to let the workroom know how much space it has to work with above the window. If there are any crown mouldings around the tops of your walls, only measure up to the bottom edge of the crown moulding.

Measurement F is the measurement from the bottom outside edge of the window to the floor. Do not subtract any allowance for baseboards. Always measure all the way to the floor.

Measurement G is the measurement from the top outside edge of the window to the floor, again not making any allowance for baseboards.

Measurements H and I are the clearances on the left and right side of the window. Measure the distance from the outside edge of the window to any point that marks the end of the clear wall space: a corner, a bookcase, a piece of furniture, another window, a door, etc. These measurements tell you how much clear wall area you have available for the stackbacks of draperies or vertical blinds.

"Is there any existing hardware?" You should note any existing drapery rods or other drapery hardware that has already been mounted to the wall.

If you give the workroom the width of your rod (excluding any decorative finials), the diameter, the return, and the distance from the top of the rod to the floor, the workroom can make your new draperies the correct size to fit your old rod. Also, give the type of rod in the space provided: plain traverse rod, decorative curtain rod with rings, whatever.

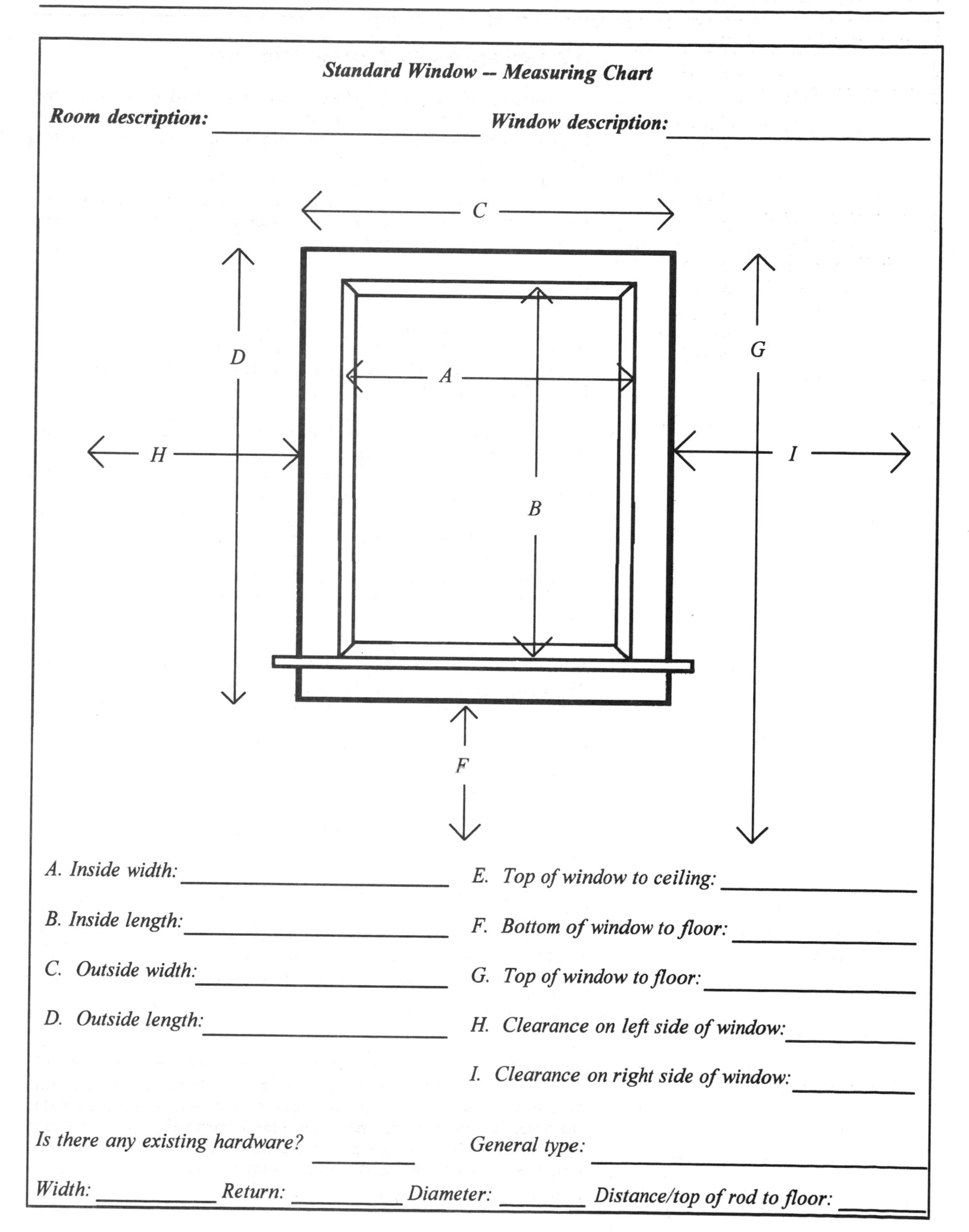

Standard Window -- Measuring Chart

Room description: ______________________ **Window description:** ______________________

A. Inside width: ______________________

B. Inside length: ______________________

C. Outside width: ______________________

D. Outside length: ______________________

E. Top of window to ceiling: ______________________

F. Bottom of window to floor: ______________________

G. Top of window to floor: ______________________

H. Clearance on left side of window: ____________

I. Clearance on right side of window: ____________

Is there any existing hardware? ________

General type: ______________________

Width: __________ *Return:* __________ *Diameter:* ________ *Distance/top of rod to floor:* ________

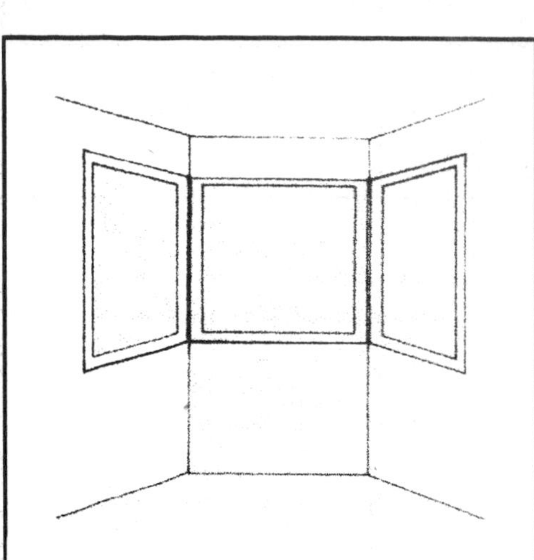

In this example, there is no clear wall space between the windows.

In a case like this, the wall clearance measurements on your chart should be recorded as follows:

Left window: *H* is measured normally. *I* is zero inches.

Center window: *H* and *I* are both zero inches.

Right window: *H* is zero inches. *I* is measured normally.

Bay windows:

Bay windows are slightly more complicated. In addition to the usual measurements -- inside width and depth, outside width and depth, distances to the ceiling and floor, and clear wall space on either side -- you must also measure the angles of the corners.

Measurements A through I should be taken for each individual window in the bay, in exactly the same way as they are taken for standard windows. Please refer to pages 134-135 for full instructions.

If there is no clear wall space between the windows and the corners, as in the bay window shown at left, the wall clearances on the appropriate sides of the windows will be zero. Follow the example at left.

Angles You also have to take the angle measurement of the left and right corner. Don't go looking for your protractor from high school geometry class -- there is a better way. This is how most professional interior designers and interior decorators take these angle measurements:

To take a corner angle measurement, just get two small pieces of heavy paper or cardboard and a stapler. Business cards work well for this. Just hold one card perpendicularly against the wall with the point right at the corner of the wall. Then, hold the other card on top of the first card, perpendicularly against the other wall with the point right at the corner of the wall. They will form an angle. Staple the cards together to hold the angle in place.

That's it. Make an angle guide this way for both corners. Don't worry about not knowing the exact angle degree measurement, as you would if you used a protractor. It doesn't matter. The workroom will use your cardboard angle guide as a pattern when making any necessary corner adjustments on your treatments.

Be sure to label each guide. The workroom or seamstress must know which is for the right corner and which is for the left corner, as noted on the measurement chart. Staple the angle guides to your measuring chart so they don't get separated from the correct chart.

You don't have to worry about labeling the top and bottom. It doesn't matter if the angle guide is turned upside-down. The measurement will be the same either way.

As with the standard window, be sure to note whether or not there is any drapery hardware already present, and be sure to write down its type and measurements.

Bay Window -- Measuring Chart

Room description: ________________ **Window description:** ________________

Left window

A. Inside width: ____________

B. Inside length: ____________

C. Outside width: ____________

D. Outside length: ____________

E. Top of window to ceiling: ________

F. Bottom of window to floor: ________

G. Top of window to floor: ________

H. Clearance on left side: ________

I. Clearance on right side: ________

Existing hardware? ____________

General type: ____________

Distance/top of rod to floor: ________

Width: ____________

Return: ______ Diameter: ______

Center window

A. Inside width: ____________

B. Inside length: ____________

C. Outside width: ____________

D. Outside length: ____________

E. Top of window to ceiling: ________

F. Bottom of window to floor: ________

G. Top of window to floor: ________

H. Clearance on left side: ________

I. Clearance on right side: ________

Existing hardware? ____________

General type: ____________

Distance/top of rod to floor: ________

Width: ____________

Return: ______ Diameter: ______

Right window

A. Inside width: ____________

B. Inside length: ____________

C. Outside width: ____________

D. Outside length: ____________

E. Top of window to ceiling: ________

F. Bottom of window to floor: ________

G. Top of window to floor: ________

H. Clearance on left side: ________

I. Clearance on right side: ________

Existing hardware? ____________

General type: ____________

Distance/top of rod to floor: ________

Width: ____________

Return: ______ Diameter: ______

Palladian windows:

These are windows that have a separate arched area at the top.

Measurements A through I are exactly like the measurements of the standard window, described on page 134. The only extra measurements that need to be taken are the size and shape of the arch itself and the distance from the top of the arch to the floor.

Measurement J on the Palladian chart is the distance from the outside top of the arch to the floor. Do not make any allowance for baseboards -- measure all the way to the floor.

Measurement K is the vertical distance between the bottom of the arched portion of the window and the top of the lower portion of the window.

Often, this area will be covered with a decorative moulding. If so, don't make any allowance for it.

This measurement is essential if you plan to use a valance over the lower portion of the window and leave the arched portion uncovered.

Measuring the arch is only necessary if you plan to cover it with a treatment. It's fine to leave the arch uncovered if you wish. If you do plan to cover the arch, you must make a template.

Simple measurements of the height and width of the arch aren't enough. These arches are rarely perfect half-circles, even when they look perfectly round and symmetrical. Arched treatments are mounted on non-returnable custom-bent rods that must exactly fit the arch. Don't take shortcuts here -- make a template. This way, you can avoid expensive mistakes.

Take a piece of newspaper (kraft paper, etc.) and tape it to the wall completely covering the arch. Use masking tape and press lightly so that you don't damage the paint.

Trace around the inside and outside edge of the arch, including the straight edge along the bottom of the arch. If the arch has no moulding around the edge, there won't be any outside edge to trace. Take the template down and trim it to a manageable size.

Make sure you label the template clearly so that the workroom will know which window chart it goes with. Also, be sure to mark the right and left side. You don't want to take a chance on the seamstress or workroom inadvertently using the template upside down. In this case, it is very important not to accidentally turn the template upside-down -- these arched windows are usually not perfectly horizontally symmetrical.

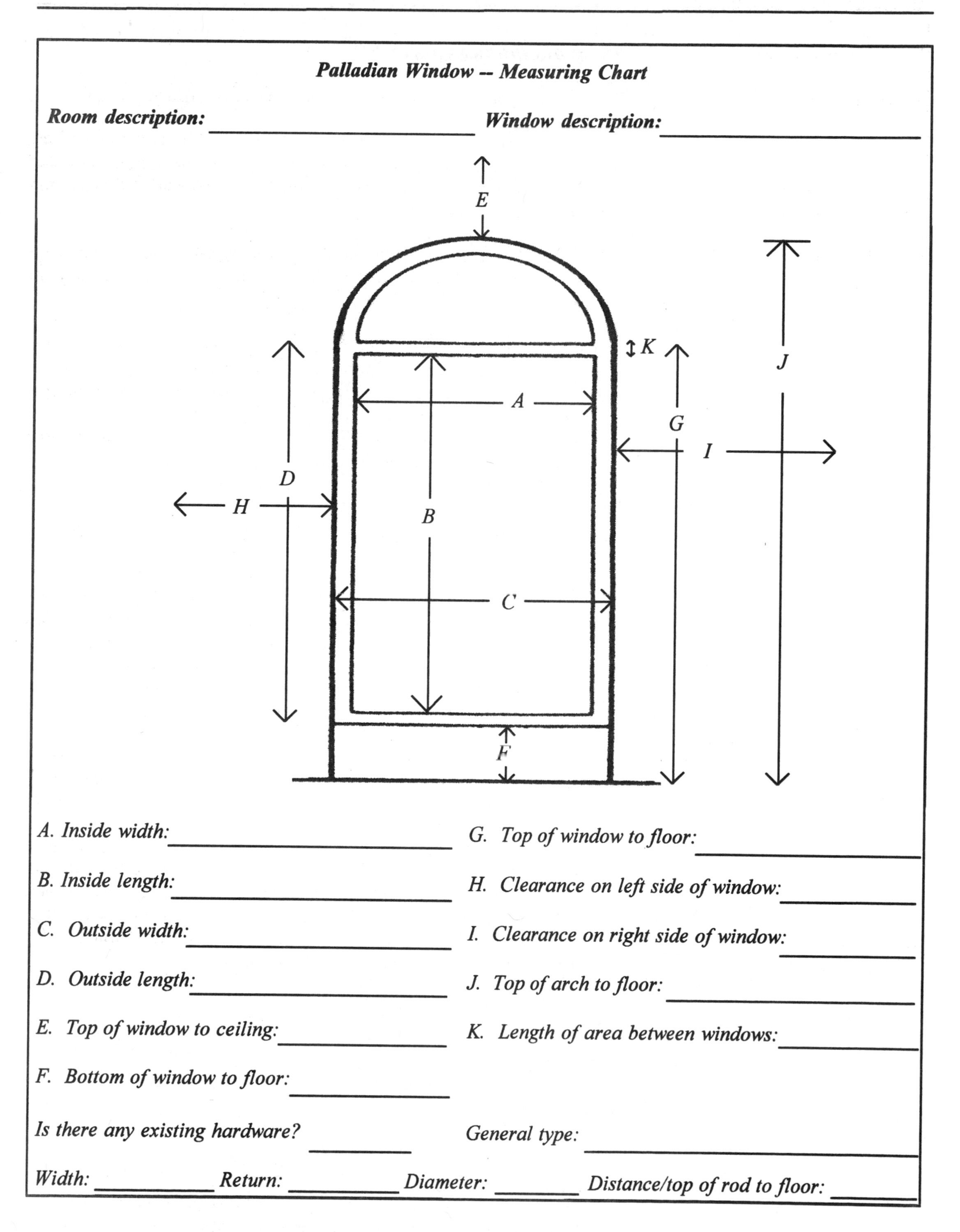

Palladian Window -- Measuring Chart

Room description: ____________________ **Window description:** ____________________

A. Inside width: ____________________

B. Inside length: ____________________

C. Outside width: ____________________

D. Outside length: ____________________

E. Top of window to ceiling: ____________________

F. Bottom of window to floor: ____________________

G. Top of window to floor: ____________________

H. Clearance on left side of window: ____________________

I. Clearance on right side of window: ____________________

J. Top of arch to floor: ____________________

K. Length of area between windows: ____________________

Is there any existing hardware? __________ General type: ____________________

Width: __________ Return: __________ Diameter: __________ Distance/top of rod to floor: __________

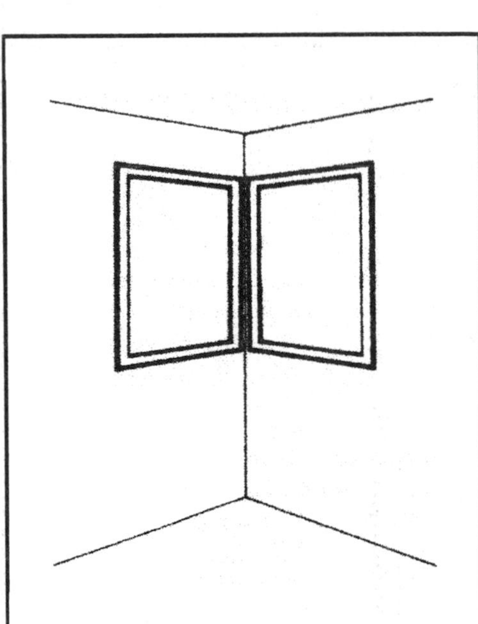

In this example, there is no clear wall space between the windows.

In a case like this, the wall clearance measurements on your chart should be recorded as follows:

Left window: *H* is measured normally. *I* is zero inches.

Right window: *H* is zero inches. *I* is measured normally.

Corner windows:

This is just an arrangement where two standard windows come together at a corner.

Measurements A through I are identical to the measurements described for the standard window measurement chart on page 134.

It is best to record the measurements for both windows together on this chart, instead of recording them individually on the standard window chart, because you will usually have one unified treatment made to cover both windows. By recording the measurements together this way, you can eliminate any possible confusion that the workroom might have about the exact window arrangement.

If there is no clear wall space between the windows, as in the corner illustration at left, the clearances on the appropriate sides of the windows will be zero. Follow the example at left.

Angle If the corner isn't 90 degrees, as might happen in an oddly-shaped room, you will need to make an angle guide for the corner just like the ones described on page 136 for bay window measurements. If no angle measurement is specified, the workroom will assume that the corner is 90 degrees.

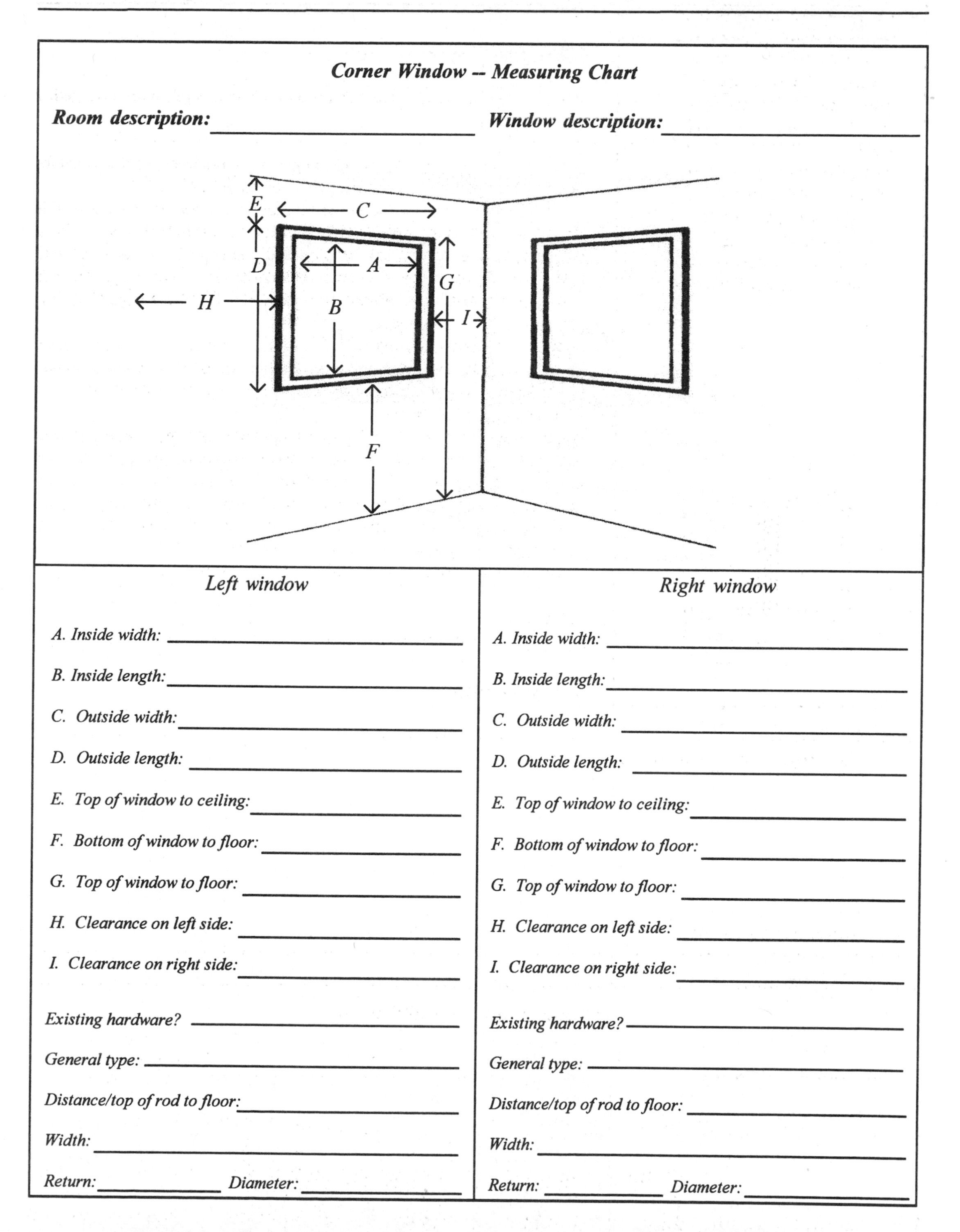

Corner Window -- Measuring Chart

Room description: ____________________ **Window description:** ____________________

Left window	*Right window*
A. Inside width: ______	*A. Inside width:* ______
B. Inside length: ______	*B. Inside length:* ______
C. Outside width: ______	*C. Outside width:* ______
D. Outside length: ______	*D. Outside length:* ______
E. Top of window to ceiling: ______	*E. Top of window to ceiling:* ______
F. Bottom of window to floor: ______	*F. Bottom of window to floor:* ______
G. Top of window to floor: ______	*G. Top of window to floor:* ______
H. Clearance on left side: ______	*H. Clearance on left side:* ______
I. Clearance on right side: ______	*I. Clearance on right side:* ______
Existing hardware? ______	*Existing hardware?* ______
General type: ______	*General type:* ______
Distance/top of rod to floor: ______	*Distance/top of rod to floor:* ______
Width: ______	*Width:* ______
Return: ______ *Diameter:* ______	*Return:* ______ *Diameter:* ______

Sliding glass doors:

The sliding glass door measuring chart is very much like the standard window measurement chart, with a few exceptions:

Measurements A and B You don't need the inside width and length. You can't mount inside-mounted window treatments on a sliding glass door.

Measurement F You don't need to record the distance from the outside bottom edge of the window to the floor because there isn't any.

Measurement G You don't need to record the distance from the top of the window to the floor because, in this case, it is the same as measurement D.

"Which way does the door open?" You do need to note which way the door opens.

If you are having pinch-pleated draperies or vertical blinds made for the door, you may want them to stackback entirely to one side. If so, you will want them to stackback on the side of the door that you don't normally walk through.

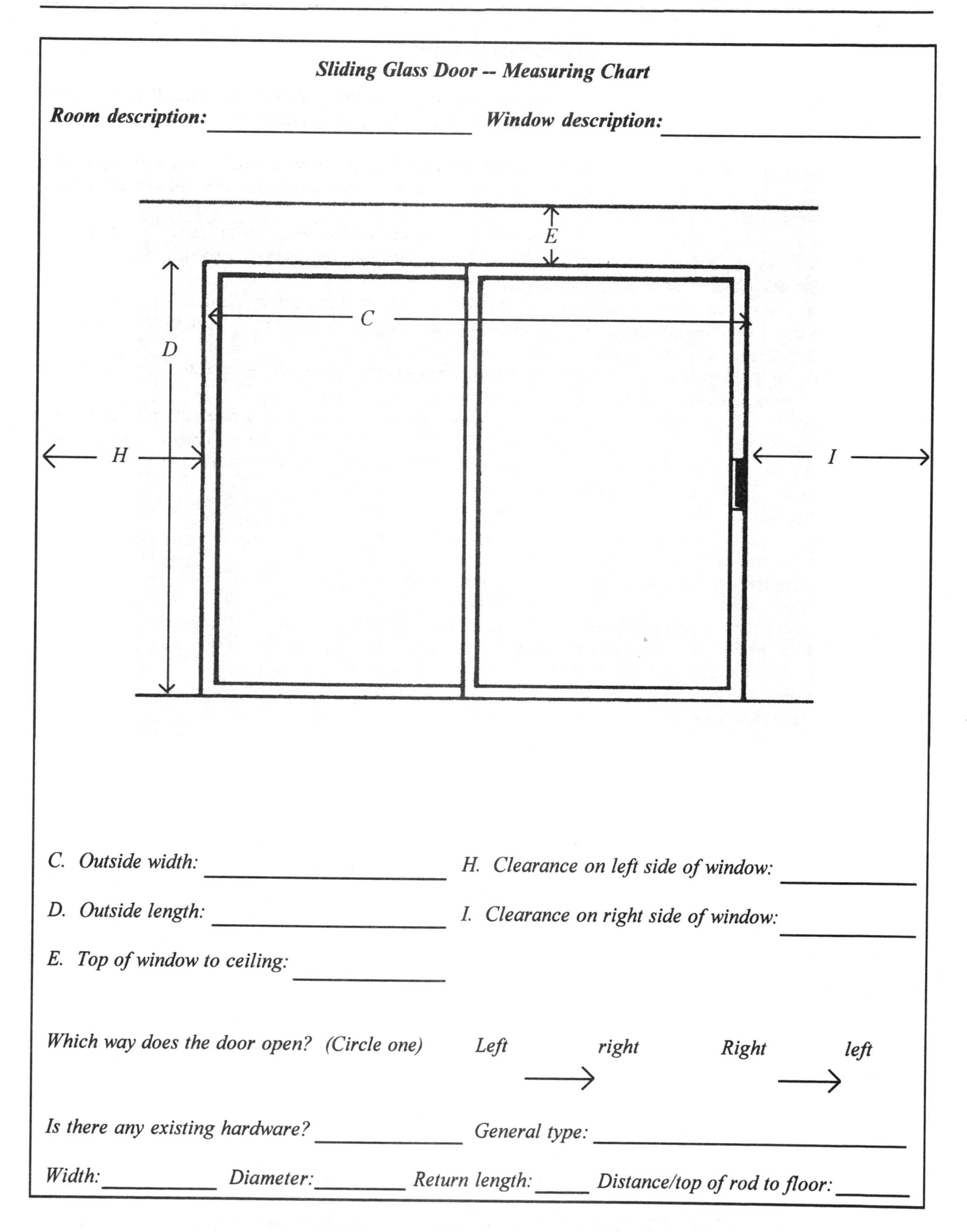
Sliding Glass Door -- Measuring Chart
Room description: ______
Window description: ______
E
C
D
H
I
C. Outside width: ______
D. Outside length: ______
E. Top of window to ceiling: ______
H. Clearance on left side of window: ______
I. Clearance on right side of window: ______
Which way does the door open? (Circle one)
Left
right
Right
left
Is there any existing hardware? ______
General type: ______
Width: ______
Diameter: ______
Return length: ______
Distance/top of rod to floor: ______

French doors:

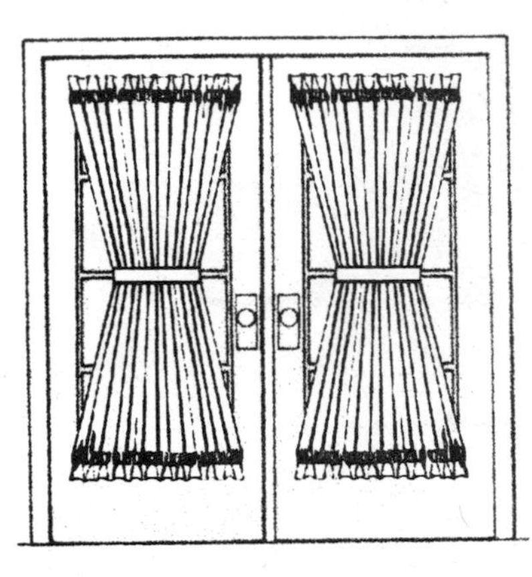

French Door With Hour-Glass Panels

This door measurement is also very much like the standard window measurement chart.

Measurements A, B, F, and G As with the sliding glass door chart, you do not need measurements A, B, F, or G from the standard window chart. It isn't possible to install inside-mounted window treatments on a French door. Measurement F (the distance from the bottom of the window to the floor) is irrelevant in this case. Measurement G (the distance from the top of the window to the floor) is the same as measurement D (the outside length of the window) in this case, so you don't have to take it again.

Measurements J, K, L, and M If you plan to install any treatments on the door itself, such as the hour-glass panels illustrated at left, you also need a few additional measurements.

Measurements J, K, L, and M are the width and length of each door panel. The measurements should be taken about one to two inches outside the glass area of the door, as illustrated at right. You will need these measurements to note the proper placement of any panels or valances, or to determine if you have room to mount these treatments at all. Study the picture of the treatment you have chosen to determine how it should be placed on the door.

"Which way does the door swing open?" You do need to note which way the door swings open.

As you stand in front of the door facing the door on the side on which you plan to mount the window treatment, note whether the door swings open toward you or away from you. It's fine to mount a window treatment on the side that swings open toward you, but you do have to be careful that the draperies or valance will not snag the door in any way.

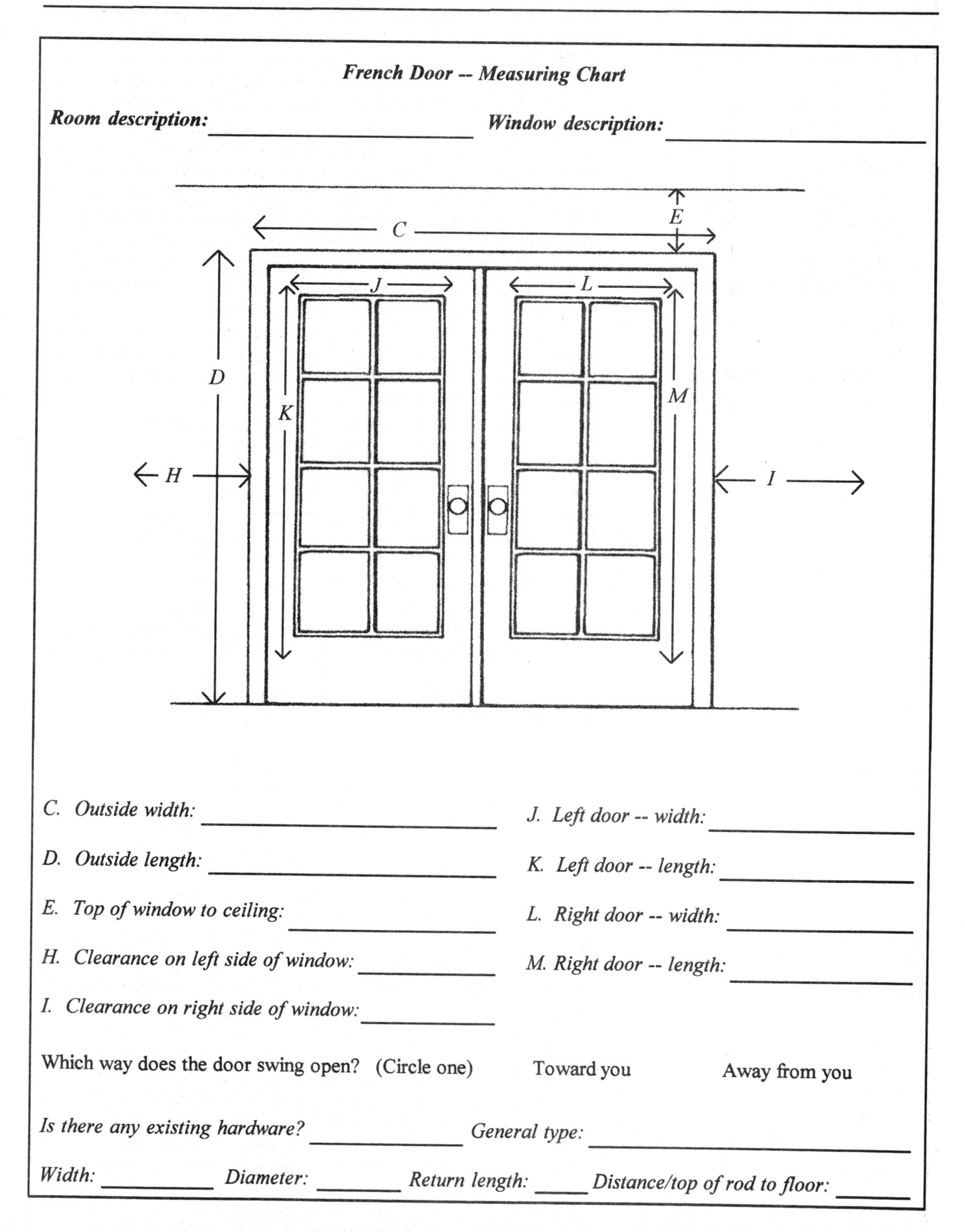

French Door -- Measuring Chart

Room description: ____________________ **Window description:** ____________________

C. *Outside width:* ____________________

D. *Outside length:* ____________________

E. *Top of window to ceiling:* ____________________

H. *Clearance on left side of window:* ____________________

I. *Clearance on right side of window:* ____________________

J. *Left door -- width:* ____________________

K. *Left door -- length:* ____________________

L. *Right door -- width:* ____________________

M. *Right door -- length:* ____________________

Which way does the door swing open? (Circle one) Toward you Away from you

Is there any existing hardware? ______________ *General type:* ____________________

Width: ________ *Diameter:* ________ *Return length:* ________ *Distance/top of rod to floor:* ________

How To Choose The Right Style

There have been many books written on choosing attractive window treatment styles. Many of them are available at your local library and bookstore. You can also get good ideas from the many interior design magazines available at your local library and newsstand.

Some styles are appropriate for traditional rooms. Others look best with contemporary decor. You do need to give some thought to which window treatments will work best with your other furnishings.

However, don't be overly intimidated by all of the choices. This is not rocket science. There are only a few hard and fast rules about what types of treatments you should and should not use with certain types of decor, and they have all been written about extensively in the basic interior design books found in most public libraries. Usually, the window treatments chosen by professional interior designers and interior decorators are simply the ones that their clients expressed a preference for.

In this book, we are discussing practical considerations only. There are very few to keep track of when you are choosing your drapery styles:

View Don't feel compelled to cover up a gorgeous view. If your living room faces out onto a beautiful lake, and you don't require much privacy in that room, just put a simple valance across the top of the window to give it a ''finished'' look.

Of course, it's still a good idea to provide some way of covering the window completely at night or when you will be away. You don't want your home to appear deserted -- this can encourage burglaries. Mini-blinds or pleated shades are inexpensive and very effective. You can keep them pulled up underneath the valance during the day.

Privacy Keep this in mind when you are choosing your fabrics and linings. When you are designing your window treatments for bedrooms and bathrooms, make sure that you choose fabrics and linings that are thick enough not to cast obvious shadows from the inside of the house at night. Naturally, thicker fabrics can't be used with certain styles, as discussed later in the chapter.

Or, if you want to use a softly draped style in a lightweight fabric or lace, you can put a mini-blind or pleated shade behind the soft window treatment and raise it out of sight underneath the valance during the day.

Sunlight Sunlight will fade many of your furnishings. If a room is in strong sunlight, you should consider ordering a window treatment that can be completely closed when the sunlight is at its most intense, such as well-lined draperies or a blackout pleated shade. Otherwise, you may find that your bedcoverings and upholstered furniture are badly faded within a very short time.

Heating and cooling bills Sunlight can substantially increase the internal temp-erature of your home. You should consider having window treatments that can be completely closed during the hottest parts of the day. During winter, this can work in reverse. Bare windows can let a lot of heat escape from your home.

You should also consider having your window treatments made with energy-efficient or blackout linings, as discussed later in the chapter. These specialized drapery linings do have a high initial cost, but you can usually more than recoup their cost in the savings on your heating and cooling bills. Pleated shades are also available with special energy-efficient or blackout linings.

Safety Be sure that your window treatments don't cover any heating elements, such as heating registers or radiators. Some fabrics can melt or catch fire if they hang too close to a heating element.

Accessibility If you are designing treatments to be installed over a set of French doors, make sure that the treatment doesn't block or snag the door in any way.

Flexibility If you are living in an apartment and expect to move into a home soon, or if your job requires you to move frequently, stick to treatments that can be easily moved from place to place. Rod-pocket curtains and valances are ideal. The rods are usually adjustable -- when you buy the rod, you will note on the box that it telescopes to fit a range of window sizes.

Many rod-pocket curtains and valances are also adjustable, unlike treatments such as cornice boards and pinch-pleated draperies that are made to one specific size. Most rod-pocket treatments are intended to be ruched or bunched-up on the rod. This makes them adjustable in width to some extent.

So, if you move to a new home and your new kitchen window is six inches wider than your old one, you should have no problem extending the rod a bit and spreading out your ruched window treatment to cover the extra rod length. Your window treatment won't be quite as full as it was, but this should not be noticeable.

If you had a static window treatment, such as a mini-blind or board-mounted valance, you would usually have no choice but to have a new window treatment made. It is pretty rare to be able to transfer a window treatment that can't have its width adjusted to another home or apartment.

Ease of use If you or a family member are elderly or handicapped, you may wish to choose a style of window treatment that can be automatically opened and closed with a remote control. Remote controls are available for most standard drapery rods and pleated shades.

You should allow a drapery workroom to order the remote control equipment for you, even if you become your own licensed decorator. The equipment is relatively expensive, somewhat complicated, and non-returnable. This is one of those times when paying for a little extra help is a smart idea.

Ask your local drapery workroom for the exact price of the window treatment, including the remote control equipment and professional installation. Remote-controlled window treatments should be installed by a professional drapery installer.

Also, the workroom will need to know that the window treatment is going to be used with automatic equipment. This can sometimes make a difference in the exact way that the treatment is put together.

How To Choose Appropriate Fabrics

Again, we aren't talking about choosing fabric patterns and colors that complement your other furnishings. There are a wide variety of books on that subject, many of which are available at your local library and bookstore.

A beautiful design won't become a beautiful window treatment unless it is made up in an appropriate fabric. When you arrange your own custom window treatment labor with local workrooms and seamstresses, you are responsible for making appropriate fabric choices.

There are a few general guidelines, listed below. There is another book available from this publisher that discusses specific window treatments in more detail: *The Complete Guide To Custom Window Treatments*.

1 You should choose crisp fabrics that will hold pleats well for structured window treatments. For instance, chintz is a good choice for a hobbled Roman shade.

2 You should choose softly draping fabrics for flowing window treatments. Sateen is a good choice for swags, for example.

3 Always use like fabrics together. If you are going to add extra touches, such as ruffles or banding, to a window treatment, choose fabrics for these embellishments that are similar in type and weight to the main fabric used for the window treatment. For instance, if you want to add a ruffle to a chintz drapery, choose a chintz fabric for the ruffle, not a sateen or silk.

4 Never use fabrics that have tiny patterns and highly contrasting colors on large window treatments. Avoid using tiny patterns, such as pinstripes or small houndstooth checks, in highly contrasting color schemes, such as black-and-white or red-and-yellow, on any window treatment that will cover a large area, such as curtains or draperies. These patterns give some people a headache.

Sheets

Sheets are fine for a few treatments, such as pouf valances and simple curtains, but you really shouldn't use them for most styles.

Standard cotton sheeting material is an extremely low-quality decorative fabric, and no amount of skill on the workroom's part can ever change that. No matter how much money you invest in skilled custom sewing, your draperies will still look cheap if you don't use quality decorative fabrics. You can't pick a beautiful flowing drapery style out of a design magazine, have it made up in sheets, and expect it to look anything like the treatment in the picture. It won't.

If you just want to have a simple valance in an appropriate style made out of a sheet to match a ready-made bedspread or comforter set, and you aren't going to any major expense for the custom sewing labor, it's fine. Just realize that window treatments that are made out of sheets will never look as good or wear as well as window treatments that are made out of decorative fabrics.

Should You Line Your Window Treatments?

Definitely. Yes, there will be some extra cost -- about $2.00 to $3.00 per yard for standard drapery lining. However, there are many benefits to lining your window treatments. There are four basic reasons to line your window treatments:

1 Many neighborhood associations have rules stating that your window treatments must present a uniform appearance when seen from the street. This means white or off-white linings on your window treatments.

In most areas of the country, an association can (and occasionally will) sue you if you don't comply with the rules -- especially if you live in a historic district. Apartment leases usually have similar requirements.

2 Your window treatments will look much better if they are lined. Decorative fabrics are meant to be used with proper linings. Many of these fabrics have a "cheap" appearance if they are used without a lining in window treatments, tablecloths, or dust ruffles.

Also, many treatments will show unattractive dark shadows where widths of fabrics have been seamed together if no lining is used and light is allowed to shine through the window treatment.

3 Many workrooms, seamstresses, interior decorators, interior designers, and retail stores won't have anything to do with unlined window treatments because they are afraid of harming their business reputations. Allowing the wrong side of the decorative fabric to be seen from the street is considered to be in very poor taste in the U. S. Many of these businesses simply refuse to make or sell unlined treatments because they do not want their businesses to be associated in any way with what is considered in the industry to be substandard workmanship.

4 Energy-efficient and blackout linings can actually save you money over the long run. While the initial cost will be higher, you should recoup the cost of the lining many times over in the savings on your heating and cooling bills. Windows are essentially big holes in your insulation. A single pane of glass doesn't help hold in your heat or air conditioning very well. Energy-efficient drapery linings can make a big difference.

Ask your workroom about the drapery linings it has available. Some buy linings in bulk and can give you a very good price. Home seamstresses generally do not stock linings -- they expect their customers to provide all necessary materials.

Many telephone fabric ordering services carry a variety of standard, energy-efficient, and blackout drapery linings. Unless you can get a better deal through your workroom, these services will normally be the cheapest places to buy lining.

Local fabric stores also carry a variety of drapery linings, but they generally have higher prices than workrooms or telephone ordering services.

No-Sew Window Treatments

There have been a number of books written about no-sew window treatments. Many of them should be available at your local library and bookstore.

They have some excellent suggestions, and instructions, for creating a variety of simple and elegant window treatments without going to the expense of custom sewing.

Some treatments lend themselves well to no-sew construction. Poor-boy swags come immediately to mind.

Most local fabric stores carry a variety of special kits and drapery brackets that are designed to help you make your own window treatments. Most are easy to use and very effective.

Drapery Hardware

You may or may not need to buy separate drapery hardware. Board-mounted window treatments, such as cornice boards and most swags, don't need a separate drapery or curtain rod. All you need are brackets and screws to mount the treatment to your walls.

Other treatments will require a curtain rod, drapery rod, or swagholders to mount them to your walls. Drapery hardware comes in an infinite variety of shapes, sizes, styles, and colors, but it all boils down to a very few basic types.

Chapter 10 discusses drapery hardware in more depth: where to buy it, what styles are available, and how to get the best bargains. There are a few general points to be aware of:

1 Try to get the hardware for board-mounted treatments provided free with your order. You could buy these "L-brackets" and screws at your local hardware store very inexpensively, but you might be able to get the work-room or seamstress to include them with your order. Some professional interior decorators and interior designers ask the workroom or seamstress to supply these.

Ask. If the seamstress or workrooms agrees, make sure your contract specifies that all hardware, including screws and brackets, will be included on board mounted treatments. If there is an extra charge, and you might be able to persuade the seamstress or workroom not to charge for this during the slow business seasons of winter and summer, it shouldn't exceed $5.00 per treatment.

2 Buy your drapery hardware before you order your custom window treatments. You should always give the measurements of the drapery rods or other hardware to the seamstress or workroom. These measurements, especially diameter, do occasionally vary -- particularly on wrought-iron or wooden rods.

Do wait, however, to actually put the hardware up on your walls. It is best to wait until you have the finished window treatments in hand to install your drapery hardware.

3 When considering prices, don't forget the drapery hardware. Some types of window treatments can be made to be mounted on a separate drapery rod or pre-mounted on a covered board. You can choose either one, but you should be sure that you are comparing all of the costs involved when you make your decision.

The price of the covered board is normally included in the labor price of board-mounted treatments. The price of the drapery rod is normally not included in the labor price of rod-mounted treatments. When you are deciding whether you want a board-mounted treatment or a rod-mounted treatment, don't forget to factor the price of the separate drapery rod into your decision.

For instance, if you are comparing costs of a board-mounted swag treatment versus a rod-mounted swag treatment, take the cost of the separate rod into consideration. It won't do you any good to save $20.00 on the labor price by choosing the rod-mounted treatment if you then have to go and buy a $30.00 rod to hang it on.

Should You Install Your Own Custom Window Treatments?

Yes. Most window treatments are very easy to install. The only exceptions are motorized window treatments, such as the remote-controlled treatments discussed on page 147, and some of the more unusual and unique treatments. You should be able to install any basic treatment by yourself.

However, if you have a more unusual window treatment, such as a swag treatment or balloon valance, or if your window is an unusual size or shape, you may need to hire a professional installer or consult a book about window treatment installation.

There are a few types of window treatments that require some extra work when they are put up, particularly pinch-pleated draperies. Some window treatments have to be arranged or "trained" after they have been installed, or they won't look right.

I have written another book, *The Complete Guide To Custom Window Treatments*, that discusses all of the different types of window treatments in detail, including specific installation instructions for each. We have installed just about every type of window treatment that a customer could dream up over the years, so this book covers virtually any possible window treatment type or special installation circumstances that could apply to your decorating job.

There are normally no special tools required for installation. A screwdriver should be all you need. If you have a drill with a screwdriver attachment or an automatic screwdriver, you will find that this makes the job easier and faster. Drapery hardware normally comes with complete installation instructions and all necessary screws and brackets.

In a few cases, such as mounting window treatments in a concrete block room or in a room with extremely tall windows, you may need extra help. In this case, ask the workroom or seamstress to refer you to a local drapery installer. Read Chapter 18 thoroughly for further instructions on getting the best work at the best price from any local craftsperson.

Unless you have a very unusual home, you should certainly be able to do your own installation. Installation isn't difficult as long as you have the correct instructions. Before hiring an installer, study the instructions on page 152 about board-mounted treatments, the package inserts that come with your drapery hardware, or the instructions in *The Complete Guide To Custom Window Treatments*. Don't hire an installer unless you really need one.

When you are deciding which treatments to order for your home, don't forget to include any installation charges in your price comparisons. Most drapery installers will charge you at least $50.00 just to come out to your home, plus an added charge for each treatment. Most window treatments will cost you at least $20.00 each to have professionally installed -- more if the treatment is unusually large, complex, or installed on a hard-to-reach window. Find out what extra installation expenses (if any) might be involved before choosing the types of window treatments you wish to order.

Installing Board-Mounted Treatments

Sunbursts, shades, pelmets, cornice boards, many swag treatments, and many valances are board-mounted. Installation is very simple, and very similar for all of these treatments.

The technique does vary slightly depending on whether the treatment is inside-mounted (as with sunbursts, some pelmets, and some valances) or outside-mounted (shades, cornice boards, swag treatments, some pelmets, and many valances).

Hardware All you need are "L-brackets", illustrated at top right, and screws. Some stores call these brackets "angle irons". You can buy these at any hardware store or home center. You might be able to get the workroom or seamstress to include these with your order. Some stock them anyway, and you might as well save yourself a trip.

L-bracket

If you do have to buy your own hardware, choose L-brackets that are about three inches long on each side. This is just a general size range -- don't worry if the size varies a bit on the L-brackets carried at your local hardware store. If you must vary from the standard size, go smaller rather than bigger. Bigger L-brackets can sometimes create problems with installing layered window treatments.

Also, make sure that the screws are not so long that they will go completely through the board. Measure the thickness of the boards on your finished window treatments before buying the screws. Most window treatment boards are 3/4 inch thick, so you will probably choose 1/2 to 5/8 inch screws. It doesn't make a bit of difference what kind of screws you buy, although you will usually find Phillips-head screws a bit easier to install.

Inside-mounted board-mounted treatment

Inside-mount Inside-mounted treatments are installed inside the window frame, as illustrated at right. The front of the window treatment should be approximately flush with the wall or window moulding. Never allow an inside-mounted window treatment to project out into the room -- it looks sloppy.

Your window treatments will be already attached to the board, of course. The window treatments aren't shown in the illustrations at right so that you can see the proper placement of the board.

Attach one side of each L-bracket to the underside of the window treatment board, as shown at center right. Position each bracket at the center of the short side of each board.

Then, have a helper position and hold the board in the window and screw the other side of each L-bracket to the wall inside your window frame.

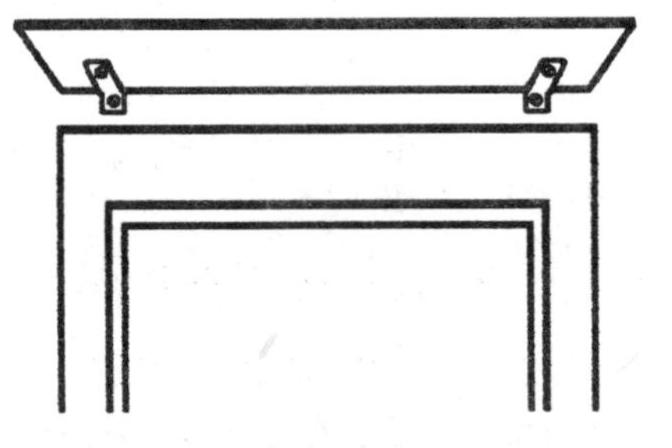

Outside-mounted board-mounted treatment

Outside-mount Outside-mounted treatments are installed outside the window and any window mouldings or other outside-mounted treatments, as shown at below right.

Attach the brackets to the wall first. Hold the window treatment up to the wall and position it properly. Use a pencil to lightly trace a line on the wall along the bottom edge of the board. This line will mark the place where the angle of the bracket should be mounted. Attach the brackets to the wall.

Set the board on the brackets, position it properly, and screw the brackets to the underside of the board.

How Much Will Your Window Treatments Cost?

That is a book in itself. There are so many variations: size, style, extra touches, etc. You will have to discuss prices directly with the workroom or seamstress you choose to work with.

There are a few general points that we can discuss here:

1 If you are having many window treatments made at the same time, for several rooms at once, you should be able to negotiate a better price for the treatments as a group than if you price the treatments out individually. Always ask for a total quote for your entire window treatment order.

Most seamstresses and workrooms want very much to get these large jobs -- they don't come along as often as you might think. Many of these businesses will go to greater lengths to get a large job, and that often means being willing to give a bigger discount. Your chances of getting a good discount improve greatly during slow business seasons of summer and winter. Chapter 18 discusses bargaining with workrooms and seamstresses in much greater detail.

2 Sometimes, a home seamstress will give you a better price than a wholesale workroom on the same job because seamstresses tend to be more limited in their ways of getting customers and tend to get fewer offers of work. They have a greater need for your job, and are therefore more likely to give you the best price. Sometimes, but not always.

3 Workrooms can sometimes give you a better price on certain kinds of window treatments because they usually have better and more specialized equipment than a home seamstress. The superior automation of a workroom often permits the workroom to give customers a better price on certain furnishings than a home seamstress can.

How To Properly Order Custom Window Treatments

You need to specify several things about your window treatments in your contract with the seamstress or workroom: finished width, finished length, return length (if applicable), rod-mounted or board-mounted, the specific type and size of drapery hardware you plan to use (if applicable), placement of any embellishments such as ruffles or trim, and the exact style of window treatment.

Most disputes over incorrect window treatment orders are the result of misunderstandings, not deliberate fraud or sloppiness on the part of the workroom or seamstress. Most of these disputes can be prevented before they happen if you plan ahead. There are many simple things you can do to eliminate confusion and potential mistakes on your order:

1 Many workrooms and seamstresses will have special forms for you to fill out with these details. If not, just write them down clearly on a sheet of paper. Always put the details of each window on a separate sheet of paper. This can prevent many mistakes and mix-ups.

2 Describe the fabric that will be used for the window treatment on your order form: "*rose-colored chintz*", "*small gold paisley on a blue background*", etc. This can help prevent mix-ups that can occur if your order becomes separated from your fabric.

3 Cut a small swatch of your fabric, about two inches square, and staple it to your order. Staple a small swatch of any trims, fringes, or accent fabrics to your order, too.

4 Enclose a photocopy or sketch of the treatment you wish to order. Most of you will be ordering window treatments from pictures in books and magazines, so this won't be difficult.

If you see an attractive window treatment in a model home, ask permission to take a snapshot. Most model home salespeople will allow this. Enclose a copy of the snapshot with your order.

5 Enclose a copy of your measurement chart for each window with your order. Remember that it is your responsibility to specify all necessary details to the seamstress or workroom. Leave nothing open to misunderstanding.

6 Take a few minutes to discuss your order with the seamstress or workroom. When you drop off your fabrics and paperwork, take about five minutes to read over your order with the seamstress or workroom manager to make sure that there are no misunderstandings or omissions.

7 Never pay in full in advance. A deposit equal to one-half of the labor charge is the most you should ever pay up front. Holding back one-half of the total labor price is customary in the trade, when a deposit is required at all, and it's your best insurance against getting stuck with an incorrectly made order.

You may or may not have to pay a deposit. Most home seamstresses don't ask for deposits. Some workrooms do. Read Chapter 18 for more details about deposits paid to local workrooms and craftspeople.

8 Take the standard delivery times into consideration. Most custom window treatment orders will take about three to four weeks to have delivered, a bit less in the summer and winter.

Around the end of September, many seamstresses and workrooms will start taking longer to complete orders because they are inundated with orders to be delivered before Thanksgiving and Christmas. Some workrooms and seamstresses stop taking any new orders around the middle of November because they already have all of the work they can handle before Christmas. The waiting time is usually about the same from home seamstresses and workrooms.

Curtains vs. Draperies

Many consumers use these terms interchangeably, but there is a difference. If you can pull on a cord and have the window treatment automatically open and close -- it's a drapery. If you have to pull the panels open and shut by hand -- it's a curtain. It's important not to confuse these terms when you are discussing your decorating job with a seamstress or workroom.

When you are deciding whether or not you want a drapery or a curtain, give a lot of thought to how often you will be opening and closing the draperies. In some homes, I see expensive, custom-made, pinch-pleated draperies that are held open with decorative tiebacks and are never closed. Often, the homeowner has sheer draperies, blinds, or pleated shades underneath that can be closed for privacy. This is a big waste of money.

There is no point in having expensive draperies made and buying an expensive drapery rod if you never plan to close the draperies. You would be much better off to buy a less expensive curtain rod and have side curtain panels made for your window.

Are "Designer Mistakes" a Good Buy In Window Treatments?

They certainly can be. Fabric stores in some areas have recently begun advertising returned and incorrectly-made window treatments at up to 90% off retail. You certainly could get an incredible bargain. However, there are a couple of limitations you should be aware of.

You are likely to find that the selection is extremely sparse. There really aren't that many returned and incorrectly-made window treatments out there. Custom-made window treatments are virtually never returnable -- usually when customers have a change of heart, they are stuck.

Also, incorrectly-made draperies are usually altered. Most mistakes can be fixed, and it is usually more cost-effective for the designer or decorator to pay to have the mistakes fixed than to try and sell the incorrectly-made window treatment and pay to have a whole new window treatment made up.

Watch out for window treatments that "only need a little alteration" to be right for your home. Sometimes, those little alterations are more expensive than the original window treatment. Some window treatments cannot be altered at all.

If you buy a window treatment that needs to be cut down to fit your windows, it usually isn't simply a matter of chopping off a few inches. In most cases, the window treatment will have to be taken completely apart and remade. Often, this is actually more expensive than just having a window treatment made up in the correct size to begin with.

If you find a returned or incorrectly-made window treatment that is the right style, color, and size for your window (you probably have a better chance of winning the lottery), buy it. This is your lucky day.

However, if you find a window treatment that needs any adjustments to be usable in your home, no matter how simple or slight the adjustments seem, call a seamstress or workroom in your area to find out what the alterations are likely to cost before you buy it.

Ready-made Window Treatments

You can find a limited variety of window treatments at linens stores and factory outlets. Often, bedding manufacturers will make a simple rod-pocket curtain and valance to match a ready-made bedding ensemble. If you are looking for a window treatment to match ready-made bedding, you will usually find that it is cheaper to buy one of these ready-made treatments -- assuming that one is available in the style and size you want -- than it is to buy a sheet and have one custom-made.

Other than that, there really aren't any ready-made treatments out there.

Most styles must be made to fit your windows, which makes them unsuitable for mass production.

Factory Outlets

There are a few factory outlets out there that carry a limited number of sizes, colors, and styles. If you are nearby and you are looking for a very simple window treatment, such as a beige rod-pocket curtain, check these outlets out. Don't travel a long way to visit these outlets without calling ahead. They are unlikely to have what you need and, if they do, the total dollar savings compared to other discount sources won't be much.

Ready-made window treatments that are made to match ready-made bedding are normally sold at bedding factory outlets. These outlets are listed in Chapter 8.

Home Decor
Peach Factory Stores
Exit 46 off I-75
Byron, GA 31008
(912) 956-1855

Home Decor
Lake Park Factory Stores
Exit 2 off I-75
Lake Park, GA 31636
(912) 559-1177

Curtain Factory Outlet
Wampanoag Mill Factory Outlet Center
Alden St. and Quequechan St
Fall River, MA 02721
(508) 678-6996

Drapery Outlet
2320 Maple Ave.
Burlington, NC 27216
(910) 222-6090

Interior Designers, Interior Decorators, and Retail Stores

Never have your window treatments made at any of these businesses. It is standard practice in the industry for these businesses to hand your order over to a local seamstress or workroom and collect a 100% commission for their trouble. It is a ridiculous and totally unnecessary waste of money.

You should have no difficulty finding at least one seamstress or wholesale workroom in your area that is willing to work directly with you, especially if you are well-informed about window treatments and shop during the slow seasons of the year. Read Chapter 18 for complete instructions on finding and working with local seamstresses and workrooms.

Of course, if you become your own decorator, you can work with local seamstresses and wholesale workrooms at straight wholesale prices any time of year. Read Chapter 19 for complete instructions on becoming your own decorator.

If you hire an interior designer or interior decorator to have an unusual window treatment made for you, there is a very high probability that the decorator or designer will simply call up the workroom or seamstress for advice, and collect a 100% commission for making a simple phone call that you could easily have made for yourself. That was the standard procedure with most of the designers and decorators we worked with over the years.

Wholesale

As discussed in this chapter, you should always have your custom window treatments made by a wholesale seamstress or workroom. It is not necessary to be a decorator in order to do this. You should have no difficulty finding at least one seamstress or workroom that will work directly with consumers, often at straight wholesale prices, particularly during the slow business seasons of summer and winter.

It generally isn't practical to buy ready-made window treatments wholesale, even if you become your own decorator. Companies that sell ready-made window treatments usually sell in bulk to large retail stores and store chains. Professional interior decorators and interior designers rarely order ready-made treatments for their clients. They almost always have these window treatments custom-made.

Recommendations

1 Take your own window measurements, select your own window treatment styles, and choose your own fabrics. This is not difficult. Everything you need to know is available in this and other books.

2 If you want a ready-made style, such as simple rod-pocket curtains or a pouf valance, check out factory outlets.

3 Don't overlook "designer mistakes". They can be incredible bargains, IF (and this is a big IF) you can find exactly what you need. Be very wary of buying any designer mistakes that must be altered for use in your home. Always check with a workroom or seamstress first to find out how much those alterations are likely to cost.

4 If you want custom-made window treatments, deal directly with a local wholesale workroom or seamstress. This is becoming more and more common these days. Consult a book about custom window treatments, such as *The Complete Guide To Custom Window Treatments*, for instructions on ordering more complex window treatments, such as swags and balloon valances.

5 Never waste your money buying custom window treatments through an interior decorator, interior designer, or retail store.

Chapter 8

Bed Treatments

Interior decorators, interior designers, and retail stores order their custom bed treatments -- bedspreads, comforters, shams, dust ruffles, etc. -- from wholesale custom workrooms. So can you, at a savings of up to 50% off retail. There is no need to pay any commissions to middlemen. Many custom workrooms will sell directly to consumers. Others only work with wholesale customers, so you may wish to become your own decorator, as discussed in Chapter 19.

Most major manufacturers of ready-made bed treatments sell directly to the public through factory outlets all over the United States. There are many telephone ordering services that have great bargains, too -- even on luxury bedding imported from Italy and Switzerland. There is no reason to ever pay retail for ready-made bedspreads, comforters, dust ruffles, shams, or sheets. You can easily save up to 50% off retail on new first quality bedding. You can usually save up to 75% if you purchase seconds or closeouts.

This chapter will show you how to get great deals on bed treatments, no matter what type you are looking for.

How To Properly Measure For Custom Bed Treatments

There are a few general guidelines you need to be aware of:

1. Always make up your bed with any linens or blankets that you would normally use in the winter before measuring for custom bed treatments.

2. Always use a steel tape measure, never cloth or plastic, because cloth and plastic can stretch and give inaccurate measurements.

3. Always record measurements in inches only, never feet and inches. This is standard in the industry. It is best to record the measurements in inches as you are taking them. If you record them in feet and inches and have to recalculate the measurements later, you might make an expensive math error.

Measuring Chart

You may photocopy the chart at right. Fill in the measurements and give the chart to the workroom or seamstress stapled to your custom bed treatment order. This will eliminate a lot of the confusion that can occur with bed treatment orders.

Be sure to clearly identify the bed the chart belongs with in the blanks marked ***Room description*** and ***Bed description***. These are provided in case you have a situation where there is more than one bed in the same room -- two twin beds in a guest room, for instance.

Measurement A and B are the width and length of the mattress. Nothing complicated there.

Measurement C is the distance from the top of your mattress to the floor. This measurement is used only for bedspreads.

Measurement D is the distance from the top of your mattress to the top of the box springs. If you have a bed with side rails, such as a poster bed, you will instead take the measurement from the top of your mattress to the top of the rail. This measurement is only used for coverlets and comforters.

Measurement E is the distance from the top of your box springs to the floor. If you have a bed, usually a traditional wooden bed, with rails down either side, make sure that you measure over the railing, not under it. If you were to measure underneath the rails, straight down to the floor, your dust ruffle would be too short when you actually put it on the bed.

Custom Bed Treatments

You can have virtually any type of custom bed treatment made by a seamstress or workroom: bedspreads, comforters, duvet covers, dust ruffles, pillow shams, accent pillows, even sheets.

Custom bedding is an enormous topic to discuss, much too complex for this book. I have written another book, *The Complete Guide To Custom Bed Treatments*, that discusses all types of custom bedding in much greater detail. It is available from this publisher.

I recommend that you not hire an interior designer or interior decorator to help you design your custom bed treatments. They typically have no training whatsoever in the proper manufacture of custom furnishings.

Down Comforters and Pillows

Down comforters and pillows are very easy to order directly from the manufacturer. These factories have been at the forefront of the movement to sell directly to the consumer and cut out the middlemen. Delivery times on most merchandise is very quick -- about a week to ten days.

Although there are down bedding manufacturers who sell only to the trade, their prices are only very slightly lower than the prices from manufacturers who also sell to the public.

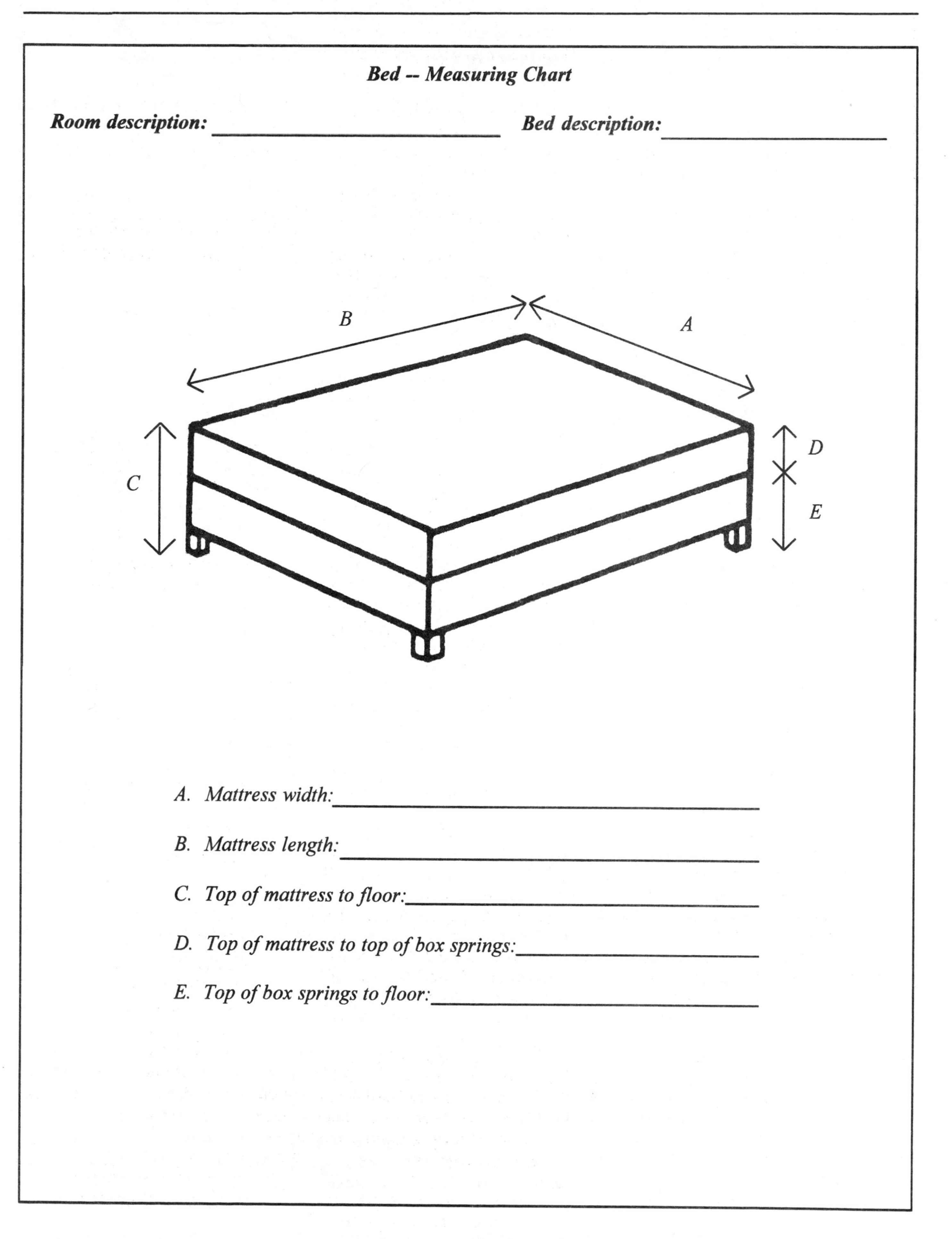

Bed -- Measuring Chart

Room description: ______________________ **Bed description:** ______________________

A. *Mattress width:* ______________________

B. *Mattress length:* ______________________

C. *Top of mattress to floor:* ______________________

D. *Top of mattress to top of box springs:* ______________________

E. *Top of box springs to floor:* ______________________

Telephone Ordering Services

Down Products

Coming Home By Lands' End
(Call for free catalog)
1 Lands' End Lane
Dodgeville, WI 53595
(800) 345-3696

The Company Store
(Call for free catalog)
500 Company Store Rd.
LaCrosse, WI 54601
(800) 323-8000

Cuddledown of Maine
(Call for free catalog)
312 Canco Rd.
Portland, ME 04104
(800) 323-6793

Heavenly Down
(Call for free catalog)
7245 Whipple Ave. NW
N. Canton, OH 44720
(800) 898-3696

J. Schachter Co.
(Send $1.00 for catalog)
85 Ludlow St.
New York, NY 10002
(800) INTO-BED

You will usually be better off to stick to the companies that will sell directly to consumers because you will be able to enjoy the protection of using your credit card. The companies listed at left all have generous return policies, as enforced by federal laws regarding mail order sales and credit card purchases.

This is particularly important when you are buying down. You don't want to buy a down comforter only to find that you or a member of your family are allergic to it. If you use your credit card to buy from the companies listed below and you later find that you are allergic to down, you won't be stuck with products you can't use.

If you already know that you are allergic to down, or later find that you are, the J. Schachter Co. and Cuddledown of Maine (left) each carry a hypo-allergenic synthetic down substitute in a variety of comforters, pillows, and other bedding products.

Cleaning down Down can be machine-washed and dried, but manufacturers recommend that you do this only when the down product has been stained. They recommend that you do not wash down on a regular basis as you would other types of linens.

You should always use pillowcases and comforter covers (also called duvet covers) to cover your down product during use. Then the cover can be washed regularly instead of the down itself, greatly extending the useful life of your down comforter or pillow.

A special trick you can use to keep down from clumping when you wash it is to put a couple of clean tennis shoes or tennis balls in the dryer with your down product. These objects will break up any clumps in your down comforter or pillow that may have formed during washing.

Many manufacturers recommend that you not dry clean your down furnishings because dry cleaning strips the down of essential natural oils and reduces its quality and useful life.

Special Considerations For Children Never allow a baby to play or sleep on a featherbed. They are very soft, and can cause a baby to smother. Some down catalogs feature cute pictures of babies on featherbeds, not always with an accompanying warning.

A thick down comforter could also pose the same threat of smothering for a baby. It is best to use blankets that are relatively thin and that the baby cannot bury his or her face in. There are down comforters that are specifically made to be used in cribs, but I recommend against using them.

You may wish to avoid buying down of any kind for a baby or small child, unless your child's pediatrician approves.

There are some doctors who believe that exposing babies and small children to allergenic substances, such as down, can actually cause or exacerbate life-long allergies.

Some down manufacturers readily acknowledged these problems when I called them -- others denied that they exist. Get your own doctor's advice to be certain that down is safe for your child.

Special Note For Parents

You will have no difficulty finding seamstresses who are willing to make custom comforters, bumpers, canopies, or any other furnishings to be used in and around your baby's crib, but it's not a good idea.

Most parents would find custom crib bedding ridiculously expensive, anyway, and not buy it on that basis. However, our custom workroom did get several requests each year for custom canopies, bumpers, comforters, etc., "for the baby who has everything". So, although custom baby bedding is something most of you would never consider from a cost standpoint, I still feel compelled to point out some safety concerns that most parents are probably unaware of.

Ready-made bedding that is intended to be used in a crib has to meet strict federal safety standards. All fabrics must be fire-retardant (most decorative fabrics are not). All embellishments -- such as ribbons, ruffles, and buttons -- must be very firmly attached to ensure that the baby cannot remove them and possibly choke on them. Bumpers and canopies must be made in such a way that the baby cannot become entangled in them and possibly strangle. All seams must be very secure -- there have been cases of babies pulling stuffing material out of comforters or bumpers through a hole in the seam and choking on it.

Most home furnishings seamstresses and workrooms have no training or experience whatsoever in properly making bedding for babies. This is a relatively rare request from customers. There is no governmental regulation or inspection of general home furnishings workrooms and seamstresses to ensure that custom crib bedding is being made to federal child safety standards.

Many seamstresses and workrooms will take your money without protest, but you really should not approach them with this kind of work. Our workroom always refused these jobs. We didn't feel qualified to do this type of work to adequate safety standards. We felt that we should leave this kind of work to those companies who do this type of work every day, have to meet federal guidelines and pass safety inspections, and are very familiar with the proper safety standards that need to be met.

You can also receive a safety brochure by sending a self-addresses stamped envelope to the Juvenile Products Manufacturers Association at the following address:

JPMA Safety Brochure
236 Route 38 W., Suite 100
Moorestown, NJ 08057

You may also phone them at (609) 231-8500 if you have any concerns that are not addressed in the brochure. The JPMA is a private association of manufacturers that certifies all types of juvenile products for safety.

Ready-Made Bed Treatments

You should always buy ready-made bedspreads, comforters, shams, dust ruffles, and sheets from factory outlets and telephone ordering services. Any other source is going to charge you way too much, up to twice as much as you would pay for the very same product at an outlet or from a telephone ordering service. Factory outlets and telephone ordering services will be discussed further later in the chapter.

Major Bedding Mfrs

Burlington Industries
1345 Avenue of the Americas
New York, NY 10105
(212) 621-3000

Dan River
1001 W. Main St.
Danville, VA 24541
(804) 799-7256

Fieldcrest-Cannon
P. O. Box 107
Highway 14
Eden, NC 27288
(919) 627-3444

J. P. Stevens
1185 Avenue of the Americas
New York, NY 10036
(212) 930-2000

Nettle Creek
P. O. Box 9
2200 Peacock Rd.
Richmond, IN 47374
(317) 962-1555

Revman
1211 Avenue of the Americas
New York, NY 10036
(212) 840-7780

Royalton
Division of the Bibb Company
1301 Avenue of the Americas
New York, NY 10019
(212) 247-0466

Springmaid-Wamsutta
1285 Avenue of the Americas
New York, NY 10019
(212) 903-2073

Westpoint-Pepperell
P. O. Box 609
Lanette, AL 31833
(706) 645-4000

How To Locate Bedding With Your Child's Favorite Cartoon Character

What do you do when your child insists on having bedding with a favorite cartoon or television character, and you can't find it at the store? After all, stores tend to carry only the few most popular characters. What about all of the other ones? And you can forget trying to get your child to make an easier-to-find selection.

Calling local stores to ask probably won't help you unless products featuring that character are actually on the shelf. There is no easy way for store salespeople to look this information up to special-order bedding, although there should be because I have needed it on several occasions. I once helped one of our staff designers get very big decorating job for our outlet store because I was able to track down a ''Cinderella'' bedspread for the homeowner's daughter.

Now, there is a catalog devoted to Disney products where you can order bedding, among other things, featuring Disney characters. You can receive information or a free catalog by calling (800) 328-0612. They even have stores in some cities.

If your child wants bedding with a specific cartoon character on it (other than Disney characters), and your local linens store doesn't have it in stock, there is still a way to locate it.

At the end of the television show (there's always a television show) featuring the character, you will see the name of the production company. You can usually get the production company's phone number from Los Angeles information at 213-555-1212.

Call the production company and ask which bedding manufacturer is licensed to produce bedding with that particular character, and then call that bedding manufacturer to ask where the retailer closest to you is located. You can also check the list of factory outlets given later in this chapter. An outlet might or might not have the exact cartoon you are trying to locate -- call ahead to check. The major ready-made bedding manufacturers and their phone numbers are listed at left.

Only the most popular cartoon characters will have ready-made bedding available on the shelf at local linens stores, but almost all cartoon characters are licensed somewhere. Bedding that depicts them can usually be special-ordered if you can track down the manufacturer.

Sheets

There is just no good reason to buy sheets at retail. ''Regular'' sheets such as those you find in department stores and linens stores can be purchased at wholesale, or near wholesale, prices from factory outlets and telephone ordering services. Luxury sheets can purchased through telephone ordering services and wholesale showrooms at huge discounts.

Regular sheets Please see the list on page 167 to determine if the particular brand name or designer name of the sheets you wish to have is readily available through a telephone ordering service.

Please see the list on page 170 and the factory outlet listings on pages 171 to 180 to determine if the sheets you want are available through a factory outlet. Most brand names and designer names are.

There really are no quality considerations for regular sheets. All brands are of satisfactory quality. Even irregular or second-quality sheets, such as those you may find at a factory outlet, usually have very minor flaws or irregularities that will not affect the looks or wear of the sheets.

The only concern you may have is if you have a pillowtop mattress. Pillowtop mattresses are much thicker than the average mattress. Often, regular ready-made fitted sheets won't quite fit them. Ready-made patterned sheets are usually not made to accommodate extra-thick mattresses, but there are some brands of solid-color sheets that are made with deep corner pockets for just this purpose. Many telephone ordering services have their own generic "house brand" sheets that are usually available in a deep-pocketed style -- check the catalog. Flat sheets will fit thicker mattresses just fine.

You may have to buy solid-color fitted sheets and matching patterned flat sheets if you have an extra-thick mattress. If you are set on having patterned fitted sheets, you can purchase a flat sheet in whatever size your bed is and have a drapery workroom or seamstress stitch elastic to the corners to make a deep-pocketed fitted sheet for you. You should be able to have this done for no more than $15.00 per sheet. Be sure to measure the thickness of the mattress and provide this measurement to the seamstress or workroom and pre-shrink the sheets before having them sewn.

Luxury sheets There are many different kinds of luxury sheets: lace, cutwork, embroidered, damask, etc. Here, quality can vary somewhat. If you are going to spend more, you should make sure that you are getting more. You don't want to pay luxury prices for something that is nothing more than a regular quality sheet in a fancy package (unfortunately, this does occur).

Quality check #1: Make sure that the sheets have a thread count of at least 250. The higher this number is, the better. The thread count refers to the number of threads per square inch. The very best sheets have thread counts of around 300.

Quality check #2: Look for 100% long-staple Egyptian cotton. This is the best. "Long-staple" means that the cotton fibers themselves are unusually long. This minimizes the fuzzy look that sheets get when they are beginning to wear out. Sheets made from long-staple cotton look newer, longer. It also allows the sheets to be thinner and more delicate while still wearing well for a long time.

Quality check #3: Don't buy sheets that have any polyester in them. Most luxury sheets don't, but there are a few manufacturers that try to sneak in polyester. Cotton/polyester blends look good initially and are sometimes less expensive, but will not wear as well as 100% cotton.

Domestically produced luxury sheets Some of the major "regular" bedding manufacturers also have higher quality luxury products. Fieldcrest, Springmaid, Wamsutta, J. P. Stevens, and Martex (Westpoint-Pepperell) all manufacture luxury sheets.

Cannon, Fieldcrest, Martex (Westpoint-Pepperell), Wamsutta, and

Springmaid all have factory outlets throughout the United States. Please see pages 171 to 180 for a list of factory outlets. Many products from these companies are also available by phone from the services listed on page 168.

The quality is usually somewhere between that of regular sheets and the imported brands. These sheets are nice but not as luxurious as the imported European brands. If you are going to buy luxury sheets, you will probably want to order the really plush stuff from France or Switzerland.

Imported luxury sheets

By phone: Many brands of imported luxury sheets can be purchased over the telephone at a discount of 30% to 40% off retail through the J. Schachter Co. The address and ordering information can be found on page 240. J. Schachter can order many imported and domestic luxury brands: Anichini, Bischoff, Bruna, Malabar Grove, Palais Royal, Paper White, Peacock Alley, Peter Reed, Sferra Brothers, Sufolla, and others.

Make sure you know exactly what you want when you call to order. J. Schachter does not show most of these imported items in its catalog. Shop around at luxury bedding stores in your area, or at the local wholesale design center if it hosts special shopping days to the public, and write down all product information when you decide what you want. Be sure to note the manufacturer's name, style name or number, size, color, and any other details that seem important.

You will be in for a small wait for your order because most of these imported brands are not carried in stock by J. Schachter. Most must be special ordered from the manufacturer at a wait of up to 4 to 6 weeks. Still, the savings are excellent, so, you will have to decide whether or not you really mind waiting.

Wholesale: Many imported luxury brands are available at wholesale showrooms in design centers throughout the United States. If are your own decorator (as explained in Chapter 19), you can go right in and order them wholesale. The usual wholesale price on bed linens is 40% to 50% off retail, depending upon the quantity you purchase. You will normally still have to wait several weeks for the linens to be shipped from the manufacturer.

You will often be able to get the very best price on luxury bedding by buying it wholesale. Wholesale showrooms for many different brands of luxury linens and bedding all over the United States are listed in the National Directory of Wholesale Home Furnishings Sources and Showrooms.

Please read Chapter 19 carefully before shopping at a wholesale showroom or placing a mail order with a wholesale company.

Some design centers have certain days when they are open to the public. On these special shopping days, consumers receive a partial trade discount, usually about 20% off retail. Often, you will be better off to write the product information down and place your order with J. Schachter if you cannot get the full trade discount of 40% to 50% of retail. Check prices and compare carefully. Please see page 399 for a list of design centers around the United States that are open to the public on certain days.

Retail Stores, Department Stores, and Interior Designers

Avoid buying bedding from these places. You will be paying a completely unnecessary commission to these middlemen.

You can get custom bedding made far more cheaply at a workroom. Retail businesses and interior designers virtually never manufacture their own custom products. They usually job them out to a local workroom. You can skip this extra step, and the extra commission, by going directly to the workroom yourself in the first place.

You can buy ready-made bedding, even luxury bedding, far more cheaply from a telephone ordering service or factory outlet.

Linens Stores

There are a variety of "category-killer" stores devoted to linens and bedding, such as Linens 'N Things and Linen Supermarket. "Category-killer", in the home furnishings industry, means a store that stocks a very narrow range of products in great quantities in order to offer extremely low prices.

Some of these stores even operate out of factory outlet centers, although I do not include them in the list of factory outlets later in this chapter because they do not have prices that are comparable to those at true outlet stores. They do come real close, though.

While the prices at these stores are low, the prices from telephone ordering services and factory outlets are usually even lower. If you must have whatever you need immediately and do not wish to wait a few days for shipment from a telephone ordering service or drive to a factory-outlet, these stores will be your best local bet to buy ready-made bedding.

Telephone Ordering Services

Telephone ordering services are the best places to order ready-made bed treatments, including down-filled products, if traveling to an outlet is not practical for you. The names and addresses of these services are listed on the next page.

Many popular brand names are available from these services, listed opposite. The typical discount is about 40% off of the retail list price on major brands and up to 75% off the comparable retail for various in-house and generic brands of linens.

The vast majority of telephone ordering services that carry bed treatments also sell matching sheets, ready-made window treatments, tablecloths, and other home furnishings.

Most services do not carry the imported brands such as Sferra Brothers and Bruna. To order imported bedding, your best bet (other than buying it wholesale) is to call the J. Schachter Co. (listed on page 168).

All of the services listed on page 168 carry all types of bed treatments. Many services carry most of the major brand names of bedding, but some specialize in certain types or brands. Any special focus of the service is noted in italics under the company name.

The list at right identifies the major brands and designers whose

Brand Names By Phone

Adrienne Vittadini
Alexander Julian
Andre' Richard
Bill Blass
Bruna
Burlington House
Cannon
Carrington
Claude Montana
Collier Campbell
Court of Versailles
Croscill
Crown Crafts
Dakotah
Dan River
Di Lewis
Echo
Eileen West
Fendi
Fieldcrest
Gear
Jay Yang
Jessica McClintock
J. G. Hook
J. P. Stevens
Laura Ashley
Liberty of London
Louis Nichole
Mario Buatta
Martex
Paint the Town
Palais Royale
Perry Ellis
Peter Reed
Polo
Ralph Lauren
Revman
Robert Stern
Royalton
Sanderson
Saturday Knight
Sferra Brothers
Springmaid
Springs
Sufolla
Utica
Wamsutta
Waverly By Fieldcrest

products are available by phone. As you can see, nearly any brand or designer name you might be interested in can be ordered over the phone at huge discounts.

These services usually do not sell down. Telephone ordering services that specialize in down products, and usually manufacture most of the products as well, are listed on page 162.

All of the services listed accept credit cards. These services are all well-established with good reputations for customer service.

Telephone Ordering Services

Bedroom Secrets
(Call with product information)
P. O. Box 529
Fremont, NE 68025
(800) 955-2559

Coming Home By Lands' End
(Call for free catalog)
1 Lands' End Lane
Dodgeville, WI 53595
(800) 345-3696

Custom Windows and Walls
(Call with product information)
32525 Stephenson Hwy.
Madison Heights, MI 48071
(800) 772-1947

Designer Secrets
(Call with product information)
P. O. Box 529
Fremont, NE 68025
(800) 955-2559

Domestications
(Call for free catalog)
P. O. Box 41
Hanover, PA 17333
(800) 782-7722

Eldridge Textile Co.
(Send $3.00 for catalog)
277 Grand St.
New York, NY 10002
(212) 219-9542

Harris Levy
(Call for free catalog)
278 Grand St.
New York, NY 10002
(800) 221-7750

J. Schachter Co.
(Send $1.00 for catalog)
85 Ludlow St.
New York, NY 10002
(800) INTO-BED

Laura Ashley By Post
Laura Ashley products only
(Call for free catalog)
P. O. Box 891
Mahwah, NJ 07430
(800) 367-2000

The Linen Source
(Call for free catalog)
5401 Hangar Ct.
Tampa, FL 33631
(800) 431-2620

P. and J. Home Furnishings and Fabric Outlet
(Call with product information)
4114 Highway 70 S.
Hickory, NC 28602
(704) 326-9755

Virginia Goodwin
Fishnet canopies only
(Call for free brochure)
Route 2, Box 770
Boone, NC 28607
(800) 735-5191

Factory Outlets

Bedding is the most common type of home furnishing available directly to the public through factory outlets. There is just no good reason to ever buy ready-made bed treatments at a retail store. Factory outlets across the U. S. are listed on pages 171 to 180, organized by state and city.

Finding particular brands Most major brand names can be traced back to a few major manufacturers, most of which offer their products directly to the public through factory outlets. The chart on page 170 matches up many popular brand names of bedding with the manufacturers that actually produce them.

Brands not available from outlets Some brands are not listed. Many of these, such as Sferra and Carrington, are imported and have no factory outlet in the United States. Others, such as Palais Royale and Malabar Grove, are small companies that do not have factory outlets, although these and most other small manufacturers have wholesale showrooms all across the United States.

Typical savings You can save approximately 50% to 75% on most items at these stores.

Typical selection Some items will be second-quality, and the selection will not be as broad as the selection available through telephone ordering services.

You will find a broad variety of first-quality goods in most outlets. Factory outlets have transcended their original purpose of disposing of substandard merchandise. Outlets are now a billion-dollar industry. Manufacturers use outlets to move a significant amount of first-quality current merchandise in addition to seconds and discontinued merchandise.

Flaws in second-quality merchandise are usually slight, but it is your responsibility to make sure that the condition of any merchandise you buy is acceptable to you. Flaws may or may not be clearly marked by the store. Merchandise is generally sold ''as-is'' with no returns allowed, so inspect everything carefully.

Payment Many of the stores listed accept credit cards. Most do not accept out-of-state personal checks, although a few will make an exception if you have two forms of picture I. D.

Not-quite-outlets A few of the stores listed on pages 171 to 180 are not true factory outlets. Bed and Bath Fair and the Sears Catalog Outlet Store liquidate second-quality merchandise and returns from Sears. The J. C. Penney Catalog Outlet store liquidates second-quality merchandise and returns from J. C. Penney.

I have included these stores here because their prices are comparable to those at manufacturer-owned factory outlets.

Bedding Designed By Clothing Designers

Bedding marketed under the names of clothing designers is normally available at the outlet of the bedding manufacturer, not at the outlet of the clothing designer. Usually the clothing designer only licenses his or her name to a bedding manufacturer and has some design input. The designer usually has nothing to do with the actual manufacturing and sale of the bedding.

For instance, you will generally not find J. G. Hook licensed bedding in the J. G. Hook clothing factory outlets across the United States. You would have to go instead to a Fieldcrest-Cannon factory outlet because Fieldcrest-Cannon actually produces the bedding. Use the cross-reference list on page 170 to track down the appropriate manufacturer's factory outlet for any designer bedding you are interested in purchasing.

Getting to the Source

Brand Name	***Manufacturer***
Adrienne Vittadini	Fieldcrest-Cannon
Alexander Julian	Fieldcrest
Andre' Richard	Springmaid-Wamsutta
Anichini	Anichini
Bill Blass	Springmaid-Wamsutta
Burlington House	Burlington Industries
Cannon	Fieldcrest-Cannon
Claude Montana	Royalton
Collier Campbell	Westpoint-Pepperell
Court of Versailles	Fieldcrest-Cannon
Croscill	Croscill
Crown Crafts	Crown Crafts
Dakotah	Dakotah
Dan River	Dan River
Di Lewis	Croscill
Echo	Revman
Eileen West	J. P. Stevens/Westpoint-Pepperell
Fendi	Royalton
Fieldcrest	Fieldcrest-Cannon
Jay Yang	Springmaid-Wamsutta
Jessica McClintock	Royalton
J. G. Hook	Fieldcrest-Cannon
J. P. Stevens	J. P. Stevens/Westpoint-Pepperell
Laura Ashley	Revman
Liberty of London	Westpoint-Pepperell
Mario Buatta	Revman
Martex	Westpoint-Pepperell
Paint the Town	Fieldcrest-Cannon
Perry Ellis	Westpoint-Pepperell
Polo	Polo/Ralph Lauren
Ralph Lauren	Polo/Ralph Lauren
Revman	Revman
Robert Stern	Westpoint-Pepperell
Sanderson	Westpoint-Pepperell
Springmaid	Springmaid-Wamsutta
Springs	Springmaid-Wamsutta
Utica	J. P. Stevens/Westpoint-Pepperell
Wamsutta	Springmaid-Wamsutta
Waverly By Fieldcrest	Fieldcrest-Cannon

Factory Outlets

Alabama

Fieldcrest-Cannon
Boaz Outlet Center
Exit 183 off I-59
Boaz, AL 35957
(205) 593-9306

The Interior Alternative
601 Elizabeth St.
Boaz, AL 35957
(205) 593-8887

Westpoint-Pepperell
Boaz Outlet Center
Exit 183 off I-59
Boaz, AL 35957
(205) 593-1696

Westpoint-Pepperell
Riviera Centre Factory Stores
Highway 59 South
Foley, AL 36535
(800) 5-CENTRE

Springmaid-Wamsutta
USA Factory Stores
Exit 62 off I-85
Opelika, AL 36803
(205) 749-9068

Arizona

Springmaid-Wamsutta
Tanger Factory Outlet Center
Exit 198 off I-10
Casa Grande, AZ 85222
(520) 836-0897

Westpoint-Pepperell
Factory Stores of America
Exit 194 off I-10
Casa Grande, AZ 85222
(602) 421-0112

Arizona (cont.)

Westpoint-Pepperell
Wigwam Outlet Stores
I-10 and Litchfield Rd.
Goodyear, AZ 85338
(602) 935-9733

Fieldcrest-Cannon
Factory Stores of America
Superstition Fwy. and Power Rd.
Mesa, AZ 85208
(602) 984-1179

Arkansas

Fieldcrest-Cannon
Hot Springs Factory Outlet Stores
Highway 7 South
Hot Springs, AR 71913
(501) 525-9171

California

Polo/Ralph Lauren
Shasta Factory Outlets
I-5 and State Rd. 273
Anderson, CA 96007
(916) 365-1090

Polo/Ralph Lauren
Atascadero Factory Outlets
Del Rio Exit off 101 Fwy.
Atascadero, CA 93422
(805) 461-5155

Fieldcrest-Cannon
Factory Merchants
I-15 and Lenwood Rd.
Barstow, CA 92311
(619) 253-3591

California (cont.)

Polo/Ralph Lauren
Factory Merchants
I-15 and Lenwood Rd.
Barstow, CA 92311
(619) 253-5333

Westpoint-Pepperell
Desert Hills Factory Stores
48400 Seminole Dr.
Cabazon, CA 92230
(909) 849-6641

Fieldcrest-Cannon
Folsom Factory Outlets
Hwy. 50 and Folsom Blvd.
Folsom, CA 95630
(916) 351-0849

Laura Ashley
Outlets At Gilroy
Highway 101 and Leavesley Rd.
Gilroy, CA 95020
(408) 848-5470

Springmaid-Wamsutta
Outlets At Gilroy
Highway 101 and Leavesley Rd.
Gilroy, CA 95020
(408) 847-3731

Springmaid-Wamsutta
Lancaster Factory Stores
A. V. Freeway 14
Lancaster, CA 93536
(805) 942-7897

I. D. Bedding
The Cooper Building
860 S. Los Angeles St.
Los Angeles, CA 90014
(213) 624-3821

Factory Outlets (cont.)

California (cont.)

Springmaid-Wamsutta
Factory Stores of America
at Nut Tree
321-2 Nut Tree Rd.
Vacaville, CA 95687
(707) 451-9970

Stroud's Linen Outlet
Factory Stores of America
at Nut Tree
321-2 Nut Tree Rd.
Vacaville, CA 95687
(707) 451-4781

Colorado

Springmaid-Wamsutta
Castle Rock Factory Shops
Exit 184 off I-25
Castle Rock, CO 80104
(303) 660-2070

Springmaid-Wamsutta
Rocky Mountain Factory Stores
I-25 and U. S. Hwy. 34
Loveland, CO 80538
(970) 679-4600

Connecticut

Bed, Bath, and Beyond
Factory Outlets at Norwalk
Exit 16 off I-95
Norwalk, CT 06855
(203) 853-6224

Delaware

The Interior Alternative
Bellvue Ave.
Newark, DE 19713
(302) 454-3232

Delaware (cont.)

Lots of Linens
Ocean Outlets
Route 1
Rehoboth Beach, DE 19971
(302) 226-9223

Florida

Springmaid-Wamsutta
Gulf Coast Factory Shops
Exit 43 off I-75
Ellenton, FL 34222
(813) 729-1715

Fieldcrest-Cannon
Sanibel Factory Stores
Exit 21 off I-75
Fort Myers, FL 33908
(941) 454-7461

Fieldcrest-Cannon
Manufacturer's Outlet Center
Exit 65 off I-95
Fort Pierce, FL 34945
(407) 466-4013

Fieldcrest-Cannon
Kissimmee Manufacturers' Mall
2517 Old Vineland Rd.
Kissimmee, FL 34746
(813) 396-8900

Fieldcrest-Cannon
Coral Isle Factory Stores
S. R. 951
Naples, FL 33961
(813) 775-9251

Fieldcrest-Cannon
Belz Factory Outlet World
I-4 and International Dr.
Orlando, FL 32819
(407) 345-9405

Florida (cont.)

Westpoint-Pepperell
International Designer Outlets
I-4 and International Dr.
Orlando, FL 32819
(407) 354-0707

Laura Ashley
St. Augustine Outlet Center
Exit 95 off I-95
St. Augustine, FL 32092
(904) 823-9533

Westpoint-Pepperell
St. Augustine Outlet Center
2700 State Rd. 16
St. Augustine, FL 32092
(904) 829-1500

Westpoint-Pepperell
Sarasota Outlet Center
Exit 40 off I-75
University Park, FL 34201
(941) 359-2444

Springmaid-Wamsutta
Horizon Outlet Center
S. R. 60 and I-95
Vero Beach, FL 32966
(407) 562-5770

Georgia

Fieldcrest-Cannon
Peach Factory Stores
Exit 46 off I-75
Byron, GA 31008
(912) 956-1855

Home Decor
Peach Factory Stores
Exit 46 off I-75
Byron, GA 31008
(912) 956-1855

Factory Outlets (cont.)

Georgia (cont.)

Springmaid-Wamsutta
Calhoun Outlet Center
Exit 129 off I-75
Calhoun, GA 30701
(800) 969-3767

Fieldcrest-Cannon
Tanger Factory Outlet Center
Exit 53 off I-85
Commerce, GA 30529
(706) 335-4537

The Interior Alternative
3004-B Parquet Rd.
Dalton, GA 30720
(706) 217-6544

Westpoint-Pepperell
Dalton Factory Stores
Exit 136 off I-75
Dalton, GA 30720
(706) 275-6217

Polo/Ralph Lauren
Magnolia Bluff Factory Shops
Exit 10 off I-95
Darien, GA 31305
(912) 437-2700

Springmaid-Wamsutta
Magnolia Bluff Factory Shops
Exit 10 off I-95
Darien, GA 31305
(912) 437-2700

J. C. Penney Catalog Outlet
5500 S. Expressway
Forest Park, GA 30050
(404) 363-3855

Fieldcrest-Cannon
Alpine Village Factory Outlets
Hwy. 17
Helen, GA 30545
(706) 878-1922

Georgia (cont.)

Home Decor
Lake Park Factory Stores
Exit 2 off I-75
Lake Park, GA 31636
(912) 559-1177

Polo/Ralph Lauren
Lake Park Mill Store Plaza
Exit 2 off I-75
Lake Park, GA 31636
(912) 559-6822

Westpoint-Pepperell
Lake Park Mill Store Plaza
Exit 2 off I-75
Lake Park, GA 31636
(912) 559-6822

J. C. Penney Catalog Outlet
2434 Atlanta Rd.
Smyrna, GA 30080
(770) 432-5231

Idaho

Fieldcrest-Cannon
Boise Factory Outlets
I-84 at Gowen Rd.
Boise, ID 83705
(208) 343-7740

Fieldcrest-Cannon
Post Falls Factory Stores
Exit 2 off I-90
Post Falls, ID 83854
(208) 777-9266

Illinois

Lands' End
2121 N. Claybourn
Chicago, IL 60614
(312) 281-0900

Illinois (cont.)

Dan River
K Square Factory Outlet Mall
Exit 160 off I-57/70
Effingham, IL 62401
(217) 342-4737

Lands' End
Seconds and irregulars only
816 1/2 Church St.
Evanston, IL 60201
(708) 328-3009

Bed, Bath, and Beyond
Gurnee Mills
I-94 and Route 132
Gurnee, IL 60031
(800) YES-SHOP

The Bedding Experts
Gurnee Mills
I-94 and Route 132
Gurnee, IL 60031
(800) YES-SHOP

J. C. Penney Clearance Center
Gurnee Mills
I-94 and Route 132
Gurnee, IL 60031
(800) YES-SHOP

Lands' End
Gurnee Mills
I-94 and Route 132
Gurnee, IL 60031
(800) YES-SHOP

Lands' End
20 Yorktown Convenience Center
Butterfield and Highland
Lombard, IL 60148
(708) 953-8855

Factory Outlets (cont.)

Illinois (cont.)

Lands' End
7205 W. Dempster St.
Niles, IL 60714
(708) 470-0320

Lands' End
Woodfield Village Green
1522 E. Golf Rd.
Schaumburg, IL 60173
(708) 413-0100

Indiana

Springmaid-Wamsutta
Indiana Factory Shops
I-69 and Route 67
Daleville, IN 47334
(317) 378-1300

Fieldcrest-Cannon
Horizon Outlet Center
Exit 76B off I-65
Edinburgh, IN 46124
(812) 526-2887

Fieldcrest-Cannon
Lighthouse Place
6th St. and Wabash St.
Michigan City, IN 46360
(800) 866-5900

Polo/Ralph Lauren
Lighthouse Place
6th St. and Wabash St.
Michigan City, IN 46360
(800) 866-5900

Polo/Ralph Lauren
Tanger Factory Outlet Center
Exit 50A off I-65
Seymour, IN 47274
(812) 522-6922

Iowa

Lands' End
10 S. Clinton St.
Iowa City, IA 52240
(319) 338-2660

Fieldcrest-Cannon
Factory Stores of America
Exit 124 off I-35
Story City, IA 50248
(515) 733-5242

Lands' End
2700 University Ave.
Suite 114
West Des Moines, IA 50266
(515) 226-0200

Fieldcrest-Cannon
Tanger Factory Outlet Center
Exit 220 off I-80
Williamsburg, IA 52361
(319) 668-2811

Laura Ashley
Tanger Factory Outlet Center
Exit 220 off I-80
Williamsburg, IA 52361
(319) 668-2811

Polo/Ralph Lauren
Tanger Factory Outlet Center
Exit 220 off I-80
Williamsburg, IA 52361
(319) 668-2811

Kansas

Fieldcrest-Cannon
Lawrence Riverfront
Factory Outlets
Exit 204 off I-70
Lawrence, KS 66044
(913) 841-8209

Kansas (cont.)

Springmaid-Wamsutta
Tanger Factory Outlet Center
Exit 204 off I-70
Lawrence, KS 66044
(913) 842-6290

Kentucky

Factory Linens
Factory Stores of America
Exit 126 off I-75
Georgetown, KY 40324
(502) 863-3660

Louisiana

Fieldcrest-Cannon
Tanger Factory Outlet Center
Exit 177 off I-10
Gonzales, LA 70737
(504) 647-0521

Fieldcrest-Cannon
Factory Stores of America
Exit 43 off I-10
Iowa, LA 70647
(318) 582-3568

Westpoint Pepperell
Slidell Factory Stores
Exit 263 off I-10
Slidell, LA 70458
(504) 646-0756

Maine

Bed & Bath Outlet Store
Exit 19 off I-95
Freeport, ME 04032
(207) 865-4820

Factory Outlets (cont.)

Maine (cont.)

Cannon Sheets, Towels, & More
Exit 19 off I-95
Freeport, ME 04032
(207) 865-1243

Cuddledown of Maine
Exit 19 off I-95
Freeport, ME 04032
(207) 865-1713

Laura Ashley
Exit 19 off I-95
Freeport, ME 04032
(207) 865-3300

Polo/Ralph Lauren
Exit 19 off I-95
Freeport, ME 04032
(207) 865-4176

Polo/Ralph Lauren
Kittery Outlet Village
Exit 3 off I-95
Kittery, ME 03904
(207) 439-6664

Massachusetts

The Interior Alternative
5 Hoosac St.
Adams, MA 01220
(413) 743-1986

Curtain Factory Outlet
Wampanoag Mill
Factory Outlet Center
Alden St. and Quequechan St.
Fall River, MA 02721
(508) 678-6996

Luxury Linens
Tower Outlet Mill
Pleasant St. and Quarry St.
Fall River, MA 02721
(508) 678-8411

Massachusetts (cont.)

Bed, Bath, and Beyond
Worcester Common
Fashion Outlets
Exit 16 off I-290
Worcester, MA 01608
(800) 2-SAVE-ALOT

Michigan

Fieldcrest-Cannon
Outlets At Birch Run
Exit 136 off I-75
Birch Run, MI 48415
(517) 624-5601

Laura Ashley
Outlets At Birch Run
Exit 136 off I-75
Birch Run, MI 48415
(517) 624-9297

Springmaid-Wamsutta
Outlets At Birch Run
Exit 136 off I-75
Birch Run, MI 48415
(517) 624-1222

Westpoint-Pepperell
Outlets At Birch Run
Exit 136 off I-75
Birch Run, MI 48415
(517) 624-4114

Westpoint-Pepperell
Horizon Outlet Center
Exit 11 off I-75
Monroe, MI 48161
(313) 241-4500

Fieldcrest-Cannon
Horizon Outlet Center
Exit 269 off I-94
Port Huron, MI 48060
(810) 364-9449

Michigan (cont.)

Polo/Ralph Lauren
Tanger Factory Outlet Center
Exit 212 off I-75
West Branch, MI 48661
(517) 345-4437

Minnesota

Fieldcrest- Cannon
Horizon Outlet Center
Exit 251 off I-94
Woodbury, MN 55125
(612) 738-8673

Westpoint-Pepperell
Horizon Outlet Center
Exit 251 off I-94
Woodbury, MN 55125
(612) 730-0002

Missouri

Fieldcrest-Cannon
Factory Merchants Branson
West Hwy. 76 and Pat Nash Dr.
Branson, MO 65616
(417) 335-4587

Polo/Ralph Lauren
Tanger Factory Outlet Center
Highway 76
Branson, MO 65616
(417) 337-9327

Springmaid-Wamsutta
Tanger Factory Outlet Center
Highway 76
Branson, MO 65616
(417) 337-9327

Fieldcrest-Cannon
Sikeston Factory Outlet Stores
Exit 67 off I-55
Miner, MO 63801
(314) 472-3616

Factory Outlets (cont.)

Missouri (cont.)

Laura Ashley
Factory Outlet Village
Highway 54
Osage Beach, MO 65065
(314) 348-1333

Polo/Ralph Lauren
Factory Outlet Village
Highway 54
Osage Beach, MO 65065
(314) 348-0386

Springmaid-Wamsutta
Factory Outlet Village
Highway 54
Osage Beach, MO 65065
(314) 348-1468

Nebraska

Fieldcrest-Cannon
Nebraska Crossing Factory Stores
Exit 432 off I-80
Gretna, NE 68028
(402) 332-5843

Nevada

Springmaid-Wamsutta
Belz Factory Outlet World
I-15 and Warm Springs Rd.
Las Vegas, NV 89123
(702) 896-5599

Westpoint-Pepperell
Factory Stores of America
Exit 33 off I-15
Las Vegas, NV 89123
(702) 897-9090

New Hampshire

Polo/Ralph Lauren
Red Barn Factory Stores
Route 16/302
North Conway, NH 03860
(800) 4-TANGER

Anichini
Powerhouse Mall
West Lebanon, NH 03784
(603) 298-8656

New Jersey

Westpoint-Pepperell
Princeton Forrestral Village
Route 1 and College Rd. W.
Princeton, NJ 08540
(609) 799-7400

Bed, Bath, and Beyond
Harmon Cove Outlet Center
20 Enterprise Ave.
Secaucus, NJ 07094
(800) 358-2373

New York

Lots of Linens
Woodbury Common
Factory Outlets
Exit 16 (Harriman exit) off I-87
Central Valley, NY 10917
(914) 928-7331

Westpoint-Pepperell
Woodbury Common
Factory Outlets
Exit 16 (Harriman exit) off I-87
Central Valley, NY 10917
(914) 928-4598

New York (cont.)

Springmaid-Wamsutta
Miromar Factory Outlet Center
Exit 42 off I-87
Champlain, NY 12919
(518) 298-2731

Leejay Linens Outlet
Cohoes Commons
43 Mohawk St.
Cohoes, NY 12047
(518) 237-8400

Polo/Ralph Lauren
Cohoes Commons
43 Mohawk St.
Cohoes, NY 12047
(518) 233-0307

Polo/Ralph Lauren
Rainbow Centre Factory Outlet
302 Rainbow Blvd. N.
Niagara Falls, NY 14303
(716) 285-9758

Westpoint Pepperell
Rainbow Centre Factory Outlet
302 Rainbow Blvd. N.
Niagara Falls, NY 14303
(716) 285-9758

Springmaid-Wamsutta
Tanger Factory Outlet Center
Exit 73 off I-495 East
Riverhead, NY 11901
(516) 369-2724

North Carolina

Polo/Ralph Lauren
Shoppes on the Parkway
Hwy. 321 Bypass
Blowing Rock, NC 28605
(704) 295-4248

Factory Outlets (cont.)

North Carolina (cont.)

Plej's Textile Mill Outlet
Burlington Manufacturers
Outlet Center
Exit 145 off I-85/40
Burlington, NC 27216
(910) 227-2872

Westpoint-Pepperell
Burlington Manufacturers
Outlet Center
Exit 145 off I-85/40
Burlington, NC 27216
(910) 227-2872

P. and J. Home Furnishings
and Fabric Outlet
4114 Highway 70 S.
Hickory, NC 28602
(704) 326-9755

Cannon Bed & Bath Outlet
Cannon Village
120 West Ave.
Kannapolis, NC 28081
(704) 939-2869

Dan River
Triangle Factory Shops
Exit 284 off I-40
Morrisville, NC 27650
(919) 380-9819

Polo/Ralph Lauren
Soundings Factory Stores
U. S. 158 and U. S. 264
Nags Head, NC 27959
(919) 441-7395

Carolina Linens
Factory Stores of America
Exit 95 off I-95
Smithfield, NC 27577
(919) 934-9446

North Carolina (cont.)

Beacon
202 Whitson Ave.
Swannanoa, NC 28778
(704) 686-5445

Ohio

Dan River
Jeffersonville Outlet Center
Exit 69 off I-71
Jeffersonville, OH 43128
(614) 426-9797

Laura Ashley
Ohio Factory Shops
Exit 65 off I-71
Jeffersonville, OH 43218
(614) 948-2015

Springmaid-Wamsutta
Ohio Factory Shops
Exit 65 off I-71
Jeffersonville, OH 43218
(614) 948-9100

Oklahoma

Fieldcrest-Cannon
Tanger Factory Outlet Center
Exit 179 off I-44
Stroud, OK 74079
(918) 968-3566

Oregon

Springmaid-Wamsutta
Tanger Factory Outlet Center
Hwy. 18 and Norton Lane
McMinnville, OR 97128
(503) 472-5387

Pennsylvania

Springmaid-Wamsutta
Grove City Factory Shops
Exit 31 off I-79
Grove City, PA 16127
(412) 748-4770

Springmaid-Wamsutta
Factory Stores at Hershey, PA
Hwy. 22
Hershey, PA 17033
(717) 520-0191

Dan River
Tanger Factory Outlet Center
Route 30 East
Lancaster, PA 17602
(717) 392-7202

Laura Ashley
Rockvale Square Outlets
U. S. Hwy. 30 and Hwy. 896
Lancaster, PA 17601
(717) 397-7116

Polo/Ralph Lauren
Tanger Factory Outlet Center
Route 30 East
Lancaster, PA 17602
(717) 392-7202

Factory Linens
Rockvale Square Outlets
U. S. Hwy. 30 and Hwy. 896
Lancaster, PA 17601
(717) 392-5459

Westpoint-Pepperell
Rockvale Square Outlets
U. S. Hwy. 30 and Hwy. 896
Lancaster, PA 17601
(717) 290-7920

Factory Outlets (cont.)

Pennsylvania (cont.)

Polo/Ralph Lauren
Bald Eagle Factory Outlets
McElhatten Exit off Route 200
McElhatten, PA 17745
(717) 769-0550

Bed, Bath, and Beyond
Franklin Mills
I-95 and Woodhaven Rd.
Philadelphia, PA 19114
(800) 336-6255

J. C. Penney Catalog Outlet
Franklin Mills
I-95 and Woodhaven Rd.
Philadelphia, PA 19114
(800) 336-6255

Fieldcrest-Cannon
VF Factory Outlet Village
Hwy. 422 W.
Reading, PA 19610
(800) 772-8336

Laura Ashley
Reading Outlet Center
801 N. 9th St.
Reading, PA 19604
(610) 478-9604

Polo/Ralph Lauren
Reading Outlet Center
801 N. 9th St.
Reading, PA 19604
(610) 373-5900

Fieldcrest-Cannon
Georgian Place Outlet Center
Highway 601 N.
Somerset, PA 15501
(800) 866-5900

South Carolina

Dan River
Low Country
Factory Outlet Village
Highway 278
Bluffton, SC 29910
(803) 837-5399

Laura Ashley
Low Country
Factory Outlet Village
Highway 278
Bluffton, SC 29910
(803) 837-2366

The Interior Alternative
1 Frederick Dr.
Richburg, SC 29729
(803) 789-6655

South Dakota

Dakotah
Highway 12
Webster, SD 57274
(605) 345-3700

Tennessee

Polo/Ralph Lauren
Warehouse Row
Factory Shops
1110 Market St.
Chattanooga, TN 37402
(615) 267-7656

Fieldcrest-Cannon
Factory Stores of America
Exit 320 off I-40
Crossville, TN 38555
(615) 484-7165

Tennessee (cont.)

Dan River
Factory Stores of America
Exit 215 off I-40
Nashville, TN 37202
(615) 885-5140

Fieldcrest-Cannon
Pigeon Forge
Factory Outlet Mall
2850 Parkway
Pigeon Forge, TN 37863
(615) 453-1692

Springmaid-Wamsutta
Tanger Factory Outlet Center
Hwy. 441 and Davis Rd.
Pigeon Forge, TN 37863
(615) 428-7001

Westpoint-Pepperell
Belz Factory Outlet World
2655 Teaster Lane
Pigeon Forge, TN 37863
(615) 453-1041

Dan River
Five Oaks Factory Stores
U. S. Hwy 441
Sevierville, TN 37862
(615) 453-1822

Polo/Ralph Lauren
Five Oaks Factory Stores
U. S. Hwy 441
Sevierville, TN 37862
(615) 429-1226

Factory Linens
Factory Stores of America
Exit 66 off I-81
Tri-Cities, TN 37617
(615) 323-4419

Factory Outlets (cont.)

Texas

The Interior Alternative
2626 Northhaven Rd.
Dallas, TX 75229
(214) 241-5422

Springmaid-Wamsutta
Gainesville Factory Shops
Exit 501 off I-35
Gainesville, TX 76240
(817) 665-1180

Westpoint-Pepperell
New Braunfels Factory Stores
Exit 188 off I-35
New Braunfels, TX 78130
(210) 625-5289

Fieldcrest-Cannon
Tanger Factory Outlet Center
Exit 200 off I-35
San Marcos, TX 78666
(512) 396-7444

Laura Ashley
San Marcos Factory Shops
Exit 200 off I-35
San Marcos, TX 78666
(800) 628-9465

Springmaid-Wamsutta
San Marcos Factory Shops
Exit 200 off I-35
San Marcos, TX 78666
(800) 628-9465

Fieldcrest-Cannon
Factory Stores of America
Exit 124 off I-30
Sulphur Springs, TX 75482
(903) 885-0015

Utah

Westpoint-Pepperell
Factory Stores at Park City
Exit 145 off I-80
Park City, UT 84060
(801) 647-0300

Virginia

Springmaid-Wamsutta
Massaponax Outlet Center
Exit 126 off I-95
Fredericksburg, VA 22401
(703) 373-8853

Linens and Things
Williamsburg Outlet Mall
Exit 234 off I-64
Lightfoot, VA 23090
(804) 565-1220

J. C. Penney Clearance Center
Potomac Mills Outlet Center
Exit 156 off I-95
Prince William, VA 22192
(800) VA-MILLS

Laura Ashley
Potomac Mills Outlet Center
Exit 156 off I-95
Prince William, VA 22192
(800) VA-MILLS

Linens and Things
Potomac Mills Outlet Center
Exit 156 off I-95
Prince William, VA 22192
(800) VA-MILLS

Westpoint-Pepperell
Great American Outlet Mall
Exit 4 off Hwy. 58
Virginia Beach, VA 23452
(804) 463-8665

Washington

Fieldcrest-Cannon
Centralia Factory Outlets
Exit 82 off I-5
Centralia, WA 98531
(360) 736-3327

Fieldcrest-Cannon
Factory Stores of America
Exit 31 off I-90
North Bend, WA 98045
(206) 888-4505

Wisconsin

Lands' End
17925 Blue Mound Rd.
Suite 400
Brookfield, WI 53045
(414) 879-2000

Lands' End
113 N. Iowa St.
Dodgeville, WI 53533
(608) 935-9053

Lands' End
8777 N. Port Washington Rd.
Brown Port Shopping Center
Fox Point, WI 53217
(414) 247-8880

The Company Store
Factory Outlet Center
I-94 and Highway 50
Kenosha, WI 53142
(414) 857-7027

Fieldcrest-Cannon
Factory Outlet Center
I-94 and Highway 50
Kenosha, WI 53142
(414) 857-2729

Factory Outlets (cont.)

Wisconsin (cont.)

The Company Store
301 Sky Harbor Dr.
Lacrosse, WI 54603
(608) 783-6646

The Company Store
Walnut Grove Shopping Center
4032 University Ave.
Madison, WI 53705
(608) 238-9338

Lands' End
6755 Odanna Rd.
Madison, WI 53719
(608) 833-3343

Lands' End
Seconds and irregulars only
411 S. State St.
Madison, WI 53703
(608) 257-4900

Fieldcrest-Cannon
Horizon Outlet Center
U. S. 41 and Hwy. 44
Oshkosh, WI 54904
(414) 426-5704

Lands' End
Horizon Outlet Center
U. S. 41 and Hwy. 44
Oshkosh, WI 54904
(414) 424-7800

The Company Store
901 S. Main
Oshkosh, WI 54901
(414) 426-1443

Wholesale

The only ready-made bedding that is practical to buy at wholesale is luxury bedding. There are many showrooms that specialize in luxury sheets, dust ruffles, shams, bedspreads, coverlets, and comforters, all over the United States. Most of them work with decorators and will sell you anything one at a time. The normal trade discount is 40% to 50% off retail.

There are very few ultra-exclusive bedding brands that are restricted only to selected interior designers. The vast majority of luxury bedding manufacturers will sell to any wholesale buyer.

Luxury bedding showrooms all over the country are listed in the National Directory Of Wholesale Home Furnishings Sources and Showrooms, by William Graham, which is available from this publisher. There is an order form in the back of this book.

If you are planning to spend a substantial amount of money ($300.00 or more) on ready-made luxury bedding you should consider becoming your own decorator and buying it directly from the manufacturer, by mail or through a wholesale showroom near you -- unless you can order the brand you want from the J. Schachter Co. Call the J. Schachter Co. (listed on page 162) and compare the excellent discount you will usually receive from them as a consumer with the wholesale discount you could get as a decorator, and decide which route is best for the particular product you plan to purchase.

Either way you buy luxury bedding, the waiting time won't vary much. Wholesale showrooms don't usually keep bedding in stock. You will still have to wait about four weeks to receive your order from most manufacturers.

Recommendations

1 You should always contact wholesale workrooms and local home seamstresses to have your custom bed treatments made. Some will work with consumers directly. You have a good chance of finding at least one workroom or home seamstress in your area that will give you a straight wholesale price on custom labor if you shop during the slow business periods of summer and winter, especially January and July.

If you decide to become your own decorator, as discussed in Chapter 19, you can have your custom work done at wholesale prices any time of year.

It is very important to have a thorough understanding of custom bed treatments before hiring a workroom or seamstress to make them. When you make your own direct arrangements to have custom furnishings made, you are responsible for making sure that you have chosen appropriate styles and fabrics. The Complete Guide To Custom Bed Treatments covers this topic in depth.

2 It isn't worth becoming your own licensed decorator just to buy standard ready-made bedding at wholesale. There is already a well-established network of factory outlets that sell directly to the public at prices that are near wholesale. Also, the manufacturers that make most standard ready-made bedding do not usually accept small orders from interior decorators and interior designers -- they usually sell in bulk to large stores and store chains.

3 Luxury bedding is another story entirely. If you are interested in buying luxury sheets and comforters from high-brow manufacturers such as you can benefit by becoming your own decorator.

These, and many other, small manufacturers have wholesale showrooms that cater to interior designers and interior decorators. They also usually accept small wholesale orders by mail.

The usual discount to the trade is 40% to 50% off retail. If you are going to become your own decorator for the purpose of buying other types of furnishings, by all means buy your luxury bedding directly at a full trade discount.

The *National Directory of Wholesale Home Furnishings Sources and Showrooms*, by William Graham, lists and cross-indexes thousands of wholesale showrooms all over the U. S. that sell all types of home furnishings products and services. The *Directory* is a complete resource for designers and decorators who wish to buy all types of luxury and custom bedding, as well as other types of home furnishings. It's available from this publisher. There is an order form in the back of this book.

If you are considering becoming your own decorator only to buy luxury bedding, call the J. Schachter Co. first. You won't get straight wholesale, but you might get enough of a discount to make becoming your own decorator impractical in this particular situation. It will just depend on the price and amount of luxury bedding you intend to buy.

4 Interior designers, interior decorators, and retail stores usually have the very worst deals available on custom or ready-made bedding. Don't waste your money at these sources.

Chapter 9

Custom Accessories

Other custom accessories are available at or near wholesale prices, too: decorative pillows, chair cushions, and decorative tablecloths. These extra touches can really make a room look complete.

You do have to be extra careful about bargain shopping, however. Typically, the smaller an item is, the larger the middleman markup. You definitely don't want to have any of these furnishings made through a designer or retail store. Always go directly to a local wholesale workroom.

Decorative Pillows

There are an infinite variety of styles. Each workroom will have its own menu of styles and sizes, and its own specific yardage requirements. Contact a workroom in your area for the choices they have available. Read Chapter 18 for complete information on finding and working with local workrooms.

Chair Cushions

Prices and yardages for custom cushions will have to be individually quoted by the workroom. Make a newspaper template of the shape of your chair seat and bring it with your old cushion to the workroom. They can recommend an appropriate style and quote you the correct yardage.

Tablecloths

These are decorative tablecloths, designed to be used on small occasional tables. If you don't have one, you can get a particle board table very inexpensively at most home centers.

Tablecloths for dining room tables will have to be quoted individually by the workroom.

Sources These also should be made by a local workroom.

Styles There are only two basic styles, each with a few embellishments. You will find some more complex styles in design books and magazines. Ask the workroom for a price and yardage quote on the fancier styles.

Round: Round tablecloths normally fall all the way to the floor. When stretched out flat, this type of tablecloth is just a big hemmed circle of fabric.

Square: This is just a hemmed square of cloth draped over the table. Normally, the corners fall about halfway down the table.

Finished measurements You need to tell the workroom the diameter of the tabletop and the distance from the top of the table to the floor (called the "drop").

Round: The workroom will need to know the total finished diameter of the tablecloth.

You can figure this by doubling the distance from the top of the table to the floor, adding this figure to the diameter of the table top, and subtracting one inch. The inch you subtract will allow a one-half inch clearance all around the tablecloth to keep it from dragging on the floor.

For example, if your table is 18 inches across the top and 21 inches from the top of the table to the floor, the finished diameter of the tablecloth would be calculated as follows:

2 X distance from top of table to floor:	42 inches
Add diameter of table top:	+ 18 inches
	60 inches
Subtract one inch for clearance:	- 1 inch
Finished diameter of tablecloth:	59 inches

Make sure that the workroom knows that you have already subtracted an inch for clearance so that they won't duplicate this step.

Square: The workroom will need to know how long the side of the square should be. Most workrooms keep charts of appropriate table square sizes. Give them the measurements of your table and let them figure the correct size of the table square.

Yardage The standard yardage requirements are as follows:

Round: Any tablecloth up to 96 inches in diameter will require 5 1/2 yards of fabric. This assumes that you are using standard 54 inch wide decorative fabric.

If your fabric is an odd width or your tablecloth will be larger than 96 inches in diameter, ask the workroom for a custom yardage estimate.

Square: 2 yards is fine for most table squares. Ask the workroom.

Embellishments If you want to add any embellishments -- such as ruffles, tassels, drapery trim, welt, shirred welt, etc. -- to your tablecloth or table square, you will need to ask the workroom for a custom yardage estimate.

Drapery Trim

Drapery trim, fringe, rope trim, decorative tiebacks, tassels, etc. can be purchased from a variety of sources for your window treatments, bed treatments, and decorative accessories. Many local fabric stores in your area carry them, at very good prices. This will normally be your best source. Call ahead -- not all stores carry these products.

If you decide to become your own decorator, you will be able to browse through the many independent showrooms and design center showrooms that carry all kinds of decorative drapery trims. This is not a way to find a bargain -- most simple styles of trim are available at prices that are just as low at your local fabric store. However, wholesale shopping is a way to have access to the many unique styles and colors that are normally available only to decorators and designers.

Wholesale trim showrooms, manufacturers, and distributors all over the United States are listed in the *National Directory of Wholesale Home Furnishings Sources and Showrooms*, which is available from this publisher.

Interior Designers, Interior Decorators, and Retail Stores

No. Never. These sources often triple the real costs of these furnishings. My parents and I saw it all the time with our own products.

Ready-Made Accessories

About the only reasonably priced ready-made pillows, cushions, and tablecloths that you will find are in bedding factory outlets. These stores often carry a few basic styles and colors as well as accessories that match many of their ready-made bedding ensembles. If you live near a bedding factory outlet, check them out. They are listed on pages 171 to 180 .

Recommendations

1 If you live near a bedding factory outlet and you want a basic style or a style to match a ready-made bedding ensemble, check the outlet.

2 If you can't find what you want at an outlet, or if you want certain styles and fabrics to match your other furnishings, go to a local wholesale workroom.

3 Never have these accessories made through a retail store, interior designer, or interior decorator. Their middleman markups are unreal.

Chapter 10

Drapery Hardware

Drapery hardware comes in a wide variety of sizes and styles. There are even swagholders that allow you to create and install your own free-form swag treatments. There are also many reproduction antique and other unique styles available.

Types of Drapery Hardware

There are four basic types of drapery hardware: traverse rods, curtain rods, swagholders, and holdbacks. Each comes in a wide variety of shapes, sizes, and styles.

Traverse rods: These are drapery rods. They are designed with a pull cord on the side that pulls your draperies open and closed. They can be plain white, wood, or brass.

Curtain rods: These come in a wide variety of sizes and shapes, as well. Some are meant to be hidden in a rod pocket; others are made to show off.

Of the rod-pocket type, standard curtain rods are one inch in diameter. Flat curtain rods that are meant to be used with rod-pocket sleeve treatments come in widths of 2 1/2 inches and 5 inches. Sash rods are small (1/2 inch wide or so) flat rods that are meant to be mounted very close to the wall. They are ideal for double-rod pocket panels.

Decorative curtain rods can have decorative rings included, or not. Some companies package the rings separately. If you are having a tab curtain made, you don't need curtain rings. So, make sure you buy a rod that doesn't come with rings included if you don't need them. They are often available for a lower price.

Swagholders: These are very popular right now. The swag-it-yourself movement has really taken off in the 90's. There is a very wide variety of styles available -- everything from reproduction antique styles to contemporary shapes and colors.

Holdbacks: There are two types -- hidden and decorative. Hidden tieback holders are a very basic type of hardware that hold back drapery or curtain panels underneath a decorative fabric tieback. The decorative tieback is then attached over the tieback holder, according to the particular manufacturer's instructions.

Decorative holdbacks are very much like swagholders. In fact, some fixtures can be used as either. They also hold back drapery or curtain panels, except that they are meant to be seen.

Custom Drapery Hardware

You can order traverse rods and curtain rods in special shapes and sizes. You should allow the drapery workroom to arrange this for you. They will earn a small commission on the sale, but it's worth it. Custom rods are complicated and unreturnable. This is one of those times when you should pay for a little extra help.

Should You Install Your Own Drapery Hardware?

Yes. Most types of drapery hardware are very easy to install and come with complete instructions. The instructions will vary according to the particular type and brand you purchase, so we won't go over that here.

You don't need any special tools. A simple screwdriver is all you need, although an automatic screwdriver or a drill with a screwdriver attachment can make the job easier and faster.

Hardware Stores and Home Centers

These will normally be your cheapest local sources for most of your drapery hardware. About the only kinds they don't usually carry are unique decorative or reproduction antique hardware and custom cut rods.

Discount Stores

Local discount stores in your area, such as Wal-Mart and Target, are great sources for plain curtain and drapery rods. Sometimes, they even have better prices on these very basic types of hardware than hardware stores and home centers.

Interior Designers, Interior Decorators, and Retail Stores

Never buy drapery hardware from these sources. The standard middleman markup is at least 100% (sometimes more) on decorative hardware.

If you want to purchase high-style brands that you might have seen in a design magazine or wholesale showroom, you should either become your own decorator and buy it directly or ask the drapery workroom to order it for you. Normal workroom markups are usually a lot less than the markups charged by decorators, designers, and retail stores.

Factory Outlets

There generally aren't any factory outlets for drapery hardware. However, I did locate one company that sells its own line of wood and wrought-iron drapery rods by mail. Contact them directly for ordering information.

South Bound Millworks
P. O. Box 349
Sandwich, MA 02563
(508) 477-9355

Wholesale

There are a wide variety of wholesale companies that sell gorgeous decorative drapery hardware directly to decorators and designers. This is one product type that designers and decorators have kept a tight grip on. Until now.

There is a list of consumer-friendly wholesale design centers that will allow consumers to shop at a discount of approximately 20% off retail on page 328. Also, if you become your own decorator (as discussed in Chapter 19), you can buy your decorative hardware at trade discounts of 40% to 50% off retail.

Hundreds of decorative hardware manufacturers, independent showrooms, and design center showrooms are listed in the *National Directory of Wholesale Home Furnishings Sources and Showrooms*, which is available from this publisher. There is an order form in the back of this book.

Hardware stores, home centers, and discount stores are still your best bet for plain drapery hardware. Major hardware manufacturers that sell basic drapery and curtain rods generally do not sell directly to decorators.

Recommendations

1 Shop at your local hardware store, home center, or discount store first. This is normally the cheapest source for basic drapery hardware.

2 If you can't find what you need, or if you are looking for a fancier style, check out a design center near you that is open to the public.

3 If there isn't one, and depending on how much decorative hardware you plan to buy, consider becoming your own decorator and shopping at the many sources in your area that serve local decorators and designers.

Chapter 11

Hard Window Treatments

The hard window treatment industry has a well-established system for selling to consumers at deep discounts. Telephone ordering services will be your best bet in most cases. You will also find a variety of ready-made window treatments that can be purchased right off the shelf at many home centers (such as Home Depot). Custom shutters can be ordered at rock-bottom prices from home centers and local wholesale shutter manufacturers.

There aren't any scams to speak of in this part of the home furnishings industry. Buying hard window treatments is pretty straightforward. There are some safety concerns for children that you should be aware of. More on that later in the chapter.

Like the ads say: shop in your neighborhood, record product information, and then head straight for the discounters and wholesale sources.

Horizontal Blinds

Types Horizontal blinds come in a variety of slat widths, ranging from about 1/2" to 2". The slats are usually aluminum, although they are also available in plastic and wood.

Horizontal blinds are the cheapest and most widely available of the hard window treatments. Blinds made from all three types of materials will last for many years under normal use. Plastic slats are the cheapest, followed by aluminum. Wooden blinds are the most expensive type of horizontal blinds.

Ready-made blinds Ready-made horizontal blinds in an array of standard sizes are widely available in discount stores and home centers. These blinds usually have plastic slats and can be inside or outside mounted. They are normally available in white, off-white, black, light blue, rose, and dark green. Most stores carry a variety of standard sizes.

If these sizes and colors suit your home, you will usually be best off to buy ready-made blinds. If the standard sizes don't match your windows, you can always buy a size slightly larger than your windows and outside-mount the blinds. These blinds are not inferior in quality in any significant way to the more expensive custom-made blinds.

The only major difference is that ready-made blinds usually have plastic slats and custom-made blinds usually have aluminum slats, but both materials are very durable. Save the difference in money and spend it somewhere else where it will be more likely to be noticed.

Custom-made blinds If you do not wish to use ready-made blinds, most brands, styles, and colors can be ordered in any size you wish from a telephone ordering service or home center. This is the next-cheapest alternative to ready-made blinds.

Unusual window shapes Horizontal blinds are available in odd sizes to cover unusually shaped windows, such as palladian windows and angled window s. These treatments are significantly more expensive than standard rectangular blinds and must always be custom-made. There are a variety of soft-window treatments that can be used to cover these types of windows much more cheaply.

Other details

1 A small valance made of two slats will be provided at no charge by most companies. However, you must specifically request this.

2 Hold-down brackets are available that attach the bottom of the blind to the door or window frame and prevent the blind from flapping whenever the door is opened or a breeze is blowing. These are usually provided free upon request, but you must specifically ask for them when you place your order.

Vertical Blinds

Vertical blinds are also a relatively inexpensive way to cover a window. You will be able to find a few sizes and colors ready-made at discount stores and home centers. These can be outside-mounted if the standard sizes do not exactly match your windows.

Types Although vertical blinds can be made from a wide variety of materials, PVC (polyvinyl chloride) and woven polyester are the most common. You may wish to avoid aluminum vertical blinds because of the tendency of the louvers to clang against each other loudly when there is a breeze. PVC vanes will make a slight noise, but this is rarely bothersome. Woven polyester usually makes no noise at all.

The more exotic materials, such as wood, macrame', and custom fabrics and wallpapers to match those in your home, can be quite a bit more expensive and often must be ordered through an interior designer or retail blinds store.

Ready-made blinds Vertical blinds made from PVC in a few sizes and colors can be purchased ready-made at discount stores and home centers. If these ready-made blinds are the correct size and color for your home, you can save a lot of money by using them. The quality of these blinds is almost comparable to that of custom-made blinds. If the ready-made sizes will not quite fit your window, the blinds can be outside-mounted.

Custom-made blinds If you do not wish to use ready-made blinds, most brands, styles, and colors can be ordered in any size you wish from a telephone ordering service or home center. This is the next-cheapest alternative to ready-made blinds.

Unusual window shapes Custom-made verticals can be made to fit angled windows, although this is a relatively expensive way to cover this type of window. If you must completely cover the window, there are a variety of soft-window treatments that can do the job for much less money. Angled verticals must usually be ordered through an interior designer or retail blinds store.

Pleated Shades

Pleated shades are slightly more expensive than blinds. They are, however, much better suited to traditionally decorated rooms. Horizontal and vertical blinds are considered to be contemporary style furnishings and should not be used in more formal or traditional rooms.

Types Pleated shades range from totally opaque to very translucent. The opaque shades block most light, but some light will come in through the small holes that the control strings pass through and around the edges of the shade. If you must completely darken a room, you would be better off to buy a blackout roller shade or a blackout honeycomb-pleated shade.

Most pleated shades are made from polyester cloth in a variety of thicknesses and textures. It is possible to have shades made from custom decorative fabric or wallpaper to match other furnishings in your home, but these are very expensive and must usually be ordered through a retail blinds store or interior designer.

In addition to standard pleated shades, shades are also available in a double or triple-honeycomb pattern, as shown below. Honeycomb shades are slightly more expensive than standard pleated shades, but they have some advantages. They can be made to completely blackout light because the control strings are embedded inside the honeycombed layers. Also, they are more energy-efficient than most other types of window treatments because they trap air inside the honeycomb structure, similar to the way a thermal blanket works. Air is an excellent insulator.

Ordering Pleated shades are generally not available ready-made. However, a wide variety of brands, styles, and colors can be ordered in any custom size from telephone ordering services and home centers. These sources will generally offer you the best prices on these treatments.

Unusual window shapes Pleated shades can be made to fit oddly-shaped windows, such as those shown below. However, like blinds, this is a relatively expensive way to treat unusual windows. These treatments often must be ordered through retail blinds stores and interior designers.

Make Sure Your Window Treatments Have Child-Safe Tassels

Over the last decade, many children have strangled to death after putting their heads through the double tassel cords on many types of hard window treatments.

In response to this, window treatment manufacturers have developed a special tassel that will separate under pressure to avoid any future tragedies. The new tassels should be on display at most home centers and blinds stores.

All new hard window treatments are supposed to have the new tassels. However, because some businesses will not want to throw away the old tassels, they are certain to be sold to some consumers. Double-check any treatments you purchase. The tassel should separate into two parts when you pull the strings apart. If not, don't buy the treatments from that business.

Be sure to inform the business owner about the old tassels. Despite the massive information campaign that has been implemented by the Window Covering Safety Council, it is possible that the business owner might not know about the new tassels.

If you already own hard window treatments that have the old, unsafe tassels, you can get new child-safe tassels at many home centers, including Home Depot.

Shutters

Interior shutters are relatively expensive window treatments. However, they will usually last a lifetime and can add to the resale value of your home (especially plantation shutters).

All shutters have a center control bar that allows the slats to be tilted open and shut. Some shutters open outwards from the center. Others open in a fan-folding pattern. Sliding or double-hung shutters have panels that slide across one another.

Shutters come in a variety of slat widths. Standard traditional shutters have slats that are between one and one-half inch wide. Plantation shutters have slats that are between two and four inches wide. Plantation shutters have a more expensive and elegant look and retain more of their value when you resell your home.

Sizes Shutters are normally inside-mounted, which means that they must usually be custom-made. However, there are a limited variety of shutters available in a few standard sizes and colors at some home centers. If your windows are the right size, you might be able to use the ready-made shutters instead of custom-ordering them.

Installation Simple ready-made shutters can be installed by most consumers. Instructions are included with the shutters. You shouldn't require any tools other than a screwdriver and, perhaps, a drill.

However, there are a few situations in which you might need a professional installer. If your windows are not perfectly square, you may have difficulty hanging the shutters properly. Sliding and double-hung shutters can be difficult to fit together properly. If you run into trouble, especially with sliding shutters, stop and call an installer. If you damage the shutters, they might be completely ruined.

Because of the relative expense of the shutters themselves and the difficulty of installing some types of custom shutters, you should usually purchase custom shutters from a local shutter manufacturer. These companies usually sell to interior designers and interior decorators, but some will also sell directly to the public.

Sources Many home centers can order custom shutters for you, but because they are such large businesses and carry a wide-variety of merchandise that is in demand year-round, they are largely invulnerable to seasonal slumps. Small local shutter manufacturers usually only sell one product, so they are very vulnerable to the usual January and July slumps.

Throughout the year, you will usually find slightly cheaper prices on custom shutters at home centers, but in July and January, you can often get local wholesale shutter manufacturers to give you a great discount which makes them a better choice. You also have a good chance of getting the small shutter manufacturer to throw in free installation if they really need the business. Compare prices carefully at both types of businesses, no matter when you shop.

Wholesale Some small local shutter manufacturers will sell directly to consumers who approach them. They generally do not advertise for retail business because this would jeopardize their wholesale business. Some of these manufacturers advertise in the Yellow Pages under "*Shutters-Wholesale*". Hundreds more are listed in the *National Directory of Wholesale Home Furnishings Sources and Showrooms*, by William Graham, which is available from this publisher.

As always when dealing with any wholesale business, you should be as well-prepared as possible when you approach the shutter manufacturer. Look through shutter samples in retail shutter stores. Write down all brand, style, size, and color information from the sample you select. Have all of your window measurements ready when you place your order.

Most national brands will be available from any local manufacturer. Many local manufacturers also have their own in-house brands which may be comparable to the national brands but less expensive.

If you can get the shutter manufacturer to throw in free installation, as you might during the slow seasons, take it. If they won't do it free, try to install them yourself. Basic shutters aren't difficult to install. Make sure that you receive an installation instruction sheet when you place your order.

Please read Chapter 18 carefully. The instructions and suggestions for dealing with local drapery and upholstery workrooms apply to local shutter manufacturers as well. The better prepared you are when you approach a wholesale business, the more likely they are to want to work with you.

How To Properly Measure Your Windows

See pages 134 to 145 for basic window measurement instructions. The same instructions apply for hard and soft window treatments.

Bear in mind that exact measurements are very important for hard window treatments. Record all measurements exactly, to the nearest eighth of an inch. Never round measurements up or down.

Fill out one copy of the appropriate measuring chart for each window. Bring copies of these charts with you when you place your order at any local source. Have them in front of you when you place your order with a telephone ordering service.

Outside Installation vs. Inside Installation

Inside installation is preferable from an aesthetic standpoint. It will eliminate the need for any additional window treatments, which may be installed on top of the hard window treatment, to be set very far out from the wall. If you outside-mount your hard window treatments, any valances or other overtreatments will have to be set an additional three inches away from the wall. This can look bulky.

If you use inside-mounted treatments, it is not necessary to use an additional overtreatment, such as a valance or curtains. Inside-mounted treatments are usually more expensive because they must be custom-made to exactly fit the window frame.

Outside installation can save you money. There is no need to exactly fit the window frame, so you can use a standard size. You will be able to make use of inexpensive ready-made blinds sold at discount stores, if you wish. However, there will usually be a gap along either side of the treatment. You

Don't Be Too Impressed By a Huge "Discount"

Retail prices for blinds and pleated shades are often inflated beyond all recognition. Everyone, even interior designers, will give you 50% off the "retail" list prices set by many manufacturers.

You should expect to receive a discount of at least 75% to 80% off retail on most blinds and pleated shades, but not shutters. Shutters are usually not priced so unrealistically.

will have to use some type of side curtains over the treatment in order to maintain privacy.

These ready-made window treatments will rarely fit your window exactly, but this is fine within reason. If you cannot find a ready-made treatment in a size that is fairly close to the size of your window (no larger than three inches beyond the window frame on each side), you will have to have the treatments made in a custom size. If the hard window treatments extend too far beyond the window frame, any overtreatments you use will look strange and oversized compared to the window frame. This is rare. You can find ready-made treatments that are appropriate for most windows.

If you plan to use a plain hard window treatment, such as horizontal blinds or vertical blinds in a standard solid color, with an overtreatment, you can usually save money by buying ready-made blinds at a discount store or home center and mounting them outside the window frame. You can often find some styles of shutters in ready-made sizes, too. If you do not plan to use an overtreatment, you will want to order inside-mounted hard window treatments.

If you plan to order pleated shades, you will want to order them inside-mounted because these types of hard window treatments are usually not available in less-expensive ready-made versions. You will have to have them custom-made, anyway.

How To Properly Place Your Custom Order

Aside from the manufacturer's name, style name or number, and color name or number, which will all be listed on the window treatment samples you will be looking at, there are a few other features that must be clearly specified on your custom order:

1 State your measurements in the proper order and clearly specify them: It is customary to state the width first and then the length. If you simply ordered a 36" by 54" blind, the manufacturer would assume that the width is 36" and the length is 54". If this was not correct, your order would be unusable, and the manufacturer would probably refuse to correct it because it would consider the problem to be your fault.

To avoid confusion, always state the width first. Also, clearly state which is the width and which is the length to avoid any expensive misunderstandings.

2 You need to specify on which side you would like the controls (which raise and lower your treatments and turn the louvers in the case of blinds) located on all treatments except shutters.

The proper terms are "left hand controls" and "right hand controls". There is no one best way, except that you should make sure that you will be able to easily reach the controls from wherever the blinds will be mounted.

3 You need to specify the "draw" for vertical blinds. "Split draw" (sometimes called "center draw") means that the blinds are in two panels and open from the center. "One-way draw -- left" means that the blinds are in a single panel and stack back to the left hand side of the window when they are opened. "One-way draw -- right" means that the blinds stack

back to the right hand side of the window.

If you have a very wide window or glass door and you plan to use side curtains, you should order split draw. One-way drawn blinds on a wide window or door can have a very bulky stackback that might not be covered by your side curtains.

4 You must also specify clearly whether the treatment is to be installed inside or outside the window frame. The correct abbreviation for inside-mount is "IB" which means "inside bracket". The correct abbreviation for outside-mount is "OB" which means "outside bracket". It is very important to make this notation so that the manufacturer will know whether or not an allowance will need to be made in your measurements.

5 When you are ordering inside-mounted treatments, list the exact inside width and length of the window frame on your order form. It is customary for the manufacturer to make the allowance necessary for your treatments to fit properly. On most treatments, the manufacturer will subtract about one-half inch from your width measurements. On vertical blinds, the manufacturer will also subtract about one-quarter to one-half inch from your length measurements.

6 The proper way to order outside-mounted treatments is to specify the exact measurement you want them to finish. The manufacturer will not make any allowances or adjustments if you have specified outside brackets. You should add three inches to the measurement of the OUTSIDE width of your window frame and two inches to the length of your window from the outside of the top frame to the sill.

It is very, very rare that you would ever order custom-made outside-mounted hard window treatments. Virtually the only reason why you would ever want to use outside-mounted treatments is to be able to use inexpensive ready-made treatments from a home center.

If you have very shallow windows (less than an inch deep), you will have to use outside-mounted treatments. I have only seen such windows a few times -- this is extremely rare. If, in addition to this problem, you cannot find ready-made treatments in the style and color you want, you will have to order custom-made outside-mounted treatments.

Should You Do Your Own Installation?

Yes. Installing hard window treatments is very easy. You will usually receive complete written instructions with your order, and they are very easy to follow. All necessary screws, brackets, and other necessary hardware should be included with your order. All you should have to supply are the tools.

You will usually only need a screwdriver, although a drill can make the job easier by allowing you to drill "pilot" holes (shallow holes to start the screws in). If you have a power screwdriver, this can sometimes take the place of a drill. If you are installing treatments on an extremely hard surface, such as a cinder-block wall, you must use a drill.

If you don't own a drill, you can rent one at many hardware stores, home centers, and equipment rental businesses.

How To Find A Reputable Installer

If you cannot do your own installation, or just don't want to, you can hire a professional. These people normally work for interior designers and interior decorators, but many of them will work for you, too. Of course, if you are your own decorator, this problem won't ever come up.

Professional drapery installers usually install hard window treatments, as well. If you are already working with a home seamstress or drapery workroom, they will often be able to put you in touch with a reputable local drapery installer. If you aren't, call a workroom anyway. Most are happy to refer an you to a reputable installer. You may rarely see a wholesale drapery installer advertised in the Yellow Pages.

Interior Designers, Interior Decorators, and Retail Stores

Don't buy blinds here. You will be paying at least twice as much as you have to, or possibly even more.

Blinds Stores

Believe it or not, these places usually don't have the best prices on blinds. Their prices are good, but you can do better.

Discount Stores

Discount stores, such as Wal-Mart and Target, usually carry a variety of ready-made horizontal and vertical blinds at great prices.

Hardware Stores and Home Centers

Most home centers and many hardware stores carry a variety of ready-made horizontal and vertical blinds. Some also carry ready-made shutters. The prices are very good and the quality is perfectly adequate.

They often sell custom-made blinds, shutters, and pleated shades, as well. Their prices on custom-made window treatments in the most common styles and colors are very low, sometimes as low as telephone ordering services. Telephone ordering services usually have the best prices on a much wider range of styles and colors. You should contact both types of businesses and compare prices carefully when ordering custom-made blinds and pleated shades.

If you are shopping during the slow seasons, you should compare prices on custom shutters with a local wholesale shutter manufacturer. They will often give you a better deal than a home center during the usual seasonal business slumps.

Telephone Ordering Services

These services will give you the best prices by far in all but the most common styles and colors.

The quality of window treatments sold by these services is fine. In fact, they normally sell the very same brands of window treatments that interior designers and retail stores sell. The savings you will receive are due to the services buying in bulk and maintaining low overhead expenses, not due to any reduction in the quality of their products.

Before calling the service, you should first measure your windows, decide whether you want inside or outside-mounted treatments, decide what type of controls and draw you want (if applicable), and decide which brand, style, and color you want.

Brand, style, and color information can be found on samples used in blinds stores, retail home furnishings stores, and interior design shops. Be sure to write down the manufacturer's name, the style name, the style number, and the color of the sample you select. If you have any doubt as to whether a description or number is important, write it down.

Don't worry about phony brand names or item numbers. This just isn't done for the most part in the hard window treatment industry. Any telephone ordering service should have no difficulty filling your order based on the product information as it appears on the sample.

Telephone Ordering Services

"A" Window Treatment Company
525 Bright Leaf Blvd.
Smithfield, NC 27577
(800) 552-5463

American Blind and Wallpaper Factory
28237 Orchard Lake Rd.
Farmington Hills, MI 48334
(800) 735-5300

American Discount Wall and Window Coverings
1411 Fifth Ave.
Pittsburgh, PA 15219
(800) 777-2737

American Wallcovering Distributors
2260 Route 22
Union, NJ 07083
(800) 843-6567

Blind Busters
10858 Harry Hines Blvd.
Dallas, TX 75220
(800) 883-5000

Blind Center USA
7013 3rd Ave.
Brooklyn, NY 11209
(800) 676-5029

Custom Windows and Walls
32525 Stephenson Hwy.
Madison Heights, MI 48071
(800) 772-1947

The Decorator's Edge
509 Randolph St.
Thomasville, NC 27360
(800) 289-5589

Designer Secrets
P. O. Box 529
Fremont, NE 68025
(800) 955-2559

Headquarters Window and Walls
8 Clinton Place
Morristown, NJ 07960
(800) 338-4882

Telephone Ordering Services (cont.)

MDC Direct
22 Trammel St.
Marietta, GA 30062
(800) 892-2083

Mary's Wallcoverings
400 Galleria, Suite 400
Southfield, MI 48038
(800) 521-3393

National Blind and
Wallpaper Factory
400 Galleria, Suite 400
Southfield, MI 48038
(800) 477-8000

New England Blinds
7013 3rd Ave.
Brooklyn, NY 11209
(800) 676-5029

Peerless Wallpaper and
Blind Depot
39500 14 Mile Rd.
Walled Lake, MI 48390
(800) 999-0898

Pintchik Homeworks
222 Avenue "U"
Brooklyn, NY 11223
(800) 847-4199

Post Wallcoverings
333 Skokie Blvd.
Northbrook, IL 60062
(800) 322-5400

Shriber's Discount
Wallcoverings and Blinds
3222 Brighton Rd.
Pittsburgh, PA 15212
(800) 245-6676

Silver's Wholesale Club
3001-15 Kensington Ave.
Philadelphia, PA 19134
(800) 426-6600

Smart Wallcoverings
400 Galleria, Suite 400
Southfield, MI 48038
(800) 677-0200

Smith and Noble
P.O. Box 1838
Corona, CA 91718
(800) 248-8888

Style Wallcoverings
and Blinds
400 Galleria, Suite 400
Southfield, MI 48038
(800) 627-0400

Three Day Blinds
2220 E. Cerritos Ave.
Anaheim, CA 92806
(800) 800-3DAY

USA Blind Factory
1312 Live Oak
Houston, TX 77003
(800) 275-3219

Wallpaper Xpress
1723 Jericho Rd.
Aurora, IL 60506
(800) 288-9979

Wells Interiors
7171 Amador Plaza Rd.
Dublin, CA 94568
(800) 547-8982

Window Scene
9833 Pacific Heights Blvd.
San Diego, CA 92121
(800) 786-3021

Worldwide Wallcoverings
and Blinds
333 Skokie Blvd.
Northbrook, IL 60062
(800) 322-5400

Yankee Wallcoverings
109 Accord Park Dr.
Norwell, MA 02061
(800) 624-7711

Wholesale

There are wholesale sources for hard window treatments, but most of them aren't worth bothering with. You can get prices that are just as low on blinds and pleated shades by shopping with a telephone ordering service or a local home center. Plus, you will be able to pay with your credit card.

The only exceptions to this are custom shutters. Custom shutters are relatively expensive, and you can sometimes save money by buying them wholesale.

Of course, if you buy shutters wholesale, you will have to give up the protection of using your credit card. Weigh the loss of this protection carefully against the wholesale discount you will receive (compared to the price that you would receive at a local home center). If the difference in price isn't very much, you might want to stick with your local home center and use your credit card.

Recommendations

1 Shop in your neighborhood and record product information for the styles you prefer: manufacturer, brand, style, color, etc.

2 Measure your own windows, and do your own installation (unless you are purchasing a complicated type of shutters). Be extremely careful and precise when taking your window measurements.

3 You will normally get the best prices from telephone ordering service for blinds and shades, and from home centers for custom shutters. If you are shopping during a seasonal slump (summer and winter, especially during January and July), also check shutter prices with local wholesale shutter manufacturers.

Chapter 12

Lighting

Lighting and fans seem to go together in the home furnishings industry so we will discuss them together in this chapter. Virtually all of the various discount sources in this chapter carry both.

How To Make Sure You Are Buying Quality Products

Very simple. Look for the UL approval seal or tag. Most lighting and fan manufacturers display it. Quality is really not a major concern when you are buying this type of furnishing. If the product carries UL approval, you can rest assured that you are getting a quality product. Just look for the style you find most attractive.

Should You Install Your Own Lighting Fixtures and Fans?

Ceiling fans and ceiling mounted lighting fixtures are often not difficult to install, but there is a risk of electrocution. The source you order your fixtures from should be able to provide you with adequate written installation instructions when you receive your order. There are also several books on the subject available in libraries and bookstores.

Professional installers are not cheap, so there is a compelling financial reason to try to "do-it-yourself". Before you attempt this, please read the instructions that arrive with your order very carefully and make absolutely certain that there is no danger of electrocution.

Turn the power off at the fuse box, of course, but also check wires directly before you handle them. Hardware stores sell an inexpensive tool that can test wires before you touch them and determine if there is any current running through them. You may wish to pick one up and discuss your installation with your local hardware store while you are there.

Home Depot stores all over the United States offer free classes in many subjects, including installing ceiling fans and lighting fixtures. Call the

Home Depot store in your area for information about upcoming classes. You can also contact community colleges and technical schools in your area. Many offer low-cost classes on these topics.

Many consumers safely install their own lighting fixtures and ceiling fans each year even though they have no training as electricians. However, each year there are also a number of injuries and deaths. Hire professional help if you have any doubt whatsoever about your ability to do this job on your own.

How To Hire a Professional Installer

Any electrician should be able to install your lighting fixtures and ceiling fans. You can usually find the least expensive electricians in your area by asking for a referral at your local hardware store.

You should ask for at least three referrals from previous customers, as always. Also, check with the Department of Professional Regulation or business license office in your county. Most counties inspect and license electricians, although the specific department that handles this will sometimes vary from county to county. You should make sure that the electrician is properly licensed and has no record of problems.

Retail Stores and Interior Designers

Needless to say, you should avoid shopping here, unless you can arrange to purchase something another customer has returned or failed to pay for.

Small items like lighting and fans often carry the highest middleman markups from these sources because they often pass through two levels of middlemen between the manufacturer and you. Many lighting and fan manufacturers sell to wholesale distributors, who then sell to retail stores and designers, who then sell to consumers. Each level of middlemen collects an extra commission at the consumer's expense. You can do much better.

Telephone Ordering Services

Unless you live within a reasonable driving distance of a factory outlet or deep discount store, telephone ordering services will normally be your best source for lighting and fans. There is a well established system of discounters that sell directly to the consumer at up to 50% off. Even high-style designer brands, such as Frederick Cooper and Stiffel, are carried by these companies.

Shop at lighting stores, furniture stores, fan stores, and general retail home furnishings stores in your area to collect product information. Write down the brand name, style name or number, size, and color (if applicable).

Browse through interior design magazines. Most have a resource page in the back that lists the correct manufacturer name and style name or number for most of the products featured in the magazine. Don't worry if the magazine has a "T" notation after the particular item you want to order, meaning that the product is supposedly available only to the trade. Many of those "trade" products ARE available from telephone ordering services. Call several services to see if they carry it.

Watch out for phony style names and numbers. Manufacturer identities are generally not falsified or hidden on samples of lighting or fans in retail stores and interior design studios, but style names and numbers sometimes are. Magazines and wholesale showrooms never falsify product information.

If you see that the original manufacturer's product information has been marked out and replaced with the store's own style names and numbers, shop somewhere else. There are still some stores that do not alter their samples this way.

If there is a wholesale design center near you that is open to the public on certain days, you can browse through many lighting and fan showrooms there. Wholesale showrooms usually don't alter product information. There is a listing of wholesale design centers that have open shopping days on page 399.

These services are generally very reliable, but you should still always use your credit card. Read Chapter 16 for general tips on dealing with any telephone ordering service.

Your order will normally be shipped within four to six weeks. A few of the more expensive lighting brands take up to eight weeks because each lighting fixture is custom-made.

Most of the services listed on page 206 ask that you have all necessary product information ready when you call, unless noted otherwise. A few services have a catalog available for a fee, although these services can usually process your order if you just call them with the product information instead of ordering a catalog.

Telephone Ordering Services

American Lighting
521- D West Market St.
Suite 803
Greensboro, NC 27409
(800) 741-0571

Barnes & Barnes Fine Furniture
(Call for free brochure)
190 Commerce Ave.
Southern Pines, NC 28387
(800) 334-8174

Blackwelder's
Route 18, Box 8
Statesville, NC 28677
(800) 438-0201

Boyles Distinctive Furniture
Hickory Furniture Mart
Hickory, NC 28602
(704) 326-1740

Corner Hutch Furniture
Highway 21 North
Statesville, NC 28677
(704) 873-1773

The Decorator's Edge
509 Randolph St.
Thomasville, NC 27360
(800) 289-5589

Designer Secrets
P. O. Box 529
Fremont, NE 68025
(800) 955-2559

Edgar B.
P. O. Box 849
Clemmons, NC 27012
(800) 255-6589

European Furniture Importers
(Send $3.00 for catalog)
2145 W. Grand Ave.
Chicago, IL 60612
(800) 283-1955

Golden Valley Lighting
(Send $3.00 for catalog)
274 Eastchester Dr.
High Point, NC 27262
(800) 735-3377

Lamp Warehouse
1073 39th St.
Brooklyn, NY 11219
(800) 525-4837

Lighting By Gregory
158 Bowery
New York, NY 10012
(800) 796-1965

Loftin-Black Furniture
111 Sedgehill Dr.
Thomasville, NC 27360
(800) 334-7398

Mallory's Fine Furniture
2153 Le Jeune Blvd.
Jacksonville, NC 28546
(910) 353-1828

Mecklenburg Furniture
7203 Statesville Rd.
Charlotte, NC 28213
(800) 541-9877

Nationwide Lighting
1073 39th St.
Brooklyn, NY 11219
(800) 52-LITES

Quality Furniture Market
2034 Hickory Blvd. SE
Lenoir, NC 28645
(704) 728-2946

Studio of Lights
2418 S. Main St.
High Point, NC 27263
(910) 882-6854

Sutton-Councill Furniture
421 S. College Rd.
Wilmington, NC 28403
(910) 799-9000

Triad Furniture Discounters
9770 North Kings Hwy.
Magnolia Plaza
Myrtle Beach, SC 29577
(800) 323-8469

Turner Tolson Furniture
U. S. Hwy. 17 S
New Bern, NC 28562
(919) 638-2121

Tyson Furniture
109 Broadway St.
Black Mountain, NC 28711
(704) 669-5000

Factory Outlets

If you are within a reasonable driving distance to any of the factory outlets listed below, you should check them out. Each carries a limited variety of irregular and closeout products at up to 75% off retail. You can find some great bargains.

However, most of you will be better off to order your lighting fixtures and fans from a telephone ordering service, especially if there is no outlet in your city. The prices are nearly as low on most styles and you will have access to a much wider variety of brands and styles.

California

Stained Glass Factory Outlet
Factory Stores of America
at Nut Tree
321-2 Nut Tree Rd.
Vacaville, CA 95687
(707) 448-5706

Georgia

Hampstead
4505-E Peachtree Industrial Blvd.
Norcross, GA 30092
(770) 447-1700

Illinois

Stained Glass Factory Outlet
Gurnee Mills
I-94 and Route 132
Gurnee, IL 60031
(800) YES-SHOP

Maine

Stained Glass Factory Outlet
Factory Stores of America
Exit 3 off I-95
Kittery, ME 03904
(207) 439-3221

Michigan

Stained Glass Factory Outlet
Outlets At Birch Run
Exit 136 off I-75
Birch Run, MI 48415
(517) 624-4578

Missouri

Stained Glass Factory Outlet
Factory Merchants Branson
West Hwy. 76 and Pat Nash Dr.
Branson, MO 65616
(417) 339-2854

New Jersey

Shady Lamp Shop
Liberty Village Factory Outlets
Route 31 and Route 202
Flemington, NJ 08822
(908) 788-5200

New York

Shady Lamp Shop
Woodbury Common Factory Outlets
Exit 16 (Harriman exit) off I-87
Central Valley, NY 10917
(914) 928-6676

North Carolina

King's Chandelier Co.
Highway 14
Eden, NC 27288
(910) 623-6188

Beacon Hill Factory Outlet
Hickory Furniture Mart
Hickory, NC 28602
(704) 324-2220

North Carolina (cont.)

Home Outfitters
Hickory Furniture Mart
Hickory, NC 28602
(704) 324-2220

Pennsylvania

Antique Hardware Store
Reproduction lighting only
9730 Easton Rd.
Kintnersville, PA 18930
(800) 422-9982

Virginia

Solid Brass of Williamsburg
Williamsburg Outlet Mall
Exit 234 off I-64
Lightfoot, VA 23090
(804) 565-1177

Lamp Factory Outlet
Potomac Mills Outlet Center
Exit 156 off I-95
Prince William, VA 22192
(800) VA-MILLS

Wisconsin

Shady Lady Outlet
1670 Pleasant Valley Rd.
Grafton, WI 53024
(800) 343-1954

The Brighter Side
Factory Outlet Center
I-94 and Highway 50
Kenosha, WI 53142
(414) 857-7724

Deep Discount Stores

These stores buy in bulk directly from manufacturers and sell at up to 50% off retail. Many stores carry a limited variety of irregulars and closeouts at up to 75% off retail. Catalog clearance stores, such as Sears Catalog Clearance Center and J. C. Penney Catalog Outlet, sell customer returns at about 50% to 75% off retail.

If you are within a reasonable driving distance from any of these sources, you should check them out. They have some truly spectacular bargains.

However, many of you will be better off to order from a telephone ordering service. The savings are not quite as great, but you will have access to a much wider variety of brands and styles. You can also avoid the hassle and expense of traveling to the discount store.

Deep Discount Stores

California

Sears Catalog Clearance Center
14500 E. Hatch Rd.
Modesto, CA 95351
(209) 538-0579

Sears Catalog Clearance Center
3450 College Ave.
San Diego, CA 92115
(619) 583-9802

Sears Catalog Clearance Center
2750 E. Main St.
Ventura, CA 93003
(805) 643-8661

Georgia

Ballard's Backroom
Catalog Clearance Center
1670 De Foor Ave.
Atlanta, GA 30318
(404) 352-2776

J. C. Penney Catalog Outlet
5500 S. Expressway
Forest Park, GA 30050
(404) 363-3855

Georgia (cont.)

Design Center Outlet
6315 Spalding Dr.
Norcross, GA 30092
(770) 825-0020

J. C. Penney Catalog Outlet
2434 Atlanta Rd.
Smyrna, GA 30080
(770) 432-5231

Illinois

European Furniture Importers
2145 W. Grand Ave.
Chicago, IL 60612
(800) 283-1955

North Carolina

Tyson Furniture
109 Broadway St.
Black Mountain, NC 28711
(704) 669-5000

The Furniture Patch
10283 Beach Dr. SW
Calabash, NC 28467
(910) 579-2001

Deep Discount Stores (cont.)

North Carolina (cont.)

Mecklenburg Furniture
7203 Statesville Rd.
Charlotte, NC 28213
(800) 541-9877

House Dressing
International Furniture
3608 W. Wendover
Greensboro, NC 27407
(800) 322-5850

Priba Furniture Sales
5-A Wendy Ct.
Greensboro, NC 27409
(910) 855-9034

Designer Creations
Hickory Furniture Mart
Hickory, NC 28602
(704) 327-9933

Alan Ferguson Associates
422 S. Main St.
High Point, NC 27260
(910) 889-3866

Arts By Alexander
701 Greensboro Rd.
High Point, NC 27260
(910) 884-8062

Black's Furniture
2800 Westchester St.
High Point, NC 27262
(910) 886-5011

Boyles Furniture Co.
727 N. Main St.
High Point, NC 27262
(910) 889-4147

Dallas Furniture Store
215 N. Centennial St.
High Point, NC 27260
(910) 882-2654

North Carolina (cont.)

Gibson Interiors
417 S. Wrenn St.
High Point, NC 27260
(910) 883-4444

High Point Furniture Sales
2000 Baker Rd.
High Point, NC 27260
(800) 334-1875

Kathryn's Collection
781 N. Main St.
High Point, NC 27262
(910) 841-7474

Main St. Galleries
430 S. Main St.
High Point, NC 27260
(910) 883-2611

Payne Furniture
2904 N. Main St.
High Point, NC 27265
(910) 887-4444

Rose Furniture
916 Finch Ave.
High Point, NC 27263
(910) 886-6050

Rose Furniture Clearance Center
1813 S. Main St.
High Point, NC 27260
(910) 886-8525

Studio of Lights
2601 S. Main St.
High Point, NC 27263
(910) 882-6854

Utility Craft Inc.
2630 Eastchester Dr.
High Point, NC 27265
(910) 454-6153

North Carolina (cont.)

Wood Armfield Furniture
460 S. Main St.
High Point, NC 27260
(910) 889-6522

Young's Furniture and Rug Co.
1706 N. Main St.
High Point, NC 27262
(910) 883-4111

Mallory's Fine Furniture
2153 Le Jeune Blvd.
Jacksonville, NC 28546
(910) 353-1828

Furnitureland South
5635 Riverdale Rd.
Jamestown, NC 27282
(910) 841-4328

Quality Furniture Market
2034 Hickory Blvd. SE
Lenoir, NC 28645
(704) 728-2946

Homeway Furniture
121 W. Lebanon St.
Mount Airy, NC 27030
(800) 334-9094

Turner Tolson Furniture
U. S. Hwy. 17 S
New Bern, NC 28562
(919) 638-2121

A. & H. Wayside Furniture
1086 Freeway Dr.
Reidsville, NC 27320
(910) 342-0717

Trott Furniture
Hwy. 258
Richlands, NC 28574
(910) 324-4660

Deep Discount Stores (cont.)

North Carolina (cont.)

Barnes and Barnes Furniture
190 Commerce Ave.
Southern Pines, NC 28387
(800) 334-8174

Furniture Barn of Forest City
Hwy. 74 Bypass
Spindale, NC 28160
(704) 287-7106

Corner Hutch Furniture
Highway 21 North
Statesville, NC 28677
(704) 873-1773

Holton Furniture
805 Randolph St.
Thomasville, NC 27361
(800) 334-3183

Loftin-Black Furniture
111 Sedgehill Dr.
Thomasville, NC 27360
(800) 334-7398

Murrow Furniture
3514 S. College Rd.
Wilmington, NC 28412
(910) 799-4010

Sutton-Councill Furniture
421 S. College Rd.
Wilmington, NC 28403
(910) 799-9000

Oklahoma

Sears Catalog Clearance Center
5644 W. Skelly Dr.
Tulsa, OK 74107
(918) 446-1681

Pennsylvania

QVC Network Clearance Center
Rockvale Square Outlets
U. S. Hwy. 30 and Hwy. 896
Lancaster, PA 17601
(717) 293-9595

J. C. Penney Catalog Outlet
Franklin Mills
I-95 and Woodhaven Rd.
Philadelphia, PA 19114
(800) 336-6255

Sears Catalog Clearance Center
Franklin Mills
I-95 and Woodhaven Rd.
Philadelphia, PA 19114
(800) 336-6255

South Carolina

Triad Furniture Discounters
9770 North Kings Hwy.
Magnolia Plaza
Myrtle Beach, SC 29577
(800) 323-8469

Virginia

Sears Catalog Clearance Center
Potomac Mills Outlet Center
2700 Potomac Mills Circle
Prince William, VA 22192
(800) VA-MILLS

Washington

Sears Catalog Clearance Center
8720 S. Tacoma Way
Tacoma, WA 98499
(206) 584-8160

Wholesale

You will usually get the best deals on major brands of lighting and fans from telephone ordering services. Their prices are about as low as the prices charged to interior decorators and interior designers by wholesale distributors for the very same brands and styles.

You usually cannot buy lighting or fans directly from major manufacturers. Their minimum purchase requirements are just too large to be practical for anyone decorating a single house at a time. Even interior decorators and interior designers usually must order these brands through wholesale distributors.

The only reason for you to become your own decorator, as far as lighting is concerned, is to buy lighting or fans from small manufacturers that have more unique products. There are many small manufacturers all over the U. S. that have some beautiful and unique creations. Some show their products in wholesale design center showrooms; others use independent showrooms.

The *National Directory Of Wholesale Home Furnishings Sources and Showrooms*, by William Graham, lists hundreds of showrooms and manufacturers that sell directly to decorators. You can order the directory from this publisher. There is an order form in the back of this book.

Before you buy your license and order your business cards, you may wish to check out the local design center, if it is open to the public on certain days. There is a list of design centers that have open shopping days on page 328. You are likely to find that you have already seen most styles of lighting fixtures and fans at local stores and in magazines.

The only reason to go the wholesale route for these products is if you want a unique and unusual style from a small manufacturer, and you don't want to pay a designer to buy it for you.

Recommendations

1 If there are any factory outlets or deep discount stores near you, check them out. They have the very best bargains on lighting and fans from major manufacturers. Even wholesale sources usually won't beat the prices you get over the phone.

2 If you don't find what you want there, or if there are no outlets or deep discount stores near you, your next best choice is a telephone ordering service. Browse through local retail stores and design studios to find the styles you want. Also, consult interior design magazines. Carefully record all product information, and then call several services to get the best price. Even many of the high-style brands shown at wholesale design centers are available from these services, at about the same price a wholesale design center showroom would charge a professional interior designer for the very same product.

3 If you still haven't found what you want, consider becoming your own decorator and checking out wholesale sources. There are some small lighting and fan manufacturers that do not display their products directly to the public.

Chapter 13

Decorative Accessories

In this chapter, we will discuss ways to save on decorative accessories: rugs, silk flowers, mirrors, clocks, artwork, baskets, crystal and glassware, and other accessories.

These are often carried by the same sources, so we will discuss these furnishings as a group. Most of the discount sources listed in this chapter carry most or all of these things, unless otherwise noted.

You should do most of your accessory shopping at factory outlets and from telephone ordering services. There are hundreds of sources out there that sell accessories at rock-bottom prices -- usually about 50% to 75% off retail.

Quality Considerations

These are fairly obvious and self-explanatory. There aren't any particular quality checks to look for. This is a fairly uncomplicated segment of the home furnishings industry.

I am familiar with most of the brands carried by the sources in this chapter. I don't expect you to have any problems with quality. Just look everything over carefully, especially in a factory outlet. If it looks like it's in good shape, you can rest assured that it probably is.

Interior Designers, Interior Decorators, and Retail Stores

No surprises here. The very worst deals on accessories are usually found at these places. Many decorative accessories are sold to designers, decorators, and stores through distributors which adds an extra middleman markup to the prices consumers pay.

In addition to this, many of these retail businesses take extra-high markups on decorative accessories, often as much as 200% over and above the distributor price. It was commonplace for designers, decorators, and stores who bought furnishings from my parents' factory to charge their retail customers three times what we charged our wholesale customers for decorative pillows and chair cushions.

The upshot of all of this is that you usually pay between 200% and 500% of the manufacturer's price when you buy accessories from interior decorators, interior designers, and retail stores -- depending upon the number of middlemen the furnishings have to go through and the markup each middleman takes. You can do much better.

Telephone Ordering Services

You can get good deals on all types of decorative accessories through telephone ordering services. Most of these services can save you up to 50% off of the manufacturer's suggested retail price on accessories.

The deals you can get here, however, don't match the prices at factory outlets. There are so many factory outlets available for all kinds of decorative accessories that sell new merchandise at rock-bottom prices right alongside the discontinued and second-quality items. Check out factory outlets first, if possible. Only buy accessories from telephone ordering services if you can't find the brand you want from an outlet or if there isn't an outlet near your home. Please read Chapter 16 for more detailed information on dealing with telephone ordering services.

Most telephone ordering services ask that you call with all product information for the items you wish to order. A few sources have catalogs or brochures about their products. Of course, you can often call these sources, too, and check prices if you already have the product information for what you want.

Before you call, shop in your neighborhood and record product information for the items you wish to purchase. Interior design magazines are good sources for product information, as are high-end furniture stores. Interior designers usually don't stock many samples of decorative accessories, but they do often have wholesale catalogs from a wide variety of manufacturers.

If there is a wholesale design center near you that is open to the public on certain days (as listed on page 328), you can browse through many accessory showrooms there. Make sure you write down the manufacturer's name, style, color, size, and any other information that seems important.

Look out for falsified product information. Some retail stores alter or conceal the manufacturer's identity and item names or numbers on their samples, usually to hinder consumers from comparing prices with telephone ordering services and other discounters. Some interior designers and interior decorators hide or falsify manufacturer and product information in their wholesale catalogs. Usually, this practice is very obvious (crossed out information, little stickers covering everything, etc). If you see that product information has been altered, move on to another store or design studio. You can also check interior design magazines and wholesale showrooms -- these sources virtually never falsify product information.

If you have any doubt as to whether the product information marked on the sample is correct or not, write down the information that is on the tag and also write down a general description of the item. Many of these telephone services can help you find out the correct manufacturer's item names and numbers if you have the correct manufacturer's name and a clear description of the item.

Telephone Ordering Services

Barnes & Barnes Fine Furniture
(Call for free brochure)
190 Commerce Ave.
Southern Pines, NC 28387
(800) 334-8174

Blackwelder's
Route 18, Box 8
Statesville, NC 28677
(800) 438-0201

Boyles Distinctive Furniture
Hickory Furniture Mart
Hickory, NC 28602
(704) 326-1740

Capel Rug Mill Outlet
121 E. Main St.
Troy, NC 27371
(800) 425-7847

Charles W. Jacobsen
Rugs only
(Call for free brochure)
401 N. Salina St.
Syracuse, NY 13203
(315) 422-7832

Corner Hutch Furniture
Highway 21 North
Statesville, NC 28677
(704) 873-1773

The Decorator's Edge
509 Randolph St.
Thomasville, NC 27360
(800) 289-5589

Designer Secrets
P. O. Box 529
Fremont, NE 68025
(800) 955-2559

Edgar B.
P. O. Box 849
Clemmons, NC 27012
(800) 255-6589

Ellenburg's Furniture
I-40 and Stamey Farm Rd.
Statesville, NC 28677
(704) 873-2900

European Furniture Importers
(Send $3.00 for catalog)
2145 W. Grand Ave.
Chicago, IL 60612
(800) 283-1955

Faucet Outlet
Decorative kitchen and bath fixtures only
(Call for free catalog)
P. O. Box 547
Middletown, NY 10940
(800) 444-5783

Loftin-Black Furniture
111 Sedgehill Dr.
Thomasville, NC 27360
(800) 334-7398

Mallory's Fine Furniture
2153 Le Jeune Blvd.
Jacksonville, NC 28546
(910) 353-1828

National Carpet and Rug
Carpeting and rugs only
1384 Coney Island Ave.
Brooklyn, NY 11230
(718) 253-5700

Quality Furniture Market
2034 Hickory Blvd. SE
Lenoir, NC 28645
(704) 728-2946

Sutton-Councill Furniture
421 S. College Rd.
Wilmington, NC 28403
(910) 799-9000

Old Town Clock Shop
Clocks only
3738 Reynolda Rd.
Winston-Salem, NC 27106
(910) 924-8807

The Time Gallery
Clocks only
3121 Battleground Ave.
Greensboro, NC 27408
(910) 282-5132

Triad Furniture Discounters
9770 North Kings Hwy.
Magnolia Plaza
Myrtle Beach, SC 29577
(800) 323-8469

Turner Tolson Furniture
(Call for free brochure)
U. S. Hwy. 17 S.
New Bern, NC 28562
(919) 638-2121

Tyson Furniture
109 Broadway St.
Black Mountain, NC 28711
(704) 669-5000

Factory Outlets

Factory outlets for all types of decorative accessories are within easy reach of most consumers. The typical discount on most outlet merchandise is about 50% off retail, and occasionally as much as 75% off retail. Most accept credit cards and sell a wide variety of new first-quality merchandise in addition to second-quality and discontinued items.

Most of the merchandise you will find in these outlets is first-quality. Many factory outlets have expanded beyond their original purpose of disposing of closeout or second-quality merchandise. Many manufacturers make full use of their outlets to move large amounts of first-quality merchandise. Seconds are normally marked, but double-check just in case. Most sales are "as-is" and unreturnable.

Outlets all over the U. S. are listed on pages 217 through 238.

Factory Outlets

Alabama

Carolina Clock and Rug Outlet
Factory Stores of America
Exit 183 off I-59
Boaz, AL 35957
(205) 593-2930

The Crystal Corner
317 Billy Dyar Blvd.
Boaz, AL 35957
(205) 593-6169

Global Rug Outlet
Exit 183 off I-59
Boaz, AL 35957
(205) 593-9549

The Interior Alternative
601 Elizabeth St.
Boaz, AL 35957
(205) 593-8887

Lenox Factory Outlet
214 S. McKlesky St.
Boaz, AL 35957
(205) 593-6461

Libbey Glass Outlet
Boaz Outlet Center
Exit 183 off I-59
Boaz, AL 35957
(205) 593-9306

Mikasa Factory Store
Tanger Factory Outlet Center
Exit 183 off I-59
Boaz, AL 35957
(205) 593-9038

Pfaltzgraff Factory Outlet
Boaz Outlet Center
Exit 183 off I-59
Boaz, AL 35957
(205) 593-9306

Alabama (cont.)

Reading China and Glass
Boaz Outlet Center
Exit 183 off I-59
Boaz, AL 35957
(205) 593-9306

Welcome Home
Tanger Factory Outlet Center
Exit 183 off I-59
Boaz, AL 35957
(205) 593-9038

Mikasa Factory Outlet
Riviera Centre Factory Stores
Highway 59 South
Foley, AL 36535
(800) 5-CENTRE

Pfaltzgraff Factory Outlet
Riviera Centre Factory Stores
Highway 59 South
Foley, AL 36535
(800) 5-CENTRE

Welcome Home
Riviera Centre Factory Stores
Highway 59 South
Foley, AL 36535
(800) 5-CENTRE

Carolina Clock and Rug Outlet
USA Factory Stores
Exit 62 off I-85
Opelika, AL 36803
(205) 742-9388

Libbey Glass
USA Factory Stores
Exit 62 off I-85
Opelika, AL 36803
(205) 749-2701

Alabama (cont.)

Welcome Home
USA Factory Stores
Exit 62 off I-85
Opelika, AL 36803
(205) 742-0966

Arizona

Brass Factory
Factory Stores of America
Exit 194 off I-10
Casa Grande, AZ 85222
(602) 421-0112

Mikasa Factory Outlet
Tanger Factory Outlet Center
Exit 198 off I-10
Casa Grande, AZ 85222
(520) 836-0897

Pfaltzgraff Factory Outlet
Tanger Factory Outlet Center
Exit 198 off I-10
Casa Grande, AZ 85222
(520) 836-0897

Royal Doulton Factory Outlet
Factory Stores of America
Exit 194 off I-10
Casa Grande, AZ 85222
(602) 421-0112

Welcome Home
Factory Stores of America
Exit 194 off I-10
Casa Grande, AZ 85222
(602) 421-0112

Welcome Home
Tanger Factory Outlet Center
Exit 198 off I-10
Casa Grande, AZ 85222
(520) 836-0897

Factory Outlets (cont.)

Arizona (cont.)

Mikasa Factory Outlet
Wigwam Outlet Stores
I-10 and Litchfield Rd.
Goodyear, AZ 85338
(602) 935-9733

Welcome Home
Wigwam Outlet Stores
I-10 and Litchfield Rd.
Goodyear, AZ 85338
(602) 935-9733

Dansk Factory Outlet
Oak Creek Factory Outlets
Hwy. 179
Sedona, AZ 86351
(520) 284-6830

Mikasa Factory Outlet
Oak Creek Factory Outlets
Hwy. 179
Sedona, AZ 86351
(520) 284-9505

Welcome Home
Oak Creek Factory Outlets
Hwy. 179
Sedona, AZ 86351
(520) 284-1314

Arkansas

Welcome Home
Hot Springs Factory Outlet Stores
Hwy. 7 South
Hot Springs, AR 71913
(501) 525-9161

California

Home Again
Shasta Factory Outlets
I-5 and State Rd. 273
Anderson, CA 96007
(916) 378-0937

California (cont.)

Mikasa Factory Outlet
Shasta Factory Outlets
I-5 and State Rd. 273
Anderson, CA 96007
(916) 378-0937

Welcome Home
Atascadero Factory Outlets
Del Rio Exit off 101 Fwy.
Atascadero, CA 93422
(805) 461-5155

Mikasa Factory Outlet
Tanger Factory Outlet Center
I-15 and Lenwood Rd.
Barstow, CA 92311
(619) 253-4812

Lenox Factory Outlet
Factory Merchants
I-15 and Lenwood Rd.
Barstow, CA 92311
(619) 253-7668

Royal Doulton Factory Outlet
Factory Merchants
I-15 and Lenwood Rd.
Barstow, CA 92311
(619) 253-2161

Welcome Home
Factory Merchants
I-15 and Lenwood Rd.
Barstow, CA 92311
(619) 253-2117

Welcome Home
Tanger Factory Outlet Center
I-15 and Lenwood Rd.
Barstow, CA 92311
(619) 253-4812

California (cont.)

Mikasa Factory Outlet
Desert Hills Factory Stores
48400 Seminole Dr.
Cabazon, CA 92230
(909) 849-6641

Pfaltzgraff Factory Outlet
Desert Hills Factory Stores
48400 Seminole Dr.
Cabazon, CA 92230
(909) 849-6641

Royal Doulton Factory Outlet
Desert Hills Factory Stores
48400 Seminole Dr.
Cabazon, CA 92230
(909) 849-6641

Welcome Home
Desert Hills Factory Stores
48400 Seminole Dr.
Cabazon, CA 92230
(909) 849-6641

Brass Factory Outlet
13000 Folsom Blvd.
Folsom, CA 95630
(916) 985-7438

Glassware House
Folsom Factory Outlets
Hwy. 50 and Folsom Blvd.
Folsom, CA 95630
(916) 985-4075

Home Again
Folsom Factory Outlets
Hwy. 50 and Folsom Blvd.
Folsom, CA 95630
(916) 351-1214

Factory Outlets (cont.)

California (cont.)

Home Again
Pacific West Outlet Center
Highway 101 and Leavesley Rd.
Gilroy, CA 95020
(408) 842-9044

Lenox Factory Outlet
Outlets At Gilroy
Highway 101 and Leavesley Rd.
Gilroy, CA 95020
(408) 847-1181

Mikasa Factory Outlet
Pacific West Outlet Center
Highway 101 and Leavesley Rd.
Gilroy, CA 95020
(408) 842-4641

Pfaltzgraff Factory Outlet
Pacific West Outlet Center
Highway 101 and Leavesley Rd.
Gilroy, CA 95020
(408) 848-3696

Reed and Barton
Outlets At Gilroy
Highway 101 and Leavesley Rd.
Gilroy, CA 95020
(408) 847-5454

Welcome Home
Lake Arrowhead Village
Hwy. 18
Lake Arrowhead, CA 92352
(800) 800-6792

Libbey Glass
Lancaster Factory Stores
A. V. Freeway 14
Lancaster, CA 93536
(805) 942-7897

California (cont.)

Welcome Home
Lancaster Factory Stores
A. V. Freeway 14
Lancaster, CA 93536
(805) 942-7897

Mikasa Factory Outlet
20642 S. Fordyce Ave.
Long Beach, CA 90810
(310) 537-9344

Home Again
Great Mall of the Bay Area
Montague Expressway
Milpitas, CA 95035
(408) 956-9740

Dansk Factory Outlet
Napa Factory Stores
1st St. exit off Hwy. 29
Napa, CA 94558
(707) 226-9876

Home Again
Napa Factory Stores
1st St. exit off Hwy. 29
Napa, CA 94558
(707) 259-1779

Mikasa Factory Outlet
Napa Factory Stores
1st St. exit off Hwy. 29
Napa, CA 94558
(707) 254-7614

Welcome Home
Plaza Continental Factory Stores
I-10 and Haven Ave.
Ontario, CA 91764
(909) 980-6231

California (cont.)

Welcome Home
Oxnard Factory Outlet
Hwy. 101/Ventura Freeway
Oxnard, CA 93030
(805) 988-1837

Home Again
American Tin Cannery
Factory Outlets
125 Ocean View Blvd.
Pacific Grove, CA 93950
(408) 375-3461

The Housewares Store
American Tin Cannery
Factory Outlets
125 Ocean View Blvd.
Pacific Grove, CA 93950
(408) 372-0446

Royal Doulton Factory Outlet
American Tin Cannery
Factory Outlets
125 Ocean View Blvd.
Pacific Grove, CA 93950
(408) 372-1793

Mikasa Factory Outlet
2500 N. Palm Canyon Dr.
Palm Springs, CA 92262
(619) 778-1080

Home Again
Petaluma Village Factory Outlets
Highway 101
Petaluma, CA 94952
(707) 765-2570

Mikasa Factory Outlet
Petaluma Village Factory Outlets
Highway 101
Petaluma, CA 94952
(707) 766-8073

Factory Outlets (cont.)

California (cont.)

Welcome Home
San Diego North County
Factory Outlet Center
1050 Los Vallecitos
San Marcos, CA 92069
(619) 595-5222

Mikasa Factory Outlet
San Diego Factory Outlet Center
4498 Camino De La Plaza
San Ysidro, CA 92173
(619) 428-2022

Welcome Home
San Diego Factory Outlet Center
4498 Camino De La Plaza
San Ysidro, CA 92173
(619) 690-2944

Dansk Factory Outlet
Old Mill Shops
Hwy. 101 and Hwy. 246
Solvang, CA 93463
(805) 688-7488

Pfaltzgraff Factory Outlet
The Pfaltzgraff Building
Hwy. 101 and Hwy. 246
Solvang, CA 93463
(805) 688-7112

Mikasa Factory Outlet
2011 Lake Tahoe Blvd.
South Lake Tahoe, CA 96150
(916) 541-7412

Brass Factory Outlet
Factory Stores of America
at Nut Tree
321-2 Nut Tree Rd.
Vacaville, CA 95687
(707) 447-5670

California (cont.)

Mikasa Factory Outlet
Factory Stores of America
at Nut Tree
321-2 Nut Tree Rd.
Vacaville, CA 95687
(707) 446-8485

Pfaltzgraff Factory Outlet
Factory Stores of America
at Nut Tree
321-2 Nut Tree Rd.
Vacaville, CA 95687
(707) 446-4984

Royal Doulton Factory Outlet
Factory Stores of America
at Nut Tree
321-2 Nut Tree Rd.
Vacaville, CA 95687
(707) 448-2793

Stained Glass Factory Outlet
Factory Stores of America
at Nut Tree
321-2 Nut Tree Rd.
Vacaville, CA 95687
(707) 448-5706

Colorado

Mikasa Factory Outlet
Castle Rock Factory Shops
Exit 184 off I-25
Castle Rock, CO 80104
(303) 688-1109

Pfaltzgraff Factory Outlet
Castle Rock Factory Shops
Exit 184 off I-25
Castle Rock, CO 80104
(303) 660-9246

Colorado (cont.)

Royal Doulton Factory Outlet
Castle Rock Factory Shops
Exit 184 off I-25
Castle Rock, CO 80104
(303) 660-1601

Villeroy & Boch
Castle Rock Factory Shops
Exit 184 off I-25
Castle Rock, CO 80104
(303) 688-1101

Welcome Home
Castle Rock Factory Shops
Exit 184 off I-25
Castle Rock, CO 80104
(303) 688-6689

Dansk Factory Outlet
Rocky Mountain Factory Stores
I-25 and U. S. Hwy. 34
Loveland, CO 80538
(970) 593-0021

Lenox Factory Outlet
Rocky Mountain Factory Stores
I-25 and U. S. Hwy. 34
Loveland, CO 80538
(970) 663-0879

Mikasa Factory Outlet
Rocky Mountain Factory Stores
I-25 and U. S. Hwy. 34
Loveland, CO 80538
(970) 663-1717

Welcome Home
Rocky Mountain Factory Stores
I-25 and U. S. Hwy. 34
Loveland, CO 80538
(970) 593-0613

Factory Outlets (cont.)

Connecticut

Brass Factory Outlet
249 W. Main St.
Branford, CT 06405
(203) 483-8026

Royal Doulton Factory Outlet
Factory Outlets at Norwalk
Exit 16 off I-95
Norwalk, CT 06855
(203) 838-7859

Delaware

The Interior Alternative
Bellvue Ave.
Newark, DE 19713
(302) 454-3232

Glass Resort
Ocean Outlets
Route 1
Rehoboth Beach, DE 19971
(302) 226-9223

Pfaltzgraff Factory Outlet
Ocean Outlets
Route 1
Rehoboth Beach, DE 19971
(302) 226-9223

Welcome Home
Ocean Outlets
Route 1
Rehoboth Beach, DE 19971
(302) 226-9223

Wicker Outlet
Ocean Outlets
Route 1
Rehoboth Beach, DE 19971
(302) 226-9223

Florida

Baldwin Brass Home Accents
Gulf Coast Factory Shops
Exit 43 off I-75
Ellenton, FL 34222
(813) 723-1566

Mikasa Factory Outlet
Gulf Coast Factory Shops
Exit 43 off I-75
Ellenton, FL 34222
(813) 723-2706

Royal Doulton Factory Outlet
Gulf Coast Factory Shops
Exit 43 off I-75
Ellenton, FL 34222
(813) 729-2076

Villeroy & Boch
Gulf Coast Factory Shops
Exit 43 off I-75
Ellenton, FL 34222
(813) 723-1880

Welcome Home
Gulf Coast Factory Shops
Exit 43 off I-75
Ellenton, FL 34222
(813) 723-2099

Mikasa Factory Outlet
Florida Keys Factory Shops
U. S. 1 and the Florida Turnpike
Florida City, FL 33034
(305) 248-4727

Welcome Home
Florida Keys Factory Shops
U. S. 1 and the Florida Turnpike
Florida City, FL 33034
(305) 248-4727

Florida (cont.)

Reed and Barton
Sanibel Factory Stores
Exit 21 off I-75
Fort Myers, FL 33908
(941) 454-5150

Welcome Home
Sanibel Factory Stores
Exit 21 off I-75
Fort Myers, FL 33908
(941) 454-3133

Welcome Home
Manufacturer's Outlet Center
Exit 65 off I-95
Fort Pierce, FL 34945
(407) 489-6637

Emperor Clocks
Kissimmee Manufacturers' Mall
2517 Old Vineland Rd.
Kissimmee, FL 34746
(813) 396-8900

Dansk Factory Outlet
Coral Isle Factory Stores
S. R. 951
Naples, FL 33961
(813) 793-5533

Mikasa Factory Outlet
Coral Isle Factory Stores
S. R. 951
Naples, FL 33961
(813) 793-7171

Villeroy & Boch
Coral Isle Factory Stores
S. R. 951
Naples, FL 33961
(813) 732-5522

Factory Outlets (cont.)

Florida (cont.)

Welcome Home
Coral Isle Factory Stores
S. R. 951
Naples, FL 33961
(813) 775-2140

Lenox Factory Outlet
International Designer Outlets
I-4 and International Dr.
Orlando, FL 32819
(407) 354-5233

Mikasa Factory Outlet
Belz Factory Outlet World
I-4 and International Dr.
Orlando, FL 32819
(407) 351-1783

Pfaltzgraff Factory Outlet
Belz Factory Outlet World
I-4 and International Dr.
Orlando, FL 32819
(407) 345-9313

Tropic Art
Belz Factory Outlet World
I-4 and International Dr.
Orlando, FL 32819
(407) 352-0746

Villeroy & Boch
International Designer Outlets
I-4 and International Dr.
Orlando, FL 32819
(407) 352-7633

Welcome Home
Belz Factory Outlet World
I-4 and International Dr.
Orlando, FL 32819
(407) 351-0855

Florida (cont.)

Mikasa Factory Outlet
St. Augustine Outlet Center
Exit 95 off I-95
St. Augustine, FL 32092
(904) 823-1190

Welcome Home
St. Augustine Outlet Center
Exit 95 off I-95
St. Augustine, FL 32092
(904) 823-8516

Dansk Factory Outlet
Sarasota Outlet Center
Exit 40 off I-75
University Park, FL 34201
(941) 359-2284

Lenox Factory Outlet
Sarasota Outlet Center
Exit 40 off I-75
University Park, FL 34201
(941) 359-8655

Pfaltzgraff Factory Outlet
Sarasota Outlet Center
Exit 40 off I-75
University Park, FL 34201
(941) 351-7885

Reading China & Glass
Sarasota Outlet Center
Exit 40 off I-75
University Park, FL 34201
(941) 355-4485

Welcome Home
Sarasota Outlet Center
Exit 40 off I-75
University Park, FL 34201
(941) 351-9695

Florida (cont.)

Mikasa Factory Outlet
Horizon Outlet Center
S. R. 60 and I-95
Vero Beach, FL 32966
(407) 563-2588

Reed & Barton
Horizon Outlet Center
S. R. 60 and I-95
Vero Beach, FL 32966
(407) 564-9923

Libbey Glass Factory Outlet
Factory Stores At Palm Beach
Exit 99 off Florida Turnpike
West Palm Beach, FL 33417
(407) 683-6007

Royal Doulton Factory Outlet
Factory Stores At Palm Beach
Exit 99 off Florida Turnpike
West Palm Beach, FL 33417
(407) 687-4600

Welcome Home
Factory Stores At Palm Beach
Exit 99 off Florida Turnpike
West Palm Beach, FL 33417
(407) 686-1742

Georgia

Welcome Home
Peach Factory Stores
Exit 46 off I-75
Byron, GA 31008
(912) 956-1855

Mikasa Factory Outlet
Calhoun Outlet Center
Exit 129 off I-75
Calhoun, GA 30701
(800) 969-3767

Factory Outlets (cont.)

Georgia (cont.)

Royal Doulton Factory Outlet
Calhoun Outlet Center
Exit 129 off I-75
Calhoun, GA 30701
(800) 969-3767

Welcome Home
Calhoun Outlet Center
Exit 129 off I-75
Calhoun, GA 30701
(800) 969-3767

Mikasa Factory Outlet
Tanger Factory Outlet Center
Exit 53 off I-85
Commerce, GA 30529
(706) 335-4537

Welcome Home
Tanger Factory Outlet Center
Exit 53 off I-85
Commerce, GA 30529
(706) 335-4537

Bearden Brothers
Carpet & Textile Corp
3200 Dug Gap Rd. SW
Exit 135, off I-75
Dalton, GA 30720
(800) 433-0074

The Interior Alternative
3004-B Parquet Rd.
Dalton, GA 30720
(706) 217-6544

Johnson's Carpets
3239 S. Dixie Rd.
Dalton, GA 30720
(800) 235-1079

Georgia (cont.)

Welcome Home
Dalton Factory Stores
Exit 136 off I-75
Dalton, GA 30720
(706) 278-3308

Fragile Outlet Store
Magnolia Bluff Factory Shops
Exit 10 off I-95
Darien, GA 31305
(912) 437-2700

Welcome Home
Magnolia Bluff Factory Shops
Exit 10 off I-95
Darien, GA 31305
(912) 437-2700

Brass-N-Things
Lake Park Factory Stores
Exit 2 off I-75
Lake Park, GA 31636
(912) 559-1177

Carolina Pottery
Factory Stores of America
Exit 2 off I-75
Lake Park, GA 31636
(912) 559-6177

Carpet and Rug Outlet
Lake Park Factory Stores
Exit 2 off I-75
Lake Park, GA 31636
(912) 559-1177

Emperor Clock
Factory Stores of America
Exit 2 off I-75
Lake Park, GA 31636
(912) 559-6177

Georgia (cont.)

Lenox Factory Outlet
Lake Park Mill Store Plaza
Exit 2 off I-75
Lake Park, GA 31636
(912) 559-6822

Pfaltzgraff Factory Outlet
Lake Park Mill Store Plaza
Exit 2 off I-75
Lake Park, GA 31636
(912) 559-6822

Mikasa Factory Outlet
Tanger Factory Outlet Center
Exit 68 off I-75
Locust Grove, GA 30248
(770) 957-0238

Welcome Home
Tanger Factory Outlet Center
Exit 68 off I-75
Locust Grove, GA 30248
(770) 957-0238

Georgia Clock and Rug
Peachtree Factory Stores
Exit 9 off I-85
Newnan, GA 30264
(770) 253-7005

Design Center Outlet
6315 Spalding Dr.
Norcross, GA 30092
(770) 825-0020

Icefields Marble Outlet
5182-A Brookhollow Pkwy.
Norcross, GA 30071
(770) 729-9868

Factory Outlets (cont.)

Idaho

Libbey Glass Factory Outlet
Boise Factory Outlets
I-84 at Gowen Rd.
Boise, ID 83705
(208) 331-1785

Welcome Home
Boise Factory Outlets
I-84 at Gowen Rd.
Boise, ID 83705
(208) 331-1654

Dansk Factory Outlet
Factory Outlets
Exit 2 off I-90
Post Falls, ID 83854
(208) 773-2000

Libbey Glass Factory Outlet
Post Falls Factory Stores
Exit 2 off I-90
Post Falls, ID 83854
(208) 777-1067

Mikasa Factory Outlet
Factory Outlets
Exit 2 off I-90
Post Falls, ID 83854
(208) 773-1675

Pfaltzgraff Factory Outlet
Factory Outlets
Exit 2 off I-90
Post Falls, ID 83854
(208) 773-1638

Royal Doulton Factory Outlet
Factory Outlets
Exit 2 off I-90
Post Falls, ID 83854
(208) 773-5090

Idaho (cont.)

Welcome Home
Factory Outlets
Exit 2 off I-90
Post Falls, ID 83854
(208) 773-2396

Illinois

Welcome Home
K Square Factory Outlet Mall
Exit 160 off I-57/70
Effingham, IL 62401
(217) 342-6367

Artworks
Gurnee Mills
I-94 and Route 132
Gurnee, IL 60031
(800) YES-SHOP

Oriental Weavers
Gurnee Mills
I-94 and Route 132
Gurnee, IL 60031
(800) YES-SHOP

Picture Us
Gurnee Mills
I-94 and Route 132
Gurnee, IL 60031
(800) YES-SHOP

Prints Unlimited
Gurnee Mills
I-94 and Route 132
Gurnee, IL 60031
(800) YES-SHOP

Stained Glass Factory Outlet
Gurnee Mills
I-94 and Route 132
Gurnee, IL 60031
(800) YES-SHOP

Illinois (cont.)

Waccamaw
Gurnee Mills
I-94 and Route 132
Gurnee, IL 60031
(800) YES-SHOP

Welcome Home
Gurnee Mills
I-94 and Route 132
Gurnee, IL 60031
(800) YES-SHOP

Mikasa Factory Outlet
Huntley Factory Shops
I-90 and Route 47
Huntley, IL 60142
(708) 669-0077

Welcome Home
Huntley Factory Shops
I-90 and Route 47
Huntley, IL 60142
(708) 669-8618

Pfaltzgraff Factory Outlet
Piano Factory Outlet Mall
410 S. 1st St.
St. Charles, IL 60174
(708) 584-4800

Mikasa Factory Outlet
Factory Stores at Tuscola
Exit 212 off I-57
Tuscola, IL 61953
(217) 253-5268

Welcome Home
Factory Stores at Tuscola
Exit 212 off I-57
Tuscola, IL 61953
(217) 253-4868

Factory Outlets (cont.)

Indiana

Mikasa Factory Outlet
Indiana Factory Shops
I-69 and Route 67
Daleville, IN 47334
(317) 378-1300

Welcome Home
Indiana Factory Shops
I-69 and Route 67
Daleville, IN 47334
(317) 378-1300

Brass Factory
Horizon Outlet Center
Exit 76B off I-65
Edinburgh, IN 46124
(812) 526-6281

Welcome Home
Horizon Outlet Center
Exit 76B off I-65
Edinburgh, IN 46124
(812) 526-5760

Mikasa Factory Outlet
Horizon Outlet Center
I-69 and I-80/90
Fremont, IN 46734
(219) 833-4145

Welcome Home
Horizon Outlet Center
I-69 and I-80/90
Fremont, IN 46734
(219) 833-2037

Factory Direct Table Pad Co.
1501 W. Market St.
Indianapolis, IN 46222
(800) 428-4567

Crystal Works Factory Outlet
917 Lighthouse Place
Michigan City, IN 46360
(219) 872-2294

Indiana (cont.)

Dansk Factory Outlet Center
Lighthouse Place
6th St. and Wabash St.
Michigan City, IN 46360
(800) 866-5900

Royal Doulton Factory Outlet
Lighthouse Place
6th St. and Wabash St.
Michigan City, IN 46360
(800) 866-5900

Welcome Home
Lighthouse Place
6th St. and Wabash St.
Michigan City, IN 46360
(800) 866-5900

Mikasa Factory Outlet
Tanger Factory Outlet Center
Exit 50A off I-65
Seymour, IN 47274
(812) 522-6922

Welcome Home
Tanger Factory Outlet Center
Exit 50A off I-65
Seymour, IN 47274
(812) 522-6922

Iowa

Mikasa Factory Outlet
Tanger Factory Outlet Center
Exit 220 off I-80
Williamsburg, IA 52361
(319) 668-2811

Welcome Home
Tanger Factory Outlet Center
Exit 220 off I-80
Williamsburg, IA 52361
(319) 668-2811

Kansas

Welcome Home
Whites Factory Outlet Center
Exit 53 off I-70
Colby, KS 67701
(913) 462-2227

Mikasa Factory Outlet
Lawrence Riverfront Factory Outlets
Exit 204 off I-70
Lawrence, KS 66044
(913) 749-5948

Mikasa Factory Outlet
Tanger Factory Outlet Center
Exit 204 off I-70
Lawrence, KS 66044
(913) 842-6290

Villeroy & Boch
Lawrence Riverfront Factory Outlets
Exit 204 off I-70
Lawrence, KS 66044
(913) 843-8999

Welcome Home
Lawrence Riverfront Factory Outlets
Exit 204 off I-70
Lawrence, KS 66044
(913) 843-7529

Welcome Home
Tanger Factory Outlet Center
Exit 204 off I-70
Lawrence, KS 66044
(913) 842-6290

Kentucky

Mikasa Factory Outlet
1102 Fashion Ridge Rd.
Dry Ridge, KY 41035
(606) 824-6800

Factory Outlets (cont.)

Kentucky (cont.)

Carolina Pottery
Factory Stores of America
Exit 126 off I-75
Georgetown, KY 40324
(502) 863-3660

Louisiana

Mikasa Factory Outlet
Tanger Factory Outlet Center
Exit 177 off I-10
Gonzales, LA 70737
(504) 647-0521

Welcome Home
Tanger Factory Outlet Center
Exit 177 off I-10
Gonzales, LA 70737
(504) 647-0521

Libbey Glass Factory Outlet
Slidell Factory Stores
Exit 263 off I-10
Slidell, LA 70458
(504) 646-0756

Welcome Home
Slidell Factory Stores
Exit 263 off I-10
Slidell, LA 70458
(504) 646-0756

Maine

Dansk Factory Outlet
Exit 19 off I-95
Freeport, ME 04032
(207) 865-6125

Mikasa Factory Outlet
Exit 19 off I-95
Freeport, ME 04032
(207) 865-9441

Maine (cont.)

Villeroy & Boch
Exit 19 off I-95
Freeport, ME 04032
(207) 865-6684

Crystal Works
Spruce Creek Outlet Center
Exit 3 off I-95
Kittery, ME 03904
(207) 439-0416

Dansk Factory Outlet
Dansk Square
Exit 3 off I-95
Kittery, ME 03904
(207) 439-0484

Lenox China Outlet
Tidewater Outlet Mall
Exit 3 off I-95
Kittery, ME 03904
(207) 439-0232

Mikasa Factory Outlet
The Maine Outlet
Exit 3 off I-95
Kittery, ME 03904
(207) 439-6550

Pfaltzgraff Factory Outlet
Tidewater Outlet Mall
Exit 3 off I-95
Kittery, ME 03904
(207) 439-4728

Reed & Barton
Tidewater Outlet Mall
Exit 3 off I-95
Kittery, ME 03904
(207) 439-4907

Maine (cont.)

Royal Doulton Factory Outlet
Kittery Outlet Center
Exit 3 off I-95
Kittery, ME 03904
(207) 439-4760

Stained Glass Factory Outlet
Factory Stores of America
Exit 3 off I-95
Kittery, ME 03904
(207) 439-3221

Villeroy & Boch
Manufacturer's Outlet Mall
Exit 3 off I-95
Kittery, ME 03904
(207) 439-6440

Maryland

Mikasa Factory Outlet
1596 Whitehall Rd.
Annapolis, MD 21401
(410) 757-8400

Brass Factory Outlet
Perryville Outlet Center
I-95 and Hwy. 222
Perryville, MD 21903
(410) 378-9399

Mikasa Outlet
Perryville Outlet Center
I-95 and Hwy. 222
Perryville, MD 21903
(410) 378-9399

Brass Factory Outlet
68 Heather Lane
Perryville, MD 21903
(410) 378-4731

Factory Outlets (cont.)

Maryland (cont.)

Brass Factory Outlet
Chesapeake Village Outlet Center
441 Chesapeake Village Rd.
Queenstown, MD 21658
(410) 827-8699

Wicker Outlet
Chesapeake Village Outlet Center
441 Chesapeake Village Rd.
Queenstown, MD 21658
(410) 827-8699

Massachusetts

The Interior Alternative
5 Hoosac St.
Adams, MA 01220
(413) 743-1986

Felicia's Gifts & Housewares
Quality Factory Outlets
Quequechan St.
Fall River, MA 02721
(508) 679-9650

Glaser Glass Factory Outlet
Pleasant St. and Quarry St.
Fall River, MA 02721
(508) 676-1464

Libbey Glass Factory Outlet
Quality Factory Outlets
Quequechan St.
Fall River, MA 02721
(508) 679-2647

Luxury Linens
Tower Outlet Mill
Pleasant St. and Quarry St.
Fall River, MA 02721
(508) 678-8411

Massachusetts (cont.)

Stevens Linen Mill Outlet
Quality Factory Outlets
Quequechan St.
Fall River, MA 02721
(508) 324-0165

Baldwin Brass
Worcester Common Fashion Outlets
Exit 16 off I-290
Worcester, MA 01608
(800) 2-SAVE-ALOT

Dansk Factory Outlet
Worcester Common Fashion Outlets
Exit 16 off I-290
Worcester, MA 01608
(800) 2-SAVE-ALOT

Mikasa Factory Outlet
Worcester Common Fashion Outlets
Exit 16 off I-290
Worcester, MA 01608
(800) 2-SAVE-ALOT

Welcome Home
Worcester Common Fashion Outlets
Exit 16 off I-290
Worcester, MA 01608
(800) 2-SAVE-ALOT

Michigan

Brass Factory Outlet
Outlets At Birch Run
Exit 136 off I-75
Birch Run, MI 48415
(517) 624-4744

Dansk Factory Outlet
Outlets At Birch Run
Exit 136 off I-75
Birch Run, MI 48415
(517) 624-1055

Michigan (cont.)

Lenox Factory Outlet
Outlets At Birch Run
Exit 136 off I-75
Birch Run, MI 48415
(517) 624-6170

Mikasa Factory Outlet
Outlets At Birch Run
Exit 136 off I-75
Birch Run, MI 48415
(517) 624-9341

Pfaltzgraff Factory Outlet
Outlets At Birch Run
Exit 136 off I-75
Birch Run, MI 48415
(517) 624-4623

Pilgrim Silk Flowers
Outlets At Birch Run
Exit 136 off I-75
Birch Run, MI 48415
(517) 624-5858

Royal Doulton Factory Outlet
Outlets At Birch Run
Exit 136 off I-75
Birch Run, MI 48415
(517) 624-1011

Villeroy & Boch
Outlets At Birch Run
Exit 136 off I-75
Birch Run, MI 48415
(517) 624-4477

Welcome Home
Outlets At Birch Run
Exit 136 off I-75
Birch Run, MI 48415
(517) 624-9023

Factory Outlets (cont.)

Michigan (cont.)

Brass Town
Horizon Outlet Center
U. S. 31 and James St.
Holland, MI 49423
(616) 394-0034

Pfaltzgraff Factory Outlet
Horizon Outlet Center
U. S. 31 and James St.
Holland, MI 49423
(616) 394-0711

Royal Doulton Factory Outlet
Horizon Outlet Center
U. S. 31 and James St.
Holland, MI 49423
(616) 394-9680

Welcome Home
Horizon Outlet Center
U. S. 31 and James St.
Holland, MI 49423
(616) 396-8035

Brass Factory Outlet
Horizon Outlet Center
Exit 11 off I-75
Monroe, MI 48161
(313) 242-3299

Mikasa Factory Outlet
Horizon Outlet Center
Exit 11 off I-75
Monroe, MI 48161
(313) 241-6565

Welcome Home
Horizon Outlet Center
Exit 11 off I-75
Monroe, MI 48161
(313) 242-2124

Michigan (cont.)

Next To Nature
Horizon Outlet Center
Exit 269 off I-94
Port Huron, MI 48060
(810) 364-1960

Welcome Home
Horizon Outlet Center
Exit 269 off I-94
Port Huron, MI 48060
(810) 364-3188

Dansk Factory Outlet
Horizon Outlet Center
U. S. 31
Traverse City, MI 49684
(616) 935-1490

Welcome Home
Horizon Outlet Center
U. S. 31
Traverse City, MI 49684
(616) 922-2867

Welcome Home
Tanger Factory Outlet Center
Exit 212 off I-75
West Branch, MI 48661
(517) 345-4437

Minnesota

Mikasa Factory Outlet
Medford Outlet Center
Medford, MN 55049
(507) 451-1939

Welcome Home
Tanger Factory Outlet Center
Exit 147 off I-35
North Branch, MN 55056
(612) 674-5885

Minnesota (cont.)

Welcome Home
Horizon Outlet Center
Exit 251 off I-94
Woodbury, MN 55125
(612) 739-3176

Missouri

Brasscrafters
Factory Merchants Branson
West Hwy. 76 and Pat Nash Dr.
Branson, MO 65616
(417) 336-8791

Mikasa Factory Outlet
Tanger Factory Outlet Center
Highway 76
Branson, MO 65616
(417) 337-9327

Stained Glass Factory Outlet
Factory Merchants Branson
West Hwy. 76 and Pat Nash Dr.
Branson, MO 65616
(417) 339-2854

Vermillion
Factory Merchants Branson
West Hwy. 76 and Pat Nash Dr.
Branson, MO 65616
(417) 335-5156

Welcome Home
Tanger Factory Outlet Center
Highway 76
Branson, MO 65616
(417) 337-9327

Libbey Glass
Sikeston Factory Outlet Stores
Exit 67 off I-55
Miner, MO 63801
(314) 471-3340

Factory Outlets (cont.)

Missouri (cont.)

Welcome Home
Sikeston Factory Outlet Stores
Exit 67 off I-55
Miner, MO 63801
(314) 472-3232

Welcome Home
Factory Outlet Village
Highway 54
Osage Beach, MO 65065
(314) 348-9015

Mikasa Factory Outlet
190 Mall Parkway
Wentzville, MO 63385
(314) 327-7167

Nebraska

Mikasa Factory Outlet
Nebraska Crossing Factory Stores
Exit 432 off I-80
Gretna, NE 68028
(402) 332-3722

Royal Doulton Factory Outlet
Nebraska Crossing Factory Stores
Exit 432 off I-80
Gretna, NE 68028
(402) 332-4280

Welcome Home
Nebraska Crossing Factory Stores
Exit 432 off I-80
Gretna, NE 68028
(402) 332-4374

Welcome Home
Whites Factory Outlet Center
Exit 177 off I-80
North Platte, NE 69101
(308) 532-4532

Nevada

Libbey Glass Factory Outlet
Factory Stores of America
Exit 33 off I-15
Las Vegas, NV 89123
(702) 897-9090

Mikasa Factory Outlet
Factory Stores of America
Exit 33 off I-15
Las Vegas, NV 89123
(702) 897-9090

Pfaltzgraff Factory Outlet
Belz Factory Outlet World
I-15 and Warm Springs Rd.
Las Vegas, NV 89123
(702) 896-5599

Welcome Home
Factory Stores of America
Exit 33 off I-15
Las Vegas, NV 89123
(702) 897-9090

Brass Factory Outlet
105 Sparks Blvd.
Sparks, NV 89434
(702) 331-5211

New Hampshire

Welcome Home
North Hampton Factory
Outlet Center
Route 1/Lafayette Rd.
North Hampton, NH 03862
(603) 964-2216

Mikasa Factory Outlet
Lakes Region Factory Stores
Exit 20 off I-93
Tilton, NH 03276
(603) 286-7880

New Hampshire (cont.)

Welcome Home
Lakes Region Factory Stores
Exit 20 off I-93
Tilton, NH 03276
(603) 286-7880

New Jersey

Mikasa Factory Outlet
95 Main St.
Flemington, NJ 08822
(908) 788-3620

Petals Factory Outlet
Liberty Village Factory Outlets
Route 31 and Route 202
Flemington, NJ 08822
(908) 788-5256

Pfaltzgraff Factory Outlet
Mine St.
Flemington, NJ 08822
(908) 782-2918

Royal Doulton Factory Outlet
Liberty Village Factory Outlets
Route 31 and Route 202
Flemington, NJ 08822
(908) 788-5677

Shady Lamp Shop
Liberty Village Factory Outlets
Route 31 and Route 202
Flemington, NJ 08822
(908) 788-5200

Villeroy & Boch
Liberty Village Factory Outlets
Route 31 and Route 202
Flemington, NJ 08822
(908) 788-5609

Factory Outlets (cont.)

New Jersey (cont.)

Mikasa Factory Outlet
1407 Atlantic Ave.
Manasquan, NJ 08736
(908) 223-0340

Dansk Factory Outlet
Princeton Forrestral Village
Route 1 and College Rd. W.
Princeton, NJ 08540
(609) 799-7400

Welcome Home
Princeton Forrestral Village
Route 1 and College Rd. W.
Princeton, NJ 08540
(609) 799-7400

Mikasa Factory Outlet
25 Enterprise Ave. N.
Secaucus, NJ 07094
(201) 867-6805

Welcome Home
Harmon Cove Outlet Center
20 Enterprise Ave.
Secaucus, NJ 07094
(800) 358-2373

New Mexico

Dansk Factory Outlet
Santa Fe Factory Stores
Exit 278 off I-25
Santa Fe, NM 87505
(505) 474-4288

Royal Doulton Factory Outlet
Santa Fe Factory Stores
Exit 278 off I-25
Santa Fe, NM 87505
(505) 474-3688

New Mexico (cont.)

Villeroy & Boch
Santa Fe Factory Stores
Exit 278 off I-25
Santa Fe, NM 87505
(505) 471-7303

Welcome Home
Santa Fe Factory Stores
Exit 278 off I-25
Santa Fe, NM 87505
(505) 474-0369

New York

Dansk Factory Outlet
Woodbury Common Factory Outlets
Exit 16 (Harriman exit) off I-87
Central Valley, NY 10917
(914) 928-9003

Mikasa Factory Outlet
Woodbury Common Factory Outlets
Exit 16 (Harriman exit) off I-87
Central Valley, NY 10917
(914) 928-4428

Petals Factory Outlet
Woodbury Common Factory Outlets
Exit 16 (Harriman exit) off I-87
Central Valley, NY 10917
(914) 928-6520

Royal Doulton Factory Outlet
Woodbury Common Factory Outlets
Exit 16 (Harriman exit) off I-87
Central Valley, NY 10917
(914) 928-2434

Shady Lamp Shop
Woodbury Common Factory Outlets
Exit 16 (Harriman exit) off I-87
Central Valley, NY 10917
(914) 928-6676

New York (cont.)

Villeroy & Boch
Woodbury Common Factory Outlets
Exit 16 (Harriman exit) off I-87
Central Valley, NY 10917
(914) 928-4558

Dansk Factory Outlet
Miromar Factory Outlet Center
Exit 42 off I-87
Champlain, NY 12919
(518) 298-3339

Welcome Home
Miromar Factory Outlet Center
Exit 42 off I-87
Champlain, NY 12919
(518) 298-2780

Mikasa Factory Outlet
Manufacturer's Outlet Center
Exit 4 off I-684
Mt. Kisco, NY 10549
(914) 241-8503

Welcome Home
Manufacturer's Outlet Center
Exit 4 off I-684
Mt. Kisco, NY 10549
((914) 241-8503

Mikasa Factory Outlet
Niagara Factory Outlets
Exit 22 off I-190
Niagara Falls, NY 14202
(716) 298-5014

Pfaltzgraff Factory Outlet
Niagara Factory Outlets
Exit 22 off I-190
Niagara Falls, NY 14202
(716) 297-5706

Factory Outlets (cont.)

New York (cont.)

Welcome Home
Niagara Factory Outlets
Exit 22 off I-190
Niagara Falls, NY 14202
(716) 297-0324

Mikasa Factory Outlet
Tanger Factory Outlet Center
Exit 73 off I-495 East
Riverhead, NY 11901
(516) 369-2724

Pfaltzgraff Factory Outlet
Tanger Factory Outlet Center
Exit 73 off I-495 East
Riverhead, NY 11901
(516) 369-2724

Welcome Home
Tanger Factory Outlet Center
Exit 73 off I-495 East
Riverhead, NY 11901
(516) 369-2724

North Carolina

Royal Doulton Factory Outlet
Shoppes on the Parkway
Hwy. 321 Bypass
Blowing Rock, NC 28605
(704) 295-4248

Welcome Home
Shoppes on the Parkway
Hwy. 321 Bypass
Blowing Rock, NC 28605
(704) 295-4248

Mikasa Factory Outlet
Burlington Manufacturers
Outlet Center
Exit 145 off I-85/40
Burlington, NC 27216
(910) 227-2872

North Carolina (cont.)

Welcome Home
Tanger Factory Outlet Center
Exit 145 off I-85/40
Burlington, NC 27215
(800) 4-TANGER

Karastan Rug Outlet
4309 Wylie Davis Rd.
Greensboro, NC 27407
(800) 877-1955

Capel Rug Mill Outlet
605 Greenville Blvd. SE
Greenville, NC 27858
(919) 756-5436

Beacon Hill Factory Outlet
Hickory Furniture Mart
Hickory, NC 28602
(704) 324-2220

Home Outfitters Factory Outlet
Hickory Furniture Mart
Hickory, NC 28602
(704) 324-2220

La Barge Factory Outlet
Hickory Furniture Mart
Hickory, NC 28602
(704) 324-2220

Maitland-Smith Factory Outlet
Hickory Furniture Mart
Hickory, NC 28602
(704) 324-2220

Zaki Oriental Rugs
1634 N. Main St.
High Point, NC 27262
(910) 968-0088

North Carolina (cont.)

Karastan Rug Outlet
Cannon Village
120 West Ave.
Kannapolis, NC 28081
(704) 933-3474

Waccamaw
Cannon Village
120 West Ave.
Kannapolis, NC 28081
(704) 932-3474

Reading China and Glass
Triangle Factory Shops
Exit 284 off I-40
Morrisville, NC 27650
(919) 481-3222

Welcome Home
Triangle Factory Shops
Exit 284 off I-40
Morrisville, NC 27650
(919) 460-9007

Pfaltzgraff Factory Outlet
Soundings Factory Stores
U. S. 158 and U. S. 264
Nags Head, NC 27959
(919) 441-7395

American & Oriental Rug Outlet
1924 Capital Blvd.
Raleigh, NC 27604
(919) 839-0925

Carolina Clock and Rug Outlet
Factory Stores of America
Exit 95 off I-95
Smithfield, NC 27577
(919) 934-9446

Factory Outlets (cont.)

North Carolina (cont.)

Carolina Pottery
Factory Stores of America
Exit 95 off I-95
Smithfield, NC 27577
(919) 934-9446

Royal Doulton Factory Outlet
Factory Stores of America
Exit 95 off I-95
Smithfield, NC 27577
(919) 934-9446

Old Town Clock Shop
3738 Reynolda Rd.
Winston-Salem, NC 27106
(910) 924-8807

Ohio

Aurora Furniture & Interiors
Aurora Farms Factory Outlets
Exit 13 off Ohio Turnpike
Aurora, OH 44202
(216) 562-9400

Mikasa Factory Outlet
Aurora Farms Factory Outlets
Exit 13 off Ohio Turnpike
Aurora, OH 44202
(216) 995-0400

Pfaltzgraff Factory Outlet
Aurora Farms Factory Outlets
Exit 13 off Ohio Turnpike
Aurora, OH 44202
(216) 562-1223

Royal Doulton Factory Outlet
Aurora Farms Factory Outlets
Exit 13 off Ohio Turnpike
Aurora, OH 44202
(216) 995-0202

Ohio (cont.)

Wayside Workshop
Aurora Farms Factory Outlets
Exit 13 off Ohio Turnpike
Aurora, OH 44202
(216) 562-4800

Welcome Home
Aurora Farms Factory Outlets
Exit 13 off Ohio Turnpike
Aurora, OH 44202
(216) 562-2271

Baldwin Brass
Ohio Factory Shops
Exit 65 off I-71
Jeffersonville, OH 43218
(614) 948-2900

Lenox Factory Outlet
Ohio Factory Shops
Exit 65 off I-71
Jeffersonville, OH 43218
(614) 948-2120

Mikasa Factory Outlet
Jeffersonville Outlet Center
Exit 69 off I-71
Jeffersonville, OH 43128
(614) 426-6688

Reading China & Glass
Ohio Factory Shops
Exit 65 off I-71
Jeffersonville, OH 43218
(614) 948-2035

Reed & Barton
Ohio Factory Shops
Exit 65 off I-71
Jeffersonville, OH 43218
(614) 948-2814

Ohio (cont.)

Royal Doulton Factory Outlet
Ohio Factory Shops
Exit 65 off I-71
Jeffersonville, OH 43218
(614) 948-9200

Villeroy & Boch
Ohio Factory Shops
Exit 65 off I-71
Jeffersonville, OH 43218
(614) 948-2985

Welcome Home
Jeffersonville Outlet Center
Exit 69 off I-71
Jeffersonville, OH 43128
(614) 426-9238

Welcome Home
Ohio Factory Shops
Exit 65 off I-71
Jeffersonville, OH 43218
(614) 948-9322

Mikasa Factory Outlet
11001 U. S. Hwy. 250 N.
Milan, OH 44846
(419) 499-4907

Oklahoma

Mikasa Factory Store
Whites Factory Outlet Center
Exit 222 off I-35
Blackwell, OK 74631
(405) 363-1161

Welcome Home
Whites Factory Outlet Center
Exit 222 off I-35
Blackwell, OK 74631
(405) 363-1437

Factory Outlets (cont.)

Oklahoma (cont.)

Mikasa Factory Outlet
Tanger Factory Outlet Center
Exit 179 off I-44
Stroud, OK 74079
(918) 968-3566

Vermillion
Tanger Factory Outlet Center
Exit 179 off I-44
Stroud, OK 74079
(918) 968-3566

Welcome Home
Tanger Factory Outlet Center
Exit 179 off I-44
Stroud, OK 74079
(918) 968-3566

Oregon

Dansk Factory Outlet
Bend Factory Outlets
Hwy. 97
Bend, OR 97702
(503) 382-1127

Welcome Home
Bend Factory Outlets
Hwy. 97
Bend, OR 97702
(503) 389-7050

Mikasa Factory Outlet
Factory Stores at Lincoln City
1510 E. Devils Lake Rd.
Lincoln City, OR 97367
(503) 996-5000

Pfaltzgraff Factory Outlet
Factory Stores at Lincoln City
1510 E. Devils Lake Rd.
Lincoln City, OR 97367
(503) 996-5000

Oregon (cont.)

Royal Doulton Factory Outlet
Factory Stores at Lincoln City
1510 E. Devils Lake Rd.
Lincoln City, OR 97367
(503) 996-5000

Welcome Home
Factory Stores at Lincoln City
1510 E. Devils Lake Rd.
Lincoln City, OR 97367
(503) 996-5000

Welcome Home
Tanger Factory Outlet Center
Hwy. 18 and Norton Lane
McMinnville, OR 97128
(503) 472-5387

Mikasa Factory Outlet
Columbia Gorge Factory Stores
Exit 17 off I-84
Troutdale, OR 97060
(503) 669-1884

Welcome Home
Columbia Gorge Factory Stores
Exit 17 off I-84
Troutdale, OR 97060
(503) 669-9714

Pennsylvania

Baldwin Brass Home Accents
Grove City Factory Shops
Exit 31 off I-79
Grove City, PA 16127
(412) 748-4770

Mikasa Factory Outlet
Grove City Factory Shops
Exit 31 off I-79
Grove City, PA 16127
(412) 748-4770

Pennsylvania (cont.)

Pfaltzgraff Factory Outlet
Grove City Factory Shops
Exit 31 off I-79
Grove City, PA 16127
(412) 748-4770

Royal Doulton Factory Outlet
Grove City Factory Shops
Exit 31 off I-79
Grove City, PA 16127
(412) 748-4770

Welcome Home
Grove City Factory Shops
Exit 31 off I-79
Grove City, PA 16127
(412) 748-4770

Irish Crystal Factory Outlet
104 Broadway
Hanover, PA 17331
(717) 632-9412

Dansk Factory Outlet
Factory Stores at Hershey, PA
Hwy. 22
Hershey, PA 17033
(717) 533-9795

Libbey Glass
Factory Stores at Hershey, PA
Hwy. 22
Hershey, PA 17033
(717) 533-6541

Mikasa Factory Outlet
Factory Stores at Hershey, PA
Hwy. 22
Hershey, PA 17033
(717) 520-0637

Factory Outlets (cont.)

Pennsylvania (cont.)

Pewtarex
Factory Stores at Hershey, PA
Hwy. 22
Hershey, PA 17033
(717) 520-0552

Pfaltzgraff Factory Outlet
Factory Stores at Hershey, PA
Hwy. 22
Hershey, PA 17033
(717) 520-0515

Welcome Home
Factory Stores at Hershey, PA
Hwy. 22
Hershey, PA 17033
(717) 520-0404

Dansk Factory Outlet
Rockvale Square Outlets
U. S. Hwy. 30 and Hwy. 896
Lancaster, PA 17601
(717) 299-2771

Lenox Factory Outlet
Rockvale Square Outlets
U. S. Hwy. 30 and Hwy. 896
Lancaster, PA 17601
(717) 393-2400

Petals Factory Store
Rockvale Square Outlets
U. S. Hwy. 30 and Hwy. 896
Lancaster, PA 17601
(717) 392-5910

Pewtarex
Rockvale Square Outlets
U. S. Hwy. 30 and Hwy. 896
Lancaster, PA 17601
(717) 392-4108

Pennsylvania (cont.)

Pfaltzgraff Factory Outlet
Rockvale Square Outlets
U. S. Hwy. 30 and Hwy. 896
Lancaster, PA 17601
(717) 299-6803

Reading China & Glass
Rockvale Square Outlets
U. S. Hwy. 30 and Hwy. 896
Lancaster, PA 17601
(717) 393-9747

Reed & Barton
Rockvale Square Outlets
U. S. Hwy. 30 and Hwy. 896
Lancaster, PA 17601
(717) 399-3485

Timeworld
Rockvale Square Outlets
U. S. Hwy. 30 and Hwy. 896
Lancaster, PA 17601
(717) 393-5917

Welcome Home
Rockvale Square Outlets
U. S. Hwy. 30 and Hwy. 896
Lancaster, PA 17601
(717) 299-5885

Wholesale Rug Outlet
Rockvale Square Outlets
U. S. Hwy. 30 and Hwy. 896
Lancaster, PA 17601
(717) 295-9078

Welcome Home
Tanger Factory Outlet Center
Route 30 East
Lancaster, PA 17602
(717) 392-7202

Pennsylvania (cont.)

Welcome Home
Bald Eagle Factory Outlets
McElhatten Exit off Route 200
McElhatten, PA 17745
(717) 769-7620

David's Crystal Factory Outlet
2001 N. 13th St.
Reading, PA 19604
(215) 921-0201

Instant Decor
VF Factory Outlet Village
Hwy. 422 W.
Reading, PA 19610
(800) 772-8336

Mikasa Factory Outlet
VF Factory Outlet Village
Hwy. 422 W.
Reading, PA 19610
(800) 772-8336

Reading China & Glass
VF Factory Outlet Village
Hwy. 422 W.
Reading, PA 19610
(800) 772-8336

Mikasa Factory Outlet
Georgian Place Outlet Center
Highway 601 N.
Somerset, PA 15501
(800) 866-5900

Welcome Home
Georgian Place Outlet Center
Highway 601 N.
Somerset, PA 15501
(800) 866-5900

Factory Outlets (cont.)

Pennsylvania (cont.)

Pfaltzgraff Factory Outlet
2900 Whiteford Rd.
York, PA 17402
(717) 757-2200

South Carolina

Belgian Rug Co.
Outlet Marketplace
Exit 90 off I-77
Fort Mill, SC 29715
(803) 548-6512

Carolina Pottery
Outlet Marketplace
Exit 90 off I-77
Fort Mill, SC 29715
(803) 548-7075

Timepieces
Outlet Marketplace
Exit 90 off I-77
Fort Mill, SC 29715
(803) 548-1976

Dansk Factory Outlet
Shoppes On the Parkway
William Hilton Parkway
Hilton Head Island, SC 29926
(803) 686-6233

Lenox Factory Outlet
Shoppes On the Parkway
William Hilton Parkway
Hilton Head Island, SC 29926
(803) 686-6233

The Interior Alternative
1 Frederick Dr.
Richburg, SC 29729
(803) 789-6655

South Carolina (cont.)

Brass Factory Outlet
Santee Village Square
Santee, SC 29142
(803) 854-4685

Tennessee

Villeroy & Boch
Warehouse Row Factory Shops
1110 Market St.
Chattanooga, TN 37402
(615) 267-3878

Welcome Home
Warehouse Row Factory Shops
1110 Market St.
Chattanooga, TN 37402
(615) 265-2039

Dan's Factory Surplus
114 N. 14th Ave.
Humboldt, TN 38343
(901) 784-3883

Welcome Home
Outlets LTD Mall
Exit 78 off I-24
Murfreesboro, TN 37129
(615) 895-4966

Libbey Glass Factory Outlet
Factory Stores of America
Exit 215 off I-40
Nashville, TN 37202
(615) 885-5140

Welcome Home
Factory Stores of America
Exit 215 off I-40
Nashville, TN 37202
(615) 885-5140

Tennessee (cont.)

Factories Outlet China & Gift Mart
2680 Parkway
Pigeon Forge, TN 37863
(615) 453-5679

Mikasa Factory Outlet
Pigeon Forge Factory Outlet Mall
2850 Parkway
Pigeon Forge, TN 37863
(615) 453-5482

Old Time Pottery
Belz Factory Outlet World
2655 Teaster Lane
Pigeon Forge, TN 37863
(615) 453-6882

Pfaltzgraff Factory Outlet
Pigeon Forge Factory Outlet Mall
2850 Parkway
Pigeon Forge, TN 37863
(615) 428-3028

Royal Doulton Factory Outlet
Belz Factory Outlet World
2655 Teaster Lane
Pigeon Forge, TN 37863
(615) 428-0977

Lenox Factory Outlet
Five Oaks Factory Stores
U. S. Hwy 441
Sevierville, TN 37862
(615) 428-4745

Reed & Barton
Five Oaks Factory Stores
U. S. Hwy 441
Sevierville, TN 37862
(615) 453-2043

Factory Outlets (cont.)

Tennessee (cont.)

Villeroy & Boch
Five Oaks Factory Stores
U. S. Hwy 441
Sevierville, TN 37862
(615) 429-8423

Carolina Clock and Rug Outlet
Factory Stores of America
Exit 66 off I-81
Tri-Cities, TN 37617
(615) 323-4419

Carolina Pottery
Factory Stores of America
Exit 66 off I-81
Tri-Cities, TN 37617
(615) 323-4419

Texas

The Interior Alternative
2626 Northhaven Rd.
Dallas, TX 75229
(214) 241-5422

Dansk Factory Outlet
Gainesville Factory Shops
Exit 501 off I-35
Gainesville, TX 76240
(817) 668-1037

Mikasa Factory Outlet
Gainesville Factory Shops
Exit 501 off I-35
Gainesville, TX 76240
(817) 665-3064

Welcome Home
Gainesville Factory Shops
Exit 501 off I-35
Gainesville, TX 76240
(817) 668-1276

Texas (cont.)

Mikasa Factory Outlet
2225 Strand St.
Galveston, TX 77550
(409) 765-1760

Mikasa Factory Outlet
SW Outlet Rd.
Hillsboro, TX 76645
(817) 582-7453

Brass Factory Outlet
14037 Delaney St.
La Marque, TX 77568
(409) 935-6776

Pfaltzgraff Factory Outlet
Factory Stores of America
Exit 13 off I-45
La Marque, TX 77568
(409) 938-3333

Pfaltzgraff Factory Outlet
New Braunfels Factory Stores
Exit 188 off I-35
New Braunfels, TX 78130
(210) 620-4242

Welcome Home
New Braunfels Factory Stores
Exit 188 off I-35
New Braunfels, TX 78130
(210) 620-7956

Mikasa Factory Outlet
6100-K Alternate Ave.
Plano, TX 75074
(214) 881-0019

Fitz and Floyd Factory Outlet
San Marcos Factory Shops
Exit 200 off I-35
San Marcos, TX 78666
(800) 628-9465

Texas (cont.)

Lenox Factory Outlet
Tanger Factory Outlet Center
Exit 200 off I-35
San Marcos, TX 78666
(512) 396-7444

Mikasa Factory Outlet
San Marcos Factory Shops
Exit 200 off I-35
San Marcos, TX 78666
(800) 628-9465

Pfaltzgraff Factory Outlet
Tanger Factory Outlet Center
Exit 200 off I-35
San Marcos, TX 78666
(512) 396-7444

Reading China and Glass
San Marcos Factory Shops
Exit 200 off I-35
San Marcos, TX 78666
(800) 628-9465

Villeroy & Boch
San Marcos Factory Shops
Exit 200 off I-35
San Marcos, TX 78666
(800) 628-9465

Welcome Home
San Marcos Factory Shops
Exit 200 off I-35
San Marcos, TX 78666
(800) 628-9465

Welcome Home
Tanger Factory Outlet Center
Exit 200 off I-35
San Marcos, TX 78666
(512) 396-7444

Factory Outlets (cont.)

Texas (cont.)

Mikasa Factory Outlet
Tanger Factory Outlet Center
Exit 501 off I-20
Terrell, TX 75160
(214) 524-6255

Welcome Home
Tanger Factory Outlet Center
Exit 501 off I-20
Terrell, TX 75160
(214) 524-6255

Utah

Mikasa Factory Outlet
Factory Stores at Park City
Exit 145 off I-80
Park City, UT 84060
(801) 645-9750

Welcome Home
Factory Stores at Park City
Exit 145 off I-80
Park City, UT 84060
(801) 649-5171

Virginia

Pfaltzgraff Factory Outlet
10334 Main St.
Fairfax, VA 22030
(703) 591-6141

Welcome Home
Factory Merchants Fort Chiswell
Exit 80 off I-81
Fort Chiswell, VA 24360
(703) 637-6519

Libbey Glass
Massaponax Outlet Center
Exit 126 off I-95
Fredericksburg, VA 22401
(703) 373-8853

Virginia (cont.)

Welcome Home
Massaponax Outlet Center
Exit 126 off I-95
Fredericksburg, VA 22401
(703) 373-8853

Pfaltzgraff Factory Outlet
Rte. 60
Lightfoot, VA 23090
(804) 564-3064

Solid Brass of Williamsburg
Williamsburg Outlet Mall
Exit 234 off I-64
Lightfoot, VA 23090
(804) 565-1177

Waltham Clock Factory Outlet
Williamsburg Outlet Mall
Exit 234 off I-64
Lightfoot, VA 23090
(804) 565-3378

Welcome Home
Williamsburg Outlet Mall
Exit 234 off I-64
Lightfoot, VA 23090
(804) 565-3884

Adler's Art and Frame
Potomac Mills Outlet Center
Exit 156 off I-95
Prince William, VA 22192
(800) VA-MILLS

Art Plus
Potomac Mills Outlet Center
Exit 156 off I-95
Prince William, VA 22192
(800) VA-MILLS

Virginia (cont.)

Brass Factory
Potomac Mills Outlet Center
Exit 156 off I-95
Prince William, VA 22192
(800) VA-MILLS

Brassworks
Potomac Mills Outlet Center
Exit 156 off I-95
Prince William, VA 22192
(800) VA-MILLS

Brewster Glassmith
Potomac Mills Outlet Center
Exit 156 off I-95
Prince William, VA 22192
(800) VA-MILLS

China Carpet and Imports
Potomac Mills Outlet Center
Exit 156 off I-95
Prince William, VA 22192
(800) VA-MILLS

Oriental Weavers Carpet
Potomac Mills Outlet Center
Exit 156 off I-95
Prince William, VA 22192
(800) VA-MILLS

Waccamaw
Potomac Mills Outlet Center
Exit 156 off I-95
Prince William, VA 22192
(800) VA-MILLS

World Accents
Potomac Mills Outlet Center
Exit 156 off I-95
Prince William, VA 22192
(800) VA-MILLS

Factory Outlets (cont.)

Virginia (cont.)

Welcome Home
Great American Outlet Mall
Exit 4 off Hwy. 58
Virginia Beach, VA 23452
(804) 463-8665

Brass Factory Outlet
5699 Richmond Rd.
Williamsburg, VA 23188
(804) 565-4549

Mikasa Factory Outlet
5711 Richmond Rd.
Williamsburg, VA 23188
(804) 565-2976

Washington

Mikasa Factory Outlet
Pacific Edge Outlet Center
Exit 229 off I-5
Burlington, WA 98233
(800) 969-3767

Pfaltzgraff Factory Outlet
Pacific Edge Outlet Center
Exit 229 off I-5
Burlington, WA 98233
(800) 969-3767

Royal Doulton Factory Outlet
Pacific Edge Outlet Center
Exit 229 off I-5
Burlington, WA 98233
(800) 969-3767

Welcome Home
Pacific Edge Outlet Center
Exit 229 off I-5
Burlington, WA 98233
(800) 969-3767

Washington (cont.)

Pfaltzgraff Factory Outlet
Centralia Factory Outlets
Exit 82 off I-5
Centralia, WA 98531
(360) 736-3327

Pilgrim Glass
Centralia Factory Outlets
Exit 82 off I-5
Centralia, WA 98531
(360) 736-3327

Welcome Home
Centralia Factory Outlets
Exit 82 off I-5
Centralia, WA 98531
(360) 736-3327

Omid Oriental Rugs
Factory Stores of America
Exit 31 off I-90
North Bend, WA 98045
(206) 888-4505

Welcome Home
Factory Stores of America
Exit 31 off I-90
North Bend, WA 98045
(206) 888-4505

Wisconsin

Libbey Glass Factory Outlet
Factory Outlet Center
I-94 and Highway 50
Kenosha, WI 53142
(414) 857-2964

Mikasa Factory Outlet
11211 120th Ave.
Kenosha, WI 53142
(414) 857-2003

Wisconsin (cont.)

Pfaltzgraff Factory Outlet
Factory Outlet Center
I-94 and Highway 50
Kenosha, WI 53142
(414) 857-6755

Welcome Home
Factory Outlet Center
I-94 and Highway 50
Kenosha, WI 53142
(414) 857-2924

Dansk Factory Outlet
Horizon Outlet Center
U. S. 41 and Hwy. 44
Oshkosh, WI 54904
(414) 426-5522

Lenox Factory Outlet
Horizon Outlet Center
U. S. 41 and Hwy. 44
Oshkosh, WI 54904
(414) 426-4499

Royal Doulton Factory Outlet
Horizon Outlet Center
U. S. 41 and Hwy. 44
Oshkosh, WI 54904
(414) 231-1141

Welcome Home
Horizon Outlet Center
U. S. 41 and Hwy. 44
Oshkosh, WI 54904
(414) 231-3101

Deep Discount Stores

These stores generally do not sell seconds and discontinued items, as outlets often do, but they do still have good prices on many types of accessories. Most of the savings come from the stores buying in bulk.

A few stores do have great deals on a limited number of closeouts and customer returns, at savings of up to 50% off retail. Clearance centers for catalogs, such as Charles Keath and Spiegel, sell overstocked items and customer returns. Furniture chains, such as Haverty's and Bombay Company, also have clearance centers. The QVC shopping channel has an clearance center. These sources have great bargains, but you should check everything over carefully in case there is any hidden damage.

Check out factory outlets and telephone ordering services before moving on to deep discount stores. Most of the stores listed here accept credit cards.

Deep Discount Stores

Colorado

Spiegel Catalog Clearance
Center
Rocky Mountain Factory Stores
I-25 and U. S. Hwy. 34
Loveland, CO 80538
(970) 663-1717

Florida

Haverty's Direct Clearance
Center
7720 Phillips Hwy.
Jacksonville, FL 32216
(904) 731-9160

Spiegel Catalog Clearance
Center
8427 Cooper Creek Blvd.
University Park, FL 34201
(813) 359-0519

Georgia

Ballard's Backroom
Catalog Clearance Center
1670 De Foor Ave.
Atlanta, GA 30318
(404) 352-2776

Georgia (cont.)

Spiegel Catalog Clearance
Center
Dalton Factory Stores
Exit 136 off I-75
Dalton, GA 30720
(706) 279-1500

Spiegel Catalog Clearance
Center
Magnolia Bluff Factory Shops
Exit 10 off I-95
Darien, GA 31305
(912) 437-2700

J. C. Penney Catalog Outlet
5500 S. Expressway
Forest Park, GA 30050
(404) 363-3855

Bombay Company Clearance
Center
4101 Roswell Rd.
Suite 401
Marietta, GA 30062
(770) 509-7008

Charles Keath Clearance Center
1265 Oakbrook Dr.
Norcross, GA 30093
(800) 241-1122

Deep Discount Stores (cont.)

Georgia (cont.)

J. C. Penney Catalog Outlet
2434 Atlanta Rd.
Smyrna, GA 30080
(404) 432-5231

Illinois

European Furniture Importers
2145 W. Grand Ave.
Chicago, IL 60612
(800) 283-1955

J. C. Penney Clearance Center
Gurnee Mills
I-94 and Route 132
Gurnee, IL 60031
(800) YES-SHOP

Spiegel Catalog Clearance Center
Gurnee Mills
I-94 and Route 132
Gurnee, IL 60031
(800) YES-SHOP

Michigan

Spiegel Catalog Clearance Center
Outlets At Birch Run
Exit 136 off I-75
Birch Run, MI 48415
(517) 624-1100

Spiegel Catalog Clearance Center
Horizon Outlet Center
U. S. 31 and James St.
Holland, MI 49423
(616) 396-1327

Spiegel Catalog Clearance Center
Horizon Outlet Center
Exit 11 off I-75
Monroe, MI 48161
(313) 457-2530

Minnesota

Spiegel Catalog Clearance Center
Horizon Outlet Center
Exit 251 off I-94
Woodbury, MN 55125
(612) 730-0187

North Carolina

Tyson Furniture
109 Broadway St.
Black Mountain, NC 28711
(704) 669-5000

The Furniture Patch
10283 Beach Dr. SW
Calabash, NC 28467
(910) 579-2001

Mecklenburg Furniture
7203 Statesville Rd.
Charlotte, NC 28213
(800) 541-9877

Lake Hickory Furniture
405 Hwy. 321 S
Granite Falls, NC 28630
(704) 396-2194

Thomas Home Furnishings
401 Hwy. 321 S
Granite Falls, NC 28630
(704) 396-2147

A Classic Design
1703 Madison Ave.
Greensboro, NC 27403
(910) 274-2922

Fields Furniture Co.
2700 Randelman Rd.
Greensboro, NC 27406
(910) 273-7629

North Carolina (cont.)

House Dressing International
Furniture
3608 W. Wendover
Greensboro, NC 27407
(800) 322-5850

Priba Furniture Sales
5-A Wendy Ct.
Greensboro, NC 27409
(910) 855-9034

Designer Creations
Hickory Furniture Mart
Hickory, NC 28602
(704) 327-9933

Elizabeth Chappell
Hickory Furniture Mart
Hickory, NC 28602
(704) 326-9115

Hunt Galleries
2920 Hwy. 127 N
Hickory, NC 28601
(800) 248-3876

National Art Gallery
Hickory Furniture Mart
Hickory, NC 28602
(704) 324-9400

Palliser
Hickory Furniture Mart
Hickory, NC 28602
(704) 324-7742

Southern Designs
Hickory Furniture Mart
Hickory, NC 28602
(704) 328-8855

A. Windsor Furniture Galleries
607 Idol St.
High Point, NC 27262
(910) 883-9000

Deep Discount Stores (cont.)

North Carolina (cont.)

Alan Ferguson Associates
422 S. Main St.
High Point, NC 27260
(910) 889-3866

Arts By Alexander
701 Greensboro Rd.
High Point, NC 27260
(910) 884-8062

Black's Furniture
2800 Westchester St.
High Point, NC 27262
(910) 886-5011

Boyles Furniture Co.
727 N. Main St.
High Point, NC 27262
(910) 889-4147

Dallas Furniture Store
215 N. Centennial St.
High Point, NC 27260
(910) 882-2654

Gibson Interiors
417 S. Wrenn St.
High Point, NC 27260
(910) 883-4444

Main St. Galleries
430 S. Main St.
High Point, NC 27260
(910) 883-2611

Paynes Furniture
2904 N. Main St.
High Point, NC 27265
(910) 887-4444

Rose Furniture
916 Finch Ave.
High Point, NC 27263
(910) 886-6050

North Carolina (cont.)

Rose Furniture Clearance Center
1813 S. Main St.
High Point, NC 27260
(910) 886-8525

Utility Craft Inc.
2630 Eastchester Dr.
High Point, NC 27265
(910) 454-6153

Wood Armfield Furniture
460 S. Main St.
High Point, NC 27260
(910) 889-6522

Young's Furniture and Rug Co.
1706 N. Main St.
High Point, NC 27262
(910) 883-4111

Mallory's Fine Furniture
2153 Le Jeune Blvd.
Jacksonville, NC 28546
(910) 353-1828

Furnitureland South
5635 Riverdale Rd.
Jamestown, NC 27282
(910) 841-4328

Quality Furniture Market
2034 Hickory Blvd. SE
Lenoir, NC 28645
(704) 728-2946

Turner Tolson Furniture
U. S. Hwy. 17 S
New Bern, NC 28562
(919) 638-2121

Barnes and Barnes Furniture
190 Commerce Ave.
Southern Pines, NC 28387
(800) 334-8174

North Carolina (cont.)

Furniture Barn of Forest City
Hwy. 74 Bypass
Spindale, NC 28160
(704) 287-7106

Corner Hutch Furniture
Highway 21 North
Statesville, NC 28677
(704) 873-1773

Ellenburg's Furniture
I-40 and Stamey Farm Rd.
Statesville, NC 28677
(704) 873-2900

The Decorator's Edge
509 Randolph St.
Thomasville, NC 27360
(800) 289-5589

Loftin-Black Furniture
111 Sedgehill Dr.
Thomasville, NC 27360
(800) 334-7398

Sutton-Councill Furniture
421 S. College Rd.
Wilmington, NC 28403
(910) 799-9000

Ohio

Spiegel Catalog Clearance Center
Jeffersonville Outlet Center
Exit 69 off I-71
Jeffersonville, OH 43128
(614) 426-8685

Pennsylvania

QVC Network Clearance Center
Rockvale Square Outlets
U. S. Hwy. 30 and Hwy. 896
Lancaster, PA 17601
(717) 293-9595

Deep Discount Stores (cont.)

Pennsylvania (cont.)

Bombay Company Clearance Center
Franklin Mills
I-95 and Woodhaven Rd.
Philadelphia, PA 19114
(800) 336-6255

J. C. Penney Clearance Center
Franklin Mills
I-95 and Woodhaven Rd.
Philadelphia, PA 19114
(800) 336-6255

Spiegel Catalog Clearance Center
Franklin Mills
I-95 and Woodhaven Rd.
Philadelphia, PA 19114
(800) 336-6255

South Carolina

Triad Furniture Discounters
9770 North Kings Hwy.
Magnolia Plaza
Myrtle Beach, SC 29577
(800) 323-8469

Texas

Spiegel Catalog Clearance Center
Tanger Factory Outlet Center
Exit 200 off I-35
San Marcos, TX 78666
(512) 396-7444

Virginia

J. C. Penney Clearance Center
Potomac Mills Outlet Center
Exit 156 off I-95
Prince William, VA 22192
(800) VA-MILLS

Lillian Vernon Catalog Clearance Center
Potomac Mills Outlet Center
Exit 156 off I-95
Prince William, VA 22192
(800) VA-MILLS

Spiegel Catalog Clearance Center
Potomac Mills Outlet Center
Exit 156 off I-95
Prince William, VA 22192
(800) VA-MILLS

Wholesale

You can buy all kinds of decorative accessories at rock-bottom prices if you decide to become your own interior decorator, as discussed in Chapter 19. Most wholesale showrooms are accustomed to selling accessories one at a time, so you shouldn't run into any volume purchase requirements. Professional interior designers and interior decorators normally buy accessories one at a time.

There are thousands of wholesale showrooms and hundreds of manufacturers all over the U. S. that sell every kind of decorative accessory you can name. They are listed in the *National Directory of Wholesale Home Furnishings Sources and Showrooms*, by William Graham. This decorator reference book is available from this publisher.

You can also buy directly from the manufacturer in many instances. Some small accessory manufacturers do not sell through distributors or permanent wholesale showrooms. My family's decorative pillow factory routinely sold directly to interior decorators (and to consumers acting as their own decorators) who placed their orders by mail. Chapter 19 explains how you can do this, too.

Shopping wholesale is often the only way for you to buy higher quality decorative accessories without paying designer commissions because many accessory manufacturers don't sell through outlets or discounters, especially the more prestigious ones. Of course, a few of the most prestigious accessory manufacturers only sell their ultra-exclusive *objets* through selected interior designers -- usually the most expensive ones. However, most accessory brands will be available to you as an interior decorator.

If you decide to become your own decorator, you will often come out ahead to buy your accessories wholesale. Please read Chapter 19 for information on shopping in wholesale showrooms.

Recommendations

1 Shop factory outlets first, if there are any near your home. These stores have the best deals on many brands. You should save approximately 50% off retail. In some cases, you may be able to save as much as 75% off retail, usually on second-quality merchandise.

2 If you don't find what you want at an outlet, move on to telephone ordering services. Shop in your neighborhood to look at samples and record product information for the accessories you wish to purchase. Call a telephone ordering service to place your order. You will save up to 50% off retail, depending on the brand involved.

3 If you can't get a good discount over the phone, consider becoming your own decorator and shopping wholesale. If you shop in wholesale showrooms, you can usually get the standard 40% to 50% trade discount.

4 If a deep discount store is nearby, and none of the above sources are working out for you, try to find your accessories there. The discounts usually aren't as good as they are from any of the other sources listed above, but they are substantially better than retail.

5 Avoid retail sources at all costs. They usually take higher middleman markups on accessories than they do on any other type of home furnishings.

PART II

THE MIDDLEMEN:

THE HIGHEST PRICES
AND
THE LEAST VALUE

Chapter 14

Interior Designers and Interior Decorators

The vast majority of you do not need to hire an interior designer or an interior decorator in order to decorate your home beautifully. We've already talked about all of the ways in which you can purchase many ''to-the-trade-only'' products without paying hefty commissions to a designer or decorator. In this chapter, we will discuss all of the ways in which you can get qualified and comprehensive design advice without paying any fees to a designer or decorator.

We will also discuss the situations in which hiring professional design help is cost-effective for certain consumers. Some of you probably should hire professional help. This chapter will help you determine if hiring an interior designer is right for you.

This chapter will also explain how to find a reputable designer, how to work with an interior designer, how to negotiate a clear and fair contract with the designer, and how to make sure that the contract is being properly carried out. You will learn how to get the maximum amount of work from a designer for the least amount of money.

You will also know all of the scams and rip-offs you should look out for if you do choose to work with a professional designer. Most designers are honest, but some are not. Thousands of consumers get ripped off every year. This chapter will show you how you should be able to avoid being one of them.

Interior Designers vs. Interior Decorators

The terms ''interior designer'' and ''interior decorator'' are often used interchangeably by consumers. However, there is one important difference. Interior designers usually have a college degree in interior design, while interior decorators usually do not. In fact, it is extremely rare for a person who has invested the time and effort to earn a degree in interior design to choose the less prestigious term of ''interior decorator''.

If you are among the few customers who would benefit from hiring professional design help, you should always hire an interior designer, never an interior decorator. Interior decorators, as a group, are just pale imitations of interior designers. They generally do not have the design skills and education of an interior designer, but they have all of an interior designer's disadvantages and more.

5 Reasons Why You Should Never Hire an Interior Decorator

1 NO INTERIOR DESIGN EDUCATION: Interior decorators usually have no college interior design education. Often, they get their start working for home furnishings stores and later branch out on their own. Their fees depend more upon their sales skills than their educational background, so they are often just as expensive as an interior designer.

Access to an interior design education is one of the only reasons why anyone should shell out their hard-earned money to hire professional design help. Don't waste your money by hiring someone who probably has no more education than you do about interior design.

2 NO PROFESSIONAL REGULATION: There is no professional association of interior decorators that works to police the industry. At least when you hire an interior designer, there are an assortment of professional interior design associations that work to eliminate the "bad apples" and ensure that educational standards are upheld.

However, if an interior decorator rips you off, she has no association membership to lose. She has no privileges to be lost, such as insurance benefits or access to merchandise from certain companies.

While membership in a professional association is certainly not a foolproof way to ensure that an interior designer is competent and honest, these associations do have some influence with which to protect consumers' interests. If you hire an interior decorator, you will not have this small protection.

3 NO GOVERNMENTAL REGULATION: Interior decorators do not need a specialized design license to offer their services to the public. At least in some states, interior designers must meet certain educational and professional standards and qualify for a specialized business license to legally call themselves "interior designers".

Anyone, including you, can buy a general business license and offer his or her services as a interior decorator with no government regulation whatsoever.

You have access to regulated professionals when hiring design help. You should take advantage of that protection. If you hire an interior decorator, you will have no way of knowing what quality of service you are getting for your money.

4 NO PRACTICAL EXPERTISE: Interior decorators usually have no practical expertise in the manufacture of home furnishings. Unfortunately, neither do most interior designers.

You will be much better off to oversee the quality of your home furnishings personally. The guidelines and quality checks in Part I of this book will help you ensure that you are getting only high quality goods and services.

5 NO ACCESS TO ULTRA-EXCLUSIVE MERCHANDISE: The only reason to hire professional design help, other than access to a design education, is access to certain ultra-exclusive merchandise. There are a very few manufacturers and artists who sell their goods only through certain licensed interior designers.

If the snob appeal of these ultra-exclusive fabrics, wallpapers, and other home furnishings is important to you, you should know that interior decorators do not have access to them.

If you want to buy ultra-exclusive, one-of-a-kind, not-even-the-Queen-of-England-has-it, $1000.00 per yard fabrics, don't waste your money on an interior decorator because she won't even be able to get in the showroom door.

10 Bad Reasons To Hire an Interior Designer

Recent economic upheavals in the home furnishings industry have changed many of the old rules and customs. Many of the old reasons to hire an interior designer no longer hold true. The following are ten basic reasons why many customers hire interior designers which are now outdated.

1 SAVING MONEY: For many years interior designers have told their clients that the wholesale discounts they have access to will more than offset their fees, resulting in a net savings to the client. Until about ten years ago, this was true. Not anymore.

Thanks to discounters, consumers now have access to many home furnishings at or near wholesale prices. In addition, the recent economic decline has forced many wholesale workrooms, upholsterers, installers, and other craftspeople to look beyond interior designers for business. Many now work directly with retail customers at or near wholesale prices.

If you decide to become your own interior decorator, as discussed in Chapter 19, you can have access to straight wholesale prices on the vast majority of the home furnishings products available to interior designers. The $110.00 you would spend on your business credentials in most areas of the country is far cheaper than any interior designer's fee.

So, while it was once true that interior designers could make their services pay for themselves through trade discounts that were once available only to them, this is no longer the case because many trade discounts are now available directly to the public.

2 HAVING ACCESS TO WORKROOMS, INSTALLERS, ETC.: When the interior design industry was booming during the early to mid-1980's, most workrooms, installers, upholsterers, and other craftspeople did not work directly with the public for fear of offending the interior designers who provided the majority of their business.

Now that the interior design industry is in a severe decline, local workrooms and craftspeople must look to the retail public to make up the business they are missing. The use of interior designers and interior decorators by consumers is down by about 40% since the late 1980's. This means that wholesale businesses that work primarily for interior decorators and interior designers are also suffering a large drop in income. They have to make it up somewhere. Many quietly work directly with retail clients, often charging them the very same prices that they charge interior designers.

Some wholesale workrooms and craftspeople are listed in the Yellow Pages. The vast majority are listed in the *National Directory of Wholesale Home Furnishings Sources and Showrooms*. Some, particularly home seamstresses, list their names with local fabric stores. All you have to do is ask. These wholesale sources aren't difficult to find.

You must seek these craftspeople out, however, because they cannot jeopardize their wholesale business by seeking you out. The best ways to find and work with the same wholesale workrooms and craftspeople who work for interior designers in your area are discussed in greater detail in Chapter 18.

3 AVOIDING HASSLES WITH WORKROOMS, INSTALLERS, ETC.: It may seem that local workrooms and craftspeople might provide better service to interior designers from whom they could expect repeat business than to consumers decorating their own homes who tend to be "one-shot" deals. It makes sense on the surface, but it isn't true.

As stated above, many local workrooms and craftspeople are coming to depend more and more on direct sales to consumers to survive. An excellent source of new customers is favorable referrals from other satisfied consumers. These workrooms and craftspeople know that if you are happy with their work, you may recommend them to your friends, relatives, and co-workers. After all, a newly redecorated home is bound to be shown off to someone.

They also know that if you are unhappy with their work, you may complain to others or, even worse, to the consumer, fabric store, building contractor, publisher, or other source that recommended them to you. These sources are a major source of referrals for local workrooms and craftspeople, who generally do not advertise to the public out of fear of offending their wholesale customers.

If a source receives a complaint from a consumer, it will probably stop referring future consumers to that craftsperson. That could eliminate most or all of the workroom's or craftsperson's referrals to consumers in some towns.

Therefore, there really is no particular advantage to hiring an interior designer to avoid potential problems in this area.

4 HAVING ACCESS TO "BETTER" MERCHANDISE: It used to be true that high-quality home furnishings were usually not available directly to the general public. Not anymore.

The fabric stores, wallpaper stores, furniture warehouses, and telephone ordering services that are open to the general public carry many of the same home furnishings that are available in wholesale interior design centers.

These are not knock-offs or copies but the very same fabrics, wallpapers, and other home furnishings which are sold at the design centers. There is no longer a major distinction between the quality and style of home furnishings that are available to the general public and those that are available exclusively to interior designers.

Also, the vast majority of the home furnishings which are still restricted to the wholesale trade can now be purchased directly by consumers. Some wholesale interior design centers now have special retail shopping days on which the general public may enter and buy whatever they wish, at a partial trade discount. There is a list of these design centers on page 399.

Also, you may wish to become your own decorator, as discussed in Chapter 19, which would give you access to all but a very few ultra-exclusive home furnishings at full trade discounts (normally 40% to 50% off retail).

There are still a very few fabrics, wallpapers, and other home furnishings which can only be purchased by certain licensed interior designers. However, these goods are separated primarily by exclusivity, not by quality.

It is no longer the case that only interior designers have access to high-quality furnishings. They do still have sole access to the very few ultra-exclusive furnishings that hold "snob appeal" for their customers.

You don't need to hire an interior designer to get the best quality home furnishings. However, if you want something ultra-exclusive, like the $40,000.00 designer sterling silver ice bucket made famous in the 1980's, you will still have to pay an interior designer to buy it for you.

5 ENSURING QUALITY WORK: Surprisingly, interior designers are usually not properly instructed about the quality manufacturing of home furnishings as a part of the interior design degree program.

It is also very rare for an interior designer to have any work experience or business background in the manufacturing of home furnishings. The manufacturing and interior design segments of the home furnishings industry are worlds apart.

You must oversee the quality of your home furnishings personally. Interior designers are usually not good judges of quality because they have no insight into how home furnishings are made. Throughout Part I of this book, specific quality checks on each type of home furnishing are discussed. If you follow these guidelines, you should be secure in the knowledge that your home furnishings have been well manufactured and installed and will last for many years.

6 AVOIDING MISTAKES IN MEASURING: This also relates to interior designers' lack of manufacturing expertise. Over the years, I have seen many errors made by interior designers in taking measurements. Occasionally, measurements are just sloppy or wrong, but more often important measurements are left out because the interior designer does not realize that they are important.

Don't hire an interior designer to ensure the accuracy and completeness of measurements. They usually have no more training than you do on this subject. Use the guidelines in Part I of this book to make sure that you have taken all necessary measurements for your home furnishings. Proper measuring is not difficult. You just need someone who understands manufacturing and installing to tell you how.

7 AVOIDING MISTAKES IN PRODUCT CHOICES: Again, this goes right back to lack of manufacturing expertise. Interior designers are trained in the design and aesthetic aspects of home furnishings, not the practical aspects.

I routinely see poor product choices in books and magazine articles written by interior designers. For instance, a recent issue of a major home furnishings magazine featured a story about silk draperies. Silk fades dramatically under natural or artificial light. The very expensive draperies featured in the article would begin to fade within a few months and would probably be ready for the trash before the year was out. The article made no mention of this.

Home furnishings magazines and design magazines are great sources of design ideas, but they are often poor sources for practical advice. The spectacular rooms featured in magazine spreads only need to look good on the day the photographs are taken. How the same furnishings will look after six months of normal use in an average home appears to be of no major concern to many of these magazines or the interior designers who decorate these fantasy rooms.

This is a perfect illustration of the lack of consideration for practical matters that most interior designers seem to have. Unfortunately, you cannot rely on advice from interior designers to make sure that you are getting products that are appropriate for your home and will last a long time.

You must do your own product research to make certain that you are choosing fabrics that won't fade for your window treatments, wallpaper that can stand exposure to steam for your bathroom, and upholstery that won't shout to the world that you own a dog.

As with measuring, interior designers are usually no more expert than you are on this subject. Use the guidelines given in Part I of this book to ensure that you are purchasing the proper furnishings for your particular needs.

8 GETTING DESIGN IDEAS: Free, or almost free, design ideas are everywhere. Design magazines, books, and model homes are the best sources for design advice. The basic principles of interior design have been thoroughly discussed by many top interior designers through books and magazine articles. Unless you have a truly unusual or elaborate home, the advice from these sources should be all you need to decorate your home beautifully.

Virtually every library in the United States has at least one of the basic books used by college interior design students in its collection. Unless your home is truly a unique, one-of-a-kind, architectural creation, the basic rules of design explained in these books should be all you need.

Do you really need to pay an interior designer a high fee or commission to tell you such basic things as mounting draperies high on the wall to make your windows look bigger or how to properly arrange pictures on a wall? You can find these things out for yourself very easily and at no charge by simply reading the very same books that are used to teach interior designers in the first place.

When you pay an interior designer to parrot age-old advice from books that are widely available to anyone who has a library card, what you are really doing is paying another middleman markup.

Many model homes are decorated by the top designers in your community. You can view their work all you like, free, any day of the week. You can easily locate all of the new subdivisions in your area that have homes, and model homes, comparable to your own by looking them up in the free real estate magazines available at most local banks.

Also, many interior designers participate in "show houses" to benefit local charities. Top designers compete with each other to show their work here. The publicity is extremely valuable to them. You can get all the ideas you wish from the best designers in your community for only a few dollars. Check your newspaper for announcements of these events.

Most libraries carry the major interior design magazines, such as *Metropolitan Home* and *Architectural Digest*. Most libraries keep these magazines on display for at least two years, so you should have more design ideas available to you than you could read in a month's time. Most libraries also have a wide selection of books written by top designers, such as Terence Conran, Mary Gilliatt, and Mark Hampton. You should have no difficulty whatsoever finding a wide variety of ideas for your home, no matter what style you prefer.

Besides, many interior designers get their ideas from these sources, too. Most of the custom window treatment orders my family's wholesale workroom received from interior designers over the years were stapled to photocopies of designs from books and magazines. These designers' clients weren't even getting the original designs they are paying for. You don't need to pay anyone $50.00 per hour to "design" your furnishings by sticking a quarter in a copying machine.

If you are going to pay high fees for original design ideas, then you should get original ideas. If you are going to get copies of designs from books and magazines, which are perfectly fine for most homes, then you should keep the money you would have paid to a designer in your own pocket and run the copying machine yourself.

If you are decorating Buckingham Palace West, hire a reputable interior designer who will create original designs for your home. Otherwise, you will be better served by taking advantage of the free design advice that is widely available at your local library and at model homes and showhouses in your community.

9 MAKING SURE THAT YOUR HOME IS DECORATED "CORRECTLY": Interior designers like to create the impression that interior design is very difficult and complicated. It helps them justify their high fees. After all, if customers believed that interior design was easy, why would they be willing to pay $50.00 per hour for help?

Professionals in many fields do this all the time. This scam is as old as the world. Interior designers pretend that decorating homes is incredibly complex. Accountants pretend that if you fill out your 1040-EZ without help, the IRS will come and get you. Lawyers pretend that if you write a simple will or fill out a lease on your own, you are asking for trouble.

The harder you can convince people your job is, the more money you can get them to pay you to do it. There is a great deal of money to be made by convincing people that life is much harder than it really is.

I'll let you in on a little secret. The only actual "rules" of design are very simple and have been around for a very long time. Everything else is just someone's opinion. Interior design really isn't that difficult.

You needn't worry that your home won't look "right" if you follow your own tastes. Go to your library and check out any basic book on interior design. All of the basic rules will be right there.

10 "INTERIOR DESIGNERS HAVE A CERTAIN CREATIVE FLAIR THAT I DON'T HAVE": Wrong. Wrong. Wrong. What successful interior designers DO have that sets them apart is confidence in their creativity. There is a big, big difference.

Most people are creative to some degree. What many people do not have are confidence and sales skills. It isn't that professional interior designers are so much more creative than you are, they just have the self-assurance to go out in public and not only convince people that their design ideas are wonderful, but ask payment for them.

You may or may not be able to come up with enough new ideas (good or otherwise) on a daily basis and in a wide variety of homes to sustain an interior design business, but you almost certainly have enough good ideas to decorate your own home.

Before you spend your hard-earned money on an interior designer, at least try your own hand at decorating. Go to the library and study what professional interior designers are doing. Use your own common sense to pick out the furnishings that you like, and ignore the "design innovations" that are obviously only pictured to get attention for the designer or sell magazines.

Then, if you are still stuck on one particular portion of your home, hire help only for the portion you cannot do alone.

The Basic Problem With Interior Designers

The basic problem with most interior designers is that they've been trained in school to decorate Buckingham Palace West. However, there just aren't that many palaces to go around.

As a result, these interior designers graduate with training in art history, historical furniture periods, and drawing gorgeous pictures of fantasy window treatments and upholstery. They usually don't get much training in practicality and getting the most value for the consumer's dollar, because these skills are not in great demand at the Buckingham Palace Wests of the world.

So, when these designers get their degrees and go out into the real world, almost all of them end up decorating average homes to make a living. Only a few designers can be at the top of their profession and decorate nothing but palaces. The rest have no choice but to work with average customers decorating average homes.

Average homes need attractive, comfortable, practical, long-lasting furnishings that won't use up all of the customer's life savings. If you have an average home and must balance the needs of your family and your pocketbook against your tastes in design, an interior designer is probably not the best person to help you.

Hiring an interior designer who has intensively studied art history and historical furniture periods to decorate an average, normal home makes as much sense as hiring a neurosurgeon to treat a case of the flu. It's overkill.

Hiring a person who is vastly overqualified for the job at hand is a big waste of money. All you will end up doing is paying much more money than you have to for skills that won't be used to benefit you because they are not necessary or appropriate in your situation.

The question is not "Can an interior designer decorate my home beautifully?'' Of course they can. The question you should be asking yourself as you read this chapter is: ''Is hiring an interior designer the most cost-effective way for me to decorate my home beautifully?'' For the vast majority of you, the answer will be ''no''.

However, there are certain customers who can benefit from an interior designer's highly specialized (and highly expensive) training. There are five good reasons to hire an interior designer. In these situations, consumers will be paying for skills that they truly need and will get good value for their money.

5 Good Reasons To Hire An Interior Designer

1 DECORATING BUCKINGHAM PALACE WEST: If you are decorating a very elaborate home, in the $1,000,000.00 range, you may wish to hire an interior designer.

A one-of-a-kind home deserves one-of-a-kind furnishings. If it seems reasonable to you to spend $1,000,000.00 on a home, then it would probably also seem reasonable to you to spend $25,000.00 on a custom designed sofa or $50,000.00 on hand-painted wallpaper. Of course, if this is the category you fall into, you probably don't read consumer books like this one.

An interior designer can create unique custom window treatments, upholstery, and other furnishings. Your designer can also obtain unusual and ultra-exclusive fabrics, wallpapers, rugs, and other furnishings for you. Homes in this range often contain art collections or unusual architectural elements which require customized lighting to show them off properly.

There is a proper place for interior designers, and this is it. This exactly the kind of job they have been trained to do.

2 DECORATING A HISTORIC HOME: Interior designers receive extensive education in historical periods of art, furniture, textiles, and other home furnishings. If you are restoring the interior of a historic home, you will want to make sure that the furnishings are correct and historically appropriate.

This type of specialized information is not readily available to the average consumer. This is another situation where an interior designer's training is needed and well worth the expense.

3 SAVING TIME: A few people, usually in very highly paid professions, have more money than they have time. An interior designer can save you a great deal of legwork when selecting home furnishings. They can do all of the browsing through showrooms and then bring a few samples to you to make your final selection.

They do charge big bucks for this service, however. Usually, these services run at least $50.00 per hour from a well-established designer, plus a percentage of the furnishings' cost. Top designers charge thousands of dollars PER DAY for their time.

If you can make more than $50.00 per hour by investing your time elsewhere, then hiring an interior designer could be cost-effective for you.

4 HAVING ACCESS TO ULTRA-EXCLUSIVE MERCHANDISE: If you want to purchase ultra-exclusive merchandise, hiring an interior

designer is the only way to go. I mean that literally, not figuratively.

The manufacturers and artists who produce these ultra-exclusive fabrics, wallpapers, furniture, and other home furnishings have gone to great lengths to ensure that this merchandise cannot be purchased any other way. The added trouble and expense of acquiring these things is apparently intended to add to the furnishings' value.

If you want to purchase ultra-exclusive, $1000.00 per yard, even-the-Queen-of-England-doesn't-have-it fabrics or an ultra-exclusive dining room table made out of elk horns by a furniture "artist", you will have to pay an interior designer an additional commission to buy it for you.

By the way, that elk-horn dining room table is a real product I saw in a design center several years ago. No kidding.

5 INVESTING IN ANTIQUES: Interior designers study art history and furniture periods thoroughly in school. If you plan to decorate your home with antiques, you really should hire professional help.

Compared to the cost of the furnishings themselves, the cost of hiring an interior designer to make sure that the antiques are genuine and coordinate well with your other home furnishings is actually quite low. When you are considering purchasing a $20,000.00 antique sofa, it is well worth paying an extra $100.00 to an interior designer to verify that it is truly an antique and that it is in good condition.

Some of the antiques you purchase may require restoration. An interior designer can put you in touch with upholsterers, furniture refinishers, and other craftspeople who are trained and experienced in this type of highly specialized and exacting work. An interior designer can also locate antique fabrics to reupholster antique upholstered furniture.

This is a portion of an interior designer's education that cannot be easily condensed into a do-it-yourself book. This is a situation where the expense of the project, and the unlikelihood of having a second chance to get it right if mistakes are made, make it preferable to hire a professional.

4 Common Mistakes Interior Designers Make (At Your Expense)

The most common mistakes made by interior designers are as a result of deficiencies in their education. Interior design schools teach very little about the practical side of interior design.

I have worked with many new graduates of interior design schools -- most have a very rude awakening when they arrive in the real world. In school, interior design is all about drawing pretty pictures of fantasy rooms. In the real world, we are more concerned with practical matters such as making sure that a window treatment will look nice when it's made up in a certain fabric or that the beautiful wallpaper installed in the bathroom won't fall off the wall the first time the shower is turned on.

Most interior designers haven't a clue about sewing, installing draperies, wallpapering, or building furniture. These skills are almost never taught in interior design schools. In fact, most interior designers make a concerted effort to separate themselves from the manufacturing side of the business.

Their ignorance can cost you plenty, however. This one flaw accounts for most of the mistakes and waste that interior designers are responsible for. The four most common ways in which we have seen interior designers waste hundreds or thousands of dollars of their clients' money due to their lack of practical knowledge about home furnishings are as follows:

1 CHOOSING THE WRONG FABRIC, WALLPAPER, ETC.: On almost every home we have ever manufactured window treatments for, we see at least one instance where the interior designer has chosen an inappropriate fabric for a window treatment.

In earlier chapters, you learned how to choose fabrics and other materials that are appropriate for the specific purpose you have in mind. A soft, flowing drapery design will not look good if it is made up in a crisp fabric. A gorgeous wallpaper will not look good in a bathroom if it is not designed to withstand exposure to steam.

Recommendation: Verify for yourself that the materials you choose are appropriate for the project you have in mind. All of the practical information you need to do this is in Part I of this book.

2 NOT ORDERING ENOUGH FABRIC, WALLPAPER, ETC.: Interior designers are ill-equipped to properly estimate the amount of fabric necessary to make a specific window treatment or the amount of wallpaper necessary to wallpaper a room because they usually have no knowledge of how home furnishings are properly manufactured and installed.

If too little material is ordered, you will have little choice but to order more. Sometimes (but not always) the interior designer will pick up the extra cost. You can bet that they will hike up the price of the next job they do for you to cover the money they lose, though. The completion of your job will almost certainly be delayed while extra materials are ordered.

There is another, more serious, problem with this, however. Fabrics, wallpapers, trimmings, and other home furnishings materials are manufactured in "dye lots". This means that all of the dye is mixed at one time for a specific batch of material. It is next to impossible to mix dyes exactly the same way twice.

If an interior designer has to go back to the supplier and order more materials to complete your job, usually at least 1-2 months after the original order, the supplier will often have already sold all of the first dye lot and be selling from a new dye lot. This color of this new dye lot will almost certainly vary in from the color of the dye lot originally used on your job.

The upshot of all of this is that if your interior designer has to go back and order more materials to complete your job, you may find yourself with a drapery that is lighter or darker in patches or a room with two different shades of the same wallpaper. You will either have to learn to live with the mismatched fabric or wallpaper or tear it all out and start again. Also, you may have a very difficult time convincing the interior designer to cover the replacement cost.

This problem is the result of sheer ignorance on the part of the interior designer. The entire complicated mess of trying to order more matching fabric, wallpaper, or other materials, can be totally avoided by making sure enough materials have been ordered in the first place.

Recommendation: Verify the quantity of materials needed yourself. Complete instructions for making correct estimates are located in the prior chapters relating to each specific type of home furnishing.

3 ORDERING TOO MUCH FABRIC, WALLPAPER, ETC.: Most interior designers don't make the above mistake twice because of the embarrassment and cost.

However, there is only one way to avoid under-ordering if you don't know how to properly estimate needed materials: ALWAYS ORDER TOO MUCH! Interior designers usually order extra fabric for their clients' jobs just in case they have made any mistakes in their estimates.

We saw this all the time in our drapery workroom. Over the years, many upholsterers and wallpaper installers have told us that they have seen this scam often, too.

Please see pages 68-70 for a complete discussion of this common rip-off.

Recommendation: The best way to avoid this rip-off, which happens to most people who hire interior designers, is to determine for yourself exactly how much fabric, wallpaper, trimming, etc., should be ordered. Read Part I of this book and make your own estimates.

4 NOT PROPERLY MEASURING FOR WINDOW TREATMENTS, WALLPAPER, ETC.: Most interior designers do a poor job of taking measurements for custom home furnishings. Sometimes, the measurements are simply wrong because they were taken in a sloppy manner. More often, important measurements are not taken because the interior designer does not realize that they are important.

Recommendation: Always take your own measurements. Complete instructions on how to measure for all types of home furnishings are located in Part I of this book.

Measuring is not difficult. All you need are the proper instructions from a person who understands manufacturing and installation methods. Taking measurements to refurnish an entire house should take you no longer than 2-3 hours.

What Do All Those Letters After the Interior Designer's Name Really Mean?

Many interior designers display certificates or use the initials of various organizations after their names to convince customers that they are well qualified. You may be surprised to learn what these designations actually mean, and, more importantly, what they don't mean.

The designations most often used by interior designers are as follows:

Allied ASID: This indicates that the designer is an allied member of the American Society of Interior Designers.

Allied ASID members may have an interior design degree, however, this is not a requirement. The minimum requirement to use this designation is: six years of experience working for an interior design or architectural firm and payment of a yearly fee.

That's it. No educational requirement. No skills test. An allied ASID membership really means little as a qualification for an interior designer. It doesn't even require that the member has even attended college, to study interior design or any other field.

ASID: ASID is supposed to indicate professional membership in the American Society of Interior Designers. I have seen some allied members use this designation on their business cards and in their advertising, so double-check to be sure.

Professional ASID members usually have an interior design degree, but it is not a requirement. The minimum requirement to use this designation is: six years of experience working for an interior design or architectural firm, payment of a yearly fee, and a satisfactory grade on the National Council for Interior Design Qualification (NCIDQ) examination.

The NCIDQ exam is quite rigorous. Although an interior design degree is not required to be an ASID member, the NCIDQ exam ensures that the designer has an equivalent level of knowledge in interior design.

This is the designation which indicates the highest level of education and knowledge of design principles.

WCAA: The Window Coverings Association of America has given out many certificates to interior decorators, interior designers, and others who sell window treatments to the public. Although the WCAA does offer classes on a voluntary basis to its members, the only actual requirements to obtain their certificate of membership are the payment of a $100.00 yearly fee and a signature on the WCAA's Code of Ethics.

That's it. No test. No educational requirement. No work experience requirement. No references. Just sign the ethics pledge and send in a hundred bucks and you can get the WCAA stamp of approval. Not very reassuring, is it?

This designation is better than nothing, because, presumably, if the interior designer does not treat clients properly he or she can be thrown out of the association and lose valuable membership privileges. That is some small protection for the consumer. However, you cannot accept this designation as proof of education, experience, or competence because these qualifications are not checked by the WCAA.

The only one of these designations that provides any substantial assurance to consumers is the professional ASID designation. The ASID tests interior designers' knowledge, checks professional references and college transcripts, and verifies work experience. If you are going to hire an interior designer, make sure you hire an professional (NOT allied) ASID member.

However, this designation is not enough by itself for you to make sure that you are hiring someone who is well qualified and reputable.

How To Make Sure an Interior Designer Is Well Qualified

The best reference is from someone you know and trust. If you have a friend or relative who has recently completed decorating a home with an interior designer, and is pleased with the job that was done, you will probably be happy with that designer's work.

The only exception is if your friend or family member has radically different tastes than your own. If your friend's home is decorated in spare, modern style and you prefer soft, comfy, English country style, don't count on your friend's interior designer being able to do a good job for you. Maybe she will, and maybe she won't. Some interior designers can work well in a variety of styles, and others are more limited.

If can't get a reliable reference through a friend or relative, there are other ways to locate competent and reliable interior designers:

Magazines: Most local and national interior design magazines feature several interior designers each month. These designers are almost always well established and reputable. Just look on the resource page in the back of the magazine to contact a designer whose work you admire.

Showhouses: Throughout the year in most areas, showhouses are held to benefit local charities. The top designers in the area compete to decorate a single room in these homes. The publicity generated for participating designers at these events is very valuable. Designers fight hard for a chance to show off their talents at these events. You can count on the roster of designers featured in these homes representing the very best your area has to offer.

You will usually find these events advertised in the home and garden section or the calendar section of your local newspaper. There is normally a small entrance fee, usually $5.00 to $10.00, which goes to benefit the charity.

Model homes: Local designers compete with each other to decorate model homes in new subdivisions because they know that many of the new residents will hire them to decorate their homes also. These model homes are usually decorated by well-established, competent, and reputable designers.

There should be a wide variety of model homes in your area. The free real estate magazines found in most banks can direct you to new subdivisions, and new model homes, in your area. Find a style you like and ask which designer's work it is.

ASID referrals: The American Society of Interior Designers operates a national designer referral service. Call (800) 775-ASID for referrals to three ASID members in your area.

Do make sure that you receive referrals to professional ASID members, not "allied" members. Professional ASID members have to submit references, have at least six years of experience in the field, and pass a rigorous national exam. Allied members are not checked out as thoroughly and are generally not as qualified as professional members, although they are often just as expensive.

You can rest assured that any professional ASID member is well qualified to decorate most homes.

3 References You Should Not Trust

Referrals from real estate agents or salespeople at model homes: Note that this is not the same as finding out who ACTUALLY DECORATED the model home. That reference is fine. What I am talking about here are referrals to other interior designers by real estate agents or salespeople.

Interior designers sometimes approach real estate agents and salespeople at model homes and offer them kickbacks in return for referrals. When the real estate agent refers your job to a certain interior designer, he or she may then receive a fee of 5% to 10% of what you pay to have your home decorated.

This is a VERY common practice in the design industry. Some books, newsletters, and articles written for interior designers even recommend this method of generating referrals.

This practice has now gotten so out of hand that in some areas laws have been passed which prohibit real estate agents and model home salespeople from referring anyone to any local business. Again, this law does not prohibit telling you who actually decorated the model home.

Referrals from dry cleaners: It makes sense that dry cleaners who clean draperies from many local homes would know which interior designers do good work and which don't.

Unfortunately, interior designers know this too, and many offer kickbacks to local dry cleaners for referrals. Also, some interior designers trade customer referrals with certain dry cleaners. This is why you should never ask your interior designer to recommend someone to clean your draperies.

Referrals from furniture stores: Many interior designers also offer kickbacks to furniture salespeople. In fact, one popular trade book which teaches interior designers how to attract customers proudly recommends this method. This scam is widespread among furniture stores. Do not trust any referrals you may receive there.

How To Make Sure an Interior Designer is Reputable

When you hire an interior designer, you are placing a tremendous amount of trust in him or her. How can you make sure that you won't be ripped off? You can never be completely certain in advance that you will be dealt with fairly and honestly by any businessperson, but there are some steps you can take to eliminate most of the risk.

After you have narrowed down your selection of potential interior designers to four or five, follow these steps to make sure that they are reputable:

Contact the local Better Business Bureau: Unresolved complaints against the interior designer are a sure sign that you should look elsewhere. The Better Business Bureau gives businesses an opportunity to resolve customer complaints before adding the business to its list. An unfavorable listing is almost never the result of a misunderstanding, but an reliable indication that the business is dishonest.

Contact the local Chamber of Commerce: Your local Chamber of Commerce also records unresolved disputes against local businesses. Avoid any interior designers who have complaints against them recorded here.

Check references: After you have interviewed and selected an interior designer, and before you actually contract with them to decorate your home, check his or her references from prior customers to further ensure the designer's reputability.

3 Types Of Working Arrangements

Do you want the designer to do everything, from the measuring to the actual shopping? Do you want the designer to check in with you often to get your approval of samples and ideas? Do you want to accompany the designer to every showroom and discuss every idea in detail? Before hiring anyone, you must decide what working arrangement will suit your needs best.

These are the three basic types of arrangements that are available:

1 FULL SERVICE: The designer does everything for you. You hand over your house keys and your wallet, and just shut your eyes and hope for the best.

I strongly, strongly recommend against this method unless you either have a tremendous amount of trust in your designer (perhaps the designer is a good friend or relative) or you have such a high-paying job that you would be better off investing your time working than closely monitoring your designer.

Even if you know that you are dealing with a conscientious and trustworthy person, you will still be paying far more than you should because interior designers usually do not utilize discount sources. You will probably end up paying far more than you should for the merchandise itself, in addition to paying the designer's commission.

This method is, by far, the most expensive way to contract for design services, and it is also the most risky. With this method, you are leaving yourself wide open to all types of waste and fraud. You are asking for trouble.

If you are willing to devote even a couple of Saturdays to doing your own measuring, reading design books, and looking through showrooms, you can save about half of what the designer would charge you above the actual cost of the furnishings under a full service arrangement by making a limited service arrangement with the interior designer, instead.

When you consider that an average home costs at least $10,000.00 at retail to completely furnish through an interior designer (including carpeting, rugs, furniture, wallpaper, fabric, window treatments, upholstery, etc.), you could save about $2,500.00 off of your total decorating bill, if you are decorating an entire average home at average prices. That's a pretty good return for two days' work.

If you decide to go this route anyway, you will be best off with a cost-plus arrangement. Under a cost-plus arrangement, the designer is paid a specific percentage of the retail price above the cost of each piece of merchandise that he or she buys for you and each type of custom labor that he or she arranges for you.

The usual rate for this type of extensive service is 35% to 50% of the

RETAIL (generally double the wholesale cost) cost of the furnishings over and above the cost of the furnishings and labor themselves. This works out to a total price of about 15% off retail to full retail for the furnishings plus the designer's commission. The rate will be quoted to you as "cost-plus-[percentage]": "cost-plus-35%, "cost-plus-50%", etc.

A "cost-plus-50%" arrangement is exactly the same as the designer charging you a 100% commission over and above the actual cost of the furnishings themselves. It just sounds like less money when the designer states the price of your decorating job as "cost-plus-50%" -- which is precisely the idea.

A cost-plus arrangement is best in this situation because the designer is making a heavy investment of his or her time. An hourly fee arrangement on a full-service design job could bankrupt you. We will discuss the types of arrangements and contracts in more detail later in this chapter.

2 LIMITED SERVICE: You do what you are willing and able to do before hiring a designer. You might do your own measuring, decide what styles of furniture and window treatments you want, and even browse through showrooms and select some specific furnishings. Then, after doing what you can easily accomplish alone, you hire an interior designer design the areas of your home which you are unsure how to decorate, purchase the furnishings and arrange custom labor for you.

This is a much better alternative to the full service arrangement, even for clients who have little time to devote to decorating. This situation is best if you plan to purchase ultra-exclusive furnishings, have an unusually elaborate home, or are refurnishing a historic home.

Because this is still a somewhat time-intensive arrangement for the designer, you should negotiate a cost-plus arrangement. However, because you have done a portion of the work for the designer in advance, the percentage that the designer should be paid as a commission will be lower, about 20% to 25% of the retail price over and above the cost of the furnishings and labor -- "cost-plus-20%" to "cost-plus-25%". This works out to a total price of 25% to 30% off retail for the furnishings plus the designer's commission.

3 MINIMAL SERVICE: This is what I recommend for most consumers, if they even require the services of an interior designer at all. You do the measuring. You study the practical guidelines in this book to decide what types of furnishings best suit your family and your lifestyle. You browse through the books and magazines to choose styles you like. You browse through the showrooms to find the furnishings you want, if there is a design center near you that is open to the public on certain days. Then, hire an interior designer to look over your choices and "proof" them.

The designer can point out any design errors, such as styles that clash with each other or are inappropriate for the style of your home. He or she may point out improvements in your ideas, such as mounting draperies higher on the wall to emphasize the height of a room or scaling back window treatments to preserve a beautiful view.

You may wish to have the designer accompany you to see a certain piece of furniture or artwork before purchasing it. If you want to buy an ultra-exclusive item, you may pay the designer to accompany you to the showroom and place the order.

This approach is best for the consumer who wants to keep unnecessary expenses to a minimum but does not feel confident enough to do the entire decorating job alone. The interior designer can verify that your designs are "right" for your home.

After the designer has proofed your ideas and choices, you should do as much of your own shopping for goods and services as possible. Remember that interior designers usually have no training in the practical aspects of interior design and will be of little help in ensuring that your furnishings are manufactured and installed well.

Use the guidelines given in Part I of this book to check for quality and get the best prices available. This way, you will be able to save at least 50% off of the retail product and labor cost in addition to having saved most of the designer's commission.

This type of service should be arranged on an hourly fee basis. This type of arrangement is discussed on pages 269-270.

Before Interviewing a Potential Designer

After verifying the reputability of several candidates, there are several things you can do before you actually interview potential designers that will save a great deal of time. Also, there are some decisions which should not be made in the presence of a salesperson, which is what an interior designer really is.

The designer is trying to convince you to buy his or her services and wants you to spend as much as possible. To avoid making choices which are not in your best interests, you should decide what you and your family can afford in terms of time and money before meeting with any designers.

Collect pictures of rooms and furnishings that are attractive to you: Browse through books and magazines and collect pictures of styles and furnishings that you like. They may be pictures of specific furnishings you are considering purchasing or just pictures of rooms that look inviting.

This is the best way to communicate your tastes and wishes to a potential designer. Many consumers do not know the correct terms for styles and periods of home furnishings. Communicating with pictures can eliminate possible misunderstandings about what you really want.

Also, gather pictures of furnishings you don't like -- colors that don't appeal to you, styles that seem pretentious, or anything that just doesn't feel right to you. This is also a good way of conveying your dislikes to the designer, so that the designer will know what furnishings to avoid.

Make a firm decision on the type of work arrangement you want: Go over the previous section very carefully, bearing in mind the demands on your time and your budget. Decide now that you will not allow any designer to persuade you to make an arrangement that you cannot afford or that is not in your financial best interests.

Decide how much you can afford to spend: When you begin discussing all of the beautiful possiblilties your home has and browsing through all of those designer showrooms, your judgment is going to be tested. That is not the time to make decisions about what you can and cannot afford.

Sit down now with your family and decide what your budget will allow.

Discuss your family's decorating priorities: If you should find after you begin shopping that your decorating budget won't go as far as you thought it would, decide now what rooms or specific furnishings may have to be put on hold.

Decide which furnishings you wish to keep and which you may wish to discard: It is perfectly reasonable to expect a designer to work with some of the furnishings that you already own. Also, a designer may be able to help you update or salvage furnishings which you thought you would have to get rid of. Slipcovers on old couches and tablecloths on ugly tables can work wonders.

If you are working on a cost-plus arrangement, you should expect to pay a reasonable extra hourly rate for any updating or rearranging of your existing furniture that a designer does.

Decide whether or not you are willing to give the designer a key to your home: Many designers are accustomed to having a key to the client's home during large decorating jobs.

While this is somewhat more convenient, it also poses a substantial security risk. It isn't just a matter of trusting the designer -- you also have to be able to trust all of the installers, painters, refinishers, and other workpeople that the designer may hire. Often, these workers are not bonded or insured.

Some designers will ask for your key in a very matter of fact way when they are hired. It will be easier for you to say "no", if you wish, if you expect the question and make a decision ahead of time.

How To Interview a Potential Designer

After you have narrowed your choices down to three or four candidates, whose reputability you have carefully checked, you are ready to conduct interviews.

Don't be apprehensive about dealing with designers: Too many customers timidly approach an interior designer, asking questions such as "Can you work with furniture I already have?" and "Do you mind if I accompany you on shopping trips?".

Don't be afraid of interior designers. I realize that they can sometimes be intimidating. This is an act they have worked for years to perfect. Many trade books that teach interior designers how to deal with customers emphasize that designers must "take charge".

Well, it's your money, and you should be in charge. You decide what services you want and how involved you want to be in the design process, and then ask the interior designer what they charge for that level of service. If you run across a domineering designer who isn't interested in what you want, pick someone else. I have met some of these designers, and they are a nightmare to work with.

This is not a democracy. It's your money, it's your house, and your wishes should reign supreme.

That said, you should sit down with each designer you are considering, in your own home, and ask them the following questions. Also, just chat with them a little. You need find out how comfortable you will be working with this person. After all, most decorating jobs take at least several months to complete, and some decorating jobs last as long as two to three years. You want to make sure that working with this person will be a relatively pleasant experience, not a constant battle.

Ask to see the designer's portfolio: Good interior designers collect pictures of their work over the years. The designer may even have been featured in the newspaper or in a design magazine, which he or she will certainly be proud to show off to you.

The portfolio should give you a good idea of the styles in which the designer works best. If you don't see a reasonable number of examples of the specific style that you prefer, move on to a different designer.

Make sure that the designer shows you actual photos of his or her work, not only pictures taken from magazines or books. There is nothing wrong with using magazines and books to discuss styles and preferences, but you also need to see actual photos of the designer's work so that you can evaluate the designer's skill.

If the designer has no photos of his or her own work, you should end the interview right there. It extremely rare for an established designer not to have a portfolio. If you are going to pay big bucks for design assistance, you should be sure that you are hiring someone with experience, not someone who probably just graduated from design school.

Bring out the pictures you have collected to discuss: Early in the interview, take out the pictures you have collected of styles and furnishings which appeal to you. You may not know the correct terms for the style you prefer, but the pictures will clearly communicate your tastes to the designer.

Do not tell the designer how much you wish to spend: This is just as bad as telling a car salesman exactly how much you want to spend on a car.

If you tell a car salesman who is paid on a straight percentage commission that you are willing to spend up to $20,000.00 on a car, what do you think the odds are that he will come back and tell you that he can get you the car you want for less money? Why would he deliberately reduce the amount of his own paycheck just to help you, a person he has never met before?

When businesspeople in any field are discussing prices with you, they are thinking about getting you to pay as much as possible so that their own paychecks will be increased, not about ways they can save you money.

If you reveal how much you are able to spend on decorating your home, you will greatly reduce your chances of getting the job done for less than the figure you quote, especially when you realize that the interior designer's paycheck is usually a straight percentage of what he or she can persuade you to spend on your home.

If the interior designer were to find a way to get your job done for less money than you had anticipated, the designer would only be reducing the size of his or her own paycheck. Few salespeople will go to such lengths to save you money.

Books, magazines, and newspaper articles often recommend that you be "honest" with the designer about your budget. These books and articles are almost always written by, or with the heavy cooperation of, interior designers. They almost always use the word "honest", too, as though it were dishonest to refuse to discuss your financial state openly with a salesperson who is being paid on a straight commission.

No matter what kind of product you are buying -- a car, a stereo, home furnishings, or whatever -- openly discussing your budget with a salesperson, whose paycheck will increase according to how high a price you pay, is a bad idea. It's not smart business.

Discuss what you want with the designer, and ask for what approximate price the designer can complete the job. After all, that's what you would do if you were buying a car. You would tell the salesman what type of car you were looking for and see what price he suggests.

It just might be lower than the figure you had expected, and, since you haven't told him what your budget actually is, you can always argue that his price is too high and bargain with him for a better deal. This method works no matter what you are buying -- including home furnishings and design services.

Also, make sure that you tell the designer that you are interviewing several other designers and that you will be comparing quotes among them all. Ask the designer for his or her best quote and make sure the designer knows that there will be competition for your business. Just like you would if you were buying a car or any other expensive item.

Inform the designer exactly what work arrangement you are looking for: Some designers do not wish to work on a minimal or limited service arrangement. Some designers are uncomfortable shopping with clients. Some designers cannot work alone and must clear every tiny decision with you.

Whether you wish to be involved with or detached from the decorating job, it is important for you and the designer to be on the same wavelength.

Tell the designer clearly what your wishes and expectations are and watch his or her reaction. If you sense any hesitation or anxiety from the designer, choose someone else.

Ask for referrals: This is the best way to judge a designer's qualifications, as well as his or her honesty. Of course, a designer is only likely to offer you positive references. How can you be sure that you are getting the whole story? How can you know if the references aren't from a friend or relative?

Ask for three referrals of the designer's choosing, but also ask for referrals to all clients with whom the designer has worked during the last six months. There should be at least six to twelve referrals during a six month period. This will give you a more unbiased view of the designer's work.

Save this question for the end of the interview, and only ask if you are fairly certain that this person will be your final choice. Some designers may be skittish about giving you so many customer names. Client lists are very valuable to interior designers. They may be fearful that you are affiliated with one of their competitors.

However, this is a very legitimate request for information, and you have a perfect right to ask. If a designer does not wish to give you referrals, for whatever reason, don't hire that designer.

How To Negotiate a Clear and Fair Contract

When you have made your final selection, and you are ready to hire a designer, you must have a clear contract with all agreements clearly spelled out. Hopefully, everything will be fine. However, if there should be a disagreement at some point down the road, or if the designer turns out to be dishonest, you will be very grateful that you have a firm and clear contract. NEVER hire a designer, or anyone else, based on a smile and a handshake. Always get everything in writing.

Don't be intimidated by pre-printed contracts. Some designers do use these. Often, the terms are already spelled out in the designer's favor and are not necessarily fair to you. Sometimes, the terms are so vague that you would have a difficult time pursuing the designer in court if the job isn't done as agreed. If you don't like some of the terms, or would like to specify some terms in greater detail, don't hesitate to ask the designer to make changes. No contract is carved in stone until it's signed.

If the changes are too numerous to be made clearly on the designer's pre-printed forms, ask the designer to have a fresh contract typed up with all of the terms you have agreed upon clearly stated. Most designers will do this if asked, especially these days when the use of interior designers is down by about 40%.

Make sure that any hand-written changes are in the designer's handwriting, not your own. Otherwise, it may not be enforceable in court, should it ever come to that. Again, it's very rare to have to take a designer to court, but it does happen to thousands of consumers every year. You shouldn't have to be among them, if you are careful.

If the designer should refuse to alter a contract to make it clearer and fairer to you, don't hire that designer. If you are having this much trouble getting a clear contract, imagine what it would have been like to work with this person on your entire home! Better to find out now that this designer isn't for you.

You probably hate detailed contracts. Most people do. When you are just trying to get your windows covered and your walls painted, the last thing you will want to do is pore over a detailed contract. It's so much easier to just tell yourself that the designer seems nice enough and leave everything to trust. Many consumers do that every year. Thousands of them get ripped off. Don't let it happen to you.

Your contract with the designer should include all of the following elements:

Date the job will be completed: Do not accept a contract that gives an "estimated date" of completion. Insist on a firm, and reasonable, completion date as well as built-in penalties for not completing the job on time.

Some designers overextend themselves by taking on more jobs than they can handle properly because they can collect deposits on each new job they accept. If you let them, these designers will let your job drag on and on, taking a lower priority behind other clients who are more insistent that their jobs be completed on schedule.

A guarantee isn't much good, however, if it doesn't have any "teeth". Make sure that your contract provides penalties, usually a 5% discount off of the designer's commission for every week the job is late, if the work is not completed on time.

Do one room only, then the rest of the house: Go ahead and discuss the entire job with the designer and get a quote. Then, hire the designer to do one room only.

If the designer does a good job and proves to be reputable, then you can go ahead with the rest of the house. Many consumers I have spoken with highly recommend this strategy.

Exact product specifications: If your job is not done properly and you are forced to take legal action to have the job completed as agreed upon, you must have a clear and detailed record of exactly what was supposed to have been done.

Hopefully, everything will be fine. However, a small percentage of design jobs done each year are handled fraudulently by the interior designer. If you are one of those unlucky people, you will be very grateful that you planned ahead.

Sketches or photocopies should be included in the contract for all custom window treatments, custom upholstery, custom artwork, and custom furniture. Make sure you get a small swatch of all fabrics, trimmings, and wallpapers that are to be ordered for you. Specific measurements should be given of any custom window treatments or upholstery. Specific manufacturer or distributor names and item numbers should be listed for all fabrics, wallpapers, trims, lamps, and other furnishings.

For instance, your contract should read ''Waverly Fabrics pattern #0000'' not ''rose-colored chintz''. Such a vague description would allow a dishonest designer to substitute inferior materials and pocket the difference in cost. If your designer wants to keep his or her sources a secret, too bad. You have a right to know exactly what you are buying and to verify that you did, in fact, receive exactly what you paid for.

Some designers refuse to reveal their sources. If your designer refuses to list the correct product information on the contract, don't hire the designer.

If you are working on an hourly-fee arrangement, clearly specify what you will and will not pay for: You must have a clear understanding of what will constitute paid work time under your contract.

For instance, some designers expect to be paid for the time they travel to and from your home and the time they travel to and from suppliers on your behalf. This travel time can add up very quickly. Also, you have no reasonable way to monitor exactly how much time the designer spends on the road.

If your home is way out in the boondocks, about a half-hour or more from town, then a set transit fee is reasonable. If the designer will be traveling to a design center that is more than one hour's drive away, then a transit charge is also reasonable. However, if your home is in or near town, you should not have to pay a transit charge.

Specifically exclude transit time from your contract, except for the following two cases. If your home is an unreasonable distance from town, agree to pay a set fee for each time the designer comes out to your home at your request.

If your job requires shopping at a remote design center or other location, agree to pay a set fee for two trips only, one trip to look at samples and one trip to place the orders. Any other trips needed should be the designer's responsibility. If she has to go back again because she forgot something, it should be at her expense, not yours.

Do not pay a designer to "think" away from your home. Agree to pay her for time she actually spends in your home discussing your job with you. Keep a written record of this time.

If your job requires substantial research, such as in redecorating a historic home, ask the designer how much research time they believe they will need and agree only to pay for that amount. Do not give the designer a "blank check" to sit and muse about your home for any length of time and then force you to pay for it.

If you agree to a clause which states simply an hourly rate for work done on your behalf with no limitations or guidelines, you may get an very unpleasant surprise when the bill comes due.

I have spoken with many consumers who have been taken advantage of in this way. They were completely shocked when they received the bill for the designer's time. Don't leave any part of your contract open to misinterpretation.

Expect to pay a one-half deposit up front against the designer's costs: It is customary to pay one-half of the cost of the furnishings upon signing the contract and the remaining half upon delivery.

Some designers have been burned when customers change their minds and leave the designers stuck with custom, unreturnable furnishings. Some designers' own homes are decorated almost entirely in "the-customer-wouldn't-pay-for-it" chic.

It's also a great financial strain on many designers to provide short term credit to purchase your home furnishings pending repayment from you. It's reasonable for them to expect some money up front.

However, don't make the mistake of prepaying the entire amount in advance. This is not standard in the industry and is a sure tip-off to a dishonest designer. Your money may end up in the Bahamas instead of going to furnishings suppliers.

Sometimes, even designers who are basically honest will be tempted to pay their own bills out of your money if they are in a temporary bind. Sometimes, the temporary bind becomes permanent and the designer cannot make the final payments on your furnishings because all of your money has been spent. In all likelihood, a designer who is in this situation will shortly be out of business, and your money will probably be gone forever.

Never pay a large retainer: If a designer is going to be doing a substantial amount of research and shopping on your behalf before any payments are made toward the furnishings, it is reasonable for the designer to expect some advance payment from you. Some designers have been burned by dishonest customers who refuse to pay after the designer has done research or consultations in good faith expecting to be paid when the work is done.

However, you should not be expected to pay a large amount up front, either. That is asking for trouble.

Split the payments up. If a designer will be making a special shopping or research trip for you, pay in advance only for that day's work. Then repeat the process for subsequent work.

Don't get stuck paying for weeks or months of work in advance, and trusting the designer to hold up his or her end of the contract. A few designers don't complete their obligations after they receive the customer's money. Don't make yourself vulnerable to being ripped off.

Remember, the designer hasn't been hired until you sign the contract. Sometimes, businesspeople can be very nice and very pleasant until you start insisting on getting their promises in writing. It doesn't matter what they say, you can only depend on promises that are written down and signed by the interior designer.

Some businesspeople, usually the most dishonest ones, may downplay your concerns or attempt to pressure you into signing a contract that you don't completely understand or agree with. Never, never sign until you receive a contract that has all of the important details written in by the designer.

If the designer refuses to put promises in writing, add necessary details to the contract, or gives you the impression that he or she would prefer not to give you a detailed contract, don't sign. Walk away.

Good designers are a dime a dozen, especially in this horrible economy. Better to waste a little time having to interview a new designer than entrust thousands of dollars of your hard-earned money to a careless or dishonest designer.

Again, it is rare that a client has to sue an interior designer, especially after having checked out their qualifications and reputability in advance. However, thousands of consumers are defrauded by interior designers, and all other types of professionals, every year. If you should ever be in this situation and you have thousands of dollars at stake, you will be grateful that you took a few extra minutes to make sure that you had an ironclad contract.

Making Sure That Your Contract Is Being Properly Carried Out

After you have the right designer and the right contract, you must still supervise the job carefully to make sure that everything is being done properly and on schedule. Call the designer about once a week to check up on the job's progression.

If at all possible, arrange to pay all sources and workers personally. If your arrangement calls for the designer to pay for labor and materials out of a retainer or pending reimbursement from you, check all invoices and receipts. The designer is acting as your agent, but you are still responsible for making sure that suppliers are paid. Title (meaning "ownership") for the labor or merchandise does not pass to you until the seller has been paid.

In a worst case situation, people who did custom work on the structure of your home, such as painting, could sue you personally if they are not paid by the designer, even if you can prove that you gave the designer the money to pay them with. These people can even put a lien on your home, in some areas.

This happens to many consumers every year who entrust a third party, such as an interior designer or building contractor, to pay people who do work on their homes. Often, they end up paying for the same work twice, once to the designer or contractor and again to the people who did the work. Avoid this scam at all costs. Pay all workers personally.

Companies that provided furnishings can repossess them, even if you can prove that you paid the designer. They are usually not required to sue the designer first. They can often skip right over the designer to sue you. Often, this situation arises when the designer has gone out of business. Again, this is a rare occurrence, but you still want to be sure that this does not happen to you.

Also, if you are working on a cost-plus arrangement, you must verify the amounts that are actually paid for goods and services. You do not want to take these amounts on faith from the designer. Remember, the designer's commission is being figured according to what was spent. Some dishonest designers inflate the costs of the furnishings in order to increase their own paychecks.

Better yet, hire the designer on an hourly basis and pay the designer only for advice. Pay all sources and workers yourself. This eliminates many, many potential problems and saves you a great deal of money.

If you have been careful when hiring a designer and drawing up your contract, you should have no problems here. Most dishonest interior designers look for easier targets. You will have clearly demonstrated that you know how to take care of yourself, and are not to be messed with.

Designer Referral Services

Designer referral service pre-screen many designers, and then match them up with clients. It's sort of like computer dating, and almost as reliable.

These services usually tell their customers that they conduct thorough background checks of each interior designer to verify reliability, skill, competence, and honesty. Then, they usually turn around and tell consumers that the service bears no liability for the designer's reliability, skill, competence, or honesty. Hmm.

I would feel much better about these services if they were willing to stand behind their recommendations. It's hard to have confidence in any service that comes right out and tells you that it doesn't stand behind its own product.

Some services charge for their referrals, some don't. Those who do charge a fee can cost as much as $100.00 for a single hour-long session. However, I can't recommend paying any amount of money for a referral that the service is unwilling to stand behind.

If a referral service is willing to guarantee the reputability of the designers they recommend, their fee could be well worth paying. However, none of the services I researched make any such guarantee. You can get free referrals from the sources listed earlier in this chapter that are just as reliable as referrals from a professional designer referral service.

There are better ways to choose an interior designer. Follow the guidelines given earlier in this chapter to obtain free, unbiased referrals. Then, do your own background checks. You don't need to pay anyone $100.00 to verify that an interior designer is properly licensed and has no recorded complaints with the Better Business Bureau and the Chamber of Commerce. You can easily do that for yourself.

Exception: I do recommend the free national designer referral service offered by ASID, for two reasons. You pay nothing, and the pool of designers has been well screened for competence.

An ASID recommendation is not necessarily a guarantee of honesty and reputability, so you should still call the BBB and your local Chamber of Commerce to see if any complaints have been registered against the designer you are considering hiring.

However, ASID memberships are very expensive and the ASID does aggressively investigate ethics complaints against its members. I find it hard to believe that an ASID member would risk losing his or her very valuable ASID membership. I have never heard of any complaints of dishonesty against any ASID member.

Alternative Design Services

The recent decline of the design industry and the general belt-tightening that is happening in many households have led to the formation of many new types of design services. The entrepreneurs who create these services are finding innovative ways to provide professional design services at lower costs to the consumer.

If you don't want, or can't afford, the full treatment, but you don't want to do your own designing either, these services are worth considering:

Dial-A-Decorator
(800) 486-REDO

Dial-A-Decorator is the brainchild of interior designer Barbara Landsman. When you call her toll-free number, you will be instructed to send a letter stating your design questions and problems, any swatches you may have, and photos of your current decor along with a check for $100.00 and a self-addressed stamped envelope. Ms. Landsman will study your situation and contact you by phone to give you her design ideas.

Room Redux
(212) 534-6319

For $250.00, interior designers Joanne Eckstut and Sharon James will give you a two hour in-home consultation -- anywhere in the New York City area. Then, they'll take all of your measurements and ideas back to their studio and -- voila! -- they'll map out your dream home from top to bottom. Shortly after your interview, you will receive a complete plan for decorating your home -- complete with photos, swatches, paint chips, sketches, and resource lists. You take it from there.

Use-What-You-Have Interiors
(212) 288-8888

This service specializes in rearranging your existing furnishings. For a fee of $195.00, they will redesign any room in your home up to 19 X 19 feet. If you live in New York, New Jersey, or Connecticut, a representative will come out to your home personally. Outside of these areas, you may contact the company by mail with photos of your design problem.

While each of these services has some interesting ideas, you might be able to do better in your own hometown. Before approaching these companies, ask local designers if they would be willing to provide services on these terms. The local designer might even be cheaper.

Plus, if you are dissatisfied with the work that is done, you will have a much easier time correcting the problem with a local designer than one who is far away.

Recommendations

1 Do not hire interior decorators. They usually have no design education, no professional regulation, no governmental regulation, and no access to ultra-exclusive furnishings.

2 Do not hire an interior designer to ensure the quality of goods and services or to get the best prices available. They are usually not educated in these areas. Hire designers only to provide design advice. Follow the guidelines in Part I of this book to get the best practical and consumer advice.

3 Hire only the help you need. Basic design principles and techniques have been widely written about. Most local libraries carry one or more basic books used by interior design students. You can easily get this information for yourself. Hire designers to provide only specialized information, such as that which concerns antiques, historic homes, and the design of extremely elaborate homes.

4 If you hire a designer, get everything in writing and make sure that the terms of the contract are clear and detailed. Do not leave anything to chance or trust. Many professional design jobs will end up costing you more than a new car would cost. If you were buying a new car, wouldn't you be very careful about the fine print?

Chapter 15

Retail Stores

I highly recommend that you do not shop in retail home furnishings stores unless you are shopping for seconds and floor samples. You can do so much better with just a little extra effort.

Consignment stores are currently in vogue. These stores often sell "designer bloopers" -- furnishings that a designer or retail store made up in the wrong size, style, or color. These are another type of middlemen. You can approach designers and retail stores about any "bloopers" they may have and buy them much more cheaply if you cut out the consignment store's middleman markup.

Be sure to read the section on retail store scams. Fraud is much more commonplace among retail businesses than it is among wholesale businesses.

Why Furnishings In Retail Stores Are Often Sold At 300% Markups (Or More) Over the Manufacturer's Prices

The prices of most of the furnishings in retail stores include hefty commissions to two extra levels of middlemen: wholesale distributors and the retail store itself.

Consider how the price of an average lamp gets inflated as it works its way from the factory through the layers of middlemen to you. This average lamp costs about $50.00 from the factory itself. A wholesale distributor purchases the lamp and resells it to a retail store for $100.00, keeping a 100% commission for itself. Then, the retail store sells the lamp to you for $200.00, keeping a 100% commission for itself.

Of the $200.00 you paid, only $50.00 went to the manufacturer of the lamp. This means that you paid a total 300% markup on this lamp. The other $150.00 of your money went to support middlemen. If you had done a minimal amount of research, as this book has taught you how to do, and purchased the same lamp from the factory's outlet or from the factory itself (if you decide to become your own licensed decorator), you could have saved

75% off retail and kept the 300% middleman markup in your own pocket.

Some stores don't settle for doubling prices on the merchandise they buy from distributors. They triple the prices they pay for merchandise, resulting in a 500% markup to their customers. Many of my family's wholesale customers, especially the very high-brow high-rent stores, routinely tripled the prices on our pillows and cushions.

You will usually find the highest mark-ups over the factory price in small gift and accessory stores and on small items, such as lamps and pictures, in any home furnishings store.

Even when stores eliminate the distributor's commission, as they do when they occasionally buy merchandise in large quantities or when they buy very large items such as some types of furniture, they are still charging their clients 100% to 200% middleman markups. That is way too much for you to have to pay. You don't want between half and two-thirds of the money you spend on home furnishings to go into middlemen's pockets as pure profit.

5 Common Scams Perpetrated By Many Retail Stores

Not all retail home furnishings stores are guilty of the following unethical and dishonest practices. However, as stores are pressed on all sides by competition from discounters, scams perpetrated by dishonest retail customers, and the general bad economy, many have resorted to unethical tactics just to survive.

It is true that many stores are going out of business due to these factors, but this is not an excuse for the surviving stores to mistreat their own customers. You have a right to expect stores to be truthful and honest in their dealings with you, no matter what kind of problems they may be having.

Scam #1: Selling Used Merchandise As New

The vast majority of retail stores use floor samples to display their products and accept returns from customers who are dissatisfied with the products they have purchased. This leaves retail stores across the country with millions of dollars worth of merchandise that is no longer in new condition.

Some stores dispose of this used or damaged merchandise honestly, by selling it as seconds at periodic clearance sales or floor sample sales. Honest stores do lose money this way because the used or damaged merchandise must be sold at greatly reduced prices, sometimes even below the store's cost.

Unfortunately, to prevent losing money, some dishonest stores pass off these items as new merchandise and sell them at full price to unsuspecting customers. This is illegal and unethical, but it happens every day.

Don't just assume that items purchased in a retail store are in new condition unless they are still encased in shrink-wrap from the factory. If a package can be opened and closed, or if there is no packaging, thoroughly examine the item before you pay for it.

There are some dishonest consumers who deliberately abuse store return policies by using merchandise for some time (even years) and then returning it to the store for a refund. Some of these crooked customers have stated in newspaper and television interviews that the stores don't lose money from this practice because the damaged merchandise is simply returned to the manufacturer.

At least in regard to the home furnishings industry, this is not true. Most home furnishings manufacturers require stores to inspect deliveries upon receipt and make any claims of shortages or damaged merchandise within a certain length of time of receiving the shipment, usually no more than one week. Most home furnishings factories would never take back merchandise that was reported damaged weeks, months, or years after the shipment was received by the store.

This customer scam is most prevalent, within the home furnishings industry, around the Christmas season. Every year in our factory outlet store, we had several customers who would buy new bedspreads, pillows, and cushions right before Christmas to spruce up for holiday company and then try to return them right after the Christmas season had ended. We never accepted them because, as a factory outlet, all our sales were final. However, many home furnishings stores who do routinely accept returns are scammed in this way every year. Some of that used merchandise is probably being resold as new. Be extra careful when you buy things in January.

Also, carefully inspect merchandise to make sure that it has not been used as a floor sample. Many floor samples are slightly dirty or frayed at the bottom edges, especially bedspreads and tablecloths, from brushing on the floor and being stepped on by customers. Look for sagging upholstery or permanent indents in seat cushions from being sat on by hundreds of customers. Furniture, upholstery, and bedding floor samples sometimes have a dull, ragged, worn appearance by the time they are taken off display.

Floor samples are usually not too badly damaged and can be great bargains when you purchase them at a deep discount, but you certainly wouldn't want to get stuck with one if you are paying for a new product. As economic pressure on stores continues to increase, this scam is likely to become more prevalent. Carefully inspect everything before you buy.

Scam #2: Advertising "Free" Services That Are Not Really Free

Many retail home furnishings stores offer "free" services. Usually, these are interior design services, but sometimes stores also offer free installation of draperies or other window treatments. Nothing in life is ever really free, including these services.

You ARE charged for these services. The cost is hidden in the prices of the furnishings you purchase. I'm sure most people already realize this. I've heard many consumers speculate that the prices are hiked up an extra 15%, 20%, or even 25% to cover the cost of these "free" services. They were on the right track, but they didn't even come close to the real mark-up.

Stores that offer "free" services customarily charge a whopping 100% markup (at least) on goods and services to cover the cost of paying a designer or decorator to work with you.

This markup is not only on merchandise that is stocked in the store, but also on merchandise and labor that the store orders for you. This 100% markup is also charged by interior decorators and interior designers who work out of their homes and have no significant overhead to pay for. A 100% commission is much too high a price to pay for a store to pass your order along to a drapery workroom or furniture manufacturer.

If any store offers you anything "free", shop somewhere else. It's not true. You ARE being charged for these services, through grossly inflated prices. You will be much better off to buy furnishings from discounters, factory outlets, and wholesale showrooms at 50% to 75% off the prices retail stores charge and pay for any design help or installation help (if you need any paid help at all) by the hour.

Scam #3: Falsifying Product Information and Concealing Manufacturers' Identities

Competition from discounters has hit retail stores hard, especially during the last ten years. Stores that offer full design services and fancy showrooms complain that some dishonest customers deliberately use all of their free services and then buy their home furnishings from no-frills discounters with much cheaper prices.

There are many honest ways to cope with this problem. Full service stores could cut back on their "free" services and lower their prices accordingly. They could charge separately for services such as decorating and installation instead of raising the prices on all of their merchandise to cover the cost of providing them (which they really should do for other reasons, as well).

What the many of them do instead, which is unethical and even illegal in some cases, is falsify the manufacturer names and numbers of their products and conceal the manufacturers' identities to prevent honest consumers from comparing prices.

This practice does indeed help prevent abuse of a store's services, but it also prevents price comparisons by the majority of consumers who are honest. You have a legal right to know the correct identification and source of each item, and you have an ethical right to compare prices among various competitors, as long as you do not abuse services that are freely offered by stores if you have no intention of buying merchandise from the store.

Altered product names and numbers and concealed manufacturer identities are usually pretty obvious. You will usually see where names and numbers have been blacked out on the sample or tag. Often, stores will make up their own phony product item names or numbers and attach them over the real item names and numbers with little stickers. Then, the store keeps a decoding key hidden away in the back room that allows them to decode all of their phony product information so that orders can be placed with the manufacturer.

Don't shop at stores that falsify product information in this manner.

Scam #4: Misapplying Funds From Customer Deposits

When you order merchandise that must be ordered especially for you from the manufacturer or merchandise that must be made up in a custom size or color, such as draperies, you will normally be expected to pay a deposit of one-half of the amount in advance. This is standard practice in the industry and usually poses no problems.

However, a few dishonest stores use customer deposits to pay store expenses such as utilities or rent instead of making down payments to the manufacturer on the merchandise that should be ordered. These stores usually do not plan ahead of time to cheat their customers. Usually, this situation occurs when a store is in a temporary financial bind and borrows against the customers' deposit money in order to stay afloat. They fully believe that when the crisis is past, they will get ahead again and be able to make the down payments on their customers' orders.

However, when a store has such a severe cash flow problem that it is willing to misuse its customers' money, the temporary financial bind will often become permanent. When the customers' delivery date arrives, the orders haven't even been placed and probably never will be.

If this happens to you, suing will usually not help. You can't get blood out of a turnip, and stores that perpetrate this scam usually turn out to be turnips. By the time your case finally winds its way through the court system, the business will usually be bankrupt or even packed up and gone.

The best way to deal with this problem is prevention. This is a perfect illustration of why you should always use a credit card whenever possible. In this situation, the credit card company would arrange a refund for you, at the expense of the store's bank. It doesn't matter if the store has any money or not when you are seeking a refund on a credit card payment. Even if the store is broke, or boarded up for that matter, you will still get your money back.

Also, because so many banks have been burned by store defaults such as this, most banks now have very stringent requirements for granting merchant accounts. A "merchant account" is an arrangement with a bank which gives the store the ability to process credit card transactions. The approval process is very similar to what stores have to go through to get a bank loan. If a store accepts credit cards, you can be assured that it has been thoroughly checked out and is an unlikely candidate to even perpetrate this scam in the first place.

If you have paid your deposit by cash or check and you suspect that the store may have misused your deposit, perhaps because they keep telling you that your order has been delayed, you must take quick action. If you are right, and the store is in financial trouble, the store's money will be going fast. You must recover yours before it's all gone.

One short delay in a delivery is not too uncommon. There are many legitimate reasons for this. However, if the store calls you a second time to say that your order has been delayed again, if the store tells you that there will be a long delay in getting your order, or if the store shows signs that it may be going out of business (drastic price reductions, unusual clearance sales, empty shelves, etc.), immediately demand a refund. If for any reason the store will not, or claims that they cannot, give you an immediate refund, please read Chapter 20 carefully for ways you can try to recover your money from a dishonest business.

Scam #5: Taking Involuntary "Loans" From Customers

This is a variation on the above scam. The normal delivery time for special order home furnishings should be no longer than six months, at the absolute maximum. Custom-upholstered furniture that must be ordered from a factory in another state and also requires special-order fabric could conceivably take this long to receive. On most other types of home furnishings, the delivery time will be much less.

Some dishonest businesses quote exaggerated delivery times in order to have your deposit money to use in the meantime. This amounts to an interest-free loan of your money to the business without your consent.

Stores that do this are often on very shaky financial ground. You don't want to entrust your deposit money to such a business. Read Part I of this book to determine the appropriate waiting time for your custom-ordered or custom-made home furnishings. If a store quotes you a delivery time that is greatly out of line with the standard, such as eight or nine months, shop somewhere else.

What About "Designer Blooper" Stores?

Recently, you may have heard about consignment stores, such as Designer Bloopers in Los Angeles, that sell off designers' mistakes: furnishings made in the wrong size or the wrong dye lot and furnishings that were ordered by mistake and couldn't be returned to the manufacturer. Typically, these furnishings have no serious defects that would affect their looks or wear in your home, they were simply not right for their intended customers. These stores do have good deals, about 50% off retail, but you can do better.

As noted in various chapters, you can go directly to retail stores and interior designers and inquire about purchasing these "bloopers" directly. If you buy them through a consignment store instead, what you are doing is bringing another middleman back into the picture. As always, you can get a better price if you go directly to the source.

The consignment store isn't doing anything that you can't easily do for yourself. Simply call designers and retail stores in your area and ask if they have any customer returns or mistakes that they wish to sell. Some will. It should take you all of thirty minutes or so, and could save you as much as 80% off retail.

If you do wish to shop at one of these consignment stores, you will find them listed in the Yellow Pages under "*Consignment Stores*". Most accept credit cards, but most do not accept returns. Usually, all sales are final.

Be aware, also, that most of these stores also accept furnishings on consignment from people in the community who just want to raise some extra cash, not only from designers and retail stores. Sometimes, these furnishings are not priced realistically because many consumers tend to overestimate their value. It won't do you much good to save 50% off of an inflated price. You should also check everything carefully -- used furnishings do occasionally have hidden damage.

Compare prices carefully with comparable furniture from other sources, such as telephone ordering services and factory outlets, before buying furnishings from a consignment store to make sure that you really are getting a good deal.

Recommendations

You may wish to check out retail stores. You might find an occasional bargain on a floor sample or second or at a clearance sale, but, generally, retail stores will offer you some of the very worst deals on home furnishings.

Consignment stores are a special category of retail stores. They do have good deals, compared to retail stores, but you can do better.

Part III

Somewhere In-Between:

But With Great Prices!

Chapter 16

Telephone Ordering Services

Telephone ordering services sell all types of furnishings at deep discounts -- fabrics, wallpapers, blinds, lighting, carpeting, accessories, furniture, you name it. These services will often give you the best prices outside of a wholesale showroom or factory outlet on many products.

However, most of these companies are in a different state from where you live, so you must take precautions. Many consumers who weren't careful have been ripped off by the small percentage of dishonest telephone ordering companies that exist. As long as you are careful and follow the tips in this chapter, you should be able to enjoy the big discounts without any problems.

Always Use Your Credit Card

Using your credit card will allow you to take advantage of powerful federal consumer laws that govern purchases made with credit cards. Please read the section that explains all about credit card protections and complaint procedures on pages 344-346.

If a telephone order company offers you a small discount to pay by check or cash instead of credit card (usually 2%-5%), don't take it. It isn't worth the risk.

Watch out for the "credit-card tax". A few of these companies, especially companies that sell furniture, state that you must pay a penalty for using a credit card instead of a check, usually between 3% and 5% of your bill. Most telephone ordering services don't charge this fee, though. It's worth checking around to find one that doesn't.

Never deal with any telephone order company that expects you to pay for any portion of your order by check. Quite a few of these do exist. Many of them are reputable, but some are not. Every year, thousands of consumers get ripped off by disreputable telephone order companies because they didn't take the precaution of using a credit card.

When researching this book, I eliminated listings for all telephone ordering companies that had a stated policy of not accepting credit cards for the entire order. Most of these companies are probably honest, but I don't believe that it is in your best interests to take any chances. Of course, company policies can change at any time, so find out what the current payment policy is before ordering anything over the phone.

Dishonest telephone ordering companies do exist. Thousands of consumers are ripped off by them every year. Paying by credit card is a very effective way of protecting yourself. Use it.

You can still get great prices from many companies that will accept your credit card. You have little to gain by not taking advantage of your credit card protections, and a lot to lose. It is unnecessary for you to take any risk of being ripped off.

Beware of Boiler Rooms

There are a few telephone ordering companies that have been deliberately left out of this book because they refused to provide an address when asked. You may notice some of these companies advertised elsewhere, however.

I have a firm policy of not listing any telephone ordering company that refuses to give out an address. There are a few "boiler-room" operations out there that masquerade as legitimate home furnishings companies. They take as much money as they can from customers and then skip town without delivering orders.

This is not to say that any company that doesn't give out an address must necessarily be dishonest. However, dishonest boiler-room operations rarely give out an address, and well-established reputable businesses rarely keep their addresses a secret. Any company that wants to keep its whereabouts a secret sounds, at best, fishy.

There are many well-established companies that are open and honest about who and where they are and have great bargains. I recommend that you place your orders with them. It is unnecessary for you to risk being ripped off. You don't stand to gain anything, but you could lose a lot.

If you should see an advertisement for a service that is not listed in this book, it may be because the company is new and opened after this book was printed. It may also be that I refused to list them for the reasons stated above. Call them and compare prices, by all means, but always ask for an address. If they refuse, I recommend that you not deal with them.

Buy From Companies That Aren't Required To Charge You Sales Tax

Always find out which states require the company to levy sales tax. The law only requires companies to collect sales tax on orders from states in which they have "sufficient contact", which usually means an office or distribution center. These companies must always collect sales tax on orders from the states where they have their home offices, but orders from most other states will be exempt.

No matter what state you live in, you should have no trouble locating a company which is not required to collect sales tax from you. Think of it as a bonus discount of up to 6%, depending upon the tax rate where you live.

Don't Forget the Freight Charges

When you order merchandise over the phone, you will have to pay freight charges to have it shipped to you. This is one disadvantage of ordering merchandise over the phone instead of shopping at a local business.

Usually, the savings are so great (at least 50% off retail), that it is still much better for you to order many furnishings by phone. Always find out what the freight charges will be and take this into account when comparing prices. If you have an appropriate vehicle and accommodating friends, you might be better off to buy heavy or bulky items locally.

Shipping Methods

Home furnishings, except for large pieces of furniture, are normally sent by UPS. UPS normally takes less than a week to deliver anywhere in the lower 48 states. Deliveries to Alaska and Hawaii may take up to two weeks.

UPS has a policy of leaving packages with a neighbor if you are not home. If this poses a problem, call UPS at (800) 742-5877 to make other arrangements. UPS can usually arrange delivery in the late afternoon and on weekends, if you wish.

Large items, such as most furniture, will normally be shipped by common freight carriers or by the service's own trucks. Truck shipments are discussed thoroughly on pages 316-319.

Buy Shipping Insurance When Appropriate

If you are buying something extremely fragile or expensive, consider buying shipping insurance. You shouldn't have any problems with merchandise such as fabric, wallpaper, trimmings, bedspreads, draperies, blinds, table or bed linens, pillows, or cushions. Damage during shipment to items such as these is very rare.

However, if you are ordering lamps, chandeliers, fragile or delicate furniture, glass or porcelain of any kind, or any other fragile or expensive item, you should consider purchasing insurance at the time you place your order.

Ask the telephone ordering company for complete instructions, for the particular shipper it plans to use to ship your order, on insuring items in transit and filing a claim should any damage occur. The cost is usually quite small, and is well worth it.

Compare Prices Carefully

Prices do vary among telephone order companies, even on identical merchandise. Shop around carefully. Some companies offer guaranteed lowest prices. After you get the best price quote, call back some of the other companies that carry the same merchandise and ask them if they can beat the lowest price you have been quoted.

The Retailer Vs. Discounter Controversy

Telephone ordering services usually suggest that you "shop in your neighborhood" to look at samples and write down product information before calling them to place your order. Most interior decorators, interior designers, and retail stores hate this practice -- for obvious reasons.

The vast majority of businesses that sell retail home furnishings don't want consumers to be able to purchase them any other way. Every time a consumer buys fabric, wallpaper, furniture, carpet, lighting, or any other type of furnishings, from a telephone ordering service, retail businesses lose another sale (and another big commission check). Naturally, they would probably like to see telephone discounters vanish from the face of the earth.

Many of these retail businesses even go so far as to alter or remove the manufacturer's product tags and labels (even though this is unethical and illegal in many cases) to prevent consumers from writing down product information.

Some consumers feel that looking at samples from retail sources and then ordering their furnishings over the phone is unethical. If they had ever seen the other side of this controversy, the side that the public generally doesn't see, they would not feel this way.

Many retail businesses have successfully lobbied some manufacturers to make some of their products "exclusive". These exclusive products are not sold to consumers through telephone ordering services or any other discount source -- only through interior decorators, interior designers, and retail stores.

These exclusive products are normally priced through the roof. The vast majority of interior designers and other retail businesses take full advantage of the opportunity to gouge consumers by pricing these products at approximately double the prices of comparable non-exclusive products from the very same manufacturers.

Fabric companies provide a very good example of this. Non-exclusive patterned chintz fabrics usually sell for about $12.00 per yard through discount sources, such as telephone ordering services and deep discount stores. Exclusive patterned chintz fabrics of comparable quality (often from the very same manufacturers!) sell for about $24.00 (or more) through interior designers and interior decorators.

There is little or no difference in the quality of these exclusive and non-exclusive chintz fabrics. Consumers pay twice as much while receiving nothing extra in the way of quality. It's a very bad deal any way you look at it -- unless you are a designer or a decorator.

Many manufacturers of all types of home furnishings engage in this practice. By eliminating open competition from discounters, these manufacturers are creating an artificial monopoly on these exclusive products for the benefit of interior designers, interior decorators, and retail stores. And they benefit from it, all right.

After watching so many interior designers, interior decorators, and retail stores gouge their customers this way over the years, I am convinced that any sympathy toward them for their current discounter dilemma is misplaced. There is nothing wrong with looking at samples and comparing prices. Open price competition is the most important tool consumers have to keep prices low and quality high. You ought to use it.

Chapter 17

Antique Malls and Flea Markets

You should think of the antique malls and flea markets in your local area as mini-factory outlet malls. You can find some wonderful bargains here on brand-new merchandise -- if you know what to look for. Many small manufacturers in your area use flea markets and antique malls to liquidate irregulars, samples, and closeout merchandise.

You do need to be on the lookout for potential problems, as well. This chapter will teach you how to protect yourself from being ripped off. You will also learn how antique malls and flea markets work on the inside, so that you can make sure that you are dealing with the person who really IS in charge.

Mini-Factory Outlets

Many wholesale businesses cannot afford to operate an independent factory outlet. Outlet stores are somewhat expensive to operate. They require at least one employee, a storefront, utilities, advertising, etc. Also, many smaller wholesale businesses do not generate enough overstocked goods, seconds, and discontinued merchandise to stock an entire store.

However, all wholesale businesses generate some amount of merchandise that cannot be sold to their regular customers -- samples, closeouts, seconds, and irregulars. Some retail home furnishings businesses have merchandise that customers have returned or refused to pay for and cannot sell it directly because they do not wish to create an image that their stores sell anything less than the best quality merchandise.

Many of these businesses use antique malls and flea markets as mini-outlets. Spaces are usually small, the rent is very low, utilities and advertising are included in the rent, and there is usually no need to hire an extra employee. My parents' factory used antique malls and flea markets to sell closeouts and irregulars for years until we decided to open an independent outlet store.

What Is the Difference Between an Antique Mall and a Flea Market?

Price, mostly. Usually, you will pay a higher price for comparable merchandise if you purchase it at an antique mall rather than a flea market.

Both types of businesses sell both new and used merchandise. Some home furnishings businesses only maintain spaces at antique malls because they know they can usually get a higher price from their customers, so there will be some furnishings that you cannot get at flea markets.

Other than that, these businesses usually differ only in name. The name ''antique mall'' has snob appeal -- ''flea market'' definitely doesn't. Many consumers, unfortunately, allow the name on the storefront to influence what price they are willing to pay for merchandise that is otherwise identical.

5 Tips For Dealing With Flea Markets and Antique Malls

1 REQUEST THE DECORATOR DISCOUNT: Most flea markets and antique malls have a set decorator discount of 10% for anyone who asks. You should ask for the discount when you are ready to pay at the central checkout counter, not at the dealer's space.

They usually don't even verify your credentials to make sure that you are a licensed decorator or designer. Interior decorators and interior designers make up a large percentage of these business' customers, and these discounts are given routinely.

Since these discounts are not advertised and are generally unknown outside of the trade, many businesses just assume that if you know enough to ask, you must be a professional interior decorator or interior designer. Of course, if you ARE your own decorator, always carry a copy of your license and resale number just in case.

This discount is sometimes applied only to cash or check sales and denied on charge card sales. Also, most flea markets and antique malls set a discount ''floor'', usually $10.00 to $20.00, under which no items are discounted. So, you may not be able to get a discount on a very cheap item, such as a $10.00 pillow.

A few dealers in the flea market or antique mall may mark some or all of their merchandise with the notation ''FIRM''. This is an instruction to the checkout counter not to give a decorator discount on these particular items. It is fairly rare for this notation to be used.

2 LEAVE SMALL CHILDREN AT HOME: Unlike some retail establishments, the ''you break it, you buy it'' policy is usually very strictly enforced at these businesses. Also, most spaces will be crammed with merchandise which places more objects in easy reach of little hands.

If your child does accidentally break something, don't expect the flea market or antique mall employees to smile forgivingly like the employees do at some businesses, such as grocery stores. Be ready to get out your checkbook.

3 CHECK RETURN POLICIES BEFORE BUYING: Most flea markets and antique malls sell on a ''as-is -- all sales final'' basis. Always

check items thoroughly for any hidden defects before purchasing them.

If you want to see how an item looks in your home before purchasing it, as you might with furniture or a picture, ask the dealer at the space AND the owner of the flea market or antique mall.

Sometimes, what is acceptable to the dealer who owns the merchandise in the space is not acceptable to the owner of the flea market or antique mall. Since sales are almost always processed through a central checkout area instead of by the individual dealers, it will usually be the owner of the flea market or antique mall who will have the final say over whether you may or may not return an item. For that reason, you should make sure that you have the approval of BOTH owners before proceeding.

If this is agreeable to both owners, you will usually be expected to pay in full for the item before leaving with it. This is fine, but make sure that you pay with a credit card and that you have the owners make a notation on your receipt that you may return the item for a full refund (NOT a store credit or exchange) if it is returned undamaged within the agreed upon time.

If there is any obvious damage to the item, as there may be in a used or second quality piece, be sure that the owners note this on your receipt as well or you may find that you are refused a refund on the grounds that YOU did the damage.

Given the frequent used or second-quality condition of merchandise sold at these businesses, I strongly recommend that you always use a credit card, especially when taking items out temporarily to see how they look in your home.

4 USE YOUR CREDIT CARD: Most well-established flea markets and antique malls accept credit cards. The only exceptions are most traveling flea markets that come into town on a yearly basis.

If you use a credit card, you will usually have to give up the 10% decorator discount you could otherwise usually claim. This will have to be a judgment call on your part. If you have thoroughly examined the item, and you have no doubt that you will ever need to return it, you may wish to forego the protection of using a credit card in favor of getting a discount. It is up to you.

5 DON'T DEAL WITH TRAVELING FLEA MARKETS: In most cities, there is at least one annual flea market that breezes into town and sets up on the local fairground for a week or so. Don't buy home furnishings at these places. There are many dealers at these temporary shows that are reputable and honest, but there are too many who are not.

Most of them don't accept credit cards, so you lose valuable consumer protection in a situation when you are most in need of it. Also, stolen merchandise is sometimes displayed in these places. These traveling flea markets often do not check dealers to make sure that they are reputable and that the merchandise they are selling isn't stolen.

My parents and I once inadvertently surprised a soon-to-be-ex-employee selling pillows that she had stolen from us at one of these places. We would have been within our legal rights to have all of the merchandise confiscated, whether or not her customers had paid for it. If you buy merchandise from a thief, and the rightful owner of the merchandise decides to fully exercise his or her legal rights, the police may confiscate the merchandise from you, even if you have already paid for it. You will probably never see your money again.

Finally, if there is a problem with the merchandise at some later time, where will you find the seller to correct it? In the next state?

This just is not a good place to shop. You can get equivalent, or better, savings on a wide variety of home furnishings without putting yourself at such a high risk of being ripped off. Stick with permanent flea markets and antique malls in your area that are open daily, on weekends, or on some other regular schedule.

Part IV

The Inside Scoop:

How To Buy Home Furnishings At Wholesale Prices

Chapter 18

Wholesale Workrooms and Craftspeople

If you are in the market for custom window treatments, custom bed treatments, decorative accessories, custom shutters, or drapery installation -- you are in luck. There has probably never been a better time to be purchasing these goods and services.

Local custom workrooms and craftspeople have been suffering a severe drop in business over the last ten years or so. Use of interior decorators and interior designers by consumers has dropped by about 40% since the late eighties. Most local custom workrooms and craftspeople have experienced a similar drop in business because their customer bases used to consist almost entirely of interior decorators and interior designers.

They have to make up that lost business somewhere just to survive. As a result, many workrooms and craftspeople have begun quietly working directly with consumers. You can almost certainly find at least one business in your area that will do your custom work at wholesale prices -- if you understand how to find and deal with these businesses. This chapter will show you how.

There are a few types of businesses -- wallpaper installers, upholsterers, painters, and tile setters -- that have gone 100% retail in most areas of the country. There generally are no wholesale craftspeople in these professions. However, if you are your own decorator, you might be able to get a small decorator discount -- usually about 10%. Ask. The best place to locate these types of businesses are through referrals from friends or through the Yellow Pages. The general advice given in this chapter on verifying reputability and getting the best prices applies to these workers, also.

Must I Be a Licensed Interior Decorator To Buy Directly From These Businesses?

In many cases, no. Many of these businesses are run by one person (or sometimes by several members of the same family) as a home-based business. They are very informal, and will usually accept business from anyone whether they have a business license or not.

Attitudes vary among those workrooms and craftspeople who work out of a separate workshop or office. Many are very pleased to get any business at all during the current recession.

A few, usually the very old and well-established workrooms, won't even condescend to deal with interior decorators -- much less the public. If you run into such a business, just ignore the attitude and go on to the next one.

Most local workrooms and craftspeople need your business very much during summer and winter, especially during January and July. Most of the time, you will encounter no difficulty dealing with these businesses even though you do not have a business license. Often, you can even buy at straight wholesale.

What Do These Workrooms and Craftspeople Think About Dealing With Consumers?

In this recession, many of them will secretly worship the ground you walk on, although they will do their best not to give you this impression. When you are dealing with these businesspeople, never forget that you are in a very strong buyer's market. With the exception of the very few well-established "old money" workrooms, which you should avoid, these businesses are badly in need of your money. This is the only type of wholesale home furnishings business that will welcome you (usually while trying not to make it obvious), rather than just tolerate you.

It has been estimated that the use of interior designers and interior decorators by consumers has dropped by about 40% since about 1988. This means that the revenues of these local workrooms and craftspeople has also dropped by about 40% because interior designers and interior decorators make up the vast majority of their customers. They have to make up this business somewhere else just to survive. Many welcome interest, and business, from consumers. They will be thrilled to see you.

Often, consumers who called my family's custom workroom sounded very tentative and meek, as though they thought we would be doing them some sort of great favor to even speak to them. Nothing could have been further from the truth. Of course, we weren't going to offer these customers a discount or make any other efforts to court their business if they acted as though we were doing them a favor by agreeing to sell to them. No business would.

When you approach these businesses, act very professional but also a little bit independent. Do make certain to establish that you are a very professional, knowledgeable customer (as explained later in this chapter), but then be a little aloof. Ask for a price quote and compare quotes from several businesses before settling on one. When you get the best quote, haggle with that business. You might get them to do even better on the price, especially during the slow business periods of summer and winter.

If you have a business license, by all means, say so. However, if you don't have a license, don't think that you can't still get wholesale or near wholesale prices. Most of these businesses are in very hard financial straits, in this horrible economy. You should be able to find at least one business in your area that needs your business badly enough to give you a straight wholesale price.

It is also very important for you to realize that these businesses will not want their wholesale customers, primarily interior decorators and interior designers, to know that they are also selling to consumers. Wholesale customers would be highly offended by this.

Selling to consumers, some of whom would presumably buy these goods and services through interior designers and interior decorators if they could not buy directly from the wholesale sources, goes against the wholesale customers' business interests. These wholesale customers would almost certainly refuse to give any more jobs to a local workroom or craftsperson who they knew had sold directly to consumers because this practice cuts out the wholesale customers' profit.

This is why most local craftspeople and workrooms do not openly advertise to consumers. They can't risk losing their main source of income, which comes from their wholesale customers. However, if you quietly and discreetly approach these businesses, many of them will sell directly to you.

It is best to go directly to the business rather than calling. Some workrooms and craftspeople are so afraid of losing their wholesale customers that they won't discuss any jobs with consumers over the phone for fear that the person calling might really be a decorator or designer trying to find out if the business is selling to consumers behind its wholesale customers' backs. Business hours are normally 9 to 5, Monday through Friday.

How To Locate Local Workrooms and Craftspeople

The best referrals come from people who have recently had work done. If you have a friend or relative who has recently redecorated, ask who did his or her custom work, such as draperies or bed treatments. If this person worked through an interior designer, your friend or relative may not know who did the work. Interior designers often keep this information a secret whenever possible.

If your friend or relative does know which workroom or craftsperson did the work, contact the business quietly. Never ask a workroom representative or a craftsperson about doing work for you in front of an interior designer or interior decorator. If you do, the businessperson will usually say no because he or she will not want wholesale customers, such as interior designers or interior decorators, to know that the business is also taking on retail clients. You must be discreet.

If you cannot get a reference from a friend or relative, you have a several other options:

Check the Yellow Pages: A few workrooms and craftspeople do advertise here, although many don't. Look under "*Draperies--Wholesale*" for custom window treatment workrooms and referrals to drapery installers, "*Shutters--Wholesale*" for custom shutters and referrals to shutter installers, and "*Bedspreads--Wholesale*" for custom bed treatment workrooms.

Ask a fabric store: Home seamstresses often list their names with local fabric stores. This list may be kept behind the desk instead of being openly displayed, for discretion's sake.

Before asking this question, you should make sure that the store does not offer custom sewing or other custom labor. These stores would naturally want you to purchase these services through them. Then, they will usually pass your order along to a home seamstress who will actually make your furnishings, at a hefty commission to the store, of course.

Some stores do not offer these custom services. They will usually give you a good reference, which you can use to arrange your custom labor directly at the source, without paying extra commissions to any middlemen.
You should have no difficulty finding fabric stores in your area that do not offer custom labor through the store.

Ask a craftsperson or workroom: Once you find one good workroom or craftsperson, he or she can usually refer you to others in other fields. If you have already hired a drapery installer, home seamstress, drapery workroom, shutter manufacturer, or any other specialist, he or she will often be your best informed source to locate the best local specialists in all of the other fields.

Look it up: The National Directory of Wholesale Home Furnishings Sources and Showrooms also has comprehensive listings of the thousands of drapery workrooms, bedspread workrooms, and other craftspeople all over the United States and Canada.

How Not To Locate Local Workrooms and Craftspeople

Interior decorators and interior designers: You will be wasting your time. They consider their contacts to be very private and will usually not refer you to anyone (unless they have arranged to receive a kickback). They will probably offer to arrange these services for you, at a hefty commission, of course. You want to skip these middlemen.

Wallpaper stores: Many wallpaper stores offer custom wallpapering at a hefty commission to the store. Enough said.

Design centers, retail stores, and wholesale showrooms: Usually, these people will have anticipated customer requests such as yours long in advance and arranged to refer certain workrooms or craftspeople in return for a percentage of what you end up paying. You want to avoid paying these secret kickbacks in addition to what you pay for the actual work. Unfortunately, this is a common practice.

People in this business who actually do physical work, such as installation or sewing, usually don't deal with kickbacks. You will far be less likely to be a victim of a kickback arrangement if you get referrals from craftspeople and workrooms than if you get them from middlemen of any kind.

Your Responsibilities When Dealing With a Workroom Or Craftsperson

When dealing directly with any workroom or craftsperson, you must remember that you are assuming the role of an interior decorator. There are certain responsibilities associated with this:

1 CAREFULLY CHECK THE CONDITION OF YOUR MATERIALS: Workrooms do not inspect the fabrics, trims, and other materials that you provide them with to make up your custom furnishings. It is your responsibility to inspect your own materials before delivering them to the workroom to make sure that there are no flaws or other problems and that the quantity is correct.

Before delivering your fabric to a workroom, unroll it carefully and check that the yardage is correct. Make sure that the fabric is all in one piece -- very rarely a supplier may ship your order in two or more parts, all on the same roll. Make sure that the fabric is not wrinkled. Workrooms do not assume responsibility for ironing your fabric. Look over the fabric to make sure that there are no snags or stains.

Problems with fabric are quite rare. We have seldom encountered more than one or two defective rolls per year in all the years our workroom and factory made custom furnishings.

However, if you find that your fabric is flawed in some way after the workroom has finished making your custom furnishings, you will be out of luck. The workroom will not refund your money or offer to remake your furnishings free or at a discount. After all, the workroom has done nothing wrong.

Also, even if the flaw in the fabric is the fault of the fabric supplier, you will not be able to get a refund if the fabric has already been cut. You must inspect your fabric as soon as you receive it to make sure that it is correct. Otherwise, you stand little chance of getting the supplier to make things right.

You should also carefully inspect any trims, tassels, fringes, or other materials that you may be providing to the workroom to make sure that they do not have any defects and that you have the correct quantity.

If you do properly inspect your fabrics and other materials and contact the supplier immediately about any problems, most suppliers will correct your order at no charge and with no argument. As long as you understand the way the industry works and what is expected of you as a wholesale customer, you will usually not have any difficulty in getting suppliers to correct problems.

2 CAREFULLY CHECK ALL MEASUREMENTS: When you go it alone and have custom furnishings made without going through an interior designer, you are responsible for taking your own measurements. This is not difficult to do, but you must be very accurate and thorough. Follow the instructions throughout Part I of this book to correctly measure for all types of custom furnishings.

Unfortunately, using an interior designer is not a foolproof way of making sure that your measurements are correct. Designers often make mistakes. We saw it all the time in our workroom. However, these mistakes are usually due to the designer's ignorance of how home furnishings are made.

The instructions in Part I of this book take into account all aspects of the manufacturing process. They are based upon the real-life situations that have occurred during the many years that my family manufactured custom home furnishings. You won't have to worry about overlooking an important measurement if you follow these instructions carefully.

If your furnishings do not fit when you get them home because you did not measure properly, you will have no recourse. The workroom is only responsible for making your furnishings according to the measurements you provide. They have no legal responsibility whatsoever for making sure that the furnishings actually fit when you get them home.

If your measurements are wrong, and your furnishings must be remade, the workroom will expect to be paid to make these alterations. Often the alterations are nearly as expensive as the original work because the item may have to be completely taken apart and recut. Sometimes, remaking an item is actually more difficult and expensive than making it in the first place. Some types of furnishings cannot be taken apart at all without ruining the fabric, which means that you would be out the cost of the fabric as well. So, check and double-check your measurements.

3 MAKE SURE THAT INSTRUCTIONS ARE CLEARLY WRITTEN: It never ceased to amaze me how many custom orders we received from interior designers that we could not read! Many times when an item is incorrect and has to be remade, it is because the order was written sloppily and was misread.

Check your zeroes and sixes. These are easily confused if they are written sloppily.

Label everything. Never expect the workroom or seamstress to guess which measurements are width, length, or whatever.

Clearly specify which fabrics go where. Describe the fabrics to be used for ruffles, lining, welting, or other portions of your furnishings. Make sure that your instructions are very clear as to what fabric belongs where. Describe the placement of any trims or tassels. Enclose a sketch or picture of the item to be made if at all possible.

Take a few minutes to read over your order with the workroom representative or home seamstress when you deliver your materials to make sure that all of the details are clear. If you are shipping your materials to a distant workroom, call the workroom to discuss your order before it is processed.

If your order is vague or illegible in any way, it is not the workroom's responsibility to correctly decipher it. If your furnishings are made incorrectly, and there is any problem with the way you wrote your instructions, the workroom will deny any fault and will not correct the problem unless you are willing to pay for the alterations.

If you take the matter to court, you can expect to lose. Courts typically favor the workrooms in these cases.

4 OVERSEE ANY CRAFTSPEOPLE DOING WORK IN YOUR HOME: Wholesale home furnishings workrooms and craftspeople are rarely bonded or insured. If anything in your home is damaged or stolen while work is being done, you will have no reasonable recourse other than your own homeowner's insurance. Never let people work alone in your home.

Also, if you are present, you can oversee the stages of your job to make sure that it is progressing properly. If there should be a misunderstanding or mistake, it will be infinitely easier to correct it right when it happens than to get the workers to come back at a later date to fix it.

10 Tips For Dealing With Local Workrooms and Craftspeople

1 ACT LIKE A PROFESSIONAL: This, more than any other factor except choosing the proper time of year to shop, will help determine your success in getting the workroom or craftsperson to give you straight wholesale prices. Often, wholesale workrooms and craftspeople charge consumers a higher price than they charge interior designers and interior decorators because they anticipate having to do extra work on the consumer's behalf.

Some consumers want the workroom to help select the proper materials (fabrics, trimmings, wallpapers, etc.), take measurements, carry samples of materials out to the consumer's home, and even offer design help. All of these services take a lot of additional time and effort above what is normally required when dealing with a professional interior designer or interior decorator, and the workroom or craftsperson naturally expects to be paid extra for these additional services.

After all, these unprepared consumers are attempting to use a wholesale workroom as an retail interior design service, which is an unfair imposition. If you want to get a wholesale price, you cannot expect to receive retail services.

Based upon past experiences, some workrooms and craftspeople expect to have to go to a lot of extra work and bother when dealing with consumers, so they anticipate this and charge consumers higher prices to compensate for the extra services they sometimes demand.

You must disprove this assumption immediately. You must make it very clear to the person you are dealing with that you know exactly what you want and exactly how to properly relate this information this to the workroom or craftsperson.

Before approaching the workroom, you should already know all of the specifics about your job, such as exactly how high you would like your draperies to be mounted. If applicable, such as in the case of window treatments, you should have obtained a picture of the design you want. You should have no trouble finding a picture of what you want in a home furnishings magazine or design book. If you can't find a picture, make a clear sketch of what you want.

All of the design advice most of you will ever need is available in library books and magazines. The few of you who need special help should hire a designer to answer any design questions. All of the practical advice most of you will ever need to determine what types of materials and furnishings you should buy and where you should shop for them are in Part I of this book.

In a few cases, it is appropriate to ask the workroom or craftsperson certain questions about your job (these are questions that professional interior designers routinely ask), and these questions are noted in the appropriate chapters in Part I of this book.

You can make the proper preparations on your job with very little effort, and enjoy savings of about 50% off retail for your trouble. The effort is well worth it.

When you are ready to approach the workroom or craftsperson, you should be ready to hand them your materials along with any necessary pictures and measurements, and say "I want you to make this..." or "I want you to install this in this way...''. You should be prepared and decisive, just as professional interior designers are.

If you are unprepared, seem uncertain, or try to get free design services from the workroom or craftsperson, they will make you pay. Virtually every wholesale workroom and craftsperson in existence that accepts work from consumers has been burned by a consumer who imposed on their time and patience, and every subsequent consumer who looks like trouble ends up paying for it.

When you approach the workroom or craftsperson, simply say ''I am (whoever), and I want to get a price quote from you on making and\or installing (whatever)''.

Don't state up front that you are a consumer. If you conduct yourself just like the pros do, you may never even have to bring up the fact that you aren't a professional interior decorator or interior designer. You may be treated (and charged) just like a professional from the very beginning.

Many of these businesses, especially the home-based ones, don't inspect licenses and resale numbers. Of course, if you decide to become your own licensed decorator, you can certainly state up front that you are a decorator.

Read Chapter 19 carefully before approaching any local workrooms or craftspeople.

2 INSIST ON RECEIVING WHOLESALE PRICES: Of course, if you decide to become your own decorator, this question is irrelevant. As for the rest of you, if you are making the same order preparations and receiving the same level of service as an interior decorator or interior designer, without asking for any extra inappropriate assistance or making any extra trouble for the workroom or craftsperson, then you deserve to receive straight wholesale prices. The way in which you approach this is very important, however.

If you approach a local workroom or craftsperson, state that you are a consumer, and announce that you must receive wholesale prices right off the bat, the businessperson you are dealing with is likely to be skeptical. He or she will remember other consumers in the past who required twice as much time and effort than wholesale customers on comparable jobs. The businessperson may decide that dealing with you is not worth the trouble, especially for no extra compensation, and refuse to take your job at a wholesale price.

However, if you begin by discussing your job with the businessperson, making sure that you establish that you know exactly what you want and are well-prepared with your measurements, pictures, materials, etc. (which you can easily do with the information given in Part I of this book), you may never have to go through this argument in the first place. The businessperson may simply assume that you are a professional interior designer or interior decorator based upon your obvious expertise and give you the wholesale price to begin with.

If the businessperson does ask to verify your credentials, and you must tell him or her that you are a consumer, politely insist upon receiving the wholesale price. Since you have already allayed the businessperson's fears about dealing with an uninformed and troublesome customer, he or she may give you the wholesale price without any further argument. If not, go somewhere else. If you are properly prepared, you should be able to get your work done at wholesale prices from at least one source in your area.

How will you know what the wholesale price is? After all, many workrooms and craftspeople don't have a prepared price list. They quote prices for each job individually.

You can get an idea of what the prices are in your area (prices will normally be somewhat higher in the city than in the suburbs or rural areas) by calling a local retail business and asking what they would charge to arrange these services for you. Call an interior designer to check retail prices on window treatments, bed treatments, and window treatment installation. Call a retail shutter store to check retail prices on custom shutters and shutter installation.

When you get the going retail price in your area, divide it in half to get the going wholesale rate. Retail businesses usually double the labor cost charged by the workroom or craftsperson when setting their prices. For instance, if an interior designer tells you that a window treatment costs $100.00 to have made, shoot for a price of $50.00 when you make arrangements directly with the workroom or home seamstress.

3 SHOP IN SUBURBAN OR RURAL AREAS: Avoid purchasing custom labor or services downtown. These workrooms and craftspeople are accustomed to being paid higher rates for this type of work. Driving an extra fifteen minutes to the suburbs could save you as much as 25% off the price you would otherwise pay, depending upon the type of service or labor.

Also, because the demand for these services normally decreases the further out you are from town, workers in these areas will be less busy and more accommodating to you. They need your business much more than their counterparts downtown. This means that you will be more likely to get your job done quickly and with few complications.

If you try to work directly with a downtown workroom or craftsperson, you are likely to find that the business doesn't even condescend to deal with interior decorators, much less you. These workrooms and craftspeople are usually very loyal to interior designers and are highly unlikely to go over the designers' heads and sell directly to the public.

Suburban and rural businesses, on the other hand, tend not to be quite so chummy with the local interior design establishment. Your chances of buying direct increase greatly in the suburbs.

When you are comparing retail and wholesale prices in your area prior to placing your order, make sure to call only businesses in the general area in which you will actually be placing your order. If you call a downtown store to get the retail price of the labor you wish to have done and use half of that amount as a guideline to what you should pay at a wholesale workroom in the suburbs or rural areas, you may be paying too high a price.

4 SHOP DURING SLOW PERIODS: This is one area of the home furnishings industry where shopping during the slow periods of summer and winter will do you the most good. Many of these businesses get virtually no jobs at all from the last week of December to early February and from late June to early August.

January is the worst. I have been through a few January droughts. It always feels like business will never pick up again. Being self-employed means never getting a dependable paycheck. No customers -- no money -- too bad. Self-employed people feel this vulnerability most acutely during

What About the Sales Tax?

You may or may not owe sales tax on custom labor and installation, depending on where you live. Some states and counties exempt services from taxation.

If you decide to buy a business license and become your own decorator, call the office where you register for your resale permit to find out if you owe tax on services. If you do, just calculate the tax and send it in.

If you are purchasing services as a regular consumer, don't worry about it. It's the service provider's responsibility to know if taxes are due and collect them, not yours.

these slow business periods.

Use this to your advantage. Haggle. Press the business for a better price. You will find at least a few businesses who need your money badly enough to make you a great bargain. Better to have some work than none at all.

Also, you will usually get your job completed much faster because the local workrooms and craftspeople will have few (or no) other jobs going on at the same time. At some businesses, you may be the only customer they have during this period.

If you shop during the busiest periods of the year, from early March to early May and from late September to late November, you are almost assured of not getting a discount. You might not even be able to get a wholesale price. Some of these businesses won't deal with you at all.

Why should a business give away money in the form of a discount to get your business when it already has all the business it can handle? Why should a business take on jobs from consumers, who are sometimes troublesome and unprepared and create a risk of offending the business' wholesale customers, when the business already has enough wholesale customers to get its bills paid? This is why you need to know how the business works on the inside in order to get the best deals.

5 GET EVERYTHING IN WRITING: Always get everything in writing. This is especially important in any kind of transaction which involves custom work. It is your responsibility to make sure that all details, such as measurements and materials, have been very clearly conveyed, in writing, to the workroom.

6 DON'T BE PUT OFF BY A MESSY WORK AREA: If you walked into a retail business that looked like a fabric tornado had just blown through, you might decide not to shop there. However, this is the usual state of most workrooms. This does not indicate that the workroom has a sloppy attitude toward its work, as you might rightly assume about messy businesses in different fields.

Sewing and upholstery are just messy. Piles of thread and stuffing and fabric scraps just seem to accumulate on the floor and multiply all by themselves. Don't hold this against the business. The messiest workrooms usually produce the best work. They are too busy filling orders to stop and clean up every five minutes.

7 NEVER PAY THE ENTIRE AMOUNT IN ADVANCE: When you have custom furnishings made by a workroom or craftsperson, it is customary to pay one-half of the amount due in advance and the other half upon delivery or pick-up.

Never pay the entire amount due in advance. This is not customary in the business. Holding back that other half of your money is your best insurance against having any problems with your job.

Please note that this is a different situation than dealing with a factory or wholesale showroom. If you are ordering custom furnishings from a factory or wholesale showroom, you will have to pay entirely in advance. Many of these companies will consider that they are doing you a favor to take your order at all.

Small workrooms and craftspeople need your business, however, and usually have a much more accommodating attitude. For this reason, you should have most of your custom work done with local workrooms and craftspeople instead of factories and wholesale showrooms, with a few exceptions which are explained in the appropriate chapters in Part I of this book.

When you are having custom labor done in your home, such as drapery or wallpaper installation, it is customary to pay the entire amount immediately upon completion of the work. Most jobs will be completed in one day.

8 NEVER PAY THE BALANCE DUE UNTIL THE WORK HAS BEEN PROPERLY COMPLETED AS STATED IN YOUR CONTRACT: Always retain the balance due until the work has been properly completed. Never trust any business that says they will fix any problems after they are paid. They might, or they might not. Holding back the balance due until your job is completed as agreed is the best insurance.

The only exception to this is when the problem is your fault. If your job is incorrect because you forgot to specify a detail in your contract or you mismeasured, you are obligated to pay the balance due to the workroom or craftsperson for the original work that was done before they perform any alterations. They did the work properly as specified in the contract, and they deserve to be paid. Indeed, if you refuse to pay them, they would be within their rights to sue you.

In a case such as this. you will probably be expected to pay for any alterations entirely in advance. This is not unreasonable. If I were dealing with a customer who seemed not to know what he or she was doing, or couldn't decide what he or she wanted, I wouldn't think of touching any more work from that person without a signed contract and full payment in advance.

9 DON'T TRY TO USE A CREDIT CARD: Almost none of these businesses will accept credit cards. They just aren't set up for it. This is not an indication that these businesses might be insolvent or dishonest, as it would be if you were dealing with a retail business. Wholesale business just isn't conducted with credit cards. Period. That's just the way it is.

Don't worry about losing the consumer protections that go along with credit card transactions. You have other ways, as explained later in this chapter, to make sure that the business gives you what you pay for.

10 PROMISE TO REFER MORE BUSINESS IF YOU ARE PLEASED WITH YOUR JOB: Potential referrals for more work are a powerful financial incentive for any of these businesses to make sure they do a great job for you. Virtually all of you are in a position to refer a business to more customers if you are pleased with its work -- you may belong to the Chamber of Commerce, business clubs, the PTA, neighborhood associations, etc. If so, speak up.

How To Make Sure That Your Job Is Done Properly

Most of these businesses are honest and reliable. Con artists don't go into this type of work because it is too difficult. Con artists tend to be very lazy. They don't want to do any hard physical work such as sewing draperies or putting up wallpaper. You don't have to worry about running into any seriously dishonest businesses of this type. However, occasionally, a business may not treat you as well as it should.

Prevention is the best defense. Get everything in writing. Read the chapters in Part I to make sure that you have included all necessary details for the specific type of home furnishings you are having custom-made in your contract. The vast majority of disagreements that consumers have with these types of businesses arise from misunderstandings about exactly what was supposed to be done. Specifying all of the important details of the job in writing will prevent most disagreements from ever happening.

If you are having custom labor done in your home be sure to stay and oversee the work. It is rare for any such work to be done incorrectly, especially if your contract is written clearly. Have your contract handy to point out any mistakes while the workers are still there and can fix them.

You should stay home primarily to watch out for your other possessions. Often, workers for wholesale businesses are not bonded or insured, as workers for retail businesses often are. If you allow workers in your home to work by themselves, and later something of yours turns up stolen or broken, you will have no practical recourse.

If for some reason the work is not done properly, even after you clearly specified all details in your contract, ask the business to fix the problem. Most will do this with no argument. Custom-made furnishings can often be complicated, and it's not unusual for a workroom to make an occasional mistake, especially when you consider all of the different jobs they have going at once. The problem is most likely an error, not a deliberate rip-off.

Of course, if your job is not correct because you forgot to specify an important detail or measured incorrectly, you will have to pay the workroom to make any changes. Always read and reread your contract to make sure that all details are correctly stated and included before work is begun. Sometimes, these little alterations can be more expensive than the original cost of the entire job because the furnishings may have to be taken apart and put back together again.

If the job is not done exactly as specified in your written contract, however, it is the workroom's responsibility to fix the problem at no added expense to you.

Remember, don't pay the entire amount in advance, and don't pay the balance due until the job is properly completed. The balance due that you are holding back is your best insurance that the job will be correctly completed. Carefully inspect the completed work before paying the balance due.

If, for some reason, you discover a mistake or defect after you have paid the balance due and the workroom or craftsperson refuses to fix it, which will be extremely rare if you follow the instructions in this book, you still have one effective method of recourse left.

The single biggest threat you can pose to any of these businesses is to block future referrals of new customers. Tell the business that if the problem or defect is not corrected right away, you will complain to the person or business who referred you.

Complaining to the person or business who gave you the referral could cut off a very large percentage of the workroom's or craftsperson's future jobs, up to 50% in some small towns. This should get any business into high gear to resolve your complaint.

Chapter 19

How To Be Your Own Decorator

This is the chapter you've been waiting for -- how to buy all kinds of home furnishings from wholesale sources, just like people who work in the industry do when they are decorating their own homes.

Other decorating books have also told consumers that they could shop wholesale, but they usually didn't tell consumers HOW to shop wholesale in enough detail. How to get the proper business credentials. How to get into wholesale showrooms and design centers. What to say and do when you get there. And, more importantly, what NOT to say and do when you get there.

This chapter has ALL of the details you need to shop the way industry insiders shop.

The Best Kept Secret In Interior Decorating

Over the years, many smart consumers have purchased pillows, cushions, and window treatments directly from my family's wholesale business by becoming interior decorators themselves. It's easy.

There are no professional or educational requirements to be an interior decorator. Professional interior decorators who decorate homes for a living just have to buy a general business license, register for a resale number, and buy business cards. That's all there is to it. Many of them even work out of their homes. You don't need to have an office or storefront to be an interior decorator.

Your license and resale number will be your passport into a whole new world. You won't have to pay middlemen a high commission or markup to purchase fine home furnishings for you. You can do your own shopping, and keep the interior designer's commission in your own pocket. You can browse through showrooms that are open only to the trade. You can see the vast majority of the home furnishings available and make your own choices, instead of relying on an interior designer to bring you samples of what he or she thinks you might like. Best of all, you can use your interior decorator's trade discount, which is usually 40% to 50% (and occasionally as much as

Important Note

Being able to shop wholesale does not mean being able to buy every brand on the market directly from the manufacturer. Most of the brands available to professional interior decorators will be available to you if you become your own licensed decorator, but some will not.

As discussed throughout this book, some manufacturers make their merchandise "ultra-exclusive", which means that only certain interior designers are allowed to buy it wholesale. Many professional interior designers and all interior decorators (including you) are normally barred from buying furnishings from these companies.

Also, some manufacturers do not allow their wholesale customers to purchase in small quantities. This has the effect of restricting their products to retail stores only.

However, most brands of home furnishings can be purchased one at a time by interior decorators. These brands will normally be available to you when you shop wholesale.

It's important for you to understand ahead of time that manufacturers of ultra-exclusive furnishings will not want to sell to you and may even be rude to you when you attempt to buy from them.

Just remember that most manufacturers do want your business as long as you are properly licensed and understand how to properly shop in a wholesale setting. Then move on to one of the ultra-exclusive brand's competitors. You won't have to look far.

75%) off of retail!

Many people who work in the design industry use their own licenses and resale numbers all the time to buy furnishings at wholesale for their own homes. That's how my family and so many other families have been able to decorate our homes so inexpensively while shopping at the best wholesale designer showrooms. This chapter will teach you how to shop the way industry insiders shop. By going directly to the source, you cut out all of the expensive retail overhead and middleman profits.

Wholesale shopping is not quite as convenient as retail shopping, however. Salespeople in wholesale showrooms do not answer questions about interior design, only about the quality and manufacturing specifications of the merchandise they sell. Interior decorators are expected to come up with their own design ideas and make their own product selections.

If you want to shop wholesale, you will have to follow the guidelines in Part I of this book to make sure that you are buying furnishings that are suitable for the way they will be used in your home. You will also either have to come up with your own design ideas, by consulting the many free sources of design advice discussed in Chapter 14, or pay a designer to suggest ideas to you. Wholesale design centers and showrooms may not be quite as close by as your local furniture store, although they are present in most cities.

The rewards of buying wholesale, however, are huge. You will receive the standard trade discount of 40% to 50% off of retail. In some situations, you will be able to save even more. You will be able to browse through nearly all of the merchandise that is available to the design trade instead of trying to trace certain retail furnishings back to their sources. You won't have to pay to support the expensive retail showrooms that furniture stores and interior designers maintain. You will be able to buy most of the unique and unusual furnishings that are not available directly to the public.

You must know how to function smoothly in a wholesale atmosphere if you are going to shop as a wholesale customer. Later in this chapter, we will discuss appropriate ways to conduct business in a wholesale showroom and translate all of the "designer lingo" that will help you fit right in.

It is slightly more work for you to shop wholesale. It would be easier to just hire an interior designer to do your shopping for you. It would also be much more expensive -- at least twice as expensive as shopping wholesale, more on certain types of furnishings. You will be able to save so much money by shopping wholesale that if you are planning to spend very much at all on redecorating your home, about $300.00 or more, this is a buying method you should consider.

How To Become Your Own Decorator

Becoming a licensed interior decorator is very simple. You need three things: a general business license, a resale number, and business cards.

In this section, we will discuss exactly how you can go about getting all of these things. Don't worry if you have no prior experience in business. The instructions in this section are designed for anyone to follow. I haven't made any assumptions about what you do or don't know about getting business credentials. Every tiny detail is spelled out for you.

Now, let's get you set up to go shopping:

1 GENERAL BUSINESS LICENSE: These licenses are sold at your city occupational license office. Call city hall for the office location. What you want is a home occupational license. All this means is that you work from your home. Many interior decorators who make their living decorating homes work this way.

If you ever decide that you would like to make some extra money from your new-found shopping skills by hiring your decorating services out to the public, this license should also suffice for that purpose. There should be no need to get a separate license.

The form is very simple. It usually just asks for your name and address and the type of business you will have. Be sure to fill in "interior decorator". Some cities code their license numbers according to the type of business. Design centers and wholesale showrooms in those areas will look for the correct code.

There are a few other questions asked on many city license applications. These questions are normally used by the city to weed out businesses who may carry on activities that would be offensive to their neighbors or disrupt the normal residential atmosphere. You will be conducting all of your business (shopping) in the design centers and wholesale showrooms, so your business will not be disruptive to your neighbors in any way. The usual questions, along with the appropriate answers for your situation, are listed below:

Business name: Many interior decorators use the business name [your name] Interiors. For instance, a decorator named Jane Doe would call her business "Jane Doe Interiors". You will substitute your own name. This is the best business name for your situation.

Cities usually do not require that you register a business name as a "fictitious name" as long as the business name contains your name and obviously belongs to you.

Business phone: List your home phone number. Many professional interior decorators and interior designers who work from their homes use their home phones for business rather than installing a separate business phone line.

"Will the business activity at this location take place entirely within the dwelling?" Answer "Yes". You will not be conducting any business in your yard or driveway. This question is not referring to work you do away from your home, such as at a design center or in a customer's home.

"Will any employees, partners, or other associates other than those living in the home, come to this location for any purpose concerning the business?" Answer "No". You will not be hiring any employees, to work at your home or anywhere else.

"Give the percentage of the dwelling unit used for business." Answer "1%" The vast majority of your business activities (shopping) will take place at design centers and wholesale showrooms, not in your home. You will, occasionally, be using your home phone to call manufacturers and showrooms, however, which constitutes about 1% of the area of your home.

"Will any public contact take place at this location other than by telephone or mail?" Answer "No". You will not be receiving any customers at your home because you won't have any customers. Should you decide to hire out your decorating services to the public, you will meet with your customers in their homes, not your own.

"Will any materials, inventory, or equipment be stored anywhere at this location other than within the dwelling?" Answer "No". You will not be maintaining any outdoor storage, such as in a shed or detached garage. In fact, you won't be storing anything at all.

"State where inventory and equipment will be stored." Answer "My business does not maintain an inventory and does not use any equipment." Items that you purchase for your own use and keep in your home are not considered to be "stored" there. These are typical furnishings being used appropriately in a home. You are not storing them for resale to someone else.

"Describe all vehicles used in connection with the business and indicate who will operate the vehicles." Simply list the car you usually drive and list yourself as the driver. Presumably, this is the car you will drive when you go shopping.

This question is usually asked only to ensure that the owner of a home business does not maintain a car that would detract from the appearance of the neighborhood, such as an ice cream truck or a van with your business name plastered all over it in neon purple. That would be unfair to the neighbors.

"Date business is to begin at this address." Just state a date about two weeks after you file the application. You aren't supposed to start until you receive your license and resale number, which might be a few days after you file.

"State the type of organization: proprietorship (sometimes called a "sole proprietorship"), partnership, or corporation." Answer "proprietorship". This is the type of organization which applies to people going into business for themselves without having a partner or organizing a corporation. Most small businesses, and nearly all interior decorators and interior designers, use this type of organization.

This is the best, easiest, and most appropriate choice for your situation. Also, the many of instructions given in this chapter apply only to proprietorships.

That's all there is to it. Many cities will give you a license on the spot. Some cities will mail the license to you a few days later. Make a photocopy of the license to take with you when you shop. Leave the original at home.

The usual rate for this license in most towns is about $100.00. The fee may be more or less (usually less) depending upon where you live. The license will be effective for one year, at the end of which you will receive a renewal form in the mail.

Although city inspectors have the right to inspect your home before issuing a license, they almost never do unless they have cause for concern, such as large amounts of stored merchandise in the home that might pose a fire hazard or business activities that might pose a nuisance to your neighbors. There are no potential problems with your type of business that a city inspector is likely to be concerned about. It is extremely unlikely that an inspector would visit your home. I have never heard of an on-site inspection being conducted for an interior decorating license.

2 RESALE NUMBER: You may have also heard people speak of using a "tax number", "resale permit", or a "sales tax permit" to shop wholesale. A tax number, a sales tax permit, a resale permit, and a resale number are all one and the same thing. These names are used interchangeably all over the U. S. Wherever you live, occupational license office should be familiar with all of these terms.

Ask the occupational license office where you should register for your resale number. In some areas you will register with the state, in others you will register with the county. There is usually no charge to register.

You will fill out and send in a simple registration form, very similar to the form you filled out to get your business license. Forms used by different states and counties vary in their complexity. They are usually only a single page long.

You will be asked some basic questions, many of which don't really apply to you as a home business with no inventory or employees. Typical questions and the correct answers for your situation are given below:

"If you have a state taxpayer identifier number, enter it here": This is only for businesses with employees and corporations. It doesn't apply to you. Leave this area blank.

"Reason for application": Check "new business".

"For which type of permit are you applying?" Check "sales and use tax" or "sales tax" These terms mean the same thing, but the wording does vary among different applications. Many states and counties use a single all-purpose form for many different types of tax permit applications.

"State your legal business name": Give the business name discussed above -- "[your name] Interiors".

"State your trade name": Leave this blank. You are not applying for any type of "fictitious name" or "trade name" for your business.

"State the type of ownership (sometimes called the "type of business organization"): Answer "sole proprietorship" or "proprietorship". The wording will vary depending upon where you live.

"If this is a seasonal business, state the months in which you will be open": Leave this blank. It doesn't apply to you.

"State the last month and day of your accounting year": Answer "December 31st". You are a sole proprietorship and would normally include any business tax deductions on your regular 1040 income tax form.

Your business tax year is the same as your personal tax year, just the standard calendar year.

If you are buying furnishings only for yourself, you will have no legitimate business deductions, and the way you normally file your taxes will not change. If you should ever decide to become a professional interior decorator and charge the public for your services with the intent of making a profit, you would claim any business deductions on Schedule C of your personal 1040 form.

"State your relationship to the business": Your proper legal title is "owner".

"State the nature of your business": Your business will be 100% retail. Your business, in essence, is centered around selling home furnishings to yourself. You will be a retail business with only one customer.

If you decide to offer your decorating services to the public, you will still be a 100% retail business. You should be able to continue using the same license and tax number.

"What kind of business will you operate?" Answer "Interior decorating".

"Will you sell alcohol, tobacco, gasoline, and/or motor fuel?": Answer "No".

"When will you start selling or purchasing items subject to sales tax?": State a date a couple of weeks after you apply for the resale number to give the certificate enough time to reach you.

"What accounting method will you use?": Answer "Cash basis". Again, this really doesn't apply to you unless you decide to offer your decorating services to the public.

"Will you have employees?": Answer "No".

After your form has been received and processed by the state or county, you will receive a certificate in the mail, usually one to two weeks later, which shows your resale number. Make a photocopy of this certificate to take with you when you shop. Leave the original at home.

The resale number is what you will use to pay sales tax on the goods you purchase for your own use. When you buy goods wholesale, you are not charged sales tax at the point of purchase as you are when you buy retail. You have to send in your check for the sales tax, yourself.

If you decide to sell furnishings to friends, relatives, or even business clients (if you should decide to pursue interior decorating professionally), you still must submit the sales tax due. If you sell furnishings to others, you will charge them sales tax and submit it to the state or county, just as most retail businesses do. When you buy furnishings for yourself, you will charge yourself the sales tax and send it in.

Depending on where you live, you will receive a form either every month or every three months on which to report your purchases and pay your sales tax. The state or county you live in may operate on a quarterly basis (every three months) or a monthly basis. The forms will be sent to you automatically in the mail. You don't need to call anyone or go anywhere to get them.

The form is very simple and requires only a few minutes to fill out. You list the total retail dollar amount of the merchandise you purchased during the one month or three month period, figure the tax, and mail in a check. It's that simple.

It is very important to note that you must pay tax on the retail price of the furnishings you purchase, not the wholesale price that you actually paid. For instance, if you purchased a sofa at the wholesale design center that retails for $1,000.00, you would probably pay about $500.00 with your decorator discount. However, you don't pay your sales tax based on the wholesale price of $500.00, you calculate the tax based on the $1,000.00 retail price. This is very important.

Whenever you shop wholesale, make a note to yourself of the retail price, which is normally marked on the sample tag in most showrooms that cater to interior decorators and interior designers. If you don't see any retail price listed, which often happens in trade center showrooms, just double the wholesale price you paid to arrive at the retail price.

For example, if you purchased a sofa that retails for $600.00 and a chair that retails for $400.00, you would enter $1,000.00 on the form for your total sales. If the sales tax rate in your state or county is 5%, you would calculate the tax to be $50.00 ($1,000.00 times 0.05). Mail in the form and your check for $50.00, and you will have properly completed your legal tax obligation as a resale number holder.

These forms also often ask for the amount of your exempt sales. There are none in your situation, even if you decide to become a professional decorator. Sorry.

Some forms provide for "vendor's compensation". This is a portion of the tax (usually 1% to 5%) paid to you as compensation for having to collect tax for the state or county. You are entitled to take this deduction. Follow the instructions to properly calculate this. Please note carefully that this is a percentage of the TAX not a percentage of the sales or purchases.

In the example given above, the correct vendor's compensation you could deduct from your tax payment if you were allowed a 3% vendor's compensation deduction is $1.50 ($50.00 X 0.03), NOT $30.00 ($1,000.00 X 0.03). Not a big bonus, but it is money.

To take this deduction, just fill in the vendor's compensation amount on your sales tax form and deduct the proper amount from the tax due. In the example given above, you would deduct $1.50 from the tax amount of $50.00 and send in a check for $48.50.

Make sure that you file these forms ON TIME, as stated in the instructions you will receive with the form. Hefty penalties and interest are normally assessed if you are late. Usually, you will also lose your vendor's compensation allowance if you file late. You will normally have at least three weeks to fill out and submit these forms after you receive them in the mail.

When you make a wholesale purchase, you may sometimes be asked to fill out a small white card called a "blanket certificate of resale" by the manufacturer or showroom. This is a certification to the business you are buying merchandise from that you agree to be responsible for the sales tax. It provides a written record for the business that you have agreed to properly pay any sales tax owed on the item sold. This way, if you were to fail to pay the sales tax owed on an item, the business could not be sued for the tax money because it has a properly filled out and signed form from you agreeing to properly pay any taxes due. The showroom will show you how to fill in the card, if this is required.

3 BUSINESS CARDS: You can order basic business cards for less than $10.00 (for a minimum order) at most office supply stores. The minimum order is normally 500 cards, which should be enough to keep you shopping for the next ten years.

Colored papers, embossed logos, and drawings are unnecessary. You don't need anything fancy. Simple black and white cards are all that are needed. Of course, if you want to use colored papers or inks, that's fine, too.

You are not expected or required to present any licenses or proof of who you are in order to have these cards printed. There are no "business card police" out there checking to see what everyone is printing on their cards. All you have to do is tell the store how you want your cards to look.

You should go ahead and order your cards at the same time you order your license and resale permit. There is no need to wait until you receive your business credentials.

Interior Decorators vs. Interior Designers

You should always refer to yourself as an "interior decorator", never an "interior designer". Many people outside the trade use these terms interchangeably, but those in the trade know that there is a difference.

Interior designers usually have a college education in interior design. Interior decorators usually do not.

Interior designers are in the process of lobbying for laws that restrict the practice of interior design. At the present time, most states still have no laws at all regarding this. Seventeen states have "title" laws, which means that you cannot call yourself an "interior designer" unless you have a college degree in interior design and have met any other education and experience requirements that are mandated in that state's law. You are perfectly free to call yourself an "interior decorator" in these states, and everywhere else.

Many professional interior decorators are really just salespeople who work for fabric stores and retail furniture stores. They usually have no design education at all. Often, they have no decorating experience whatsoever prior to going to work for that store. They just have business cards printed and POOF! -- Instant Decorator.

None of the lobbying interior designers are doing has anything to do with you. You are an interior decorator. Interior decorators aren't legally required to have any specialized education or experience to work anywhere in the U. S. All you, or any of the thousands of professional interior decorators who currently work in the U. S., need are a business license, business cards, and a resale permit.

Just do be sure that you call yourself an "interior decorator" and not an "interior designer" on your license applications. The exact title you use IS important.

Common Questions

Does having a resale number make me exempt from paying sales tax? No. It is very important to pay your sales taxes truthfully and promptly.

Although when you purchase items wholesale using a resale number, you will not be charged sales tax when you make your purchases, you must properly calculate the sales tax and pay it yourself when you receive your next sales tax form in the mail.

Even if you resell the merchandise to someone else, such as a friend or business client (if you decide to become a professional interior decorator and offer your decorating services to the general public), you still must collect and pay the sales tax on these sales.

May I use any of these purchases as income tax deductions? No. If you were conducting an interior design business with the intent of making a profit by selling your design services to the public, you could deduct the cost of your license and business cards as legitimate business expenses.

However, since you are not offering your services to the public, and have no intention of producing an income from this venture, you cannot claim these costs as deductions.

Your wholesale purchases are also not eligible as business deductions. If you were purchasing goods for resale to someone else, you could deduct their cost. However, since you are purchasing goods for your own use instead of reselling them, you cannot claim their cost as a deduction.

If you do ever decide to become a professional interior decorator and offer your services to the public with the intent of making a profit, there are many tax deductions that you will be able to take advantage of.

What do interior designers and interior decorators think about this? Well, they're not happy, to put it mildly. Most interior designers and interior decorators naturally want to cling to their former monopoly on fine home furnishings. They don't want consumers to be able to purchase them any other way, whether through wholesale shopping, buying from telephone discounters, or buying directly from factory outlets. Every time someone buys home furnishings without paying a commission to an interior designer or interior decorator, they lose income.

However, you do not owe these people a living. You have no obligation to pay higher prices to support middlemen, such as interior designers and interior decorators. You have every right to find less expensive substitutes for their services by getting your own free design advice from books and magazines and by purchasing a license which will permit you to buy your furnishings directly from the source.

What do wholesale design centers think about this? Most wholesale design centers have been warming up to this idea for some time. Many wholesale showrooms are having difficulty paying their rents to the design center due to falling sales.

As a result, some interior design centers have begun allowing the public in to shop at a partial trade discount on certain days, ever since showroom revenues began dropping several years ago. The Seattle Design Center has even established a special program to welcome consumers, as described in

VISIONS Of Savings

The Seattle Design Center has established a special consumer access program, called VISIONS, to accommodate consumers who want to shop directly at the source without paying huge commissions to interior designers and interior decorators. Since this program was established in 1992, over 11,000 consumers have participated in it.

Home Design Lecture Series: This is a bi-monthly lecture series held in conjunction with special luncheons for consumers at the design center. Each luncheon seminar features a different design topic tailored to a consumer audience and is given by a local interior designer. Recent topics include: soft window treatments, custom floral arrangements, and holiday decorating. Call the SDC at (800) 497-7997 for details on the next seminar.

Design Thursdays: Every second Thursday of the month, the SDC extends its normal shopping hours to 8:00 in the evening. Between 5:00 and 8:00 PM, consumers may browse the design center and buy furnishings at about 20% off retail.

Portfolio Center: Participating designers display photographs of their recent work here. What a great place to get free design ideas!

VISIONS Resource Center: This consumer office helps consumers make purchases during normal design center hours, at about 20% off retail.

the box at left.

Many other design centers will not openly welcome consumers because they do not wish to offend the interior designers and interior decorators who shop there. However, virtually all design centers have been tolerating properly licensed and well-informed consumers who know how to properly shop wholesale for many years.

What do manufacturers and trade center showrooms think of this? Well, my family has been in manufacturing for many years, and we never minded "being shopped", as this practice is known in the trade. This happened often at our factory and at our wholesale trade center showrooms.

It made no difference to us if we sold decorative pillows to a decorator shopping for herself or to a decorator shopping for a client. A sale is a sale, after all.

Although we occasionally suspected that a decorator was a licensed consumer shopping for herself because she didn't seem familiar with wholesale customs and procedures, we usually never knew for sure if the decorator was shopping for herself or for a client. After all, the decorators don't tell us who they are shopping for. They just pay for their purchases and move on.

As long as licensed consumers conducted themselves in an appropriate and professional manner that did not disrupt the normal course of business, as we will discuss later in this chapter, there were no problems. As long as we were making sales and not experiencing any problems, we really didn't care who the decorators were shopping for.

May I pay with my own personal checks? Yes, many professional interior designers and interior decorators do. You do not need special business checks to shop from the vast majority of wholesale sources.

The few sources that do require designers and decorators to pay with a business check almost always also require large opening orders. Both of these restrictions tend to discourage sales to interior decorators and interior designers. There are a few manufacturers who are accustomed to selling in large quantities, usually to store chains, and do not wish to accept the small orders that designers and decorators usually place.

If you encounter such a manufacturer, all you can do is choose a different product and shop somewhere else. The vast majority of home furnishings are available in quantities appropriate for interior decorators to purchase.

May I pay with a credit card or cash? No.

Is there a central checkout area such as there is in some retail stores? No. You will make your purchases individually at each showroom. Showrooms do not have a designated "check-out" area. Many do not even have a central customer service desk. The salespeople just mill around. Just tell a salesperson when you are ready to make a purchase.

May I take an item home to see how it looks in my house or show it to my family before buying it? Yes, in most showrooms. Ask for a sample (called a "memo sample"). These are available for most fabrics, wallpapers, tiles, carpets, etc. You will usually not be charged for the memo sample when you take it out. However, if you keep it longer than the agreed upon time, you will usually be charged a fee.

It is considered rude and unprofessional to keep out samples longer than is absolutely necessary. Samples are very expensive, and the longer a sample is out of the showroom, the more potential sales are lost because other shoppers cannot see that particular sample. If a sample is kept out too long, the showroom will have to pay to replace it in order to prevent losing any more potential sales. You will appear more professional if you make every effort to return samples as quickly as possible.

If no memo sample is available, as will happen with some furniture and accessories, you can often arrange to take the piece home "on memo". To take out merchandise on memo, you give the showroom a check for the full cost of the item and they agree not to cash it for a given length of time, usually two to five days. Many showrooms will have a special memo form for you to fill out.

If you decide to return the item (undamaged, of course) they will return your uncashed check to you. If you damage the item, or if the showroom does not hear from you in the agreed upon time, they will deposit your check and the item will be yours to keep.

Don't worry about being ripped off by the showroom. This has been standard procedure for many years. Remember, interior decorators take goods and samples out to customers' homes on memo every day. I have never heard a decorator or designer complain that a showroom had ripped him or her off over a memo purchase.

Memo samples and the taking out of merchandise on memo are not available at trade shows.

Will I be able to take my purchases home the same day? Almost never. The items you see in a showroom are usually floor samples only. The standard procedure for making a wholesale purchase is to pay in full in advance and have the item delivered several weeks later. If the item is out of stock or must be custom-made, the wait may be as long as six to eight weeks.

Don't worry about being ripped off by paying in advance. This is standard procedure in the industry. Professional interior designers and interior decorators place orders this way every day.

Besides, you have no other choice. The only alternative is to request that you be given an open credit line, which would involve a detailed inspection of your credit record and business income. You don't have any business income because you aren't offering your decorating services for sale to the public.

Businesses that have been established for years often have difficulty getting open credit from manufacturers, especially when they only make small purchases as interior decorators usually do. You will just have to settle for being a "pro forma" customer (this is the business term for paying in advance).

It is very rare for a wholesale business to default on a prepaid order. However, you may wish to check the business out with the Better Business Bureau and the Chamber of Commerce just to provide a little extra peace of mind. When you buy wholesale, you won't be able to use many of the consumer protection measures that are available to you when you buy retail. Fortunately, there is far less incidence of fraud from wholesale businesses than there is from retail businesses.

The only items you won't have to wait to receive are show samples and floor samples, which are occasionally sold (often at great discounts) by the showrooms.

How will my purchases arrive? Most of your purchases will arrive by UPS. When packages are delivered via UPS, there is usually no extra freight charge to be paid upon delivery. UPS charges are normally already added in to the amount you prepay when you place your order.

Very large or heavy items, such as some pieces of furniture, will be delivered by truck. You will usually have to pay the freight bill when the item arrives. It is not practical for the showroom to figure these amounts in advance.

When you place your order, always look at the receipt to see if the freight charges have already been included. If not, ask the showroom for a rough estimate of what the charges should be.

You may see a notation on your receipt or order that reads "FOB". "FOB" is an industry term which means "free on board" and refers to the point to which freight charges will be paid by the seller. If your order or receipt says "FOB destination", the notation means that all freight charges have been paid to the final destination and that you will owe nothing upon delivery. If your order or receipt says "FOB factory" or "FOB (city name)", the notation means that freight charges from the factory to you have not been paid by the seller and that you must pay these freight charges when the item is delivered.

If a salesperson should ask you if you would like to have your purchase "drop shipped" to your customer, say "no". "Drop shipping" means shipping it directly to your customer's home. While this does save some time and expense for professional interior decorators and interior designers, many of them choose not to do this.

It is a widespread (and wise) practice of many interior decorators and interior designers to have all items delivered to their own addresses (whether they work out of their own homes or out of separate offices) a short time prior to the date of installation at the client's home. This allows the decorator or designer to carefully inspect all of the furnishings before taking them to the customer's home to make sure that everything conforms with what was ordered and is undamaged. If mistakes or damage are present, the decorator or designer will still have time to correct them before the customer's installation date.

If you decline drop shipment and have the item delivered to your own home, you needn't worry about tipping off the showroom staff that the item is really for you. This is a perfectly normal procedure.

When will my purchases arrive? Unfortunately, this is a lot like asking when the cable or telephone repairperson will arrive. It's hard to narrow a time down.

The vast majority of your purchases will arrive by UPS. UPS often leaves packages with a neighbor if no one is home to receive them. If this is cause for concern, call UPS at (800) 742-5877 and request that other arrangements be made.

Packages that arrive by truck will not be left with a neighbor. If you aren't home, they will be returned to the seller at great expense to you. You will have to pay the extra freight bills incurred by sending the packages back and forth.

Also, most items delivered by truck are too heavy for one person to handle. You may need to arrange to have help available when it is delivered. Truck drivers will usually not carry your packages inside for you. It is not part of their job. If you are handicapped, you should know that the laws that require businesses to provide extra help to handicapped customers do not apply to wholesale businesses, only to businesses that serve the general public.

If the showroom says that your purchase will be delivered by truck, ask the showroom to give you an approximate date of shipment. Call back several days ahead of the projected shipment date and ask the manufacturer to call you when the item is shipped so that you can make arrangements to receive it. They should do this for you. When they notify you that the item has been shipped, get the name of the trucking company and the shipment tracking number. Then, call the local office of the trucking company, which you can easily find in the Yellow Pages or white pages, and give them the tracking number. They should be able to give you a reasonable idea of when your shipment will arrive. Usually, they can narrow it down to a specific day, just like the cable company.

Many professional interior decorators and interior designers work out of their homes and cannot be home all of the time to receive shipments because they are out working with customers. Showrooms and manufacturers are accustomed to working with decorators and designers who need help scheduling deliveries.

Arranging to receive bulky packages can occasionally be a nuisance, but just keep thinking about all the money you have saved. Interior designers and furniture stores will indeed bring your purchases out to your home anytime you like and even set them up for you, but they will usually also charge at least twice as much for the furnishings.

Should I inspect the packages when they arrive? Absolutely. If there is any obvious evidence of damage, such as a wet or dented box, make certain that you note this on the deliveryperson's receipt before signing. If the furnishings inside are damaged, immediately call the manufacturer and get their instructions on filing a claim with the delivery service. You will normally not be allowed to open the packages until you after sign for them.

If items inside the box or crate are damaged, but there is no apparent damage to the box or crate itself, the delivery company normally cannot be held liable. The responsibility is considered to be the manufacturer's, probably due to improper packing. In this case, you must file a claim directly with the manufacturer.

Simply call the manufacturer and let them know about the problem. The standard procedure is for the manufacturer to arrange to pick up the merchandise at no cost to you and send you a replacement right away. This problem is extremely rare. Manufacturers are very familiar with proper packing methods for the goods they sell. They normally err on the side of caution when deciding what type of packaging to use. After all, it's much cheaper to buy an extra pound of styrofoam peanuts and not leave any doubt that delicate merchandise is well padded than it is to pay for replacements or lose customers when merchandise arrives broken. You are unlikely to have any problems due to improper packing by the manufacturer.

You might possibly have a problem with damage done by the delivery service, although this is also very rare. If you are purchasing anything that is unusually expensive and/or unusually fragile, you may wish to purchase insurance through the delivery service prior to shipment. The showroom or manufacturer can usually arrange this for you at a small additional charge.

When damage does occur during shipment, the established method used by delivery services to reimburse consumers is generally not adequate. Even when the damage is delivery service's fault, the service will normally only reimburse you up to a certain set fee which is calculated according to the contents' weight, no matter what you actually paid for the item. If you purchase insurance through the delivery service, and the delivery service damages the item, you should be reimbursed in full with no problem.

In other words, if you purchase an antique porcelain tea set that arrives in a thousand pieces and the shipping service openly admits damaging it, you still will not usually be reimbursed what you actually paid for the tea set. The shipping service will usually look up the tea set's weight and pay you a set per-pound reimbursment fee, which won't even come close to what you actually paid.

If you are shipping anything fragile or expensive, you really should consider purchasing the shipping company's insurance. I know this system sounds extremely unfair, but it's just the way it is. Your only other alternative would be to sue the delivery service for the damage, which probably would not be practical for you. It's much better and simpler to pay a small extra fee for the insurance and avoid any potential hassles.

If it makes you feel any better, my parents' factory shipped most of its packages by UPS over a twenty year period, and in that time we only had one package arrive damaged during shipment. Most home furnishings manufacturers use UPS, and we have always found them to be very reliable. I do not recall any damage ever having occurred during a truck shipment.

If the damage is determined to be the manufacturer's fault, the insurance provided by the delivery service usually will NOT reimburse you. This is very important to remember. If the box your tea set arrives in has no apparent damage, but the tea set inside is shattered, even if you purchased insurance through the shipping company, you will usually not be reimbursed by the shipping company. In this case, the damage would be assumed to be the manufacturer's fault for not properly packing the tea set. The shipping company's insurance won't pay because the damage is assumed not to have been the shipping company's fault.

This is a fairly rare occurence. Most manufacturers ship the same items over and over again and are very familiar with the proper packing methods. If this does happen to you, contact the manufacturer for a replacement. You should receive a replacement at no charge with no problem.

Will large items be unpacked, set up, or put in place when they arrive? No. Your purchases will arrive packed up. You must unpack them and put them where you want them to go.

Often, large items, such as pieces of furniture, will arrive ''knocked down'', which means that they have been taken apart to allow them to be packed in smaller packages and keep freight costs down, and must be reassembled upon delivery. You are responsible for reassembly. This is rarely difficult.

Remember that professional interior decorators and interior designers generally do not own a wide array of tools or have any specialized knowledge of building furniture. Manufacturers bear this in mind when deciding how to disassemble the furniture.

Assembling furniture, or any other item, is very easy and usually requires nothing more than a screwdriver. Just keep thinking about the 40% to 50% you saved while you are working.

Must I buy large quantities of goods to shop wholesale? No. Remember, professional interior designers and interior decorators almost always shop for furnishings for only one house at a time. Most showrooms are accustomed to selling items one at a time. This is the normal procedure at design centers and the vast majority of wholesale factory and distributor showrooms.

The only major exceptions to this custom occur at wholesale trade shows. Trade shows, which are conducted twice each year at the major trade centers such as the Atlanta Market Center and the High Point International Home Furnishings Center, feature some suppliers who are accustomed to selling in larger quantities. Furniture stores and even store chains shop at these shows, in addition to many interior decorators and interior designers.

The proper way to find out if a supplier at a trade show will sell you only one of an item is to ask "do you work with decorators?". This is code for "may I buy only one of these?". Phrasing the question in the correct way will make you sound like an insider, though.

Some showrooms even have signs which read "Designers Welcome", which means that they will sell items one at a time. Decorators such as yourself are welcome at these showrooms, too.

The signs don't read "Decorators Welcome" or "Designers and Decorators Welcome" because interior designers tend to get very insulted when they are lumped into the same category with interior decorators. If a showroom even hinted openly that it did not have a thorough understanding of the exaltedness of interior designers, no self-respecting interior designer would ever debase herself by shopping at such an ignorant and uninformed establishment again.

All of the furnishings you will see at design centers and most of the furnishings you will see at trade shows need not be purchased in large quantities. However, if you see an item at a trade show that is not available one at a time, and you are interested in it, ask if you may purchase the show sample. Show samples can often be purchased at the show. We will discuss trade shows at more length later in the chapter.

Do handicapped access laws apply to wholesale locations? No. Those laws apply only to locations which serve the general public. Some commercial buildings, especially the older ones, do not have full wheelchair access.

If you have special needs, call ahead. Most businesses will be happy to accommodate you to the best of their ability.

How To Properly Conduct Business In a Wholesale Setting

It's very important to understand that wholesale shopping locations are not at all like retail locations. A wholesale design center is not a retail shopping mall. A factory showroom is not a furniture store.

It's important for you to understand that salespeople and managers in wholesale showrooms will usually ask you to leave, or not allow you inside in the first place, if you appear disruptive in any way. Most of you have never been inside a wholesale business, so you probably don't realize some of the concerns that wholesale business owners and managers have.

You could very innocently do something disruptive simply because no one has ever told you what is expected in a wholesale setting. That is the purpose of these guidelines.

Read the list of guidelines below very carefully. Some of the guidelines may seem excessive or unfair to you. They are certainly different from the expectations in a retail store or mall. However, you must realize that these restrictions are necessary to ensure that wholesale business can be conducted smoothly.

Do not bring ten of your closest friends with you: You cannot shop wholesale as a group. Bring no more than one person with you. Interior decorators are usually allowed to bring one person only (their client or a co-worker) with them to a showroom. A few showrooms don't even allow that. Interior designers and interior decorators never shop together -- they are business competitors. It would look extremely strange for a group of people to show up together in a wholesale setting to shop, like tourists.

When you arrive at the showroom or design center, simply state that the person works with you -- if you are even asked at all. After all, this person must be helping you decorate your home or you wouldn't have brought him or her along.

Your companion will usually be given a pass in his or her own name with no problem. If you bring someone with you to a trade center show, and your friend does not have his or her own tax number and license, this person may be given a "guest" pass instead of a pass in his or her own name. Guests are not treated as well as buyers by the showrooms and are not allowed to purchase anything.

You can usually get around this problem by ordering a second set of business cards with your companion's name listed. You may wish to do this if you will be shopping with this person frequently. Don't be concerned about looking odd if your companion is a family member -- many professional interior decorating and interior design firms are family businesses.

A few showrooms, usually located in design centers and trade centers, are called "closed" showrooms. No guests, clients, or co-workers are allowed in these showrooms, only the designer or decorator. They are not usually identified by a sign. You may see someone who looks like a maitre d' standing guard at the door, though. If a showroom is closed to anyone other than a designer, either the "maitre d'" or a salesperson will usually tell you immediately. There is usually no need for you to ask.

Avoid these showrooms. They are a waste of your time because closed showrooms typically only sell to interior designers, not interior decorators. This is where you will find most of the ultra-exclusive furnishings discussed in previous chapters.

Never, ever, bring a camera to any wholesale design center, trade center, factory, independent showroom, or any other wholesale location: It might be confiscated.

This is actually not such an unreasonable thing to consider doing. Years ago, I brought a camera into a trade center showroom to take a picture of some furniture that I wished to show a client back home. Not all showrooms have pictures of every one of their products. Taking your own pictures can eliminate the need to bring a client directly to the showroom.

However, when I tried this myself, I was promptly read the riot act by the showroom manager and nearly lost my camera.

It seems that they had been having severe problems with competitors making cheap knock-offs of their products. It takes a lot of time and money to design and test market new products. Competitors that come along after all of the hard work has been done and copy the final product can severely damage the original company. They had purposely avoided distributing pictures of their products in an effort to cut down on this problem.

I can certainly see the showroom's point. They had every right to be concerned about strangers taking pictures in their showroom.

Back then, this problem was fairly rare. However, in recent years, design theft has become far more prevalent. A major trade newsletter recently reported that many European trade shows are considering banning cameras altogether, even for showroom managers and salespeople to take pictures of their own products in the course of making sales. A few design centers in the United States have also prohibited any cameras on the premises.

This is one more unfortunate side effect of the intense competition among businesses that has been going on during this recession. It's a shame that everyone has to suffer because of the actions of a few dishonest people, but that's just the way it is today. So, leave the cameras at home, please.

Do not bring children with you: Never bring children to any wholesale showroom, design center, trade center, workroom, or factory. This includes small babies who could not possibly make trouble. This includes well-behaved teenagers. This is simply NEVER DONE by decorators or designers.

If you are a nursing mother, I'm sorry. Wholesale showrooms and businesses generally do not make exceptions for this, as retail shopping locations often do.

Design centers, trade centers, and wholesale showrooms choose not to allow children. Manufacturers and workrooms have no choice. They are usually prohibited by law from allowing children on the premises. Besides, most factories and workrooms have equipment and tools around that could seriously hurt a child. You would not want to bring your child to such a dangerous place.

You may, rarely, see a child in a wholesale showroom or factory. These are the owner's children. Laws and wholesale business policies do make this one exception. So, if you should see a child, don't think that the rules have changed and that it's now OK for you to bring in your children, too. It isn't.

Do not attempt to pay by credit card: Credit cards are generally not used in wholesale transactions. Processing credit cards is expensive for businesses and is only done when the public demands it. Wholesale customers do not expect to be able to use their credit cards, so wholesale suppliers do not make arrangements to be able to process them.

Don't worry about this. Fly-by-night fraud is very rare among wholesale businesses. Not being able to use your credit card is just a trade-off you will have to make in return for getting a much lower price.

Dress in a businesslike manner: Even away from their clients, interior decorators and interior designers wear business attire when shopping wholesale. Men should wear suits. Women should wear suits or business dresses.

You may occasionally see a casually dressed person. There are a few people who are so rich and so well established in the industry that they don't care what people think about their clothes. They can get away with wearing jogging suits and sneakers to the design center or trade center. You and I can't.

Do not bring food or drinks into any wholesale business: Generally, food and drinks are prohibited in showrooms, factories, and workrooms. You will probably be asked to leave if you try this. It will almost certainly make the salespeople resent you, which isn't what you want.

Many of these salespeople and designers have also worked in retail. We all have vivid memories of one or two retail customers who dripped ice cream on our expensive furniture samples or spilled their soft drinks on our $500.00 fabric swatches.

Most retail stores have lost a lot of money due to careless damage by customers. It's one small factor in the high prices we all have to pay in retail stores. Retail stores tolerate more damage, and more potential risks, from customers, but they also charge much higher prices to everyone. If you look like an accident waiting to happen, you will bring back some very unhappy memories for the showroom staff. You will immediately look like you don't belong in a wholesale setting. You want to blend in, not stand out.

EXCEPTION: The only exception to this rule is during wholesale trade shows at trade centers. These shows are usually grueling, 12-hour-day affairs for people who make their living in the industry. Many buyers don't even slow down for lunch. Food and drinks are sold in the lobby and given away in many showrooms, and it's OK to bring them in many showrooms if you are careful. Buyers always shop with their mouths full at these events.

In fact, you should probably skip the overpriced hot dogs and Cokes in the lobby. Wait until you get upstairs where the showrooms are. I've been in showrooms where they served everything from homemade chocolate-chip cookies to falafels. Many showrooms serve every kind of free food and drink you can imagine in an effort to attract buyers. You definitely won't go hungry.

To be on the safe side, look to see if a showroom offers refreshments or if other buyers are taking food in with them before you take food into a particular showroom. There are a few trade center showrooms that don't want buyers to eat while they shop.

Don't sit on anything: I know that in many retail stores, customers routinely sit on samples of furniture, beds, and other furnishings. The store owners usually tolerate it, but they don't like it. No one can see the sample to buy from it if someone is sitting on the price tag. This also makes expensive samples look worn and unattractive.

Wholesale showrooms absolutely do not tolerate this. The salespeople will be offended and may ask you to leave. Besides, it looks unprofessional, and that isn't the image you want to project.

Most design centers have at least one coffee shop or restaurant and plenty of benches if you are tired.

Remember, nothing is returnable: It's fine to take samples out on memo, when you make prior arrangements with the showroom to do so. Aside from that, however, once you buy something, it's yours.

It is very rare for showrooms or factories to allow returns, even on items that are not custom-made. It is considered extremely unprofessional to even ask to return anything.

Also, most of the consumer laws that you are accustomed to in a retail usetting do not apply to wholesale purchases. There is no legal requirement to post signs stating that items are non-returnable before you make your purchase, as there is in retail transactions. In fact, such signs are virtually never posted in a wholesale setting. It is simply assumed that you know this because you work in the industry.

Be very sure about what you want before you make a purchase.

Do not ask the salespeople design questions: Never bring in a picture of your home and ask a salesperson what they think you should buy. Salespeople in these showrooms and factories only answer questions about the prices, manufacturing methods, specifications, contents, and delivery arrangements of the goods they sell. It is not part of their job to tell you if they think an item will match your carpet or look good in your living room.

If you shop wholesale, you will be on your own for design advice.

Never ask to use the restroom in a wholesale showroom, workroom, or factory: Most design centers and trade centers have central restrooms available for the decorators and designers. Most wholesale showrooms, workrooms, and factories do not have restrooms readily available.

The reason for this is an architectural one. Commercial buildings almost always have restrooms located in the rear of the building. This means that to get to the restrooms, you must take the grand tour of the entire establishment.

Wholesale establishments always have private work areas which they do not wish clients (much less competitors) to see. These areas contain new product designs which have not yet been unveiled, confidential customer lists, packages and papers which reveal confidential resources, office records, and other private information.

Occasionally, gossiping salesmen or competitors masquerading as customers will ask to use the restroom in a factory or workroom for the specific purpose of finding out confidential information. "Asking to use the restroom" is considered in the industry to be a very sleazy way of seeing parts of the factory, workroom, or showroom that are none of your business. If you

To the Trade Only

"To the trade only" is a common phrase that you will see on many wholesale showroom doors and mentioned in many design magazines. It means that only licensed decorators and designers are allowed inside the showroom or permitted to purchase the product or service mentioned in the magazine.

Licensed decorators. That's you. Has a nice ring, doesn't it? Walk right on in.

do this, you will offend the business owners. They may ask you to leave. Don't do it.

Don't wander around outside of the showroom area: Never wander out of the showroom into the offices, workroom areas, or factory floor of any commercial establishment. Even if you have been left alone and you don't know when the person who was helping you will be back, don't go looking for them. For the reason stated above, this is a very offensive thing to do.

You could even get hurt. Factories and workrooms usually have all kinds of dangerous equipment and tools laying around. Also, you will often be violating the business' insurance coverage.

"Going exploring" is a sure way to never be allowed in a showroom or factory again.

How To Find Showrooms For Specific Types and Specific Brand Names Of Home Furnishings

For a comprehensive directory of the thousands of wholesale custom workrooms, wholesale design centers, wholesale trade centers, home furnishings manufacturers, and wholesale showrooms all over the United States (including independent showrooms as well as those in design centers and trade centers), you may order a copy of the *National Directory of Wholesale Home Furnishings Sources and Showrooms,* by William Graham. An order form can be found in the back of this book.

The directory contains over 300 pages of wholesale sources for all types of home furnishings organized by brand name, by location, and by product or service type.

How To Get In Wholesale Design Centers

When you arrive at wholesale design centers, you will register at the front desk. Bring a photocopy of your business license, a photocopy of your resale certificate, and a business card. Upon presentation of these, the receptionist will give you a pass or badge, usually to pin on your clothing, which will allow you in the design center for the day. You keep the photocopies of your credentials. You don't need to give them to anyone. There is normally no admission charge at a design center.

If you wish to bring someone with you while you shop, simply tell the receptionist that the person works with you. After all, this person must be helping you decorate your home or you wouldn't have brought him or her along. It is preferable, but not necessary, to have business cards made up in this person's name, too -- as discussed on page 320.

You should have no problem bringing in one other person with you. Do not attempt to bring more than one person with you. Do not call this person your "friend" or "guest". Some design centers will not allow guests, only clients and people who work with you.

At this point, you will be on your own. You may travel freely, going in and out of showrooms as you wish. Most design centers have a coffee shop or restaurant if you do not wish to leave for lunch. Most design centers are open from 9:00 to 5:00, Monday through Friday. Most design centers have free parking for decorators.

A variety of pricing methods are used and will vary from showroom to showroom. The discounted prices that decorators and designers pay are never openly stated because many decorators and designers bring their retail clients with them to browse through the showrooms. If the discounted prices were stated clearly, retail clients would know just how high a markup they were paying -- and the designers and decorators simply can't have that, can they? The three main types of showrooms codes are described in the next section.

You may be asked to register in a few showrooms. A few showrooms don't allow decorators to look around unaccompanied. You may be asked to sign in and wait for a salesperson. Don't worry that a salesperson will show up on your doorstep at some point in the future if you give your name and address. That is simply not done. You may be sent literature or product announcements in the mail. Rarely, a salesperson may phone you. If this should happen, all you need to do is tell him or her that you don't need anything at that time.

When the salesperson comes to show you around, he or she will ask you what you are looking for. Tell the salesperson what you want. This is not like imposing on the staff to answer inappropriate design questions. It's fine to accept help when it is offered.

Most showrooms allow decorators to browse freely. The staff is usually indifferent to customers. You need not worry about being hounded by an too-helpful salesperson, as sometimes happens in retail stores.

Many design centers host special talks on a variety of subjects, such as Feng-shui design or trompe l'oeil accents. These presentations are often free. Many design centers also host classes on all types of design topics and projects. There may or may not be a charge to attend a class.

All of these events will normally be posted on the design center's bulletin board near the entrance and/or listed on brochures or flyers available from the receptionist at the check-in desk. Some of the topics may be too "dry" or business-oriented to be of interest to you, but many will be very informative and fascinating even to people who are not professional interior decorators or interior designers.

Some interior design centers now host special days on which the public may enter and shop at a discount, usually 20% off retail, without any need for a license or tax number.

You might wish to check out the design center in your area on one of these special shopping days before investing in your own license (if the design center in your area permits the public inside at all), however, it is better if you don't. These centers have comparatively few visitors and everyone must check in at the front desk. It would look very unusual for you to check in as a retail customer one day and as a decorator soon after.

If you do decide to invest in your own business license after visiting a design center as a retail customer, wait a few months before going back to that particular design center.

Cracking the Codes

There are three basic types of codes that are used in wholesale showrooms to hide the true cost of the furnishings from retail design clients. You will normally see these codes anywhere that decorators and designers bring in clients: design center showrooms, independent wholesale showrooms, and many factory showrooms.

You will usually not see any codes in trade center showrooms, and some factory showrooms, because retail clients are not allowed in these places (even when accompanied by a decorator or designer). These showrooms simply tag everything with the wholesale price.

The basic wholesale price codes are:

1 THE "5/10" CODE: Samples that are tagged with "5/10" coded prices look like fractions: 20/55, 60/35, etc.

To arrive at the true cost of the furnishings, you deduct $5.00 from the first number and ten cents from the second. Therefore, an item tagged "20/55" actually costs $15.45 per unit at wholesale. An item tagged "60/35" actually costs $55.25 per unit, etc.

If you are looking at fabrics, this will be the price per yard. If you are looking at a piece of furniture, this will be the price for one unit. And so on.

You don't need to ask the showroom staff if they use the 5/10 system. In fact, you shouldn't. You would sound like you didn't know what you were doing. If a showroom uses the 5/10 system of coding prices, it will be obvious from the fractions written on the price tags.

If you see actual prices marked on the samples instead of fractions, you will know that the showroom must use some type of decorator discount instead of the 5/10 system. Whenever you see prices marked in any showroom where decorators and designers are allowed to bring clients, the prices are always retail.

Ask a salesperson what your discount is, quietly and discreetly. There will probably be other decorators and designers within earshot who might have retail clients with them. No one will appreciate you asking about the wholesale discount in a way that might cause problems for other decorators and designers.

2 STRAIGHT DISCOUNTS: Often, the showroom gives decorators and designers a straight percentage discount, usually 40% to 50%. Just look at the price on the tag and deduct your discount to arrive at the true cost of the furnishings.

The showroom salesperson may answer "keystone" when you ask what your discount is. Keystone is code in the trade for a straight percentage discount of 50% off the retail price. This is a very commonly used code.

3 COMPOUND DISCOUNTS: Occasionally, a showroom may use a compound discount. When this happens, which is only in a few furniture showrooms and hard window treatment workrooms for the most part, you will be told that your discount is "50/10" or "50/50", for example.

To arrive at the true cost of the furnishings, deduct the first percentage and then deduct the second percentage from the result. For example, a "50/

10'' discount off of an item that is tagged at $100.00 retail would be: 50% off $100.00, which is $50.00, and then another 10% off of the $50.00, which is $45.00, the final wholesale cost to you.

A "50/50" discount off of an item that is tagged at $100.00 retail would be: 50% off of $100.00, which is $50.00, and then another 50% off of the $50.00, which is $25.00, the true cost of the furnishings. Note here that the retail price in this very typical hard window treatment example is FOUR TIMES what decorators and designers pay. And designers wonder why 40% of their customers have quit buying through them in the last few years!

Design Centers that Welcome Consumers

A few design centers now welcome retail consumers on certain days. These consumers do not receive the 40% to 50% trade discount that interior decorators and interior designers receive, but they do usually receive a discount of around 20% off retail.

Because the discounts given to the public at these centers are relatively low, I recommend that you visit the centers only to browse. The vast majority of the furnishings you will see are available at much bigger discounts from telephone ordering services and factory outlet stores -- 30% to 75% off retail as opposed to the design centers' puny 20% discount. Just look around and write down all of the product information when you find something you like.

I recommend that you record information for several acceptable choices instead of narrowing everything down to one final choice. The vast majority of the furnishings you see in the design center are available through other sources, but a few are not. These ultra-exclusive furnishings can only be purchased at the design center. You usually won't have any way of knowing which items are ultra-exclusive until you call a telephone ordering service or outlet.

If you find out upon calling telephone ordering services or outlets that the particular item you chose is ultra-exclusive (because you can't find any services or outlets that carry it), it will be much more convenient for you to have some alternate choices already picked out and written down. If you have a few alternatives, you won't be faced with making another trip to the design center (which might be a long way depending on where you live) to either settle for the 20% discount or make another choice that you can order at a better price.

Occasionally, these centers offer clearance sales. Most of the items sold are floor samples, but there is sometimes some new merchandise (usually discontinued styles) mixed in. Discounts during these sales are much better -- up to 75% off retail.

If you order directly from the design center, your sale will normally be arranged through a staff designer or through a special buying service established by the center. In most centers, the designer or buying service representative will escort you through the showrooms. You usually won't be allowed to look around freely. The up-side of having an escort is that the designer's advice during the tour is free in most centers. Use it.

A few centers charge a nominal fee to shop, or even to browse. Typically, this fee runs about $25.00. If you go to a center that has an entrance fee, ask that the fee be waived, or at least only charged if you actually make a purchase. Remember, this is a bad economy, and most of the design centers

Design Centers That Welcome Consumers

Boston Design Center
One Design Center Place
Boston, MA 02210
(617) 338-5062

Dallas Design District
("Design Experience")
Dallas, TX 75207
(214) 698-1350

Decorative Center of Houston
5120 Woodway
Houston, TX 77056
(713) 961-9292

Design Center South
23811 Aliso Creek Rd.
Laguna Niguel, CA 92656
(714) 643-2929

New York Design Center
200 Lexington Ave.
New York, NY 10016
(212) 679-9500

San Diego Design Center
6455 Lusk Blvd.
San Diego, CA 92121
(619) 452-7332

Showplace & Galleria Desn Ctrs
2 Henry Adams St.
San Francisco, CA 94103
(415) 864-1500
(800) 877-8522

Seattle Design Center
5701 6th Ave. S
Seattle, WA 98108
(800) 497-7997

Pacific Design Center
8687 Melrose Ave.
West Hollywood, CA 90069
(310) 657-0800

don't charge at all. Few design centers will want to lose a good sale over a $25.00 fee. You may not always succeed in getting the fee waived, but it's worth asking about.

As always, shipping costs are extra. You will usually have to wait several months to receive your purchases, depending upon the particular type of furnishings you are ordering. Except during floor sample sales, you will usually not be able to take your furnishings home the same day. If you do buy anything at a sample sale, don't forget to make arrangements to transport it home. You may need to arrange for a truck and someone to help you carry large items.

The conduct rules described earlier in this chapter apply here as well, even though you aren't shopping as a licensed decorator. It's still very important to not disrupt the normal business atmosphere. If consumers inadvertently create a significant problem with the normal flow of wholesale business at these centers, these new direct-to-the-public days might be cut out. Then, everyone would lose out on a good thing.

If you are thinking of purchasing more than about $500.00 worth of furnishings at one of these design centers, not including sample sales, STOP! You might be better off to hire a designer who works on an hourly fee or flat fee to buy the furnishings for you and pass along his or her entire 40% to 50% trade discount.

Assuming that the designer will charge you $100.00 (which is a terrific deal for the designer and for you) to process your purchases, $500.00 is the break-even point where you would be better off to pay a designer a flat fee instead of accepting only a 20% discount. This does not normally apply to sample sales because the discounts are much greater and are usually applied equally to designers and consumers.

If there isn't an accommodating design center in your area, don't despair. This phenomenon is highly likely to spread to other design centers in the very near future.

Many of these centers are only open to the public on certain days, although some do allow the public in every day. Because this is a relatively new phenomenon, schedules are changing too rapidly to print here. Call the design center directly to find out the hours or days when consumers are allowed in, and don't forget to ask about the next sample sale!

How To Get In Exclusive Wholesale Distributor Showrooms

Independent wholesale distributor showrooms are very much like mini-design centers. They may contain only one brand of furnishings or, more often, up to about ten brand names of varying types of furnishings. For instance, a showroom may feature two brands of fabric, three brands of trimmings, one brand of wallpaper, one brand of furniture, two brands of lamps, and one brand of artwork.

Most independent wholesale distributor showrooms cater primarily to interior decorators and interior designers. After checking in at the door, you will browse around and place orders just as you do at a design center. The hours are usually standard business hours, 9:00 to 5:00, Monday through Friday.

These showrooms normally tag samples at the retail price. You must then calculate your wholesale cost according to the discount you have been given by the showroom: 40% off retail, 50% off retail, or whatever. Sometimes these showrooms use keystone pricing (50% off retail). A few use the 5/10 system of pricing described on page 398.

The thousands of showrooms of this type are listed by location and cross-referenced by product type and brand name in the National Directory of Wholesale Home Furnishings Sources and Showrooms.

How To Get In Factory Showrooms

Factory showrooms only feature the brands of furnishings actually produced at the factory, usually only one brand. Many factories do not have showrooms specifically set aside. They work with interior decorators and interior designers in their offices, instead. This is how my parents' factory was set up for many years until we established a separate factory outlet.

Admission is very informal. Just show the copies of your license and resale number and your business card to the receptionist or secretary. You usually won't be given any kind of pass or badge as in other wholesale locations. Normal factory hours are 9:00 to 5:00, Monday through Friday.

Avoid going to a factory less than one hour before closing. The office staff will usually be rushing around attending to last minute details on the day's shipping. You would be in the way. Between 11:00 and 1:00, part of the staff may be out for lunch. The least intrusive times to go to most factories are between 10:00 and 11:00 in the morning and between 1:00 and 3:00 in the afternoon. Factory showrooms normally tag their samples at the wholesale price.

If the factory has no showroom and you must place your order in the office, actively avoid looking at papers on the secretary's desk, looking at packages, or taking any other inordinate amount of interest in anything else that is not related to your order. I know that the inside of a factory might be very interesting if you have never been in one before, but excessive interest can lead to resentment and misunderstandings. Resource information (which can be read off of packages), customer names (which can be read off of orders on the secretary's desk), and other information in the factory office is considered to be very private.

Occasionally, competitors are brazen enough to go in a factory's office and masquerade as customers while trying to find out all they can about the factory's private business. The manufacturing business can unfortunately be unscrupulously competitive at times. After all, a lot of money is at stake. You don't want to give the impression that you are there on behalf of a sleazy competitor.

If you are placing a custom order to be picked up at a later time, you will be expected to pay in full in advance, and you will always be given a receipt. If you purchasing an item that is in stock and you will be taking it with you right then, you may not be given a receipt. If not, don't ask for one. Factories don't keep retail receipt books because they usually have no need for them. Asking a secretary to type up a special factory invoice just for you would be considered rude and inconsiderate. Unless you are prepaying for an order that is to be custom made or picked up at a later date, you don't really need a receipt.

If the factory does not offer any customization of its products, such as changing the color of a ruffle or making something up in a special size, do not ask. It would be considered disrespectful and unprofessional. Factories have low prices because they use mass-production methods. They are not set up to process orders individually for you. Factories are not custom workrooms.

The most important thing to remember about factory showrooms is that small sales to interior decorators and interior designers make up a very, very small percentage of the factory's income. These tiny sales are not actively solicited by factories, but they are tolerated if they do not disrupt the normal course of business.

It is fine for you to approach a factory directly and ask to place a direct order, whether the factory has a showroom or not. You may be told that you must be a ''stocking dealer'', which means that you regularly purchase large quantities of the factory's products, or that you must spend a certain minimum dollar amount in order to buy directly from the factory. In that case, you will probably have to buy through a distributor of the factory's products which is accustomed to filling small orders. The factory can refer you to a distributor.

Some factories, like my parents', will allow you to make small purchases with no problem. Many factories are grateful for every little speck of business they can get during the current recession, although they would never admit this.

When dealing with any factory, it is very important not to be disruptive. If you can go in, place your order with little fuss, and leave, most factories won't mind dealing with you at all. However, if you have a thousand questions, insist on mulling over your decision forever, or in any other way disrupt the normal routine of the factory, you will probably be asked to leave. It makes no economic sense for the factory owners or supervisors to spend time with you on a $100.00 sale at the expense of not filling the $10,000.00 worth of sales that a factory may routinely fill in the same amount of time.

We had few problems with customers at my family's factory over the years. However, I do distinctly remember one retired couple who acted as though we had nothing else to do but bring out every single thing we made and help them choose two pillows from among them all. They gave the impression, perhaps unknowingly, that they were disrespectful of our time. Customers like that make factories leery of continuing to accommodate small orders.

If you are going to buy directly at the factory level, you must know exactly what you want and be prepared to place your order quickly and with little fuss and bother.

You may find that you are given more consideration during the slow periods of summer and winter, especially January and July. During these times, factories have a greater need for business and also have more time to spend working with you. If you approach a factory during the peak times of March through May and September through December, the factory might be too busy to deal with you.

Ask about seconds, discontinued items, and samples which may be available for sale. Some factories do not have outlets set up to dispose of these things and consider them a nuisance to get rid of. Amazingly, it is rare for consumers to ask factories about buying these things. You could get some beautiful, high-quality home furnishings for up to 75% off retail, sometimes even more.

How To Buy Directly From Manufacturers Without Traveling To the Showroom

It usually isn't necessary to travel to the factory showroom if you already know exactly what you want. Sometimes, the factory has only one showroom at the factory site itself, which could be on the other side of the country from you. More often, the factory will have showrooms in major cities, but this will still leave many of you several hours away from a showroom. If you already know the stock number of the item you wish to order and any other information such as the exact color or size, you may wish to place your order by mail.

If you wish to place an order with any factory by mail, here is what you should do. Call the factory and ask them if they "work with decorators". They may say "no". They may say that you must buy samples first (which is usually quite expensive) or place an initial "stocking order" which could amount to several thousand dollars of merchandise. If this is the case, you will have to settle for buying the factory's products through a distributor (middleman), or choose a similar product from a different manufacturer and try again. If you do wish to purchase the factory's products through a distributor, and pay an extra price markup to the distributor, you should ask the factory to refer you to one.

They may say "yes". Many factories do work with decorators, especially during the current recession. It is always worth your time to ask. This means that the factory will sell you one item at a time instead of requiring minimum purchase amounts or initial stocking orders. Factories that work with interior decorators usually do not require you to buy samples, either.

If the factory asks you if you would like to set up an account, say "no". "Setting up an account" means to apply for an open line of credit. This would require a careful examination of your credit and business income. You have no business income because you are not offering your services to the public. Even well-established interior decorators and interior designers who have been in business for years have great difficulty establishing open lines of credit. It is a lost cause and a waste of your time.

You should tell the factory that you are new in business (and know that you would never qualify anyway because you are so new) and that you need the merchandise as soon as possible. Open lines of credit typically take weeks to process. Many professional interior decorators would not want to delay their orders this long.

Without an open line of credit, the factory has two choices in getting payment from you: C.O.D. and "pro forma". C.O.D. means cash on delivery. You may already be familiar with this. The item will be sent to you, and you will have to pay the deliveryperson for it upon receipt. You will also have to pay a C.O.D. fee, usually $5.00 per package.

Many factories do not ship C.O.D. because of the extra paperwork and hassle involved, the fact that occasionally decorators and designers change their minds and refuse to accept the packages at some wasted expense to the manufacturer, and the unfortunate fact that some dishonest customers pay with bad checks (or worse, stop payment on their checks) after receiving the merchandise which often leaves the manufacturer with no practical recourse for getting their money or their merchandise back.

Most factories use "pro forma" billing instead of C.O.D. This means that the customer mails a check in advance for the merchandise and shipping fee, and the merchandise is shipped several weeks later. Custom-made merchandise, such as bedspreads or laminated fabric, is usually sold on a "pro forma" basis. Even when the item you want is in stock, the factory will normally wait two weeks to make sure that your check has cleared your bank before shipping your order.

Please don't take this personally. Many manufacturers have been burned repeatedly in their dealings with decorators and designers. Interior decorators and interior designers, as a group, have a bad reputation among manufacturers for defaulting on their bills. Also, manufacturers do not check credit reports on businesses that place very small orders because the expense of ordering the credit report makes it impractical. Even if you have excellent credit, the factory has no practical way of knowing that.

Don't worry about being ripped off by the factory by paying in advance. It is extremely rare for a factory to default on a pro forma payment, far more rare than defaults by retail stores. Professional interior decorators and interior designers place pro forma orders with factories all the time, and very rarely have any problems. This is the established system.

After you tell the factory what you want to order, they will either tell you the amount to mail over the phone, or they may send you a pro forma invoice with all charges listed. The factory will probably ask you to send photocopies of your resale number certificate and business license with your payment. Some factories will also want you to sign a blanket certificate of resale as discussed in the section about resale numbers early in this chapter.

Always send a written copy of your order when you mail your check, the photocopies of your credentials, and your blanket certificate. Clearly specify all colors, stock numbers, and other details.

That's it. Ordering from factories is very simple. Please refer to the information given early in this chapter for guidelines about shipping, taking care of mistakes in your order, etc.

Problems with these types of orders are very rare. However, if you should ever have a problem, please read Chapter 20 for instructions on dealing with incorrect or shoddy merchandise.

How To Attend Wholesale Trade Shows

Wholesale trade shows are where people and businesses in the industry meet to see, buy, and show all of the latest products. They are held at varying times throughout the year, and often at varying locations. The *National Home Furnishings Trade Show Newsletter* provides up-to-date information on a monthly basis about home furnishings trade shows all over the United States and Canada. An order form for the newsletter can be found in the back of this book.

Trade shows concentrate on a variety of subjects. Some cover all types of home furnishings, such as the International Home Furnishings Market at High Point, NC. Some concentrate only on certain segments of the home furnishings industry, such as the World of Window Coverings Trade Show (commonly called the "windows and walls show") and the Fabric Fair shows at the Michigan Design Center.

Many types of products are available at trade shows: fabrics, furniture, wallpapers, decorative tiles, lamps, lighting, mirrors, artwork, sculpture, ceramics, rugs, trimmings, leather, antiques, aquariums, kitchen and bath fixtures, quilts, fireplace mantels, bedspreads, pillows, cushions, window treatments, and even jewelry (we'll talk more about that later).

A few trade shows charge an entrance fee, although the vast majority do not. When charged, the fee is rarely higher than $25.00 or $30.00 per person. You may register when you arrive at the show. There will be a row of tables set up in the lobby of the convention center or other building where you will show the photocopies of your license and resale number and your business card.

Although most trade shows welcome interior designers and interior decorators and have no problem filling small orders, a few shows are tightening their entry requirements. A few trade shows have recently begun requiring interior designers and interior decorators who work from their homes to bring copies of invoices which show that substantial wholesale home furnishings purchases (usually about $2000.00) have been made during the previous year. These few trade shows often cater to stores and store chains more than they do to interior decorators and interior designers.

Most trade shows do cater mainly to interior decorators and interior designers, and are geared to their needs. These shows do not have a minimum purchase requirement.

You may be able to get past this requirement by telling the registration worker that you are new in business and have, therefore, not had enough time to purchase such a large amount of merchandise. After all, you ARE new and the date on your license and resale number certificates will verify this.

If you are refurnishing a large portion of your home, you may already have spent $2000.00 on furniture and other furnishings, in which case there is no problem. Just bring copies of the invoices or receipts for the merchandise you purchased.

Also, even though these requirements are usually announced in advance in order to scare off licensed consumers, they are not always enforced at the door. Many trade shows hire temporary workers to help with show registration. Some of these workers really don't care who does or doesn't get in as long as they get their paychecks. These workers may wave you on through.

However, if you should arrive at a trade show that has a minimum purchase requirement and strictly enforces it, you will just have to choose another show to attend. Remember, most trade shows do not have such stringent requirements.

You will usually be permitted to bring a guest or co-worker (meaning anyone who is helping you decorate your home). Guests are common at these events. Many exhibitors and some buyers bring their spouses. A few exhibitors bring their children, although buyers and guests are not allowed to bring theirs.

Many trade shows feature free talks on a variety of design topics which you may attend. Many trade shows offer classes (usually for an added fee) on a wide variety of business and design topics. You must normally register for these classes at least several weeks in advance of the show. As soon as you hear about a show that you wish to attend, contact the show's organizer to inquire about any classes that may be offered.

Although some classes concentrate on business subjects, such as keeping tax records and soliciting customers, which would be of no interest to you, many classes cover more practical topics, such as making and installing window treatments and decorative painting techniques. Classes on such specialized home furnishings topics are often not available anywhere else. You can get unique training in making and designing home furnishings that is available nowhere else.

The best bargains are often found in the temporary spaces at some trade shows. Some trade shows, such as those in High Point and Dallas, have many permanent showrooms that stay in place all year round. These markets normally also have a temporary space section which is essentially a big room filled up with small merchants at 10' X 10' booths. These temporary spaces are rented only during show days. Many trade shows are made up entirely of temporary spaces.

Manufacturers who exhibit their products on a temporary basis are usually smaller, and often newer in business, than the manufacturers who have permanent showrooms. These small manufacturers often have lower prices on their products and are more eager to please customers with small purchases (such as interior decorators) because they are trying build their customer bases. They often have the most unique products at the show.

You will also find good buys in the permanent spaces. Most of the permanent spaces welcome interior decorators, although a very few do not. A few spaces, mostly furniture showrooms, cater mostly to large furniture store chains and do not wish to fill small orders for interior decorators and interior designers.

Some spaces and showrooms require minimum purchases. This means that you must purchase at least a certain dollar amount of furnishings, usually $200.00 to $500.00 where minimums apply. This isn't too awful. These spaces usually sell furniture, lighting, artwork, or other large items that can easily total several hundred dollars. You shouldn't find this to be much of a problem.

Many of the spaces and showrooms that require minimum purchases carry several different types of merchandise, all of which usually go toward completing your minimum purchase requirement. For instance, many furniture showrooms also carry several brands of lighting, artwork, and accessories. It doesn't really take any extra space to show a lamp sitting on an end table or a picture hanging behind a sofa, and the manufacturers of these other furnishings pay the furniture manufacturer a commission in return for being allowed to show their merchandise in the space. This allows the furniture manufacturer to greatly offset the high cost of renting the space without detracting from its own products in any way or sacrificing any of its expensive showroom space.

What this all means to you is that, in our hypothetical furniture showroom, you would normally be allowed to buy a lamp, a chair, and a picture, and have them all count toward your minimum purchase requirement. This mixing of different types of furnishings in many showrooms makes it much easier for buyers to meet minimum purchasing requirements, where they do exist.

Most spaces and showrooms require no minimum purchases, especially during the current recession. These spaces often display a sign which says

"Designers Welcome". Decorators are welcome in these spaces, too. If there is no sign, the proper way to find out if a space requires a minimum purchase is to ask either "Do you work with decorators?" or "What are your minimums?". Remember, the proper phrasing of these questions is important. You want to sound like you know your way around trade shows.

You may browse all you like. Most trade shows are held over the weekend, so you may find them more convenient to visit than the design centers.

You will make your payment arrangements directly with each showroom, just as in the design centers. You will nearly always pay in full in advance for your order and have the furnishings shipped to you several weeks later. The usual discount is 50% off of retail.

Merchandise at these shows is normally tagged with the wholesale price. You don't normally deduct any discounts from the prices printed on the sample tags because these deductions have usually already been made. Wholesale prices are openly stated in these spaces and showrooms because interior decorators and interior designers are usually not allowed to bring retail clients in with them.

Most floor samples are available for sale, even in showrooms that normally require minimum purchases. It costs money to pack and ship samples back to the factory after the show ends, and often it just isn't worth the expense for the smaller and less expensive items. You can get some terrific deals on these samples. If you see something you would like to buy, ask about it as early in the show as possible. If the showroom owner is willing to sell it, you will be expected to pay for it in advance. You will not be allowed to take the item with you until the end of the last day of the show.

The showroom will need to keep the item throughout the entire show to take orders from, and the market center will not allow anyone to take items out of the building until the trade show ends (whether it's been paid for or not) as a way of reducing theft.

You are at little risk by paying in advance. This procedure has been in place for many years. I have never heard of anyone having a problem. If you choose not to pay in advance, and wait until the end of the show to approach the showroom owner, you will find that most items have already been sold.

Food and drinks are nearly always served in the lobby at these trade shows, although they can be fairly expensive. At many trade shows, you will find that many showrooms serve food and drinks at no charge to buyers. They often serve a fair amount of alcohol, too. These events are also business conventions, and serve as a sort of working vacation for some buyers and exhibitors. You may wish to bypass the lobby and just graze your way through the showrooms while you shop.

Also, there are usually several catered parties at the major trade shows, such as those at the permanent market centers in Atlanta, Dallas, High Point, Chicago, and San Francisco. Usually, all buyers are welcome to attend. The entertainment is usually pretty good at these parties, too.

If a manufacturer has a celebrity spokesperson, he or she will often attend these major trade shows. Vanna White recently attended the Atlanta Home Furnishings Market as the spokesperson for a mattress company.

So, go and have fun. Save a lot of money. Learn something about interior design or making your own furnishings. Find out how the home furnishings industry really works from the inside. Trade shows are a unique experience.

You Can Buy Wholesale Jewelry At a Home Furnishings Show?

Incredible jewelry bargains are one of the best perks of attending these trade shows. I found an accommodating gemstone wholesaler in the temporary spaces at a trade show in Atlanta several years ago. He was willing to sell even one stone to anyone who asked.

I bought three matching pairs of gemstones and had earring posts added at a local jewelry store, for a small fraction of what I would have paid if I had purchased comparable earrings at a retail jewelry store.

Most of the major trade shows at the permanent market centers in Atlanta, Dallas, San Francisco, and Chicago are attended by jewelry wholesalers who will sell single pieces of jewelry to show attendees. These jewelry wholesalers normally sell to jewelry stores, but they know that they can do a lot of business at home furnishings shows, too. They keep their permanent showrooms at the market centers open year round, no matter what kind of trade show is going on. Sometimes, you can also find jewelry wholesalers in the temporary spaces, as I once did.

Every woman I know who works in the industry and attends these shows buys all of her jewelry wholesale. I have never had to pay retail for jewelry in my life. That's one of the perks of being an interior decorator that you may not have expected.

Part V

What To Do When Things Go Wrong

Chapter 20

Troubleshooting

This is the gloom and doom chapter: wrong orders, fly-by-night con artists, shoddy workmanship, everything that can possibly go seriously wrong with your order.

I think a little perspective is in order before you read all of this. Most consumers never run into any of the problems listed in this chapter when they buy home furnishings. Most home furnishings businesses are honest, competent, and reputable. However, a few of you are bound to have a serious problem with your order, and the purpose of this chapter is to help you cope with these problems, should you ever experience any.

If you're reading this chapter before you go shopping, great. Prevention is the best defense against getting ripped off. If you follow the guidelines given in this book, I am confident that you can avoid the vast majority of the scams and rip-offs that exist in the home furnishings industry.

If you're reading this chapter because something has gone wrong with your order, I'm sorry. Unfortunately, this does occasionally happen. Sometimes, all the caution and preparation in the world won't prevent you from being taken advantage of.

Don't give up yet. There are a lot of insider tips that can help you resolve problems with home furnishings businesses. I've had a good bit of experience collecting bad debts from interior decorators, interior designers, and retail stores that defaulted on payments due to my parents' factory. There are some strategies I have learned over the years that might help you get your money back. They have often worked for me.

You Can't Afford To Be "Nice"

While working at our outlet store, I spoke with some retail customers who had been ripped off by home furnishings businesses, and businesses in other fields. Most of them were very nice, pleasant people who did not like confrontations and attempted to work out problems with businesses in a conciliatory and non-confrontational way. Every time, this "nice" attitude

The Clock Is Slower Than You Might Think

Even if you have been ripped off several years ago, it may not be too late for you to get your money back. Some of the advice in this chapter can be pursued for any length of time after the actual transaction. Courts in most areas will permit you to sue up to two to four years after you have been defrauded (other areas may have even longer statutes of limitations).

Don't just assume that it is too late. Call your local small claims court and ask about the statute of limitations on civil cases in your area. If they won't tell you (some employees of the court refuse to discuss legal matters of any kind), you should be able to look up this information at your local library. Ask the reference librarian.

backfired on these customers.

Over the years, I have pursued hundreds of retail stores and interior designers who defaulted on paying their bills for merchandise that my family's factory shipped to them on credit. Businesses that rip off their customers usually rip off their suppliers, too. I have dealt with more dishonest businesses, failed businesses, and professional con-artists in the home furnishings industry than all of the readers of this book combined are ever likely to meet. I got our money back from many of them. I know how to deal with these people.

You will always begin pursuing a refund or the correction of any problems with furnishings you have purchased in a very professional and respectful way, but if you don't get any results, you must promptly step up your efforts. It's fine to give them a second chance to get your order right, but it's a very bad idea to keep giving them third chances, and fourth chances, and so on.

The most effective con artists use your own sympathy and trust to cheat you. Crooks usually never look or sound like crooks. They are usually very nice and very pleasant and try to trick you into trusting them. Over the years, I have listened to many well-rehearsed sob stories that turned out not to be true.

Most of the people who will ask you to "work with them" and give them more time to complete their obligations to you or refund your money will be stalling you until they can close up and get out of town, taking your money with them. Most of the people who will tell you sob stories to delay refunding your money will be lying.

Yes, there are businesses that are honest and cannot complete your order or refund your money because they have truly been overwhelmed by circumstances out of their control, such as illness. In reality, these situations are very, very rare.

My family has been cheated this way dozens of times over the years. Almost every time we tried to work with a delinquent business that claimed to be the victim of some type of disaster or extreme hardship we ended up regretting it. Don't let it happen to you. Don't learn the hard way, like we did.

You may feel like a heel insisting on a refund from a store owner who insists that he was just robbed last week or that half of his employees are out sick and that he can deliver your order (or fix it) if you will just work with him and give him a little more time. If you have to tell him that you will take him to court if he doesn't refund your money immediately, you are probably going to feel like the scum of the earth.

In most cases, that's exactly how the store owner wants you to feel. The most skillful con artists know exactly how to manipulate your emotions and play on your sympathies.

Over the years, our factory lost more money to people who stalled us with these phony excuses than we did to any other type of scam.

If you have hundreds or thousands of dollars at stake, as some consumers do every year, you can't afford to learn the hard way. You must be firm, you must act quickly, and you must sometimes be very harsh and very unforgiving. The bottom line is, it works.

Go To the Top

If a salesperson won't give you your money back or correct any problems with your purchase, go immediately to the owner of the business. Sometimes, the salesperson you are dealing with is paid a low salary and couldn't care less about preserving the store's good reputation.

If the store owner is honest, you can be sure that he or she will be very interested in resolving your complaint. It is possible that the owner may never know about your problem unless you tell him or her personally. Salespeople rarely run to tell their bosses when they have offended a customer.

Most of the home furnishings businesses you will be dealing with, however, are quite small. The salesperson probably is the owner, or a member of the owner's family. The only large companies you may deal with are wholesale suppliers, which pose little risk to you.

Make Sure the Business Has Something To Gain By Helping You

When you initially confront a business owner about a problem you are having with the business, be as pleasant and professional as possible. Don't give the impression that you are already so offended that you will never shop at the business again and that you will do your best to see that your family and friends don't shop there either.

You must make the business owner believe that you still have goodwill toward the business that can be salvaged. If you make it clear that you can never be appeased no matter what the business does, the business has much less incentive to even try to make you happy. You will have given away a very useful bargaining chip.

Even if a business isn't particularly honest, letting the owner believe that you may patronize the business again in the future if everything is cleared up to your satisfaction will give the business owner a financial incentive to please you. It helps. Sometimes, this approach is all you need in order to get the problem straightened out.

Unfortunately, some businesses don't need your business badly enough or are too dishonest for this approach to work. Also, this approach won't help if a business is about to go out of business. These businesses don't care about future sales because they won't be there anyway. If this appears to be the case, proceed quickly to stronger measures. You won't have any time to waste.

Always Keep a Written Record Of Your Efforts To Resolve the Problem

You must keep a written record of the complaint process in case your complaint ever goes to court. Also, many government consumer protection agencies require that you first make an attempt to resolve your complaint in writing with the offending business before they will consider your complaint.

If you speak with the business owner by phone or in person, follow up by writing a letter that restates what was said -- ''Per our conversation in your store/on the phone on January 1st, 1995, I accept your offer to resolve my complaint by (taking some type of corrective action or making a refund) prior to (a specific date)''. Usually, in each conversation the business will promise to resolve your complaint.

Many times the business will follow through on its promises, but occasionally it won't. If the business doesn't do what it promised, by the date it was promised, the paper trail you have established will confirm the pattern of neglect and promises broken by the business.

Better yet, communicate by letter in the first place. Many people are more calm and collected when writing a letter than they are when they are speaking directly with the owner of the offending business. If you communicate in writing, there will be less chance of saying something you don't mean or being distracted from the real subject of your complaint.

Send your first letter by regular mail. However, if the business breaks its first promise to you and you have to send a second letter requesting an explanation, send the second letter and all subsequent letters by certified mail, return receipt requested. If the situation has gotten this bad with the business, you are probably on your way to court. You will need these return receipts to prove in court that you did contact the business about your complaint.

Just the fact that you are using certified mail will show the business that you know how to properly prepare to go to court and that you are seriously thinking of taking this step. This alone can convince some business owners to take your complaint more seriously.

If you ever have to go to court, this paper trail will establish that you made various attempts to resolve the problem in a reasonable and professional way before going to court. This will help prove your case that the business has deliberately neglected or ignored its obligations to you, instead of making an innocent mistake. This can only help you.

If you arrive at court and you can only tell the judge about the business' broken promises, you are likely to find that the business owner has conveniently forgotten them and says that he or she had no idea that you were having a problem in the first place.

If you have no written evidence to disprove the business' claim that it doesn't know about your problem, the judge may believe that you have not given the business an appropriate chance to resolve the problem without wasting the court's time. This can only hurt you.

In a few cases, if the business' behavior is truly outrageous, you may be entitled to additional damages. A written record of your communication with the business could be very important in proving such damages.

Needless to say, always be very professional when writing these letters. Write all complaint letters with the assumption that they will someday be read by a judge.

What To Do If You Do Get A Refund

If you do get a refund check, that's wonderful. However, if the business was reluctant to pay you or seems to be in financial trouble, there is an extra measure you should take to protect yourself.

When you get the check, immediately drive to the business' bank and exchange its check for a cashier's check that cannot bounce. It will cost you about $5.00 in bank fees, but it is well worth it. Once you have that cashier's check, it can't bounce or have its payment stopped. You will know absolutely for certain that you finally have your money. Or, if the amount isn't too large, just cash the check.

Several years ago, I finally collected a $5,000.00 check from a long overdue customer after much haranguing and hassle. I thought we were never going to be paid by this woman's business. However, when I picked up the check, the store seemed suspiciously low in inventory, with some shelves completely bare.

I was so mistrustful of this woman after all I had gone through with her that I decided on the spur of the moment to go to her bank and exchange her check for a cashier's check. Sure enough, two days later her business was packed up and gone. If I had simply deposited her check into our business account, it might not have cleared her bank in time.

Ever since that incident, if I have any doubt about a business' honesty or financial condition, I exchange the refund check for a cashier's check. Don't ask the business to pay you with a cashier's check or in cash. They may refuse, as it will put them to some trouble, and you might lose the payment they would otherwise have given you.

You will have pretty much the same assurance about your money if you accept a standard business check and then immediately go the business' bank and exchange their check for a cashier's check or cash the check.

What To Do If Your Refund Check Bounces

Sometimes, if a business is in severe financial trouble, your refund check may bounce. Or, if you go to the bank to exchange the business' check for a cashier's check or to cash the business' check, you may be told that the business does not have sufficient funds.

You could go to court over the bad check, but that might take too long. By the time your court date arrives, the business may be nothing but a faint memory. There is a better way to get your money.

"Birddog" the business' checking account. Call the business' bank and ask to "verify" a check written on the bank. Tell the bank the amount of your check, and the bank will tell you if the business has sufficient funds to cover the check. You don't need any special authorization to do this -- this is not considered to be private information.

Nearly all banks offer check verification services. Businesses use these services all the time when customers want to pay for expensive items with personal checks. Sometimes, these services are automated.

Banks generally do not notify the account holder when someone calls to verify a check drawn on the account. It is highly unlikely that the business will be aware that you are watching its checking account.

Call to verify the check every day until the money to cover your check is finally there. Then, go IMMEDIATELY to the bank and exchange the check for a cashier's check or cash the check.

You have a pretty good chance of getting your money, even from the most destitute or dishonest business. Even if the business' checking account has been empty all month, there is a good chance that funds will be deposited during the last few days of the month to cover rent and utility bills. So, if you find after checking several times that the business never seems to have ANY money, don't give up until you have checked again right around the end of the month.

Be very careful when you present a check that has already bounced once. You will only get one more chance. If the check bounces twice, the check will be stamped with a notation not to allow it to be presented again, even if funds do become available to pay it. Then, you will have no choice but to go to court, which may take too long for you to ever have any chance of getting your money. Always make sure that the money is actually in the bank before presenting a bad check to the bank a second time.

Con Artists Are Rare In Wholesale Settings

Severe consumer problems are usually the result of falling victim to a con artist, and wholesale con artists are rare. As a group, wholesale businesses tend to be honest. They have to be. Their customers are all businesspeople who are familiar with consumer laws, government regulations, standard business practices, and their legal rights.

Also, once a wholesale business gets a bad reputation in the wholesale industry, it is difficult for them to ever reopen again. Word travels fast.

However, if a retail business cheats hundreds of customers and skips town, as happens on a daily basis, there is always another town where no one knows or suspects anything. The crooks can go right in and start up the very same scam all over again.

Crooks tend to go into retail business because there are many more potential customers to victimize and because retail customers tend to be less informed about business matters. Retail customers are much easier targets than wholesale customers.

Con artists also tend to be lazy. They just want a fast buck. They generally don't build furniture, sew, or install wallpaper. That kind of work is too hard for them.

The most prevalent scam in the home furnishings industry, by far, is the retail store that opens, takes customer deposits and gets as much merchandise as possible on credit from manufacturers, and then quickly closes and skips town. I regret to say that my family has run into quite a few of these over the years.

Of all the home furnishings businesses that you may come into contact with, the ones who are the most likely to be con artists are retail stores (usually relatively small ones), followed closely by interior designers and interior decorators. You will have little to fear from wholesale showrooms, design centers, trade centers, factories, workrooms, craftspeople, and installers.

Credit Card Transactions

Federal law gives you very good protection when you shop with your credit card. Always use your credit card when you buy anything from a telephone ordering service, retail store, interior designer, or any other retail business. Businesses are checked out thoroughly by the bank that processes their credit card transactions, so you can be assured that most businesses that do accept credit cards are honest and solvent.

Wholesale businesses -- such as custom workrooms, local craftspeople, design centers, independent showrooms, trade centers, and factories -- generally do not accept credit cards. It is somewhat expensive for businesses to process credit card transactions, so businesses generally do not offer this service unless most customers demand it. Wholesale customers do not expect to be able to pay with their credit cards, so wholesale businesses don't accept them.

This is simply a trade-off that you will have to make in return for receiving a much lower price when you shop wholesale. Fortunately, you have much less need for the protections offered by credit card issuers when you shop wholesale because there is far less fraud from wholesale businesses than there is from retail businesses, as explained in the previous section.

Federal laws set out general guidelines to protect consumers and leave it to the individual credit card issuers to fill in some of the details. Consequently, dispute and refund procedures vary according to who issued your credit card. Before making any major purchase (such as furniture) with your credit card, contact your credit card issuer to receive a current written copy of its policies on complaints and disputes. Know your rights BEFORE you spend any money.

In general, you are allowed to dispute the charge for any merchandise that is not what you ordered, never arrives, or is shoddily made if you purchased it over the phone, by mail, or within 100 miles of your home if you made the purchase in person. The general guidelines for disputes and refunds are as follows:

You should first contact the seller once by certified mail (return receipt requested), specifically state exactly what the problem is (you received a red pillow instead of the blue pillow you ordered, your furniture has a large scratch, your order didn't arrive when it was supposed to, etc.), tell the seller exactly what you want it to do to correct the problem (arrange for a free pickup of the red pillow and send you a blue pillow at no charge, arrange to replace the scratched furniture at no cost to you, ship your order immediately, etc.), and state that you will file a dispute with your credit card issuer if the problem isn't corrected within a reasonable length of time (usually about four weeks).

Many credit card issuers require that you first attempt to solve the problem directly with the seller before you file a dispute. The return receipt you requested when you mailed your letter will provide proof that you contacted the seller, if proof is required by your credit card issuer.

Often, this is all you will have to do. Honest mistakes are made by all businesses. Many times, the business will correct the problem immediately as soon as it is notified that the problem exists.

However, if the problem hasn't been corrected within four weeks, you should immediately file the dispute with your credit card issuer. Many credit card issuers put a time limit on your right to dispute a charge, usually anywhere from sixty days to six months.

Make sure you understand your credit card issuer's time limits before you make any large purchase with a credit card, especially if you are dealing with a company (such as a telephone furniture ordering service) that quotes you a delivery time of several months. You want to make sure that your time limit to file a dispute doesn't run out before your order is even due to arrive.

Also, make sure that you thoroughly understand your card issuer's policies regarding credit card deposits on orders to be shipped or delivered at a later time.

When you file your dispute, make sure that you carefully read the card issuer's guidelines (which you sent away for earlier). Make sure you include all required paperwork. Whether or not the guidelines ask for it, send a copy of your letter to the seller and a copy of the return receipt that shows when and by whom it was received at the seller's place of business. Sometimes, your complaint can be handled faster if the credit card issuer has a specific person's name at the seller's office to contact.

In the vast majority of cases, this is all that is required. Credit card issuers have an excellent record of resolving these problems. In most cases, you will not have to make any payments toward the amount of the disputed transaction while the problem is being investigated. Also, since credit card issuers often have the power to withhold payment to the seller for the merchandise until the problem is corrected, it is highly likely that the defective, incorrect, or missing shipment will be corrected immediately.

If your order is wrong (or never arrives) and the business refuses to correct the situation after you properly notify it that there is a problem, you are virtually assured of getting the problem corrected if you properly pursue your rights under the law and according to your card issuer's policies. If the business should close without shipping your order or be unable to ship your order, you should receive a refund with no problem, as long as you properly comply with the law and your credit card issuer's policies. Be aware, however, that these protections do NOT apply to debit cards, even those debit cards which bear Mastercard or VISA symbols.

Debit cards are cards issued by your bank, which charge purchases directly to your checking account instead of giving you a line of credit which you may pay off monthly. They often look like credit cards, but they aren't. If you pay by debit card, federal law considers it to be a cash transaction and offers you no protection.

Never mail a check or money order (and certainly not cash) to any retail company that is not from your local area. If a telephone order company tells you that it cannot accept credit cards, you should assume the worst, that the company may not be legitimate or financially solvent, and you should not deal with them.

There certainly are many honest and solvent companies that don't accept credit cards for mail or phone orders, but it is unnecessary for you to take any chances. There are so many companies that do accept credit cards, and they have great bargains. Why take the risk? Stick with companies that accept credit cards -- it's the safest way to shop.

It doesn't matter if the business is solvent or not when you seek a refund. Your refund money comes from the business' bank, not the business itself. Even if the business is closed up and doesn't have a red cent, or if it has already taken all of its money (and your money) to the Bahamas, it doesn't matter. You will still get your money if you qualify for a refund under the card issuers guidelines.

Always Get It In Writing!

You must get every detail of any special order or custom made home furnishings purchase in writing. If you don't, and your order is not what you expected, you will probably have no legal recourse.

When placing the custom orders or special orders, these are the details you must have in writing:

Date the item will be delivered: Insist on a firm (and reasonable) delivery date, not an "expected" delivery date.

The business' complete name and address: Some businesses use standard contracts for special orders that do not have the business' name pre-printed on them. It's all right for the business to write this information in, just make sure that it is not left blank.

Where the item will be delivered: Does the price include installing or setting up the item in your home or are you expected to pick it up at the business and install it yourself?

Final total price: Some dishonest businesses will fill in extra charges for "delivery" or "installation" after you leave.

Exact measurements or sizes of the item to be made

Supplier names and item names or numbers of any materials to be ordered: "Waverly Fabrics pattern #0000", not "rose colored chintz" -- for instance. This will help prevent dishonest businesses from substituting cheaper or substandard materials behind your back.

Small swatches of all materials to be ordered: Always get small swatches of fabric, wallpaper, trimming, and other materials that are to be ordered so that you can make sure that cheaper substitutions are not made without your knowledge.

A sketch or picture of the item to be made

A statement that you may cancel the order if it is incorrect or not delivered on time: This will help prevent you from having to endure endless delays and remakes, and also gives you an opportunity to negotiate an extra discount if the item is delivered late or made incorrectly.

Always make sure that you have a copy of the contract containing all of these details before you sign anything or pay any money.

Avoid Misunderstandings

Sometimes, customers don't understand their legal rights or do not inquire about a company's policies until long after the transaction has been made, when it is too late. You must have a clear agreement with the company before you special-order merchandise or have furnishings custom-made. You must also be careful when you are contracting for services, such as wallpaper installation or interior design.

Follow the guidelines given throughout this book carefully when negotiating any agreements or contracts. This should prevent any misunderstandings.

There are two topics on which misunderstandings are widespread: returns and cancellations. Often, in these situations, customers mistakenly believe that they are in the right because they don't understand standard industry procedures regarding custom home furnishings.

You need to realize before you place your custom order that returns and cancellations are virtually never allowed on custom-made or special-order home furnishings, so that you can make your buying decisions accordingly. Wholesale businesses generally do not accept returns or cancellations at all, whether the furnishings are custom-made or not.

1 RETURNS: Many consumers believe, based on widespread experience making returns in retail stores, that they have an inalienable legal right to return anything, purchased anywhere, any time, for any reason. This is not at all true, and this misunderstanding can cause severe problems with custom-made or special-order furnishings.

Although most retail stores do routinely accept returns of in-stock, non-custom-made, merchandise as a convenience to their customers, businesses are not required to allow returns of non-defective custom-made or special-order merchandise. In virtually every case, you will be required to sign a special-order or custom-order contract that states that the item is unreturnable. Read this contract very carefully.

When you order custom-made furnishings, such as custom draperies or upholstery, you are making a commitment to the business that you will pay for the merchandise as long as it is made to a reasonable standard of quality and according to the specifications written in your contract. When the business properly fulfills your custom order, it has a legal right to be paid for its work, according to the contract it made with you and according to general business laws. The business has invested its own money and effort filling your order, and it deserves to be paid as agreed.

However, if the order was made IMPROPERLY (wrong measurements, wrong color, demonstrably shoddy workmanship, etc.), the business must correct the problem. If you have a clause written in your contract (as recommended in this book) which allows you to cancel your order if it is not correctly filled by the specified delivery date, then you could cancel your late or incorrectly made custom-made furnishings.

However, in the absence of such a statement in your contract, the business is usually at liberty to fulfill the contract any way it sees fit. The business would most likely force you to wait while it fixes your order instead of canceling your order and giving you your money back, and they would probably be within their legal rights to do so. This is why it is so important to be careful when you are signing contracts.

Special orders work the same way. When a business special-orders materials or furnishings for you (fabric, wallpaper, furniture, lamps, etc.), they are under no obligation to accept returns, unless the furnishings are defective or not the correct items as specified in your contract.

2 CANCELLATIONS: Custom-orders and special-orders are normally non-cancellable once work on them has begun. It is standard procedure to have a clause in these contracts stating this.

This is a fair arrangement because, again, the business is investing its effort and money in accordance with its agreement with you and it deserves to be paid. The business can't return the special-order furnishings or materials to the factory or undo the work it has already done just because you changed your mind.

You should always make sure that your contract states that you can cancel the order if it is not delivered on time. This is also fair and reasonable. You should not have to be held hostage for weeks or months without your furnishings or your money.

Consider what you want VERY carefully before placing any custom or special orders or purchasing anything from a wholesale business.

What To Do If Your Order Is Wrong

The best way to take care of this problem is to catch it right away. Keep in mind also that most incorrect orders are the result of honest mistakes. Usually, the business will clear up the problem right away if you just let them know about the problem.

If your order has been shipped to you by a retail business and you paid by credit card (always), simply follow the instructions given earlier in this chapter regarding credit card transactions. The problem should be cleared up right away.

If your order has been shipped to you by a wholesale business and you prepaid by check (which will virtually always be the case), contact the manufacturer or wholesale dealer right away. You should have no difficulty in getting the mistake cleared up. The standard procedure is for the wholesale business to arrange to pick up the incorrect order at no cost to you and send a replacement out as quickly as possible, as explained in the box at right.

If you are picking up your order in person, such as from a local custom workroom, carefully examine the furnishings before you pay for them. Check them over carefully to make sure that they match the specifications on your order contract. Bring a steel tape measure and check all measurements. Take your time. If the order is incorrect in any way, do not pay the balance due. Tell the business that you will pay for your order when the problem has been corrected.

This is a very rare problem. If you have clearly specified all of the details of your order as explained in this book, you shouldn't have any problems with incorrect orders.

"Call Tags"

Often, a wholesale business will tell you that it will "issue a call tag" for an incorrect order.

That is code for "we will arrange to have the shipper (usually UPS) pick up the incorrect order from your home or office and send the freight bill to us". Remember, if your are going to be your own decorator and shop wholesale, you need to know the local language.

So, if are contacting a wholesale company about a problem with your order, ask them to "issue a call tag". That is how a professional interior decorator or interior designer would normally phrase this request.

What To Do When Your Order Is Suspiciously Delayed (and Delayed, and Delayed)

You should hear warning bells ringing. One delay in delivering your custom-made or special-order furnishings is no cause for alarm -- this happens all the time for a variety of perfectly legitimate reasons. However, if your order is delayed again, for any reason, you should be suspicious.

Late deliveries are fairly rare for a legitimate, honest, financially solvent business. Good service is very important. So is good word-of-mouth advertising, especially in the home furnishings industry. Most businesses will want to avoid inconveniencing you with repeated delays at all costs.

One unavoidable delay could certainly occur with any business. But two in a row with the same customer on the same order? No way.

A few businesses, usually those that are about to go out of business, misapply their customers' deposits. Normally, when you give a business an up-front deposit on custom-made or special-order furnishings, the business will immediately use your deposit money to order materials (fabrics, trimmings, etc.) to make your furnishings or make an advance payment to the factory that will be shipping your special-order merchandise, such as fabric or wallpaper. That is what the business is supposed to do.

However, if a business is in a temporary financial bind, it may use your deposit money to pay the rent or its employees' salaries, instead. Often, the business has no deliberate intent to cheat you. It honestly believes that once the crisis is over, business will improve and it will make enough money to properly place your order. Unfortunately, if a business is so destitute that it will misuse its customers' money in this way, the temporary bind often becomes permanent.

Then, when your scheduled delivery day arrives, your order hasn't even been placed with the manufacturer. The business may panic and make all kinds of crazy excuses to stall you until it can come up with the money to place your order. It probably never will. Businesses that pull this scam are often well on the way to going out of business.

You might also be dealing with a con artist. Some con artists come into town, open up a shop, take as many customer deposits as possible, and then close and skip town without delivering anything. When the business calls you with the second, or third, or fourth excuse, they may already be packing.

Every year, customers of all types of stores lose millions of dollars in deposit money to these thieves. Suppliers lose a lot of money, too. Usually, however, I recommend that you only purchase custom-made or special-order merchandise from wholesale showrooms, discounters, local wholesale workrooms and craftspeople, and those telephone ordering services that will allow you to pay for your entire order with a credit card. It is very rare for a con artist to run these types of businesses.

If you paid your deposit by credit card, you shouldn't have any problem getting your deposit money back. Just contact your credit card issuer and ask about their procedures for filing a claim.

If you didn't pay by credit card, your chances of getting your deposit money back aren't very good, and they will only get worse. Those customers that demand their refunds first are most likely to get them.

Time is critical. If you paid your deposit by cash or check, you must get your money back before the business either leaves town or folds. When the business calls you to announce the second delay, you should immediately take your contract down to the business and demand a refund.

This is one reason why it is so important to insist that any contract you sign has a clause stating that you may cancel the order if it is not correctly delivered on or before a specified due date. Without this clause, the business is not legally obligated to refund your money. It could force you to wait.

If the business won't refund your money, and you didn't use a credit card, there isn't much else you can do except consider going to court.

This problem is very, very rare among the businesses that I advise you to deal with. The vast majority of the people who are in this horrible situation are dealing with retail stores and have paid with cash or a check. If you follow all of the advice in this book, the chances of you ever being in this situation are very, very low.

What To Do When A Business Goes Out Of Business (Taking Your Deposit Money With It)

This is very, very rare among the businesses I advise you to deal with. This is almost always a case in which a con artist has opened up a retail store to deliberately cheat consumers. You can get all types of home furnishings without ever having to risk giving a deposit to a retail store, and you can save 50% or more off of your bill to boot.

If you ever do have to give a deposit to a retail store, you can usually find one that will take credit cards. Federal laws would provide you with a refund of your credit card payment in case the business closed. This problem can almost always be prevented. However, if you are ever in this horrible predicament anyway, with any type of business, there are a few things you can do.

To begin with, don't wait until this happens. Don't give a business hundreds or thousands of dollars of your deposit money and then wait two months (or however long your delivery time is) to see them again. Go by the business briefly every week or so to check on your order's progress. Don't just call. You would miss seeing valuable clues that the business could be in trouble: empty shelves, extreme or unseasonable clearance sales (''75% off--everything must go'' sales during the height of the spring or fall selling season), no customers, etc.

Unless you are dealing with a con artist, it is rare for a business to be bustling one day and gone the next. Failing businesses decline for several weeks or months before disappearing completely. Keep an eye on them (and your money). It's a little extra trouble, but not nearly as much trouble as having to sue.

If the worst happens, and the business closes without filling your order or giving your money back, consult an attorney or a book of legal advice and consider suing. Before you sue, make sure that the business has money or assets that you can collect before you actually go to court.

When To Give Up

Sometimes, the con artists win. There are some crooked businesses that are so well organized that you just can't win. It has happened to my family several times, and it may happen to you.

There comes a time when you should give up, when you are only throwing good money after bad. Sometimes, all the money you spend on lawyers and court costs and all of the time you waste won't do you any more good. In the situations listed below, you should consider calling it a day.

If the business is a corporation, and it has closed

If the business or the business owner has declared bankruptcy

If the business or the business owner has left the state

A Final Word

This chapter is not a substitute for qualified legal advice. I am not an attorney. Neither my publisher nor I are attempting to provide legal advice to you. The information given in this chapter is based on my personal business experience and is provided for your information only.

I have pursued a lot of delinquent and dishonest home furnishings businesses over the years with a fair amount of success. I hope that the practical experience I have gained over the years will help you avoid or deal with crooked businesses, should you ever encounter one.

If you have a lot of money at stake, or if you feel any insecurity about pursuing the matter on your own, I recommend that you consult a qualified attorney in your area.

Index

Order Form

Telephone orders: Call Toll Free: 1 (800) 829-1203.
Visa, Mastercard, Discover, and American Express cards accepted.

Mail orders: Send to: Home Decor Press
P. O. Box 1514
Roswell, GA 30077

Please send the books checked below:

☐	The Complete Guide To Custom Window Treatments	$24.95
☐	The Complete Guide To Custom Bed Treatments	$24.95
☐	1995 Decorative Fabrics Cross-Reference Guide	$39.95
☐	National Directory of Wholesale Home Furnishings Sources and Showrooms	$39.95
☐	National Home Furnishings Trade Show Newsletter (issued monthly -- price is for a one year subscription)	$18.00

Subtotal	$
Please add $4.00 shipping for each book ordered	$
GA residents please add 6% sales tax	$
Total amount enclosed	$

$ **Payment:** ☐ Check ☐ Mastercard ☐ Visa ☐ Amex ☐ Discover

Card number:______________________________

Name on card:____________________ Expiration date:________

Shipping: Name______________________________

Address______________________________

City____________ State___ Zip_____ Daytime phone________

Call toll free and order now